6/06

Understanding, Assessing, and Treating Adult Victims of Childhood Abuse

Understanding, Assessing, and Treating Adult Victims of Childhood Abuse

Ofelia Rodriguez-Srednicki and James A. Twaite

JASON ARONSON

Lanham • Boulder • New York • Toronto • Oxford

Published in the United States of America
by Jason Aronson
An imprint of Rowman & Littlefield Publishers, Inc.

A wholly owned subsidary of
The Rowman & Littlefield Publishing Group, Inc.
4501 Forbes Boulevard, Suite 200, Lanham, Maryland 20706
www.rowmanlittlefield.com

PO Box 317
Oxford
OX2 9RU, UK

British Library Cataloguing in Publication Information Available

Library of Congress Cataloging-in-Publication Data

Rodriguez-Srednicki, Ofelia, 1958–
  Understanding, assessing, and treating adult victims of childhood abuse / Ofelia
Rodriguez-Srednicki and James A. Twaite.
     p. cm.
  Includes bibliographical references and index.
  ISBN-13: 978-0-7657-0393-4 (cloth : alk. paper)
  ISBN-10: 0-7657-0393-9 (cloth : alk. paper)
  1. Adult child abuse victims—Rehabilitation. 2. Adult child abuse victims—Mental
health. I. Twaite, James A., 1946– II. Title.

  RC569.5.C55R66 2006
  616.85'82239—dc22   2005034551

Printed in the United States of America

∞™ The paper used in this publication meets the minimum requirements of
American National Standard for Information Sciences—Permanence of Paper for
Printed Library Materials, ANSI/NISO Z39.48-1992.

~

Contents

CHAPTER ONE

~

The Nature, Origins, and Prevalence of Child Abuse

Evans and Sullivan (1995) have defined abuse as "the experience of highly stressful events inflicted by another person that is beyond the individual's capacity to cope and that impairs the individual's sense of well-being" (31). At least five distinct forms of abuse occurring during childhood have been identified and discussed in the literature: physical abuse, sexual abuse, abuse by omission (neglect), emotional abuse, and secondary abuse (which occurs when children observe domestic violence between parents). In this chapter each form of abuse will be described and current theoretical conceptualizations will be discussed.

Physical Abuse

The Nature of Child Physical Abuse

There is no general consensus regarding the definition of the physical abuse of a child. Johnson (2000) defined childhood physical abuse in terms of the injury sustained by the victim. According to Johnson, physical abuse of a child occurs whenever someone commits an intentional act that causes a physical injury to a child. These injuries may include bruises, burns, fractures, cuts, punctures, or organ damage. In addition, physical abuse may begin before the birth of a child if the mother uses illegal drugs, misuses medications, or fails to secure prenatal health care. Johnson's definition is not specific with respect to the age range that constitutes childhood, nor does it specify any particular groups of individuals who may be the perpetrators of the abuse.

1

Other definitions of childhood physical abuse have defined both child-hood and the individual perpetrating the abuse. For example, Garbarino and Ebata (1983) cited the New York State Family Court Act of 1976, which specified that child physical abuse occurs when a parent or other person legally responsible for a child less than eighteen years old inflicts or allows a physical injury to be inflicted upon that child by other than accidental means. Note that this definition differs from Johnson's definition not only in its specification of the age of a child and the individual(s) who can commit the abuse, but also in its expansion of the domain of abuse from acts that the responsible individual actually commits to acts that the responsible individual allows to be committed. This definition would identify as a perpetrator not only a parent who physically beats a child, but also a parent who realizes that beatings are occurring, but does nothing to prevent them.

Kaplan (1996) cited the definition of physical abuse contained in the Child Abuse Prevention, Adoption, and Family Services Act of 1988 (P.L. 100-294). This act defined physical abuse as "the physical injury of a child under eighteen years of age by a person who is responsible for the child's welfare, under circumstances which indicate that the child's health or welfare is harmed or threatened thereby, as determined in accordance with regulations prescribed by the Secretary of Health and Human Services" (2). This law specifically included in the category of responsible persons the staff members of residential facilities providing children with out-of-home care.

Other definitions have focused more on the specific acts committed by the perpetrator, as opposed to the injury to the child that occurs as a result of these acts. Straus and Gelles (1986) defined physical abuse as the use by a parent of any of the acts included in the Severe Violence Index of the Con-flict Tactics Scale. These acts include kicking, biting, hitting with a fist, hit-ting or trying to hit with an object, battering, or using or threatening to use a gun or knife. This definition is somewhat stricter than the other definitions considered above. Presumably slapping or pinching a child would not be con-sidered abuse under this definition, even if these actions were painful, left welts or bruises, or resulted in psychological trauma. This aspect of the defi-nition is problematic. It is likely that no definition focusing on the specific acts committed by the perpetrator could encompass every conceivable way that an adult could cause physical injury to a child. Therefore, it probably makes more sense to focus the definition of physical abuse on the nature and extent of injury sustained by the child.

The Origins of Physical Abuse of Children

Belsky (1980) described an ecological model to explain the occurrence of the physical abuse of children. This model conceptualizes the physical abuse of children as the result of many different variables, including the personal attributes of the abusing parent(s), the impact on the family of significant environmental stressors, and specific predisposing characteristics of the abused child.

According to the U.S. Department of Health and Human Services (1988) the personal attributes of the parent(s) that predict the physical abuse of their children include (1) becoming a parent at a very early age; (2) being a single parent; (3) having several young children who are close together in age; (4) being a substance abuser; (5) having a history of poor impulse control or violence; and (6) having suffered physical abuse as children. In addition, individuals who were sexually abused or neglected as children have been shown to have elevated risk of physically abusing their own children (Kaufman and Zigler 1987; Straus 1991).

Parents who physically abuse their children have been characterized as having inadequate repertoires of coping skills, particularly social skills (Salzinger, Kaplan, and Artemyeff 1983; Salzinger, Kaplan, and Pelcovitz 1984). These deficits lead to social isolation and a lack of opportunity to acquire appropriate parenting skills through the socialization process. Isolated parents also tend to lack realistic expectations regarding the normal course of development of their children. This may lead them to be unduly frustrated by aspects of their children's behavior that other parents recognize as normal. This frustration can be expressed in the form of severe punishments that rise to the level of physical abuse.

Physically abusive parents may be modeling violent behaviors that they have observed. Individuals who witnessed significant amounts of violence as children are disproportionately likely to physically abuse their own children, even if they were not themselves victims of violence. This applies to individuals from families in which domestic violence occurred as well as individuals who grew up in neighborhoods where violence was frequently observed on the street.

Parents who have a history of mental illness are more likely than other parents to abuse their children physically. Fathers who physically abuse their children are disproportionately likely to manifest externalizing pathologies, such as antisocial personality disorders (Kaplan, Pelcovitz, and Salzinger 1983). On the other hand, mothers who physically abuse their children have been shown to be disproportionately characterized by depression and somatic complaints (Breiner 1992). Physically abusing parents also tend to have low self-esteem (Breiner 1992).

The environmental stressors that have been shown to be related to the occurrence of physical abuse of children include (1) poverty; (2) lack of an adequate social support network; (3) unemployment; (4) homelessness or inadequate housing; (5) moving frequently; (6) acculturative stress; and (7) the experience of discrimination based on one's status as a minority group member (U.S. Department of Health and Human Services 1981, 1988).

A substantial body of empirical literature indicates that both family poverty and neighborhood poverty are related significantly to the rates of both reported and unreported child abuse (Ards, Chung, and Myers 1998, 1999; Berger 2005; Connelly and Straus 1992; Drake and Pandey 1996; Gil 1970; Hampton and Newberger 1985; Lindsey 1994; Waldfogel 1998; Whipple and Webster-Stratton 1991; Wolfner and Gelles 1993; Zellman 1992). There is also considerable evidence indicating that families who have received or are currently receiving welfare are more likely than other families to come under the scrutiny of the child welfare authorities for potential child abuse (Berrick 1999; Lindsey 1994; Pelton 1994). However, Berger (2005) pointed out that the latter relationship may be due to a direct relationship between low income status and physical child abuse, but it might also be due at least in part to "reporting or other biases within the child welfare system, such that lower income families are more likely to face reports, substantiations, or child removals" (108).

The children who are physically abused tend to be children who were unplanned and unwanted. Children who have physical or mental disabilities are physically abused disproportionately. Children who have difficult temperaments are at increased risk of being abused, as are children who manifest behavioral problems, such as attention deficit disorder with hyperactivity. Children who were born prematurely are at greater risk, possibly because prematurity is often associated with stressful medical complications and/or developmental delays. Children who fail to bond with their mothers are also more likely to be abused physically. Failure to bond may occur when mother and child are separated for an extended period shortly after birth. Such separations may result from an illness requiring either mother or child to be hospitalized for an extended period. Maternal incarceration or substance abuse may also lead to separation.

The characteristics of physically abusing parents and abused children tend to vary, depending on the age of the victim. Children who are abused as infants or toddlers tend to be from single-parent low-income households. These children are also more likely to be members of ethnic minority groups. Furthermore, these children are most likely to be abused by their mothers (Straus, Gelles, and Steinmetz 1980). In contrast, children who are adolescents when they first experience physical abuse are more likely to come from two-parent, middle-income families (U.S. Department of Health and Human Services 1988). These adolescents are also more likely to be white. Adolescents are most likely to be abused physically by their fathers rather than their mothers. Kaplan (1996) noted that it is relatively uncommon for physical abuse to begin during early childhood and continue through adolescence. Most studies of abused adolescents indicate that the physical abuse begins during adolescence.

Based on a sample of 2,760 families with children drawn from the 1985 National Family Violence Survey (NFVS), Berger (2005) concluded that in both single-parent and two-parent households, parental depression, parental alcohol consumption, and history of violence within one or both parents' families of origin were related positively to the physical abuse of children. In this survey family income was a significant predictor of physical child abuse only in single-parent families.

Prevalence of Physical Abuse of Children
Substantial data exist relevant to the prevalence of physical abuse of children. Based on responses to a national telephone survey conducted in 1985, Straus and Gelles (1986) estimated that each year 19 out of every 1,000 children between the ages of three and seventeen were physically abused. This estimate is probably quite conservative, considering the strict definition of physical abuse these investigators employed. The National Center on Child Abuse and Neglect estimated that over a million children were physically abused during the calendar year 1993 (U.S. Department of Health and Human Services 1995).

The most comprehensive and current data on the prevalence of child abuse and neglect in the United States is provided by the Administration on Children, Youth, and Families of the Department of Health and Human Services. The Child Abuse Prevention and Treatment Act (P.L. 93-247) as amended in 1996 directed the secretary of the Department of Health and Human Services to establish a national data collection and analysis program relevant to child abuse and neglect. The result was the National Child Abuse and Neglect Data System (NCANDS), which collects and publishes both aggregate data and case level data from each state on an annual basis. The most recent NCANDS report available at the time of this writing is *Child Maltreatment 2000* (U.S. Department of Health and Human Services 2002).

This report estimated that 879,000 children were victims of abuse and neglect in 2000. This is equivalent to a prevalence rate of 12.2 per 1,000 children. This estimate must be evaluated in the context of two specific aspects of the data set. First, the data do not differentiate specifically between child physical abuse and child neglect, which really comprise two separate forms of abuse. Second, the NCANDS data set reflects only cases reported to and handled by the state child protective services agencies. The failure to differentiate between physical abuse and neglect would be expected to overestimate the proportion of all children who are physically abused, since some children would be reported to child protective services for neglect only. On the other hand, the inclusion of only cases referred to child protective services agencies would be expected to underestimate substantially the actual proportion of children who are abused physically each year, since only a small proportion of child abuse cases ever comes to the attention of child protective services personnel.

Sexual Abuse

The Nature of Child Sexual Abuse

Nearly twenty years ago, Waterman and Lusk (1986) noted that child sexual abuse had been defined in many different ways by different investigators and that the definitions frequently lack precision. They complained that the lack of a precise and generally accepted definition made it very difficult to compare the findings of different studies. They suggested that "it seems important to specify some factors that vary in sexual abuse, and to keep them in mind when looking at case studies or research data" (4). Among the parameters of child sexual abuse that they considered essential to report were: the type(s) of sex acts involved; the nature of the relationship between the participants; the duration of the abuse; the degree to which violence or threats of violence were involved; the ages and the relative developmental levels of the participants; and the familial and cultural context in which the acts occurred.

Since Waterman and Lusk made these observations, little progress has been made toward the adoption of a universal definition of child sexual abuse. On the other hand, investigators have tended to be more specific in the definitions of sexual abuse that they have employed, even though they continue to employ different definitions. One area in which the definitions employed in recent studies differ is whether to consider as sexual abuse only behaviors involving actual physical contact or whether to consider noncontact sexual behaviors as abusive as well.

Green (1996) defined child sexual abuse as "the use of a child under 18 years of age as an object of gratification for adult sexual needs and desires" (73). Green suggested that both noncontact and contact acts could constitute abuse, noting that sexual abuse ranges in intensity from exhibitionism through gentle fondling to forcible rape that results in physical injury. He also provided a definition of incest, reporting that "the legal definition of incest is cohabitation between persons related to a degree where marriage would be prohibited by law" (1996, 73).

Green stated that the most common forms of sexual victimization experienced by girls are exhibitionism; fondling; masturbation; and vaginal, oral, and anal intercourse performed by a male perpetrator. Boys are also most often abused by a male perpetrator. The American Humane Association (1981) estimated that 94 percent of the perpetrators of child sexual abuse against girls and 86 percent of the perpetrators of child sexual abuse against boys are males. The most common forms of abuse perpetrated against boys are fondling, mutual masturbation, fellatio, and anal intercourse. Green (1996) noted that about half of the victims of child sexual abuse are victimized repeatedly, and that in many cases the molestation takes place over a period of years.

In a self-report study of the relationship between childhood sexual abuse and bulimia, Korte, Horton, and Graybill (1998) employed a definition that restricted sexual abuse to sexual behaviors involving physical contact. These investigators defined sexual abuse as involving "contact (e.g., fondling, intercourse) between: (a) a child twelve or under and an adult eighteen years of age or older; (b) a child twelve or under and another child or adolescent at least five years older than the victim; (c) an adolescent aged thirteen to sixteen and an adult at least ten years older; or (d) a situation in which a child or adolescent endured a consensual sexual experience in which force or coercion was used by a perpetrator of any age" (58). These authors noted that the first three categories of abuse contained in the above definition were drawn from Finkelhor's (1979) landmark study, and the fourth category was added in view of recent increased awareness of the prevalence and damaging effects of peer-perpetrated abuse (Finkelhor and Dzuiba-Leatherman 1994; Gil and Johnson 1993).

In their study of locus of control and adjustment in female adult survivors of childhood sexual abuse, Porter and Long (1999) assessed noncontact forms of sexual behavior but did not include such behaviors in the definition of sexual abuse. These investigators asked respondents whether as a child under the age of seventeen they had experienced any of a series of eight different sexual experiences, ranging from someone exposing himself/herself to the participant to having engaged in intercourse with someone. They instructed respondents to "exclude any voluntary sexual activities between themselves and a dating partner and any consensual sexual play with a peer as long as the partner, in either case, was no more than five years older than the subject" (8). Porter and Long defined sexual abuse as including contact abuse only (excluding noncontact experiences such as exhibitionism). Further, they suggested that in order to be considered child sexual abuse, the act(s) involved must have met at least one of the following criteria: (1) the abusive acts were perpetrated by a relative; (2) there was greater than five years age difference between the victim and the perpetrator; or (3) if there was less than a five-year age difference between victim and perpetrator, force or threat of force was employed.

Interestingly, in spite of the specificity of the above definition, Porter and Long (1999) also asked respondents to indicate whether they considered any of the sexual experiences they reported to be sexual abuse, whether or not the act(s) in question met the three criteria noted above. This resulted in three respondents out of eighty-four characterizing as sexual abuse an experience that did not meet the criteria contained in the definition. These respondents included a woman who reported repeated genital fondling by an unidentified perpetrator of an unknown age that ended when she was ten, and a woman who reported oral-genital contact at age eight with an eleven-year-old neighbor. These self-defined cases were also counted as constituting childhood sexual abuse in the analysis of the data.

Porter and Long categorized all the abuse experiences reported as either more severe or less severe. Sexual abuse experiences were considered more severe if three or more of the following criteria were present: (1) the abuse involved penetration; (2) the abuse involved the threat or use of force; (3) the duration of the abuse was more than one year; (4) the abuse did not end until the victim was eleven or older; and (5) the perpetrator was a family member.

In a self-report study of the relationship between childhood sexual abuse and alexithymia, Scher and Twaite (1999) included noncontact sexual behaviors in their definition of abuse. These investigators defined childhood sexual abuse as "any sexual behavior that occurs between a child under the age of sixteen and any person at least five years older than the victim" (28). Sexual behavior was in turn defined as including "sexual contact (e.g., fondling, intercourse, sodomy) and noncontact forms of sexual behavior (e.g., exhibitionism, requests for sex, lewd or lascivious jokes)" (28). Respondents were asked to read these definitions and then report whether or not they had experienced abuse defined in this manner.

However, recognizing that this is a very broad definition of child sexual abuse and that the impact of repeated intercourse over time is likely to be very different from the impact of a single lewd joke, Scher and Twaite (1999) followed the admonition of Waterman and Lusk (1986) to assess several salient parameters of the sexual abuse experience, including the duration of the abuse, the age of the victim at the time of the first occurrence of abuse, the relationship of the perpetrator to the victim, whether or not the abuse involved oral, anal, or vaginal penetration, whether the perpetrator used force, and whether or not the perpetrator used threats or coercion. These parameters of child sexual abuse were then used individually and collectively to predict the dependent variable of the study, measured alexithymia. In this way, each of these specific parameters was used as an indicator of the severity of the abuse.

The Origins of the Sexual Abuse of Children

Finkelhor (1979) estimated that 75–89 percent of child sexual abuse (CSA) is perpetrated by someone within the child's immediate social circle, including family members, relatives, friends of the family, and neighbors. However, these figures may convey the impression that most CSA is committed by close family members, and this is not the case. Fergusson and Mullen (1999) reviewed eight empirical studies on the incidence of CSA dating back to 1990. They recorded the proportion of cases in each study in which the perpetrator fell into each of the following categories: (1) natural parent; (2) stepparent; (3) sibling; (4) other relative not within the immediate family; (5) acquaintances, including friends, neighbors, boyfriends, and girlfriends; and (6) strangers who were not known to the victims prior to the abusive incident. Fergusson calculated averages of the proportions of perpetrators in each of these categories, weighted by the sample size of the study. They reported that the overall proportion of CSA cases in which the perpetrator was a natural parent was 3.3 percent, that in which the perpetrator was a stepparent was 2.7 percent, and that in which the perpetrator was a sibling was 4.5 percent. These three categories together add up to 10.5 percent. Thus a rather small proportion of CSA victims were abused by a member of their immediate family. The results indicated further that 18.3 percent of perpetrators were relatives outside the immediate family; that 47.8 percent were acquaintances; and that 23.4 percent of the perpetrators were strangers.

It is important to keep these proportions in mind as we consider the first the origins and then later the childhood and adult sequelae of CSA. The dynamics of sexual abuse that takes place at the hands of a parent or parent figure are different from those of other forms of CSA, due to the failure of trust associated with the abuse. In sexual abuse at the hands of a sibling, the issue of trust and early attachment relationships with the caretaker are not so much of an issue. However, parental abuse and sibling abuse are similar in that the close family relationship will provide the opportunity for the perpetrator to repeat the abuse many times over a prolonged period of time. As will be discussed at length in later chapters of this book, repeated and prolonged abuse has been shown to have more serious negative psychosocial adjustment consequences than circumscribed instances of abuse. CSA involving a relative who does not reside with the family may also have some potential to be repeated, but probably not as often or as regularly as abuse by a member of the household.

In spite of the fact that CSA in which the perpetrator is a parent or step-parent, incest has probably been the subject of more attention in the literature than any other form of CSA. More specifically, the form of child sexual abuse that has been discussed most frequently in the literature is father-daughter incest. Accordingly, we consider this form of CSA first.

Father–Daughter Incest

Green (1996) described the psychodynamics of "the incestuous family" in some detail. He used the term incestuous family to refer to father–daughter incest. He noted that such families are typically characterized by a rigid and authoritarian structure in which the father maintains his dominant position through coercion and violence. The authoritarian family structure is often reinforced by social isolation. The mothers in such families are typically highly dependent on the domineering spouse. These mothers may not be allowed to work outside the home or to develop other outside interests. It is quite common that the mother in the incestuous family was herself sexually abused or neglected as a child.

Often the incestuous activity is related to paternal substance abuse. Aahrens, Cameron, and Roizen (1978) estimated that 30–40 percent of all cases of child sexual abuse are related to substance abuse. Incestuous fathers are also characterized by extremely dysfunctional family histories. According to the Texas Department of Human Services (2003), at least 30 percent of such fathers had been physically abused as children. In addition, 27 percent had been sexually abused, and 23 percent had been the victims of emotional abuse or neglect. Furthermore, 37 percent of incestuous fathers had witnessed domestic violence as children, and 47 percent had been subjected to physical and/or social isolation during childhood.

Green (1996) observed that incestuous families are characterized by "role confusion and a blurring of physical and psychological boundaries" (76). In one scenario, the mother is described as emotionally unavailable to both her husband and her daughter. She may delegate many of the marital and house-keeping responsibilities to her daughter (Meiselman 1978). The father may become the primary source of nurturance for his daughter, but he provides this nurturance in a sexualized context. In effect, the father makes his daughter a surrogate wife; and he expects her to provide sexual gratification in exchange for his attention. In this circumstance the daughter often fails to develop normal adolescent peer relationships, because she is focused on the relationship with her father.

The various members of the incestuous family employ a variety of defenses to be able to live with the dysfunctional reality. Substance abusing fathers may be unaware that the sexual activity is occurring, since they may experience blackouts or dissociative episodes when the abusive behavior occurs. Perpetrating fathers who are fully aware of their behavior may rationalize the activity as a form of sex education. Mothers may employ denial, since acknowledging the incestuous behavior would threaten the dependent relationship with the husband and render undeniable their failure to protect and nurture their daughter. The victim of incest may deny the reality of the situation in order to preserve the family unit or her special status with her father. Especially in cases where the abusive sexual activity is accompanied by threats or use of force, the victim may also employ dissociative defenses to remove herself psychologically from the aversive situation.

Male Victims of CSA

Despite the focus in the literature on childhood sexual abuse involving fathers or father figures perpetrating incest upon daughters, it cannot be stressed too strongly that male children may be victims of CSA and perpetrators may be female. We first consider the issue of the gender of the victim. Fergusson and Mullen (1999) argued that the focus of the literature on victims of CSA heavily emphasized female victims, and they contended that this "gender bias has obscured issues relating to the sexual abuse of male children" (35). They cited a number of studies which indicated that a substantial minority of children exposed to sexual abuse are male (Collings 1995; Dhaliwal, Gauzas, Antonowicz, and Ross 1996; Finkelhor and Baron 1986; Watkins and Bentovim 1992). Based on review of the empirical literature available at the time of their study, Finkelhor and Baron (1986) estimated that about 29 percent of victims of CSA are male. Based on a meta-analysis of empirical studies using samples from the general population published after 1990, Fergusson and Mullen (1999) estimated that approximately 27 percent of victims of CSA are male. Fergusson and Mullen also noted that the research indicates that the proportion of victims of CSA who are male is somewhat greater among the more severe cases of sexual abuse involving sexual penetration (anal, oral, or vaginal). They estimated that the ratio of female to male victims with respect to such cases is about 1.8 to 1.0, which means that about 64 percent of the victims are female, and about 36 percent are male.

We note that males compose a substantial minority of CSA victims here to dispel the myth that only female children are abused and caution clinicians to be open to the possibility that an adult male patient might also be a survivor of CSA. Several authors have provided extensive anecdotal evidence of the negative psychosocial outcomes that characterize adult male survivors of CSA (Gartner 1999; Hunter 1990; Ray 2001). Clinicians should be aware that male survivors of CSA may be reluctant to disclose their histories of CSA, since they may regard the abuse as a threat to their masculinity (Lusk and Waterman 1986).

Female Perpetrators of CSA

Just as there has been a tendency to assume that victims of CSA are female, there has been a tendency to assume that perpetrators of CSA are male. Miletski (1995) pointed out that "Fifteen years ago, sexual abuse by a woman was hardly ever acknowledged" (16). Similarly, Fergusson and Mullen (1999) asserted that "until recently, it was believed that nearly all CSA perpetrators were male" (44). Several other investigators have also asserted that childhood sexual abuse perpetrated by women is generally ignored or denied (Araji and Finkelhor 1986; McBean 1987; Peluso and Putnam 1996; Rush 1980). However, empirical studies clearly indicate that a meaningful minority of perpetrators of CSA are women, particularly in the case of sexual abuse directed against male victims (Anderson, Martin, Mullen, Romans, and Herbison 1993; Bagley 1995; Banning 1989; Bendixen, Muus and Schei 1994; Condy, Templer, Brown, and Veaco 1987; Fergusson, Horwood, and Lynskey 1996; Finkelhor 1990; Finkelhor and Russell 1984; Fritz, Stoll, and Wagner 1981; Fromuth and Burkhart 1989; Halperin, Bouvier, Jaffe, et al. 1996; Harrison 1993; Johnson and Shrier 1987; Kinzl, Traweger, and Biefl 1995; Krugman, Mata, and Krugman 1992; Ogilvie 1996; Ogilvie and Daniluk 1995; Petrovich and Templer 1984; Rosencrans 1997).

Based on an analysis of the National Incidence Study of Child Abuse and Neglect conducted in 1981, Finkelhor and Russell (1984) concluded that 13 percent of female victims of CSA were abused by females, and that 24 percent of male victims of CSA were abused by females. Based on a meta-analysis of the literature on perpetrators of CSA conducted after 1990, Fergusson and Mullen (1999) concluded that females constituted approximately 2.5 percent of the perpetrators of childhood sexual abuse committed against females, and approximately 21.3 percent of the perpetrators of childhood sexual abuse committed against males. Ogilvie (2004) estimated that approximately 20 percent of male victims of CSA were abused by females, as were approximately 5 percent of female victims of CSA.

Despite the compelling evidence of the existence of childhood sexual abuse committed by women, some authorities on child sexual abuse still tend to minimize this form of abuse. For example, in an announcement entitled "Incest and Child Sexual Abuse Misconceptions and Facts," the website of the Texas Women's University Counseling Center (2003) stated as a straw man argument the position that "Women sexually abuse children as frequently as men." The announcement then labeled this argument a "myth," and stated that the facts indicated that "although a woman's role as primary caretaker for children offers her more opportunity to abuse, men make up 97 percent of reported sexual crimes against women and children." The manner in which this politically driven argument is presented clearly implies that CSA perpetrated by women is so uncommon as to be unworthy of our concern. What's worse, the statistic reported in support of the argument confounds sexual abuse perpetrated against children with sexual abuse perpetrated against adult women.

While there is no doubt that female perpetrators of sexual abuse against children are fewer in number than male perpetrators, we nevertheless recommend that clinicians keep in mind that CSA perpetrated by women does occur. Miletski (1995) argued that "feminist theories which emphasize female victimization and male dominance and control, especially in the sexual abuse arena, discourage awareness of female perpetrators among professionals as well as among victims themselves" (18). This argument has been made by other investigators as well (Allen 1990, 1991; Banning 1989; Harrison 1993).

The tendency of professionals to minimize childhood sexual abuse perpetrated by women has been documented by Hunter (1990) who reported that while working in a mental health clinic, on several occasions he contacted child protection workers as a mandated reporter when he suspected child sexual abuse in a family. He indicated that he noticed a "disturbing pattern" in the responses of the child protection workers:

> When I reported a case that involved a girl or a boy being abused by an adult male, there was rapid and efficient action. However, when I reported a boy being abused by an adult female, very little was done; in many cases nothing was done. My clients saw the agency's lack of concern as a sign that what had been done to them was acceptable and that they had no business calling it abuse; this only added to the trauma they had experienced. (1990, 37)

The tendency of the general public and professionals alike to minimize CSA perpetrated by females is exacerbated not only by politically driven ideological arguments, but also by the long-standing societal attitude that sex between women and boys is an initiation right and/or a form of sex education. Boys who are victimized by older women are supposed to enjoy it and consider themselves lucky. According to Hunter, "boys who do not enjoy it are likely to question their masculinity or sexual orientation" (1990, 36). Also contributing to the minimization of CSA perpetrated by females is the idea that it is not physically possible for a female to force herself on a male, because it would not be possible for a boy or a man to obtain or maintain an erection when he is threatened or attacked. Along this line, Longdon (1993) even described therapists who attempted to convince male clients that it is not possible for a female to sexually abuse a male. However, Sarrel and Masters (1982) pointed out that just as a women who are sexually assaulted sometimes lubricate and even have orgasms, so men who are forced to have sex can and do maintain erections.

For these reasons we are stressing that clinicians keep an open mind regarding the possibility of sexual abuse perpetrated by females. This is particularly important in view of the fact that clients are apt to reveal sexual abuse committed by males long before they reveal sexual abuse by women (Sgroi and Sargent 1993). It has also been reported that clients who have been abused by female perpetrators are likely to disclose the fact that they were abused before they disclose the gender of the abuser, and that they reveal the gender of the abuser only after they feel that they have gained the therapist's trust (Goodwin and DiVasto 1979; Longdon 1993).

Miletski (1995) asserted that "the current literature lacks theoretical explanations for the phenomenon of female perpetrators of child sexual abuse" (19). Nevertheless, she identified several patterns in the literature. Female sex offenders are characterized by weak ego development, low self-esteem, poor social skills, and significant interpersonal problems (Matthews, Matthews, and Speltz 1989). Furthermore, most adult female perpetrators of CSA were themselves abused sexually and/or physically as children (Matthews et al. 1989; McCarty 1986; Tardif, Auclair, Jacob, and Carpentier 2005). Finally, the great majority of the children who are sexually abused by a female perpetrator are members of the woman's immediate family (Allen 1991; Falller 1987; Wolfe 1985). The latter point merits further comment. We have already seen that relatively few victims of CSA are abused by parents or other members of the immediate family. Yet the great majority of children who are abused by female perpetrators are members of the perpetrator's immediate family. Therefore, the gender breakdown of perpetrators tends to be more equal in abuse that occurs within the family than it is in abuse in which the perpetrator is outside the immediate family. But CSA that occurs within the family is more likely to be repeated over extended periods of time, and more likely as well to be associated with severe psychosocial adjustment difficulties later in life. For all these reasons, then, clinicians should remain open to the possibility of CSA perpetrated by females. As Miletski (1995) concluded, "no matter how many women sexually abuse children, the fact is that some women do, and professionals need to be aware of it" (19).

Brother–Sister Incest

Waterman and Lusk (1986) observed that brother–sister incest is also quite common. In fact, they suggested that "brother–sister incest is thought by many to be the most common form of incest" (8). The data reported by Fergusson and Mullen (1999) referred to earlier in this chapter support this contention. They reported that in 4.5 percent of CSA cases, the perpetrator is a sibling. In contrast, in only 3.3 percent of CSA cases is the perpetrator a natural parent, and in only 2.7 percent of CSA cases is the perpetrator a stepparent.

They observed that this form of incest is substantially underreported, due to its transient nature and generally less harmful effects. However, they noted that instances of brother–sister incest fall along a continuum of severity. They noted that two preschoolers playing doctor or sexual activity between consenting adolescents at roughly the same developmental level are typically not considered to be sexual abuse. On the other hand, if there is a great discrepancy between the siblings in terms of age, development, or physical power, brother–sister incest is more problematic. Finkelhor (1980) suggested that in such cases brother–sister incest may be as damaging as father–daughter incest.

The Prevalence of Childhood Sexual Abuse

Available data indicate that childhood sexual abuse occurs frequently; and over the past thirty years estimates of the prevalence of abuse have been increasing. Finkelhor (1983) declared that in terms of reported cases, sexual abuse was the fastest growing form of child abuse. Lusk and Waterman (1986) noted that estimates of the prevalence of childhood sexual abuse are derived from two primary sources—official reports received by agencies such as the police or child protective services agencies and retrospective self-reports obtained from adults.

Based on data obtained from the American Humane Society indicating that 60,000 to 100,000 children are sexually abused each year in the United States, Bander, Fein, and Bishop (1982) estimated that between 10 and 14 percent of American families are impacted by child sexual abuse each year. The National Center on Child Abuse and Neglect estimated that 156,000 children were sexually abused in 1986 (U.S. Department of Health and Human Services 1988). This estimate represents a prevalence rate of 2.5 children per 1,000 in the population being sexually abused each year. State reports to the National Center on Child Abuse and Neglect made in 1993 indicated that 143,000 cases of child sexual abuse were reported (U.S. Department of Health and Human Services 1995).

Estimates of the prevalence of childhood sexual abuse that are based on the retrospective reports of adults are higher than estimates based on official reports. Finkelhor (1979) surveyed 795 undergraduates in the New England region. Of this group, 9 percent of the men and 19 percent of the women reported being sexually abused as children. Russell (1983) interviewed a random sample of 930 adult women in the San Francisco area. Of this group, 16 percent reported being sexually abused by a family member before their eighteenth birthday, and 31 percent reported that they had been abused by an extrafamilial perpetrator. A total of 38 percent of Russell's sample reported that before the age of eighteen they had experienced either intrafamilial sexual abuse, extrafamilial sexual abuse, or both.

Wyatt (1985) reported that 45 percent of a sample of women drawn from the Los Angeles area reported that they had experienced unwanted sexual contact as children. Siegel, Sorenson, Golding, Burnham, and Stein (1987) surveyed 3,132 adults eighteen years or older from the Los Angeles area. These authors focused on "childhood sexual assault," which they defined as "incidents before the age of sixteen which involved pressure or force for sexual contact" (1141). The proportion of the total sample who reported that they had experienced childhood sexual assault was 5.3 percent. The proportion indicating such a history was greater among females (6.8 percent) than among males (3.8 percent).

Obviously the prevalence rates that are reported vary as a function of the definition of childhood sexual abuse employed and the gender of the respondent. In the study reported by Siegel and associates, there were also differences due to the ethnic group of the respondent, the age of the respondent at the time of the study, and the respondent's level of education. Reported childhood sexual assault was higher among non-Hispanic whites (8.7 percent) than among Hispanics (3.0 percent). It was higher among respondents in the 18–39 age range (6.5 percent) than among respondents above the age of 40 (3.9 percent). Finally, the frequency of reported childhood sexual assault was related directly to level of education. It was 3.1 percent among respondents who were not high school graduates, 4.7 percent among high school graduates, 7.6 percent among respondents with some college, and 7.3 percent among respondents who were college graduates.

Of course, these differences may reflect factors other than actual experience. There may be cultural differences in what is regarded as sexual abuse that may influence responses, regardless of the investigators' efforts to define childhood sexual assault for respondents. There may also be age-related differences in the respondents' recollections of their childhood, as well as age cohort differences in the age at which respondents became aware of what behaviors constitute "pressure or force." Finally there may have been differences due to education in the respondents' ability to put aside their own idea of sexual assault in favor of the definition provided by the investigators.

Regardless of the definition of sexual abuse employed or the demographic characteristics of the group(s) that are sampled, there is good reason to believe that estimates of the prevalence of child sexual abuse are low. This applies to both estimates that are based on official reports of abuse and estimates based on retrospective self-reports. Perpetrators may take advantage of the victim's innocence to convince the child that the sexual activity is not unusual or inappropriate. Very young victims may have no idea what is considered proper and improper behavior, and even if they are uncomfortable with what is happening, they may not be able to articulate their distress. Assuming that the victim does realize that the behavior is inappropriate, he or she may nonetheless fail to disclose. Perpetrators frequently employ bribes or threats to keep their victims from disclosing abuse. In the case of father–daughter incest, the father may tell the daughter that if she discloses the abuse he will be arrested or put in jail, or he may tell her that if she discloses it will hurt her mother very much. If the victim has derived any gratification from the sexual experiences, he or she may feel guilty and fail to disclose for this reason. Male victims of male perpetrators may be particularly reticent to disclose abuse, due to the homosexual connotations of the sexual behavior.

Lusk and Waterman (1986) summarized the results of several different studies that indicated that many cases of child sexual abuse go unreported. Groth, Longo, and McFaddin (1982) surveyed convicted child molesters and reported that the typical molester reported that he had committed between two and five times as many crimes as he was ever charged with. James, Womack, and Strauss (1978) surveyed physicians in the Seattle area, asking them about their practice with respect to reporting the cases of sexual abuse that they became aware of. These investigators found that only 42 percent of the doctors they surveyed indicated that they would conform to the requirements of the law by reporting all cases of child sexual abuse they encountered. Those who indicated that they would not comply with the legal reporting requirements suggested that making an official report would be harmful to the family, and that the problem could be dealt with better without social service intervention. Based on a survey of women who had experienced childhood sexual abuse, Russell (1983) reported that only 2 percent of the women who experienced intrafamilial abuse and only 6 percent of the women who were abused by someone outside the family ever reported the abuse.

In cases where the victim does disclose the abuse, there is no guarantee that he or she will be believed or that the disclosure will ever lead to an official report. Waterman and Lusk (1986) indicated several reasons why "a huge number of cases go unreported each year" (5). For example, it may be difficult to determine whether alleged abuse actually occurred. Physical evidence is often absent, and in the absence of such evidence a child who reports having been abused is likely not to be believed. In this case, the abuse is not likely to be reported to any official agency. If the alleged abuse is intrafamilial in nature, the child's disclosure represents a threat to the parents' marriage, and possibly the threat to the continuity of family income. The spouse of the alleged abuser may consciously or unconsciously deny the validity of the child's report in an effort to ward off such significant threats to the security of the family.

Neglect

The Nature of Child Neglect

Neglect has been defined most simply as that form of abuse that occurs by omission rather than commission (Giovanni 1988). This definition has intuitive appeal, but it lacks the specificity required to be of practical use to educators, social service providers, or representatives of the legal system. Monteleone (1998) defined neglect as "reckless failure to provide, by those responsible for the care, custody, and control of the child, the proper or necessary support, education as required by law, nutrition or medical, surgical, or any other care necessary for his well-being; and food, clothing, or shelter sufficient for life or essential medical or surgical care" (57). Straus and Kantor (2005) defined neglect as "behavior by a caregiver that constitutes a failure to act in ways that are presumed by the culture of a society to be necessary to meet the developmental needs of a child and which are the responsibility of the caregiver to provide" (20).

Giardino and Giardino (2003) noted that "a component of clinical judgment is required in assessing some forms of neglect because there may be a recognition of cultural values or considerations of poverty-related causes not to provide what might be considered the necessities of life" (8). These authors noted that laws in some states exclude neglect resulting from poverty or religious beliefs or practices as constituting failure on the part of parents or legal guardians to provide necessary care. They noted that some of the controversial situations include parental refusal of medical treatment for a child on religious grounds when the child's life is threatened, and they observed that such cases are often subject to litigation between parents and child protective services professionals.

Although each state is responsible for defining child neglect, the Federal Child Abuse Prevention and Treatment Act (CAPTA) as amended by the Keeping Children and Families Safe Act of 2003, provides general guidelines regarding specific situations that constitute child neglect (National Clearinghouse on Child Abuse and Neglect Information 2004). This act defines neglect as failure to provide for a child's basic needs in one or more of four areas, as follows: (1) physical needs, including the need for food or shelter, and the need for appropriate supervision to prevent possible injury which might result from unsupervised behaviors on the part of the child; (2) medical needs, including both physical and mental health treatment; (3) educational needs, including not only regular education for most children, but also special education for children with special education needs; and (4) emotional needs.

Rosenzweig and Kaplan (1996) detailed specific categories of behavior that constitute neglect. These investigators specified several actions that would necessarily result in the failure to meet any of the child's needs. These behaviors included abandonment, which is the "desertion of a child without arranging for reasonable care and supervision" (1996, 38). A child is considered to be abandoned when a parent leaves the child somewhere or with someone for a period of forty-eight hours or more without leaving information as to their whereabouts. Another behavior that constitutes neglect is expulsion, which occurs when a parent excludes a child from the home without making adequate arrangements for care by others, or when a parent refuses to accept a returned runaway child back into the home. Disruptions associated with child custody issues may also rise to the level of neglect, as in the case where a child is shuffled repeatedly from one household to another because of the apparent unwillingness of one or both parents to maintain custody, or the case where a child is chronically and repeatedly left with others for days at a time. Still another category of neglect occurs when a parent leaves a child unsupervised or inadequately supervised for an extended period of time, or when a parent allows a child to remain away from home overnight without attempting to determine the child's whereabouts.

In the absence of abandonment, expulsion, or a failure to account for a child's whereabouts, a parent may neglect the physical needs of a child through diverse behaviors. The parent may fail to attend to conspicuous avoidable hazards in the home. The parent may fail to provide adequate nutrition, clothing, and hygiene. The parent may demonstrate a reckless disregard for the safety and welfare of the child by driving while intoxicated, leaving the child unattended in a motor vehicle, or allowing the child to engage in behaviors that carry significant risk of injury.

Neglect of medical needs may take diverse forms as well. Parents neglect their children when they do not make appropriate arrangements for preventive care, including recommended inoculations. Parents also neglect their children when they fail to seek timely medical care for a chronic or acute health problem that a reasonable layperson would recognize as requiring medical attention. Further, parents neglect their children when they fail to provide or allow to be provided such care as is recommended by competent professionals to address a physical injury, an illness, a chronic medical condition, or a physical impairment. Within the latter category of neglect would be a parental refusal to give permission for a necessary medical procedure such as a surgery or a transfusion. The National Clearinghouse on Child Abuse and Neglect Information (2004) noted that there are times when the family's cultural values may place a child at risk of neglect. In such cases, the clearinghouse asserted, "the family is in need of information or assistance" (2004, 2). Furthermore, "when a family fails to use information and resources, and the child's health or safety is at risk, then child welfare intervention may be required" (2004, 2).

Neglect of educational needs may also take a variety of forms. Parents are neglecting the educational needs of their children when they fail to enroll a child in school when that child reaches mandatory school age; and they are similarly negligent when they regularly keep a school-age child away from school for nonlegitimate reasons, including work and child care for siblings. Parents are also neglecting their children's educational needs if they allow their children to be truant from school. Rosenzweig and Kaplan (1996) asserted that allowing a child to be truant rises to the level of neglect when the parent has been informed that there has been an attendance problem, yet the child continues to be truant on an average of five or more days per month.

In addition to tolerating truancy, parents may neglect the educational needs of their children if they fail to obtain or refuse to allow the delivery of recommended remedial services, especially in connection with a diagnosed learning disability or special educational need. Discussions of neglect of educational needs typically do not extend to an implication that parents must provide an appropriate environment for study at home, attend parent–teacher conferences, and supervise homework.

Rosenzweig and Kaplan (1996) noted that "child and adolescent neglect and emotional maltreatment overlap in many areas" (37). This overlap is quite clear in the definition of emotional neglect provided by the National

Center of Child Abuse in its study of the national incidence and prevalence of child abuse and neglect (U.S. Department of Health and Human Services 1988), which states that emotional neglect is providing the child with inadequate nurturing and affection, allowing the child to misuse drugs or alcohol, allowing the child to engage in maladaptive behavior, or failing to provide the child with necessary psychological care.

Origins of Child Neglect

A variety of explanations have been offered for parental neglect of children. Some of these explanations involve the same factors as those associated with other forms of childhood abuse; but other explanations include predictors which appear to be unique to or at least particularly predictive of neglect. Nay, Fung, and Wickett (1992) attributed child neglect in part to parental substance abuse, but they also implicated external factors such as marital discord, unemployment, and financial stress.

Ethier, Palacio-Quintin, and Jourdan-Ionescu (1992) found that neglectful mothers tend to differ from physically abusive mothers in that the neglectful mothers tend to be more socially isolated and more financially disadvantaged. Paxson and Waldfogel (1999) emphasized the relationship between economic deprivation and child neglect. These authors noted that economic hardship impacted the quality of the care that parents could provide for their children both directly and indirectly, through the impact of low income on parental availability and on the quality of the time that the parent can spend with the child. For example, Paxson and Waldfogel argued that "a low-income working single mother may be short also because she may not have the physical or emotional reserves to care for her children properly at the end of the day" and similarly that "an unemployed father may provide less than adequate parenting not only because his income has been reduced, but also because of the depression and loss of self-esteem that may accompany unemployment" (1999, 239).

Zuravin (1988) focused on the psychological state of the parents as a predictor of neglect, reporting that maternal depression was a stronger predictor of maternal neglect than it was a predictor of maternal physical child abuse. It has also been argued that parental neglect of children is associated with parental intellectual impairments. For example, Taylor (1991) reported that neglectful parents are characterized by below average IQ scores.

Prevalence of Child and Adolescent Neglect

Neglect is the form of child abuse that is reported most frequently to child protective services (CPS) officials. Paxson and Waldfogel (1999) reported that

58 percent of all maltreatment cases reported to CPS fall under the category of neglect. In contrast, reports of physical abuse, the next most frequently occurring category of maltreatment, compose 22 percent of all reports. Price, Islam, Gruhler, Dove, Knowles, and Stults (2001) reported that in 1993 neglect, including physical neglect, emotional neglect, and educational neglect, was experienced by 29.2 children per 1,000 in the population. These authors also noted that neglect was the most frequently occurring form of child abuse in the United States. They reported that the prevalence rate for physical abuse was 9.1 children per 1,000; the rate for emotional abuse was 7.9 per 1,000; and the rate for sexual abuse was 4.5 per 1,000. The figures provided by Price and his colleagues indicate that approximately 2 million children experienced parental neglect each year. Clearly passive forms of child abuse are more common than active forms of abuse.

Emotional Abuse

The Nature of Emotional Abuse

Rosenzweig and Kaplan (1996) defined childhood emotional abuse as "a pattern of psychically destructive behavior inflicted by an adult on a child" (43). Johnson (2000) suggested that emotional maltreatment is "a repeated pattern of parent or caregiver behavior that conveys to a child that he or she is worthless, flawed, unloved, unwanted, endangered, or only of value to meet someone else's needs" (110). Garbarino, Schellenbach, and Sebes (1986) noted that diverse forms of adult behavior could have the effect of making a child feel worthless. These behaviors include rejection, isolation, terrorizing the child, ignoring the child, and corrupting the child.

In a report for the U.S. Department of Health and Human Services, Sedlak and Broadhurst (1996) noted several additional forms of adult behavior that are emotionally abusive to children. One of these forms of emotional abuse they referred to as "verbal or emotional assault," which was defined as "habitual patterns of belittling, denigrating, scapegoating, or other forms of overtly hostile or rejecting treatment, as well as threats of other forms of maltreatment (such as threats of beatings, sexual assault, abandonment, etc.)" (Sedlak and Broadhurst 1996, 15). Romeo (2000b) presented an extreme example of such abuse in the form of a Florida father who threatened to rape his eight-year-old daughter if she came home with a bad report card.

Sedlak and Broadhurst (1996) also included in the definition of emotional abuse forms of punishment involving the "torturous restriction of movement," including (1) tying a child's arms or legs together or binding the child to a chair or bed or (2) confining the child to an enclosed area, such as a

closet. Shull (1999) noted that these forms of abuse are not clearly enumerated in state criminal codes, and he suggested that the authorities may experience substantial difficulty in attempting to address such behavior. For example, Shull (1999) described the case of a mother in Pennsylvania who was
"charged criminally for having locked her thirteen-year-old daughter in a
closet for seventeen hours, naked, without food or water, and with only a
bucket for a bathroom" (1665). Shull noted pointedly that this mother was
acquitted of having committed any crime. Shull (1999) also described a
mother in Oregon who chained her daughter to a tree for two days and
chopped off the daughter's long ponytail with a hunting knife. Shull pointed
out that this woman was convicted of a crime, but only because she slapped
her daughter in the course of securing her to the tree. The point Shull (1999)
was making here is that these forms of abuse were not defined by legal
statutes specific enough to provide a dependable remedy for victims.

Shull (1999) asserted that few states even recognize anything specifically
called emotional or psychological child abuse. He cited the Alaska child protection statute as typical of the vast majority of states, in that child abuse
other than physical battering or sexual abuse is not defined in terms of any
specific action on the part of a perpetrator, but rather by the nature of the injury to the child. This statute states that child emotional abuse has occurred
when a child under the age of eighteen has sustained a "mental injury,"
which in turn is defined as "an injury to the emotional well-being, or intellectual or psychological capacity of a child, as evidenced by a substantial impairment in the child's ability to function" (Alaska Statutes, section
47.17.290[2] 1998). Clearly this definition implies that emotional abuse has
not occurred unless the child manifests substantial and observable negative
outcomes. Shull also referred to the Pennsylvania child abuse statute, which
states that emotional abuse has occurred when an act or failure to act results
in a "nonaccidental serious mental injury," which in turn is defined as "a psychological condition, as diagnosed by a physician or licensed psychologist,
that (1) renders a child chronically and severely anxious, agitated, depressed,
socially withdrawn, psychotic or in reasonable fear that the child's life or
safety is threatened; or (2) seriously interferes with a child's ability to accomplish age-appropriate developmental and social tasks" (PA Statutes, title
23, section 6303(b)(ii) 1998). This latter definition also depends on symptoms manifested in the child, but with the additional restriction that the
symptoms must by diagnosed by a physician or psychologist.

Thus it appears that the concept of emotional abuse has clear face validity, but the difficulties associated with defining emotional abuse make it more
difficult for the legal and social service delivery systems to take action to

protect a victim of emotional abuse than to protect victims of physical or sexual abuse. This point is made clear by Romeo (2000a) in her article on the role of the educator in reporting the emotional abuse of children. Romeo asserted that educators routinely attend in-service seminars to help them learn the behavioral indicators of physical and sexual abuse and neglect; but these in-service experiences almost never consider the problem of emotional abuse. She argued that the explanation for this discrepancy was simply that physical and sexual abuse and neglect are often indicated by easily visible external injuries, whereas indicators of emotional abuse are more difficult to identify. Wood (1999) offered further support for the view that emotional abuse can be very difficult to detect by noting that only 4 percent of all substantiated cases of child abuse are reported as emotional abuse.

Origins of Child Emotional Abuse

Rosenzweig and Kaplan (1996) suggested that parental substance abuse is often a significant predictor of child emotional abuse, just as parental substance abuse is frequently associated with the physical and sexual abuse of children. They noted that alcohol and other addictive drugs tend to lower inhibitions, and they argued that for this reason "when operating under the influence of alcohol or drugs, parents are more likely to insult, disparage, threaten, and coerce children than when in a chemical-free state of mind." They also suggested that such parents may not recall their abusive behavior when they are sober; or if they do recall it they may dismiss the abuse as the unintentional result of the substance use (e.g., "It was just the booze talking"). However, the child who is insulted or denigrated while the parent is under the influence of a substance is not capable of dismissing abusive comments on the basis of the subtle distinction that the parent was drunk or stoned and therefore somehow didn't really mean what he or she said. The child responds to parental insults with anxiety, sadness, and anger, whatever the offending parent's state of mind. The child feels unloved and unwanted and eventually fails to develop positive self-esteem.

On the other hand, the role of parental substance abuse in childhood emotional abuse can clearly be overstated, for two reasons. First, parental substance abuse has so many negative consequences that simply observing the existence of a parental substance abuse does not automatically suggest that the children will predominantly manifest symptoms of emotional abuse. The children of substance abusing parents often display a broad range of pathologies, of which poor self-concept is perhaps least noticeable and least troublesome. In addition, Renn (2000) noted that emotionally abused children often come from families in which there is no obvious problem of sub-

stance abuse. These children may perceive their families as quite normal. As a result, the children may be at a loss to understand why they always feel bad or why they chronically experience anxiety, impaired relationships, and lack of fulfillment with respect to their personal goals.

Romeo (2000b) noted that emotionally abusive parents frequently ridicule their children in front of significant others, including friends, siblings, relatives, and even teachers. Like the abused child who is the subject of the ridicule, the witnesses may tend to accept the demeaning statements as accurate, leading them to think less of the abused child. They may also model the abusive behavior, joining in the ridicule of the abused child.

In addition to insulting the target child, Romeo pointed out that emotionally abusing parents are generally emotionally cold and distant. These parents fail to demonstrate normal affection toward their children, and they fail to provide their children with support and guidance. To make matters worse, emotionally abusive parents tend to have unrealistic expectations regarding their children's behavior and accomplishments. When the abused child is successful in school or demonstrates some other significant accomplishment, the emotionally abusing parent will tend to belittle the success or raise the bar.

The Prevalence of Child Emotional Abuse

Sedlak and Broadhurst (1996) reported in the Third National Incidence Study of Child Abuse and neglect that approximately 532,200 children in the United States experienced emotional abuse each year. This translates into 7.9 children per 1,000 in the population. Moreover, these authors estimated that 204,500 of these emotionally abused children, or about 3.0 children per 1,000 in the population, suffered demonstrable harm as a result of the emotional abuse they experienced. Sedlak and Broadhurst noted further that over the period from 1986 through 1993 the numbers of cases of emotional abuse that were identified each year rose by 183 percent, and the incidence rate per 1,000 children rose by 163 percent. These increases were greater than the corresponding increases in the number and incidence of cases of physical abuse and sexual abuse over the same time period. Furthermore, Sedlak and Broadhurst (1996) specifically concluded that the increases observed in instances of emotional abuse during this period were not a statistical aberration or the result of increased awareness of emotional abuse on the part of abuse reporters. Lesnik-Oberstein, Coers, and Cohen (1994) suggested that the prevalence of emotional abuse, coupled with the severity of the damage associated with such abuse, clearly justified the need for child protective agencies to develop standards governing the conditions which justify intervention in families in which emotional abuse appears to be occurring.

Secondary Abuse

The Nature of Secondary Abuse

Geffner, Igelman, and Zellner (2003) noted that "there is now wide recognition among professionals who work with abused children and maltreating families that family violence, specifically interparental or intimate partner violence, is a problem of great magnitude that can significantly impact the short- and long-term development of children who are exposed to such violence in their homes" (1). The National Center on Child Abuse study has specifically included the exposure of a child to chronic or extreme interparental violence as a form of child abuse (U.S. Department of Health and Human Services 1988). Such exposure may be classified as a form of emotional abuse, or it may be considered under a separate heading as secondary child abuse. DeVoe and Smith (2003) pointed out that in many jurisdictions the regulations which define child abuse consider the exposure of a child to violence between his or her parents in and of itself a form of child maltreatment for which the removal of the child from the home is considered an appropriate response.

The Origins of Secondary Abuse

Secondary abuse occurs when children observe domestic violence. The risk factors most often associated with the occurrence of domestic violence are socioeconomic disadvantage, parental substance abuse, and depression (Lystad, Rice, and Kaplan 1995). Poverty is a chronic stressor that gives rise to frustration and anger, which may ultimately be expressed in violence. Unemployment can be a strong economic stressor, and Coker, Smith, McKeown, and Melissa (2000) reported a significant relationship between husbands' unemployment and violent behavior toward their wives. In addition, there is reason to believe that the power imbalance between men and women which has been associated with domestic violence tends to be greater in poorer families, and that anachronistic cultural norms which suggest that it is acceptable for husbands to abuse their wives are more deeply rooted in less affluent groups than in more affluent segments of the population (Straus and Gelles 1990; Babcock, Waltz, and Jacobson 1993).

The disinhibiting effect of intoxicating substances such as alcohol has also been shown to predict domestic violence. Roizen (1993) reported that in 45 percent of all cases of intimate partner violence the male partner had been drinking, and in 20 percent of the cases the female partner had been drinking. Hotaling and Sugarman (1986) similarly reported a significant relationship between substance abuse and husband-to-wife violence. Slade, Daniel, and Hoiser (1991) examined the relationships between the intake of alcohol and other drugs and the occurrence of domestic violence. They reported that alcohol was a factor in 85 percent of the cases of domestic violence that they studied, and that cocaine was a factor in 30 percent of the cases. They also noted that a combination of alcohol and cocaine was involved in 20 percent of the domestic violence cases that they studied. In addition, several studies have demonstrated relationships between substance use and the sexual assault of domestic partners (Campbell and Gibbs 1986; Hotaling and Sugarman 1986; Ladoner and Temple 1985). Campbell and Gibbs noted that the use of social isolation is a factor in domestic violence because isolation attenuates the restraining effect on abusive behavior of the oversight and scrutiny of other members of the community.

Prevalence of Secondary Abuse

Onyskiw (2003) described domestic violence as "a health and social issue of epidemic proportions" (12). Edelson (1999) noted that the actual number of children exposed to domestic violence is unclear because there has never been a national prevalence study. Edelson explained that the estimates of the number of children exposed to this trauma have been extrapolated from surveys of violence between adult family members. Data from these surveys is used to extrapolate estimates of the prevalence of secondary child abuse by adjusting for the average number of children in each household where domestic abuse has occurred. With these limitations in mind, it is noted that estimates of the prevalence of secondary child abuse have ranged from approximately 3.3 million per year to as many as 10 million per year (Humphreys 1997; Jaffe, Wolfe, and Wilson 1990; McFarlane, Groff, O'Brien, and Watson 2003; Straus, Gelles, and Steinmetz 1980; Straus 1992).

Fantuzzo and Mohr (1999) pointed out that estimates of the prevalence of secondary abuse vary because of differences in the way interparental violence has been operationalized in the various studies. Most typically the level of parental violence that is required for the observation of this violence to rise to the level of secondary child abuse involves punching, kicking, and/or beating of one of their parents, typically the mother (Humphreys 1997). However, Tjaden and Theonnes (2000) pointed out that regardless of the specific definition of domestic violence employed, the problem of children being exposed to violence between intimates is a significant problem. In addition, Finkelhor (1993) noted that the number of children exposed to secondary abuse is substantially underestimated, regardless of the definition employed in the estimate. The seriousness of this problem is in-dicated by the announcement in October 2003 by HHS secretary Tommy Thompson of the Safe and Bright Futures for Children initiative, which is aimed at providing treatment for child and adolescent trauma, mentoring, and mental health services aimed at breaking the cycle of violence (U.S. Department of Health and Human Services 2003).

The Initial Impact of Maltreatment on Children and Adolescents

The forms of child maltreatment defined in the previous chapter impact negatively on the individual's physical health, psychological development, and social adjustment. Browne and Finklehor (1986) distinguish between the "initial" effects of abuse and the "long-term" effects of abuse that persist into adulthood. They use the term "initial" rather than "short-term" because the latter implies that the reactions do not persist, which is certainly not the case. On the contrary, child abuse is now widely regarded as a cause of a broad range of psychosocial adjustment difficulties in adult life (Mullen and Fleming 1998). The assessment and treatment of these adjustment difficulties in adults is the primary focus of this book.

However, Latimer (1998) has argued that there is an unfortunate "tendency for people to view the effects of maltreatment as less serious if the impact appears to be temporary and disappears in the course of a child's development" (7). He suggested that childhood abuse represents traumatic experience which is painful and alarming, whether or not the effects persist into adulthood. For this reason, the present chapter has been included to describe the initial effects of child maltreatment on children's development and adjustment. These effects are also worthy of consideration in this volume because familiarity with the initial effects of child maltreatment can help the clinician better understand the meaning of the retrospective reports of their adult clients regarding experiences they had during their childhoods.

Latimer (1998) argued that some of the initial effects of child abuse are appropriately regarded as the result of maltreatment in general, whereas other effects appear to be the result of specific forms of abuse. Latimer described the general effects of child maltreatment as falling into four major categories, the including physical, behavioral, psychological, and spiritual consequences of abuse.

General Effects of Maltreatment

Physical Effects

In addition to the obvious physical injuries that result from physical abuse specifically, child maltreatment in general is associated with a number of initial manifestations that are primarily physical in nature. Children who are maltreated tend to display a variety of stress-related physical symptoms, including gastrointestinal disturbances, migraine headaches, hypertension, sleep disturbances, and aches, pains, and rashes that seem to defy diagnosis and/or treatment (Gilmartin 1994). Clinicians should be sensitive to client self-descriptions which include references to these maladies during childhood, because such references suggest the possibility of childhood abuse. Similarly, abused children often manifest weight problems. They tend to be smaller and lighter than nonabused children; and they are predisposed to specific eating disorders, such as anorexia and bulimia (Yawney 1996). Client self-references to childhood eating disorders are also appropriately viewed as indicators of possible abuse.

Behavioral Effects

Abused children display a broad range of behavioral disturbances during childhood. They are characterized by developmental delays and by difficulties socializing appropriately with peers (Feldman, Salzinger, Rosario, Alvarado, Caraballo, and Hammer 1995). Both developmental delays and inadequate socialization are associated with poor school adjustment and disruptive classroom behavior (de Paul and Arruabarrena 1995). These difficulties are in turn reflected in poor academic performance, including low scores on tests of language, reading, and math (Kurtz, Gaudin, Wodarski, and Howing 1993; Oates 1996); retention in grade (Kendall-Tacket and Eckenrode 1996); and dropping out (Latimer 1998).

During adolescence, abused children are disproportionately likely to display a variety of self-destructive behaviors, including (1) truancy and running away (Kurtz et al. 1993; Manion and Wilson 1995); (2) premature and promiscuous sexual activity (Gilmartin 1994); (3) early use of alcohol and other addictive drugs and substance use disorders (Chandy, Blum, and Resnick 1996b; Malinosky-Rummell and Hansen 1993); (4) delinquency and prostitution (Manion and Wilson 1995); (5) self-destructive behaviors such as self-mutilation, burning, and driving under the influence of alcohol or other drugs (Oates 1996); and (6) suicidal ideation and/or suicide attempts (Fergusson and Lynskey 1997).

Psychological Effects

Immediately following maltreatment, children tend to display a variety of psychological disturbances, including anxiety (Oates 1996); general fearfulness and specific phobias (Gilmartin 1994); extreme and recurrent nightmares (Oates 1996); feelings of guilt and shame (Oates 1996); bouts of sadness, depression, and social withdrawal (Mian, Marton, and LeBaron 1996); and unusually high levels of anger (Loos and Alexander 1997).

Children who are abused over long periods of time tend to develop negative self-perceptions. In an effort to maintain a positive perception of the abusing parent(s), these children frequently blame themselves for the abusive treatment they receive. As a result, they are frequently characterized by low self-esteem that sometimes reaches the level of self-hatred (Gilmartin 1994). They often have difficulty achieving a cohesive sense of ego identity (Varia, Abidin, and Dass 1996).

Following prolonged exposure to various forms of abuse, children also develop more serious psychiatric symptoms, including distorted reality testing (Gilmartin 1994), dissociative disorders (Zweig-Frank and Paris 1997), and impaired cognitive functioning, including disruptions in the ability to comprehend complex roles (Varia, Abidin, and Dass 1996).

Spiritual Effects

Latimer (1998) described the impact of maltreatment on children's spirit. He argued that "children who have been abused and neglected report having lost their sense of faith, not just a religious belief in a divine being, but also their faith in themselves, other people, and the world around them" (11). He referred to them as suffering from a "shattered soul." He stated that "systematic battering, sexual abuse, emotional attacks, or the long-term neglect of a child is likely to destroy his or her enthusiasm for life" (11). Latimer contended that the shattered soul is observed clearly among abused children, and he asserted that this effect of childhood abuse persists into adulthood and becomes an important long-term consequence of child maltreatment.

Specific Effects of Particular Forms of Child Maltreatment

In addition to the general characteristics of abused children described above, specific adjustment disorders have been linked to each of the particular categories of abuse enumerated above. These negative outcomes are described in the paragraphs that follow. These descriptions must be interpreted in the context of serious methodological limitations which characterize existing research on the immediate outcomes of the various forms of childhood abuse. These limitations include failure to control for symptoms that may have existed prior to the abusive experiences and failure to control for the frequent occurrence of multiple forms of abuse (Green 1996). These limitations make it impossible to establish a strict one-to-one correspondence between each specific form of abuse and the direct effects of that particular form of abuse. This reality makes it necessary to refer to the generalized effects of child maltreatment in order to describe adequately the immediate impact of abuse on children's development and adjustment. Nevertheless, Latimer (1998) has provided a list of the specific sequelae of childhood maltreatment that are associated *primarily* with each of the five major categories of child maltreatment. This list was used as a guide in developing the following descriptions.

Physical Abuse
In addition to obvious external physical injuries, children who are abused physically often suffer from permanent or long-term neurological damage that may lead to learning disabilities (Kaplan 1996; Kline and Christiansen 1975; Salzinger, Kaplan, and Pelcovitz 1984) as well as to impulsivity and hyperactivity (Kaplan 1996; Martin and Beezley 1977). These symptoms in turn may lead to poor school adjustment and academic underachievement.

Physical abuse of children is also associated with poor socialization, particularly in the form of uncooperative acting-out behavior and inappropriate aggression. Salzinger, Feldman, and Hammer (1993) compared a group of physically abused children to a comparable group of children who were not maltreated. They found that peers rated the children in the physically abused group as less cooperative and more aggressive than children in the nonabused group. In addition, the children in the physically abused group were rated by their teachers as more disturbed than the children in the nonabused group. Several other studies have confirmed that physically abused children are disproportionately likely to display aggressive and violent behavior (Alfaro 1978; Lewis 1985). Moreover, as these children move into adolescence, they are likely to engage in delinquent behavior and criminal activity. Truscott (1992) found that adolescent males who had been abused physically by their fathers were more likely than nonabused males to engage in violent behavior directed toward their age peers.

Sexual Abuse
Sexually abused children tend to manifest disturbances in their own sexual behavior (Browne and Finklehor 1986; Friedrich, Urquiza, and Beilke 1986;

Tufts 1984). Yates (1982) described preschool children who were victims of incest as prematurely eroticized. Yates indicated that these children were orgasmic as preschoolers, and they maintained high levels of sexual arousal. He also noted that these children were often unable to differentiate appropriate affectionate gestures from inappropriate sexual advances. As a result, these abused preschoolers tended to become sexually aroused during interactions involving routine physical or emotional closeness. Children who are victims of incest are also likely to reenact sexual experiences with other children (Brandt and Tiza 1977). This behavior is motivated not only by the inherent pleasure associated with the sexual behavior, but also as a means of establishing a sense of mastery and control following the trauma of sexual abuse.

Johnson (2002) noted a widespread belief among child protective service workers, mental health professionals, and law enforcement personnel that all children who molest other children are themselves the victims of sexual abuse, and conversely that all children who are victims of sexual abuse will molest or initiate sexual activity with other children. Johnson suggested that neither of these generalizations is accurate. The relationship between the experience of being sexually abused and subsequently engaging in sexual behaviors with other children or adolescents is far from perfect. However, Johnson does acknowledge an apparent relationship between a history of being sexually abused and the likelihood of engaging in sexual activity with other youngsters. Several studies provide evidence of this relationship (Bonner 1998; Friedrich and Chaffin 2000; Friedrich and Luecke 1988; Gray 1996; Gray, Pithers, Busconi, and Houchens 1999; Johnson 1988, 1989). Therefore the clinician who learns that a young patient has molested or otherwise engaged in sexual activity with young age peers or younger children should be mindful of the possibility that this patient may in fact have been the victim of sexual abuse.

On the other hand, the clinician should not assume that a child who molests other children has been sexually abused. Further, even if a child who molests other children does have a history of being abused sexually, the clinician should not assume that the abuse history is the sole determinant of the inappropriate sexual behavior. Johnson (2002) cautions that many of the studies reporting a relationship between a history of sexual abuse and engaging in sexual behavior with other children have failed to control for a history of other forms of child maltreatment, such as secondary abuse. Moreover, Johnson noted that "our own unpublished data shows that respondents consistently report that children who molest have witnessed violence between their parents or caretakers" (2002, 86). Thus the effects of child sexual abuse and secondary child abuse may be confounded.

Numerous studies have indicated that sexually abused children tend to display a variety of inappropriate sexual behaviors, including excessive sexual curiosity (Tufts 1984), compulsive masturbation and promiscuity (MacVicar 1979), and frequent exposure of the genitals (Tufts 1984). Friedrich and associates (1986) employed the Child Behavior Checklist to assess inappropriate sexual behaviors among sexually abused children ranging in age from three to twelve years. They found that 70 percent of the males and 44 percent of the females in the sample scored at least one standard deviation above the mean of the age group norm on the scale measuring sexual problem behaviors. Similar results were reported by Mannarino, Cohen, and Gregor (1989), who used a variety of psychological and sexual adjustment measures to compare three groups of girls: (1) a group who were known to have been sexually abused and who had been referred to a regional rape crisis center (n = 94); (2) a group who were attending an outpatient psychiatric clinic but who had not been sexually abused (n = 84); and (3) a control group selected from two schools (n = 75). They found that the sexually abused girls had significantly higher levels of sexual problems than the girls in either of the other two groups.

During adolescence, sexually abused girls are more likely than nonabused girls to be sexually active and to engage in risky sexual behavior. Stock, Bell, Boyer, and Connell (1997) reported that adolescent girls who had been sexually abused were significantly more likely than nonabused age peers to report: (1) having engaged in consensual sexual intercourse before the age of 15; (2) not using contraception at the time of last intercourse; and (3) having more than one sexual partner. These adolescents were also predictably more likely than nonabused age peers to report having been pregnant at least one time.

Several meta-analytic studies of the literature on the relationship between childhood sexual abuse and inappropriate and or risky sexual behavior during childhood and adolescence have confirmed the existence of moderately strong relationships. Based on a review and analysis of the findings of twenty-six empirical studies on the immediate effects of childhood sexual abuse, Kendall-Tackett, Williams, and Finkelhor (1993) estimated that approximately 43 percent of the variability in premature sexualized behavior in children and adolescents could be explained by a history of sexual abuse. Fergusson and Mullen (1999) also concluded that there was at least a moderate relationship among children and adolescents between risky sexual behavior and a history of sexual abuse, although they suggested that it would be desirable to determine "how many more times likely children exposed to childhood sexual abuse are to develop given outcomes when compared to nonabused children" (54).

More than any other form of child maltreatment, child sexual abuse has been linked to the emergence during childhood of a variety of psychological symptoms. Whereas physical abuse is most often associated with the emergence of externalizing pathology, sexual abuse is more frequently linked to internalizing pathologies. Physically abused children are apt to be overly aggressive, whereas sexually abused children tend to be characterized by social withdrawal, poor social skills, and failure to develop meaningful peer relationships (Adams-Tucker 1982; Tsai and Wagner 1981). Social withdrawal has been attributed in part to the tendency of incestuous families to be socially isolated (Sgroi, Blick, and Porter 1982).

Sexually abused children tend to display fearfulness and anxiety-related symptoms, including phobic avoidance of adult males (Browning and Boatman 1977; Sgroi et al. 1982), sleep disturbances such as insomnia and nightmares (Anderson 1981; Lewis and Sarrell 1969), and eating disturbances (Anderson 1981). Sexually abused children have also been described as manifesting the symptoms of Posttraumatic Stress Disorder (Goodwin 1985), including startle reactions, flashbacks, reenactment of the trauma, and depressive symptoms. Kiser, Ackerman, and Browne (1988) studied ten children between the ages of two and six years who had been sexually molested in their day care center. They found symptoms of PTSD in nine of these ten children. These symptoms included nightmares and intrusive daydreams involving the abusive experiences. The symptoms also included the fear that the traumatic abuse would be repeated, particularly following exposure to environmental cues that had been associated with the trauma. Finally, the symptoms included the avoidance of activities that reminded them of the traumatic event. McLeer, Deblinger, and Atkins (1988) studied a sample of sexually abused children who were being treated at an outpatient child psychiatry clinic. Their assessments indicated that 48 percent of these victims met the criteria of the DSM-III-R for the diagnosis of PTSD. These criteria included reexperiencing the abuse, avoidance behavior, and autonomic hyperarousal. Seventy-five percent of the children who had been abused by their biological fathers met the criteria for PTSD, whereas none of the children who had been abused by older children met the criteria.

Sexually abused children have also been shown to be disproportionately likely to display hysterical and dissociative symptoms (Goodwin, Zouhar, and Bergman 1989). Hysterical symptoms are thought to represent an effort by victims to defend against traumatic memories through the use of denial, isolation of affect, and splitting. Children who have been victims of sexual abuse display dissociative symptoms in the form of periods of amnesia, blackouts, excessive fantasizing and daydreaming, sleepwalking, and the existence of an imaginary companion. Several studies have reported the development of full-blown dissociative identity disorder (formerly referred to as multiple personality disorder) among sexually abused children.

Children who are sexually abused are particularly prone to low self-esteem, due to the stigmatization associated with being used sexually (Tong, Oates, and McDowell 1987). Sgroi and associates (1982) referred to this stigmatization as the damaged goods syndrome. Tong and associates (1987) compared sexually abused children to nonabused controls on the Piers-Harris Self-Concept Scale. They reported that the abused group scored significantly lower. Low self-esteem is associated with vulnerability to depression, and several studies have indicated elevated levels of depression among children who have been abused sexually (Browne and Finkelhor 1986; Kempe and Kempe 1978; Livingston 1987; MacVicar 1979). Livingston (1987) used the Diagnostic Interview for Children and Adolescents (DICA) to evaluate sexually abused children who were admitted to psychiatric inpatient facilities. The mean age of this sample of sexually abused children was 9.7 years. Livingston reported that this group was disproportionately likely to be classified as depressed on the basis of the DICA.

Depression among children who have been sexually abused may also lead to additional difficulties, including the use of alcohol and other drugs to anesthetize negative affect (Briere 1984; Herman 1981; Kearney-Cooke 1988). For example, Kearney-Cooke (1988) studied a sample of sexually abused children and reported that 27 percent of the sample had abused alcohol, and that 21 percent had abused other addictive drugs. Self-hatred and serious depression among sexually abused children may be associated with suicidal ideation and suicide attempts (Lukianowicz 1972).

Neglect
The immediate and long-term effects of childhood neglect have not been studied nearly as much as the effects of childhood physical abuse or the effects of childhood sexual abuse. Probably the immediate and observable effects of childhood neglect are less obvious than the immediate and observable effects of either physical abuse or sexual abuse. Latimer (1998) linked the neglect of children to developmental delays, poor school performance, and poor overall health. These effects may be attributed to poor nutrition, inadequate access to appropriate medical attention, and lack of appropriate support and supervision in relation to schoolwork and interactions with professionals in the school system.

Egeland (1985) studied the attachment patterns that characterized neglected and nonneglected infants and preschoolers. Consistent with attachment theory (Bowlby 1969), Egeland found that during the first two years of life, neglected children were significantly more likely than nonneglected children to manifest insecure attachment patterns. Furthermore, at two years neglected children were more likely than nonneglected children to be non-compliant and to display low tolerance for frustration. By forty-two months, the neglected children were additionally distinguished by low self-esteem, lack of appropriate assertiveness, lack of flexibility, and lack of self-control. At three and a half years Egeland also reported that the neglected children tended to lack enthusiasm for educational tasks. They also tended to be de-pendent. Williamson, Bordwin, and Howe (1991) found neglected adoles-cents also tended to be characterized by insecure attachment. These investi-gators also found that neglected adolescents tended to avoid close emotional contact and performed poorly on standardized cognitive tests.

Eckenrode, Laird, and Doris (1993) studied school performance and disci-plinary problems among neglected children, physically abused children, and nonabused children. They found that neglected children score lower than nonneglected children on standardized tests, and they also receive lower grades in school. These negative academic outcomes may be attributed to truancy associated with lack of parental supervision, as well as to lack of parental interest in academic performance and lack of supervision in regard to homework and school projects. Eckenrode and his associates also found that neglected children performed more poorly than physically abused chil-dren on academic outcome measures, whereas physically abused children had the worst outcomes in terms of disciplinary problems.

Ethier, Palacio-Quintin, and Jourdan-Ionescu (1992) noted that neg-lected children tend to assume a parental role in relation to their neglectful parents. The premature assumption of adult responsibility is in part an adap-tive response on the part of the child to the manifest disorganization and lack of efficacy of his or her parents. In addition, parental neglect is frequently the result of parental substance abuse and or psychopathology (Rosenzweig and Kaplan 1996). Under such circumstances, neglected children may be forced to assume adult responsibilities prematurely, effectively being robbed of their childhood.

Emotional Abuse

Latimer (1998) suggested that the immediate negative outcomes associated primarily with the experience of childhood emotional abuse include low self-esteem, poor social skills, and poor peer relationships. Low self-esteem in relation to emotional abuse is axiomatic, since the crucial element of at least one definition of emotional abuse is parental or caretaker behavior that conveys to the child the sense that he or she is worthless, flawed, unloved, or unwanted (Johnson 2002). Similarly, Romeo (2000b) described emotional abuse as "continuous behavior by the abuser that reduces a child's self-concept to the point where the child feels unworthy of respect, friendship, love, and affection" (184).

Parental behaviors that engender feelings of worthlessness in children include "habitual patterns of belittling, denigrating, scapegoating, or other nonphysical forms of overtly hostile or rejecting treatment" (Rosenzweig and Kaplan 1996, 44). Romeo asserted that "the parental abuses consist of: unrealistic expectations of the child's behavior, repeated name calling (no good, rotten, ugly, stupid, crazy), and deliberate humiliation in front of others (teachers, siblings, relatives, friends)" (2000b, 185). Romeo noted that children inherently trust and love their parents, and they lack the reasoning ability to discount or challenge parental attacks on their self-esteem. Instead, emotionally abused children are likely to accept the demeaning statements as accurate reflections of their worth, leading to the development of a negative self-image and low self-esteem.

While the effects of emotional abuse are devastating, they are more difficult to observe and identify than the effects of physical abuse, sexual abuse, and neglect. Renn (2000) argued that in our society the general consensus regarding the nature of abusive behavior involves gross physical injury. Romeo (2000b) asserted that emotional abuse leaves hidden scars that are not apparent or easy to identify. However, Romeo pointed out that emotional abuse results in behaviors and symptoms that are observable, and that experienced clinicians can use the behavioral indicators to identify victims of emotional abuse. Victims of emotional abuse may display both passive internalizing symptoms and aggressive externalizing symptoms, but it is the passive symptoms that provide the strongest indication a given child is the victim of emotional abuse specifically. These symptoms include self-deprecating remarks, expressions of inadequacy, lack of self-confidence and normal emotional responsiveness, helplessness, extreme shyness, inability to relate to and bond with other children, and being victimized or exploited by other children.

Victims of emotional abuse may also respond with aggressive, acting-out behavior, including defiance, bullying, ridiculing others, tardiness and truancy, and running away from home. However, these symptoms are also associated with forms of child maltreatment other than emotional abuse. Therefore the observation of angry, acting-out behavior does not differentially suggest the presence of emotional abuse, as opposed to physical or sexual abuse.

Sorsoli (2004) stressed the need for clinicians to make a conscious effort to be vigilant regarding behavioral indicators of emotional abuse in the children they see. This conscious effort is necessitated by the pervasive cultural norm that accords relatively great weight to physical injury, and relatively little weight to emotional injury. For example, the *Diagnostic and Statistical Manual of Mental Disorders-IV* (American Psychiatric Association 1994) defines a "traumatic" stressor as involving the experience of a physical injury or threat of such an injury. The *DSM-IV* does acknowledge that simply witnessing such an injury or learning about the occurrence of such an injury can be traumatic, but the nature of the injury must be physical rather than emotional. The *DSM-IV* states that "the victim experienced, witnessed, or was confronted with an event or events that involved actual or threatened death or serious injury, or a threat to the physical integrity of self or others" (1994, 463). The *DSM* criteria for trauma acknowledge that such events can lead to feelings of fear, helplessness, or horror; but these emotional responses are conceptualized as secondary to the nature of the events themselves, which involve actual or threatened physical injury. Sorsoli (2004) asserted that "the same emotions arising in response to events involving betrayal or humiliation would not be sufficient for those experiences to be considered 'traumatic' under these particular criteria" (2004, 2). Similarly, Hamarman and Bernet (2000) argued that childhood physical and sexual abuse are generally recognized within the medical and legal systems, but "there has been difficulty and reluctance in addressing the issue of emotional abuse in children" (928). These observations led Sorsoli (2004) to conclude that our society has failed to develop any universal sense of empathy with respect to the experience of victims of emotional abuse. This failure of empathy requires clinicians to make special efforts to sensitize themselves to the signs and symptoms of such abuse.

Secondary Abuse

During the last decade there has been a great deal of research on the social functioning and the psychological adjustment of children who have been exposed to family violence (Fantuzzo and Mohr 1999; Geffner, Igelman, and Zellner 2003; Geffner, Jaffe, and Suderman 2000; Graham-Berman and Edelson 2001; Rossman, Hughes, and Rosenberg 2000). This body of research makes it very clear that witnessing violence within the family is associated with a broad range of social, psychological, behavioral, and educational problems.

Secondary child abuse has been associated with immediate negative outcomes in the areas of physical health, internalizing psychopathology, social competence, externalizing behaviors, and cognitive capabilities. With respect to physical health, secondary abuse has been associated with increased risk of allergies, respiratory tract infections, psychosomatic ailments, gastrointestinal disorders, and sleep disorders (Davis and Carlson 1987; Wildin, Williamson, and Wilson 1991). Children who witness domestic violence have been shown to be at elevated risk of fear, anxiety, sadness, and depression (Jouriles, Norwood, McDonald, Vincent, and Mahoney 1996; Jouriles, Spiller, Stephens, McDonald, and Swank 2000; Mathias, Mertin, and Murray 1995). Children who observe interparental violence tend to be withdrawn (Wolfe, Zak, Wilson, and Jaffe 1986). They tend to handle frustration poorly and have difficulty regulating their emotions in interactions with peers (Graham-Bermann and Levendosky 1998; Jaffe, Wolfe, and Wilson 1990). Children who experience secondary abuse are more likely than nonabused age peers to choose aggressive responses to conflictual social situations (Graham-Bermann and Levendosky 1998). They are also more likely to manifest noncompliant, disruptive, and destructive behavior than comparison children from nonviolent households (Jouriles, McDonald, Norwood, Ware, Spiller, and Swank 1998; Smith, Berthelsen, and O'Conner 1997).

However, this research does not establish clear and specific causal connections between exposure to domestic violence and any particular symptom. This is because the psychosocial adjustment problems that have been linked to witnessing violent behavior in the home include virtually all of the problems that have been linked to any of the five forms of childhood maltreatment, and because research also indicates clearly that children who are raised in violent homes are at elevated risk of experiencing other forms of abuse, including physical abuse, sexual abuse, neglect, and emotional abuse (Geffner, Igelman, and Zellner 2003; McKay 1994; O'Keefe 1994). At least one study has reported that the relationship between witnessing domestic violence and acting-out behavior was not significant after controlling for the effects of parent–child aggression (Jouriles, Barling, and O'Leary 1987). This finding may be interpreted as suggesting that the relationship between secondary child abuse and immediate negative psychosocial outcomes is spurious, due only to the co-occurrence of other forms of child maltreatment. On the other hand, several studies have indicated that the relationships between exposure to parental violence and indicators of children's psychosocial adjustment remain significant, even after partialing out the effects of other forms of child maltreatment (Fantuzzo, DePaola, Lambert, Martino, Anderson, and Sutton 1991; O'Keefe 1994). These findings could be interpreted as indicating that some of the variability in negative psychosocial outcomes is attributable specifically to the observation of domestic violence.

In addition, families in which domestic violence occurs are frequently affected by numerous additional stressors, such as poverty, poor health, parental substance abuse, and psychiatric disorders (Lystad, Rice, and Kaplan 1996). These additional stressors may also promote the emergence of psychosocial adjustment disorders among children who experience secondary abuse. Evans (2004) argued that "poor children confront widespread environmental inequities. Compared with their economically advantaged counterparts, they are exposed to more family turmoil, violence, separation from their families, instability, and chaotic households" (79). Evans also noted that poor children have less social support than more affluent children, and that their parents tend to be less responsive and more authoritarian. Poor children read less, watch TV more, and have less access to books and computers. Low-income parents tend to be uninvolved in their children's schoolwork. Evans also asserted that poor children tend to live in homes that are more crowded and noisier than the homes of affluent children. Evans noted that poor children tend to go to inferior schools, and that they have poorer-quality water to drink and air to breathe. Evans asserted that each of these aspects of the life circumstances of poor children is potentially pathogenic. The multiple life stressors cited by Evans are potential confounding variables which provide alternative explanations for the psychosocial adjustment difficulties that characterize children who are exposed to domestic violence.

Three recent studies support the view that exposure to domestic violence has an effect on immediate psychosocial outcomes that is independent of stressors associated with poverty and related parental adjustment disorders (Baliff-Spanville, Clayton, Hendrix, and Hunsaker 2004; Kalil, Tolman, Rosen, and Gruber 2003; McFarlane, Groff, O'Brien, and Watson 2003). McFarlane and colleagues (2003) compared a sample of 258 children of abused women to a sample of seventy-two children of women who were not abused. All the mothers in the two groups were attending a primary care public health clinic in an urban area. Stratified sampling was used to ensure that the two samples of mothers were similar with respect to ethnicity, household income, age, and primary language. In this way, several potentially relevant demographic factors were controlled. Each mother in each group completed the Child Behavior Checklist (CBCL) for one of her children, selected randomly. This procedure ensured independence of observations for analyses comparing the two groups of children on the CBCL scales measuring internalizing behavior problems and externalizing behavior problems.

The CBCL scale measuring internalizing behavior problems includes items assessing anxiety/depression, withdrawal, and somatic complaints. The

CBCL scale measuring externalizing behavior problems includes items assessing attention problems, aggressive behavior, and rule breaking. The results of this study indicated that abused mothers rated their children significantly higher than nonabused mothers rated their children on both the internalizing behavior problem scale and the internalizing behavior problem scale. Of course, this study is weakened by the use of maternal reports, which may be affected in unknown ways by the status of the mother as either abused or not abused. Moreover, the study does not control for the presence of forms of child abuse other than secondary abuse. However, this study does provide some evidence that there is an effect of secondary abuse on children's immediate psychosocial adjustment that exists independent of stresses associated with poverty or minority ethnic or language status.

Kalil, Tolman, Rosen, and Gruber (2003) reported the results of a study of 443 mothers of preschool and school-age children drawn from the welfare role in an urban county in Michigan. The women in the sampling frame were between eighteen and fifty-five, and they each had at least one child between the ages of three and ten. Fifty-five percent of the mothers were black; and 45 percent were white. Each participating mother completed a six-item index of severe physical violence drawn from the Conflict Tactics Scale. The six items yield information on the woman's experiences of being: (1) threatened with a harmful object; (2) physically assaulted; (3) choked; (4) threatened with a weapon; (5) assaulted with a weapon; and (6) forced into sexual activity. For each of the six forms of abuse, the responding mother indicated whether she had experienced that form of abuse (1) at any point during her lifetime and (2) during the past twelve months. Based on their responses to these items, all the respondents were classified into one of three groups, as follows: (1) never experienced any of the forms of abuse listed; (2) experienced one or more of the forms of abuse at some point during her lifetime; and (3) experienced one or more of the forms of abuse during the past twelve months.

The responding mothers were assessed by means of diagnostic screening interviews for depression, generalized anxiety disorder, and alcohol/drug dependence. The mothers also completed several self-report measures of factors considered likely to impact their parenting ability. These measures were the Pearlin Mastery Scale (Pearlin, Menaghan, Lieberman, and Mullan 1981), a parenting stress scale composed of eight items drawn from Abidin's Parenting Stress Index (Abidin 1983) and the New Chance Study of disadvantaged mothers (Morrison, Zaslow, and Dion 1998), a three-item scale measuring maternal emotional warmth, and a three-item scale measuring maternal punitive discipline. The criterion measures consisted of maternal reports of children's externalizing behavior problems (ten items) and internalizing behavior problems (five items). These items were drawn from the Behavioral Problems Index (BPI; Chase-Lansdale, Mott, Brooks-Gunn, and Phillips 1991) and the Adaptive Social Behavior Inventory (ASBI; Hogan, Scott, and Bauer 1992).

The resulting hierarchical regression analyses indicated that, after controlling for a variety of demographic variables and the maternal variables, history of maternal physical abuse during the past twelve months still explained significant variability in the severity of externalizing behavior problems. In addition, externalizing behavior problems were higher among boys than among girls, and higher among younger children than among older children. Mothers who had not completed high school tended to have children with more serious externalizing pathology, as did mothers who were unemployed. Externalizing behavior problems tended to be lower among children whose mothers reported low levels of parenting stress and among mothers with higher scores for mastery. Externalizing behavior problems also tended to be lower among children whose mothers scored relatively high on maternal warmth and relatively low on punitive discipline.

The results were different with respect to internalizing behavior problems. The regression of this criterion variable indicated that history of maternal abuse was not related significantly to internalizing behavior problems. Internalizing pathology was higher among children whose mothers were unemployed. Internalizing problems were also greater among mothers with a substance abuse problem, mothers who had low scores on mastery, and mothers who scored high on the use of punitive discipline.

Thus the study reported by Kalil and his colleagues (2003) suggests that secondary abuse has an effect on externalizing pathology over and above the effects of poverty and parenting ability. However, this study does not support the relationship between secondary abuse and internalizing behavior problems.

Baliff-Spanvill and colleagues (2004) reported an experimental study in which sixty-two children who had witnessed interparental violence and fifty-three children who had not witnessed such violence were exposed to hypothetical peer conflict situations involving such issues as allocation of limited resources, exclusion, aggression, intimidation, and jealousy. The children were asked to verbalize a strategy for resolving each conflict, and these strategies were coded and summed to yield scores along an overall continuum ranging from predominantly violent strategies to predominantly peaceful strategies. Results indicated that children who had witnessed interparental violence tended to propose more violent strategies for resolving the conflicts than children who had not witnessed such violence. This was particularly the case for male children.

Thus there is ample evidence supporting the notion that children who observe domestic violence tend to experience immediate psychosocial adjustment difficulties, particularly externalizing behavior problems; and there is some evidence that this relationship exists independent of the effects of such external factors as poverty and related stressors. However, it cannot be concluded that simply observing domestic violence leads directly to externalizing behavior problems in children, because there is little or no evidence relevant to the possible confounding effects of other forms of child maltreatment.

Tangentially relevant to the issue of the confounding effects of other forms of child maltreatment is the body of literature concerned with the effects on children of interparental conflict between parents who are divorced or divorcing (Long, Forehand, Fauber, and Brody 1987; Long, Slater, Forehand, and Fauber 1988; Mechanic and Hansell 1989; Simons, Whitbeck, Beamon, and Conger 1994; Twaite, Silitsky, and Luchow 1998). These studies indicate that the psychosocial adjustment of children and adolescents is related more strongly to the level of conflict displayed by parents than to whether the parents divorced or remained married. In addition, adjustment disorders in children tend to vary in proportion to the intensity of conflict between parents, with the most serious adjustment difficulties occurring when parental conflict rises to the level of severe verbal and physical aggression. This literature is relevant to the issue of the possible causal relationship between the observation of domestic violence and the children's adjustment disorders because the conflict manifested by the couples in these studies is ostensibly related to the issue of divorce, suggesting that other potential predictors of children's maladjustment, such as other forms of child maltreatment, may be of minimal importance. However, none of these studies included formal controls for the existence of or potential impact of other forms of child maltreatment. Therefore this body of literature does not definitively establish a direct relationship between the observation of interparental violence and the immediate emergence of childhood adjustment disorders.

Theories do exist which would explain why witnessing domestic violence might lead directly to psychosocial adjustment disorders among children. For example, social learning theory suggests that children who are exposed to violence may model the use of violence and intimidation in the resolution of disputes. This learning could be reflected in subsequent antisocial behavior and aggression with peers. Although this hypothetical causal path is plausible, however, it is by no means the only necessary and sufficient explanation for aggressive acting-out behavior among children who have witnessed domestic violence. Research to date has not adequately controlled for all the potentially confounding variables that might impact the relationship between secondary child abuse and immediate negative psychosocial adjustment outcomes. Therefore viable competing explanations may be proposed for virtually all of the negative psychosocial outcomes that have been linked to secondary child abuse. Clearly, further research is required in this area. Until such studies have been reported, however, clinicians working with children who manifest adjustment disorders should be aware of the possibility of domestic violence in the family and should make a conscious effort to follow up on any indications of this problem.

~

CHAPTER THREE

Childhood Abuse and Adult Attachment Disorders

Karen: A Case of Insecure Adult Attachment

Karen is an attractive twenty-eight-year-old who sought therapy because she felt that her marriage of three years was "in trouble." She said that she worshiped her husband, William, and that when they were married she had thought that he loved her the same way. William had been very romantic during their courtship, which was brief and passionate. They had gone on several trips to exotic places, and they seemed to have similar goals for the future. They were both professionals, he an in-house attorney for a major corporation and she a school psychologist in an affluent suburban school district. They shared the American dream of a secure and comfortable life, and they had common interests in theater, cinema, and music. Karen said that during their courtship they spent "almost every hour" of their spare time together, and she felt as if he could read her mind. Karen said that she had come to believe that finally, after a long series of relationships that had gone sour, she had found her soul mate.

However, shortly after they were married, Karen said that William began to "pull away" from her. She complained that he had begun to leave her alone, at first just occasionally but recently "a lot of the time." William spent a good deal more time at work than she had imagined he would. He had explained to her during their courtship that he had chosen to work in a corporate setting because he believed that work demands of an attorney in that setting were more reasonable than the work demands he would experience in a major law firm. He said that he valued his leisure time, and that he was willing to earn a little less money in order to have time to live. Karen had assumed that this meant that William would be home relatively early every day, and that they would be able to spend a great deal of time together each day. In reality, however, William did have to work late "several nights each month and sometimes even several times in the same week." Karen said she didn't know what to do with herself on nights when she was home alone, feeling lonely and anxious. In addition, Karen said that William spent a great deal of time on weekends playing golf and attending sports events with his male friends. Recently he had informed her that he was going to spend one of the two weeks that he had for vacation on a fishing trip to Canada with his buddies. Karen said that she was hurt by his planning this trip without her. She said that she felt abandoned. She also said that William's attitude had reinforced feelings of insecurity and what Karen described as a long-standing sense of low self-esteem. Karen indicated that she really didn't feel adequate except when she was with William.

Karen also said that on some level William's planned fishing trip and her associated feelings of abandonment had raised questions in her mind about whether she could depend on William to be faithful. She also told her therapist that she felt that her relationship with William had become less passionate over the years since their marriage. She frequently went to great lengths to create romantic moments, like making special dinners and seeking to seduce William by wearing sexy negligees. She said that these efforts were often successful, but lately William was tired or preoccupied with work or other activities. Karen always felt rejected and abandoned when William did not respond as enthusiastically as she hoped he would, and she began to experience intense anxiety regarding the future of the relationship. Karen initially asked her therapist for guidance in getting William to reengage in the marriage and become the man who had courted her.

In a joint session arranged by Karen's therapist, William professed that he loved Karen very much and would never think of leaving her or being unfaithful. He said that he enjoyed the time they spent together and still found her sexually attractive. However, he felt that Karen sometimes expected too much from him; they needed to find a balance in terms of the time they each dedicated to work, to activities they engaged in together, and to activities they each found individually rewarding. He said that he didn't feel that his occasional overtime work was unusual, and he vigorously asserted his right to play golf and go fishing with his male friends.

William said that during their courtship he had not realized Karen would be so "needy," so dependent on him, or so unable to entertain herself or engage in activities with her female friends. He said he felt smothered. He said Karen had an unreasonable need to keep in touch during the day, often calling him at work repeatedly. He also said she wasn't comfortable unless she knew exactly when he would be home each night and exactly what he planned to do each day of the weekend and exactly when he planned to do it. He said she didn't understand that a round of golf didn't always take the same amount of time to play, and that she was unreasonably upset if he arrived home a bit later on a Saturday afternoon than he had planned.

William also said that he always appreciated Karen's efforts to be romantic, but sometimes on weekday evenings he was just too tired to appreciate romance. He said that when she demanded a night of romance on a Tuesday night when he was tired, it made him feel guilty if he was too tired to respond enthusiastically. He also acknowledged times when he stayed a bit later at the office than he probably needed to, because he knew that it would give him a good excuse to avoid the effort associated with such intimate evenings.

It seemed to Karen's therapist that Karen was inordinately preoccupied with being physically and emotionally close to William all the time. It also seemed that Karen lacked normal same-sex friendships, as well as the ability to entertain herself when William was not present. It seemed clear to the therapist that William's view of marriage was considerably closer to the norm than was Karen's. Her knowledge of attachment theory suggested to Karen's therapist that Karen was characterized by an "anxious-avoidant" or "preoccupied" pattern of adult attachment, which in the extreme is characterized by a lack of self-worth and self-confidence, an inordinate desire for intimacy based on the assumption that one derives value solely from involvement in a relationship with another person, feels discomfort being alone, a sense of dependency and helplessness, an intense desire for love and approval, and an overwhelming fear of abandonment. Karen's therapist was aware that this form of adult attachment has been hypothesized to result from (1) a general failure of the individual's primary caregiver to be warm, responsive, available, and sensitive and/or (2) specific experiences of childhood abuse.

Consistent acceptance over the course of Karen's treatment, coupled with appropriately paced inquiry, eventually led Karen to disclose a childhood history involving several forms of severe and prolonged abuse. Karen had been the victim of sexual abuse perpetrated by her father, beginning when she was three or four and continuing until she was eleven, when her parents were divorced and her father moved out of the house. This abuse initially took the form of fondling and oral–genital contact and eventually proceeded to full genital intercourse. Karen said that her father always told her that his sexual advances were intended to teach her about something wonderful and to save her from being initiated by some stranger whom she could not trust. Karen stated that her father had provided her with praise and rewards for complying with his sexual demands. However, especially when she was younger, he also employed physical force to hold her down while he fondled her. In addition, as she became older, he threatened to punish her in various ways if she refused his advances. He also placed her in a double bind situation with respect to her mother. He demanded that she keep their sexual behavior secret from her mother or anyone else, telling her that if she were to disclose their relationship, it would kill her mother. In addition, Karen's father made it difficult for her to establish and maintain normal peer relationships, rationalizing that one could not ever really trust "outsiders."

Karen also reported that her mother's behavior toward her alternated between intense expressions of love and angry outbursts of insults and denigration. Karen indicated that she believed her mother was aware of the incestuous relationship between Karen and her father, but that her mother was afraid to do anything about it. Karen said she often felt greater bitterness toward her mother than toward her father. Not only did she resent the fact that her mother did nothing to protect her, but she also had the vague feeling that if her mother had done more to satisfy her father sexually, then her father would probably have left her alone.

As Karen grew into adolescence, she had an intense need to establish close relationships with peers. When her father left she had a greater opportunity to socialize with peers, but her isolation throughout her elementary years left her with a deficit in the social skills that would normally facilitate the development of such relationships. In addition, she said that she thought she had been stigmatized by the incestuous relationship with her father. It wasn't that people in town knew exactly what had happened; but they seemed to have a vague sense that something was not right with her family.

Karen said she became sexually active with peers at an early age, partly because she thought that the boys would like her if she did what they wanted, and partly because she didn't really consider the option of politely refusing a boy who made sexual advances. This behavior developed into a pattern of serial revictimization. During high school, college, and graduate school Karen reported that she frequently engaged in sexual activity that she did not seek out or desire. When asked if she considered these incidents to be date rape, she said probably not, because it can't really be rape unless you actually say no. Karen said that she was always afraid to say no, because if she did the boy wouldn't like her. She always hoped that the boys with whom she had sex would become her friends, but for a long time that did not happen. Although she was intimate sexually with many men, she said that she never had a close friend, male or female.

During graduate school, Karen said that she got the idea that the way to resolve her need for intimacy as well as her tendency toward promiscuity was to find the right man and settle down. She remembered waking up one morning after a one-night stand with a man she didn't care for. Looking at him, she thought to herself that she was clearly attractive to men, and that if she could attract men she was not interested in, she probably could just as well find one that she could stay with forever. From that point on, Karen launched into a serious, sustained effort to find a man who would make a suitable husband and to seduce him. This decision led her to try four different live-in relationships in five years. In each case, Karen consciously picked out a man who had desirable attributes, seduced him, and moved in with him. Unfortunately, in each case the relationship ended quickly, either because the man wasn't ready for a lifetime commitment or because he felt smothered in much the same way William reported feeling smothered by Karen during their marriage.

This case illustrates how the traumatic experience of childhood sexual and emotional abuse can teach a child that he or she is worthless except as an object for the sexual gratification of others. Never experiencing unconditional love, children abused in this manner have an inordinate need for closeness and intimacy, yet they feel that they are not worthy of love. Accordingly, they become preoccupied with establishing and maintaining an intimate relationship. They go to extraordinary lengths to be accepted and loved. When they do establish an intimate relationship, they fear being abandoned as worthless. This fear creates anxiety and results in frantic efforts to maintain the relationship which may, paradoxically, ensure the demise of the relationship. This developmental sequence is best understood through the lens of attachment theory.

Attachment Theory

Infant Attachment

Bowlby developed attachment theory with the goal of understanding "the adverse influences on personality development of inadequate maternal care during early childhood" (1988a, 21). Bowlby (1969, 1982) argued for the existence of an "attachment behavioral system," which is a homeostatic process that regulates the infant's efforts to seek proximity to and maintain contact with one or a few caretakers who provide the infant with physical safety and psychological security. The infant initiates attachment behaviors when he or she cannot easily reach the attachment figure, or when the child feels threatened. These behaviors include crying, calling out, and touching. When proximity has been achieved, the child will switch to behaviors aimed at maintaining proximity. These behaviors include smiling, hugging, and clinging.

The activation of the attachment system is based on the child's development of "internal working models" of the attachment figure and of the interaction between the self and the attachment figure (Bowlby 1988b). These models are based on the infant's experience with the attachment figure, and they determine the infant's behavior during and after periods of separation from the attachment figure.

Ainsworth and her colleagues studied the relationship between the characteristic level of responsiveness of the attachment figure and the behavior displayed by the infant during and after separations from the attachment figure (Ainsworth, Blehar, Waters, and Wall 1978). They identified three distinct combinations of caretaker responsiveness and associated infant attachment behavior, which they named "secure attachment," "avoidant attachment," and "anxious/ambivalent attachment."

Secure Attachment

Ainsworth and her colleagues found that when the attachment figure is regularly responsive to the proximity-seeking behaviors of the infant, the infant develops "secure" attachment, which is characterized by signs of distress when the attachment figure leaves the infant alone, proximity-seeking behavior on the return of the attachment figure, and ultimately by a return to play and exploration.

Avoidant Attachment

In contrast, when the attachment figure is characteristically unresponsive and rejecting, spurning the infant's attempts to achieve proximity, the infant develops "avoidant" attachment. These infants do not manifest signs of distress when they are separated from the caretaker, and they do not seek engage in proximity-seeking behaviors on her return.

Anxious/Ambivalent Attachment

When the attachment figure responds inconsistently to the infant's signals, on some occasions being unavailable or unresponsive and on other occasions being intrusive or overly affectionate, the infant develops "anxious/ambivalent" attachment. These infants tend to manifest distress even before they are separated from the attachment figure, and they are extremely upset during separation. Following the return of the attachment figure, anxious/ambivalent infants are not easily consoled, and they remain so concerned with the caretaker's availability that they do not move away from the caretaker to explore.

Adult Attachment Patterns

Attachment patterns established during infancy tend to persist into later childhood and adulthood. Hazan and Shaver (1987) suggested that adult orientations toward heterosexual love relationships can be grouped under the same three attachment patterns that Ainsworth and associates identified in infants' behaviors toward their attachment figures—secure, avoidant, and anxious/ambivalent. They found that securely attached adults had romantic relationships characterized by "trust, friendship, and positive emotions" (1987, 513). Avoidant adults were characterized by a fear of closeness and a lack of trust. Anxious/ambivalent adults tended to experience love as a "preoccupying, almost painfully exciting struggle to merge with another person" (1987, 513). Thus Hazan and Shaver suggested that the nature of the relationship that the infant has with the attachment figure establishes an attachment style that persists in adulthood and determines the quality of one's adult heterosexual relationships.

This finding is consistent with Rutter's (1985) argument that rejection, hostility, and inconsistent responding on the part of the attachment figure have a detrimental effect on subsequent development. Thus it would appear that parental neglect and emotional abuse tend to be associated with disturbances in adult interpersonal adjustment. One would suspect that physical abuse, sexual abuse, and secondary abuse would also have a negative impact on adult attachment and interpersonal adjustment.

Other theorists have posited somewhat different models of adult attachment styles. Bartholomew and Horowitz (1991) proposed a four-category model based on the individual's internal representations of self and other. Early experiences with the attachment figure lead the child to internalize representations of self that are either positive or negative, as well as representations of the attachment figure (and other figures later in life) as either positive or negative. The combinations of positive versus negative self-representations and positive versus negative other representations define four unique patterns of adult attachment.

Secure Adult Attachment

Individuals who develop positive internal working models of both self and other are securely attached. These individuals find it easy to become emotionally close to others. They are comfortable depending on others and having others depend on them. They do not worry about being alone or about having others not accept them.

Dismissing Adult Attachment

Individuals who develop positive internal working models of self but negative internal working models of other are referred to as "dismissing." These individuals describe themselves as comfortable without close emotional relationships. These individuals feel it is important to be independent and self-sufficient. They prefer not to depend on others or to have others depend on them. These adults mirror the avoidant attachment pattern that Ainsworth and her colleagues (1978) described for infants.

Preoccupied Adult Attachment

Individuals who develop negative internal working models of self but positive internal working models of other are "preoccupied." These individuals want to be emotionally intimate with others but often find that others are reluctant to become as close as they would like. They are uncomfortable unless they have close relationships. They worry that others don't value them as much as they value others. These adults mirror the anxious/ambivalent attachment pattern that Ainsworth and associates (1978) described for infants.

Fearful Adult Attachment

Finally, individuals who develop negative internal working models of both self and other are referred to as "fearful." These individuals are uncomfortable getting close to others. They want emotionally close relationships, but they find it difficult to trust others or to depend on them. They tend to worry that they will be hurt if they allow themselves to become close to others.

Childhood Abuse and the Need to View Self Negatively

The models of adult attachment proposed by Hazan and Shaver (1987) and by Bartholomew and Horowitz (1991) are particularly relevant to the impact of child abuse on adult attachment, because the experience of being abused and/or neglected during childhood tends to foster the development of a negative self-concept in the victim. Herman (1992b) suggested that the abused child perceives daily, "not only that the most powerful adult in her intimate world is dangerous to her, but also that other adults who are responsible for her care do not protect her" (100–101). Herman posited that in this situation the child is faced with a formidable developmental task. She must find a way to form primary attachments to caretakers who are either dangerous or negligent. "She must find a way to develop a sense of basic trust and safety with caretakers who are untrustworthy and unsafe. She must develop a sense of self in relation to others who are helpless, uncaring, or cruel" (1992, 101).

Herman explained that even though the abused child will perceive herself as abandoned to a power without mercy, she must nevertheless find a way to preserve hope and meaning. This can only be done by preserving her faith in her parents. She must discard the obvious conclusion that there is something terribly wrong with them. This can only be done in two ways. Either the child resorts to the device of dissociation to wall off the abuse from conscious awareness and memory, enabling the child to believe that the abuse did not occur, or the child must construct some theory that justifies the abuse. According to Herman, "inevitably the child concludes that her innate badness is the cause" (1992, 103).

As long as the child chooses to view herself as bad, she may view her abusing parents as good. If she is bad, then she can try to be good. She may be able to change the situation. If she has driven her parents to mistreat her, she may someday be able to obtain their forgiveness and thus win the protection and care that she needs.

The tendency of the abused child to blame himself for the abuse is often exacerbated by parental scapegoating. Survivors of various forms of childhood abuse frequently described themselves as being blamed not only for their parents' violence and sexual misconduct, but for other family misfortunes as well. Because the development of a deep inner sense of badness preserves the relationship with the abusing parents, the negative self-concept is not easily given up, even after the abuse has stopped. The negative view of self tends to become a stable and resilient part of the child's personality structure that persists into adult life.

Herman's (1992) discussion of self-blame among abused children is founded in traditional psychoanalytic theory and object relations theory, rather than specifically in attachment theory. However, the theoretical difference is more semantic than substantive. Her description of the development of the abused child is clearly consistent with attachment theory:

In the course of normal development, a child achieves a secure sense of autonomy by forming inner representations of trustworthy and dependable caretakers, representations that can be evoked mentally in moments of distress . . . In a climate of chronic childhood abuse, these inner representations cannot form in the first place; they are repeatedly, violently, shattered by traumatic experience. Unable to develop a secure sense of independence, the abused child continues to seek desperately and indiscriminately for someone to depend upon. The result is the paradox, observed repeatedly in abused children, that while they quickly become attached to strangers, they also cling tenaciously to the very parents who mistreat them. (1992, 107)

This description of the development of abused children conforms closely to the descriptions of "anxious/ambivalent" attachment in children (Ainsworth et al. 1978) and adults (Hazan and Shaver 1987) presented above. The description is also consistent with the "preoccupied" attachment classification described by Bartholomew and Horowitz (1991).

The quality of desperation associated with the attachment-seeking behavior of these children once they reach adulthood helps explain the significant relationships reported by researchers between history of childhood abuse and revictimization in adulthood (Classen, Field, Koopman, Nevill-Manning, and Spiegel 2001; Gidycz, Cobel, Latham, and Layman 1993; Mayall and Gold 1995; Neumann, Houskamp, Pollock, and Briere 1996; Wyatt, Guthrie, and Notgrass 1992).

Research on the Relationship between Childhood Abuse and Adult Attachment

Bolen (2002) pointed out that there seems to be a reciprocal relationship between childhood abuse (particularly sexual abuse) and insecure forms of attachment. She noted that children characterized by anxious/ambivalent attachment tend to cling and be dependent in relationships, and she suggested that this dependence may place them at greater risk of sexual abuse by a trusted other. She also pointed out that children who are avoidantly attached "tend to be affiliative of strangers" (2002, 104), and she argued that this orientation places them at greater risk of abuse by strangers and acquaintances. On the other hand, Bolen cited a number of studies indicating that a history of childhood physical and/or sexual abuse predicted insecure forms of attachment later in life (Alexander 1993; Roche, Runtz, and Hunter 1999; Stalker and Davies 1995).

Carlson, Cicchetti, Barnett, and Braunwald (1989) reported that children who experience physical abuse and/or neglect are much more likely to display insecure attachment as adults than are children with no history of abuse. Cicchetti (1987) estimated that between 70 percent and 100 percent of maltreated children are characterized by insecure attachment, compared to approximately 30 percent of the general population. Cicchetti also noted that maltreated children are likely to demonstrate an impaired sense of self and an impaired ability to share information about their thoughts, feelings, and intentions. Based on clinical observations of adult women, Friedrich (1990 1996) reported that a history of intrafamilial sexual abuse was associated with an increase in the likelihood of insecure attachment.

Roche, Runtz, and Hunter (1999) reported the results of a cross-sectional study of the relationship between childhood sexual abuse, adult attachment, and overall psychological adjustment. Participants were 307 female undergraduate students at a Western Canadian university. Eighty-five of these participants (27.6 percent) reported a history of childhood sexual abuse. Thirty-one (10.1 percent) indicated a history of intrafamilial sexual abuse; and 54 (17.1 percent) indicated a history of extrafamilial sexual abuse. Roche and her colleagues measured adult attachment style using the Relationship Questionnaire (RQ; Bartholomew and Horowitz 1991), which classifies respondents in accordance with Bartholomew's four category adult attachment classification as secure, preoccupied, dismissing, or fearful. The investigators measured psychological adjustment using the Trauma Symptom Inventory (TSI; Briere 1995), which yields scores on ten adjustment dimensions, including anxious arousal, anger/irritability, depression, defensive avoidance, dissociation, dysfunctional sexual behavior, intrusive experiences, impaired self-reference, sexual concerns, and tension reduction behavior.

The results of this study showed that history of CSA (intrafamilial, extrafamilial, nonabused) was a significant predictor of both adult attachment classification and psychological adjustment. The women in the nonabused group had significantly more favorable representations of both self and other than those in either of the two abused groups. Thus, the nonabused women were more likely to be securely attached. In addition, the nonabused women exhibited fewer symptoms of poor psychological adjustment, as indicated by scores on the defensive avoidance, impaired self-reference, and intrusive experiences scales.

In addition, mediation analyses indicated that the effect of history of childhood sexual abuse on psychological adjustment fell to nonsignificance after partialing out the effect of adult attachment classification. This suggests that adult attachment mediates the relationship between history of childhood sexual abuse and psychological adjustment. This supports a theoretical model for the effect of history of childhood sexual abuse which posits that the experience of childhood sexual abuse leads to insecure adult attachment, which in turn results in relatively poor psychosocial adjustment.

A prospective study of the relationship between childhood abuse and adult attachment was reported by Waters, Merrick, Treboux, Crowell, and Albersheim (2000). These investigators measured attachment during infancy and again twenty years later. They found that individuals who were securely attached during infancy but not securely attached during early adulthood tended to be characterized by intervening negative life events, including the experience of physical and/or sexual abuse at some point during childhood. The results of this prospective study indicate that the experience of childhood physical and/or sexual abuse can actually alter one's attachment style, causing a securely attached individual to develop insecure attachment patterns, which we have seen to be associated with poor adjustment.

Other empirical studies have supported the significance of adult attachment as a mediator of the relationship between history of childhood physical and/or sexual abuse and adult psychosocial adjustment. Mallinckrodt, McCreary, and Robertson (1995) found that history of incest predicted the onset of eating disorders in adulthood, and that this relationship was mediated by adult attachment scores. Shapiro and Levendosky (1999) found that history of childhood sexual abuse and other forms of childhood abuse predicted various dimensions of psychological adjustment among adolescent females, and that this relationship was mediated by adult attachment classification. Similar findings were reported for general adult samples by Muller and Lemieux (2000).

Of special interest to clinicians engaged in marital therapy is a study reported by Colman and Widom (2004) indicating a relationship between childhood abuse and neglect and aspects of adult intimate relationships. Based on a community sample of 1,179 respondents, these investigators reported that married individuals with histories of childhood physical abuse, sexual abuse, and/or neglect were more likely than other married individuals to report marital dissatisfaction, incidents of marital disruption (temporary separations as well as divorce), and instances of marital infidelity. In addition, several other studies have reported that married women who have histories of childhood sexual abuse are more likely than married women with no history of abuse to report marital dissatisfaction (Finkelhor, Hotaling, Lewis, and Smith 1989; Fleming, Mullen, Sibthorpe, and Bammer 1999; Hunter 1991). These studies suggest that therapists treating individuals and couples who are experiencing relationship difficulties should be aware of the various types of adult attachment patterns, the relationships between certain adult attachment patterns and interpersonal relationship difficulties, and the role of childhood abuse and neglect in the development of these attachment patterns.

Conclusion

Childhood neglect as well as physical, emotional, and sexual abuse destroys the sense of comfort and security in relation to the primary caretaker that one needs to develop positive internal working models of self and others that characterize secure attachment. Insecure attachment patterns developed during early childhood tend to persist into adolescence and adulthood, resulting in a variety of psychosocial adjustment disorders of varying degrees of severity. The relationship insecurity manifested by Karen in the case study presented earlier in this chapter constitutes a relatively mild manifestation of the preoccupied attachment pattern that may result from childhood abuse and neglect. Clients like Karen who present with feelings and behaviors indicating such a preoccupied attachment pattern may very well have experienced some form of childhood abuse or neglect that led them to develop an insecure and negative self-concept. Clinicians who encounter such clients will want to make appropriately timed inquires aimed at assessing for such histories.

~

CHAPTER FOUR

Childhood Abuse and Borderline Personality Disorder

The next category of adult adjustment disorder associated with childhood abuse that we consider in this volume is Borderline Personality Disorder. We chose to consider this diagnosis immediately following our discussion of adult attachment disorders because we feel strongly that what clinicians describe as borderline pathology may be thought of as an extreme manifestation of the various forms of insecure adult attachment, accompanied by some posttraumatic features such as dissociation and self-injurious behavior. When you read through the following case study of John, an individual who clearly fits the diagnostic criteria for Borderline Personality Disorder, you will probably be struck first by how severe his pathology seems, in contrast to the distress manifested by Karen, whom we used in the previous chapter to illustrate insecure adult attachment. However, when we consider some of the specific aspects of John's dysfunctional feelings and behaviors, you will see that there are some striking parallels.

John: A Case of Borderline Personality Disorder

John is a forty-year-old white male who was brought to a psychiatric emergency unit by police who had responded to a neighbor's report of a shot being fired in John's house. John answered the door when the police rang. He was intoxicated and had obviously been crying. He acknowledged that he had discharged a gun and said he was glad to see them. When they went inside, they found a revolver lying on his desk and a bullet hole in the ceiling. There was an expended round on the desk next to the revolver, and there was a single cartridge in the cylinder. They concluded that John had been playing Russian roulette and was clearly in danger of committing suicide.

They told John that he needed to go to the hospital. He agreed and went along compliantly. In the hospital, he told the admitting physician that he was despondent regarding an impending divorce. He said that he had been unable to see his daughter since separating from his wife, and he feared he would be cut off from her permanently. John continued to be cooperative through the intake interview.

A decision was made to admit John for up to forty-eight hours for observation. When asked to undress to change into a hospital gown, however, John refused. When staff attempted to compel him to undress, John savagely attacked a male nurse, breaking his nose and knocking him out. It took five men to restrain John. He remained restrained through the night. The next day he was compliant once again, and was placed in a psychiatric ward for evaluation. During the observation period, staff concluded that John was not mentally disturbed. He was lucid and appropriately oriented. He was well-educated and articulate. He was extremely contrite with respect to his aggressive behavior toward the nurse, blaming it on the alcohol. John also expressed concern regarding the time he was spending in the unit. He was in business as a technical consultant, and he had a deadline for a project. Therefore he was anxious to get back to work. The staff attributed his suicide attempt to his despondency over the divorce, and they attributed his assaultive behavior to his intoxicated state. John was released to go home, with a recommendation that he seek personal counseling and consider the possibility of attending an AA meeting.

John did not go to AA, but he did begin therapy with a psychologist who had a cognitive behavioral orientation. This psychologist worked with the initial aim of helping John realize that the divorce would certainly be resolved in good time and help him formulate strategies aimed at resuming visitation and a normal relationship with his daughter. In the course of this work, however, it became clear that John had a long history of serious difficulties in the area of interpersonal relationships. He reported having no close friends during elementary or junior high school. He made friends during high school with a few young men who shared some of his academic and athletic interests, but these friendships didn't last. John's self-concept was founded on his superior intellect and his academic and athletic accomplishments. He explained that his relationships with same-sex peers would fall apart when they became "jealous" of his accomplishments, whether academic, athletic, or social. John also volunteered that he had been quite a ladies' man during high school and his male peers had a hard time with his sexual precociousness.

John indicated that he had been "on his own" a good deal during high school. His initial description of his home life was that his parents were divorced and his mother traveled extensively in connection with her work, leaving him alone to take care of himself. John portrayed this living situation in positive terms, maintaining that it had made him responsible and self-reliant. Having "a place of his own" during high school made it easy for him to "get women." He joked that the lack of parental supervision solved a teenager's two most important problems, which he described as access to alcohol and a place to have sex. John reported losing his virginity on his fourteenth birthday to an older woman who was a neighbor and a friend of his mother, and he explained with considerable pride that he was very experienced sexually by the time he finished high school.

John freely acknowledged that as an adult he tended to be somewhat contemptuous of people in general and business associates in particular. He described a period of approximately one year early in his career when he was employed by a large corporation. In this relatively brief time he had several heated altercations with coworkers who disagreed with conclusions and recommendations that John had made. John's descriptions of these incidents made it clear that he had been inappropriately condescending and angry. John described himself as "not the corporate type." He stated that his decision to work as an independent consultant was based on the idea that this work did not require him to put up with stupid people. If a client was not sufficiently respectful of John's expertise, John simply stopped working for that person.

John also reported a history of several intense adult romantic relationships that ended when he walked out. He had already been married and divorced once before. His second marriage of eight years was ending now because he was "fed up" with a wife whom he described as dull, incompetent, dishonest, and dependent, and because John was having an intense romantic affair with a colleague.

John was furious with his wife for several reasons. First, when John met his wife she was employed as an intensive care nurse. He expected that she would continue working in this profession, and that together they would build wealth. However, soon after their marriage his wife quit her well-paid job to dabble in various forms of arts and crafts activities, which produced no income. Second, at John's insistence, they had agreed explicitly before marrying not to have any children, yet within a year of their marriage his wife informed him that she had stopped taking birth control pills and was pregnant. Surprisingly, John accepted the unwanted pregnancy when it occurred, and he became a devoted and indulgent father. He described his daughter as extremely bright. He had taught her to read at the age of three, and he spent countless hours reading poetry and novels to her as she grew up. She began school a year early and by the age of seven she was in third grade. While John was caring and attentive toward his daughter, he virtually ignored his wife.

A few months before separating from his wife, John had begun an intense affair with a woman who was a professional colleague, whom he regarded as an intellectual equal. This colleague was also married, but John decided that they should be together. He left home immediately, simply informing his wife that she had not lived up to their bargain and he had found someone more appropriate. He convinced his lover to get a divorce as well, in order to be with him. However, she did not act nearly as precipitously as John. At the time John began therapy, she was still living with her husband, although they had begun mediation aimed at effecting the least acrimonious divorce possible. John's lover did not inform her husband that she wanted a divorce in order to be with another man. John expressed substantial displeasure with both the delay in her separating from her husband and the fact that he was not named as the "other man."

The immediate fallout of John's impulsive actions was a predictably contentious divorce. John's wife alleged that he had problems with alcohol abuse and anger management. It was revealed that in college he had been charged with a misdemeanor assault as a result of a bar room brawl, and in his twenties he had been convicted of driving while intoxicated. In the course of the disclosure process it also became clear that even though John earned good money as a consultant, he had saved no money, due to a history of impulsive spending. While John downplayed the seriousness of these issues, the court regarded them as sufficiently serious to give temporary custody of their daughter to his wife and to allow visitation only on the condition that John not drink alcohol when his daughter was with him. When he was informed of this decision, John was furious. He made a number of insulting remarks to the judge and declared that there was no way he would conform to such a ridiculous condition. He stated in court that, "Nobody tells me what I can and can't do." As a result of this intransigent attitude, the judge mandated that all visitation be supervised. John responded that he would not visit under these conditions, with the result that he effectively cut himself off from seeing his daughter.

Based on John's history of unstable personal relationships, angry outbursts, substance abuse, and impulsive self-destructive behavior, John's therapist quickly diagnosed John as having Borderline Personality Disorder and began to assess for other possible symptoms of the borderline condition. The therapist also sought clues regarding the etiology of John's condition. It turned out that John also had another characteristic of borderline personality disorder—a history of self-mutilation—particularly when he was younger. He would bite his nails until his fingers bled, and he would pick at wounds repeatedly so that they ultimately formed scars. Both his forearms were heavily scarred.

For some time John downplayed his mother's apparent neglect in allowing him to live by himself for long periods of time. However, his therapist pointed out to John that her extended absences constituted child abuse according to both legal and psychological definitions. The therapist also inquired regarding details of John's childhood and adolescence, in order to obtain a complete picture of the parameters of the abusive living situation. Over time, John began to accept the fact that his living situation was both abnormal and potentially damaging. He claimed that his adolescent experience had made him "extremely responsible" and pointed to the fact that he had been an excellent student and an athlete in high school. He graduated first in his class and won a full scholarship to a prestigious university. John also noted that because he was such a high achiever he had "gotten away with" several instances of inappropriately aggressive behavior that occurred during the middle school years.

Once John reframed his perception of his living situation during adolescence, he began to disclose details of his life that made it clear that he had grown up in an extremely abusive situation. From the time of her second divorce, which occurred when John was in sixth grade, his mother and he lived in a fairly luxurious but rather small (one bedroom) apartment. The bedroom was John's room. When his mother was at home, she slept in the living room on a pullout couch. John said that his mother was home a fair amount while he was in the sixth and seventh grades, but less and less frequently after seventh grade. By the time he got into high school, she was gone almost all the time, showing up just a few times a year for a week or so.

John initially described his mother in ideal terms, as very attractive and incredibly intelligent. He described her as working irregularly doing modeling and public relations work. Her extensive travels were ostensibly connected with this work. She was often away from home for three or four months at a time, and once for almost a full year. John relied on maternal grandparents who lived thirty minutes away to provide groceries and a bit of a safety net. He recalled that there were times when they had to pay the rent on the apartment. However, they never suggested that he come and live with them, for fear of alienating John's mother. John learned to cook and keep house and became very self-sufficient. He described keeping a rigid schedule in which he went to school early, stayed as late as possible by involving himself with after school athletic activities, and spent virtually all his time at home doing homework.

In time John revealed the more negative aspects of his relationship with his mom. When his mother did come home, John said that she generally arrived unannounced and often with friends. John said that when she came back he felt as if his space had been invaded. John said his mother had parties in which a lot of drinking and sexual activity occurred. She had many boyfriends and regularly had sex with them in the living room, making very little effort to be discreet. John said that he could not get into or out of his room without going through the living room, and he said that it was impossible for him to avoid seeing her there in bed with her boyfriends.

John recalled that when he was a child his mother had an inordinate concern with his physical development, often asking to see his penis to be make sure that he was "developing normally." He found this to be terribly embarrassing. He also recalled that she was generally indifferent toward him, except when she was drinking. He recalled that when she got drunk she would become affectionate, hugging and kissing him, pulling his head into her breasts, and wrapping her legs around him. He recalled times when she touched his penis. Initially he said that he thought he had always been clothed when this occurred, but later he indicated that there may have been times when he was not clothed.

John also recalled that his mother had several female friends, whom he described as "semiprofessional" prostitutes. When asked what he meant by this, he responded that they were not common hookers but attractive "party girls" who dabbled in modeling and public relations work but had rich older boyfriends who paid the rent. These women used to drink and party with his mother. These parties would often involve men, and John remembered witnessing "orgies" in the living room.

On several occasions when they were drunk these women hugged and fondled John. On more than one occasion these attentions progressed to the point where one of the women would get John in a corner or into the bathroom or into his room, where she would masturbate him and perform fellatio on him. He found these experiences frightening but at the same time exciting. He described his first orgasm as coming from being masturbated. He said he was probably eleven or twelve, and he was frightened because he didn't know what was happening. He could not remember if the woman who brought him to orgasm was his mother or one of her friends, but he remembered feeling extremely guilty. John had blocked out these memories, but once they began to come back he recalled many similar instances of abuse in great detail. He also began to dream of having sex with his mother. John also remembered that the neighbor woman with whom he had lost his virginity was his mom's closest drinking buddy. He recalled that she initiated this encounter, and that she had been masturbating him and performing fellatio on him for months before actually having sexual relations with him.

Borderline Personality Disorder

Although most individuals diagnosed with Borderline Personality Disorder are women, John's case is otherwise quite typical of Borderline Personality Disorder. It illustrates how dysfunctional and self-destructive borderlines can be. The diagnostic criteria for the Borderline Personality Disorder are fairly obvious, so there is often little doubt in making the initial diagnosis. In John's case, the therapist based his initial diagnosis on his history of volatile and unstable interpersonal relationships, his suicide attempt, his substance abuse, his inability to control his anger, his contempt for authority, and his impulsive and self-destructive behaviors manifested throughout his life but displayed in particular in regard to his marriage and the divorce process. During the first few therapy sessions, further evidence of the borderline personality emerged in the form of John's history of aggressive acting-out behavior, the risky behavior associated with driving while intoxicated, the discovery that he was an impulsive spender, and the revelation that he had engaged in extensive self-mutilating behavior as an adolescent.

This case is also typical of borderline personality disorder in that John was raised in a chaotic home environment and was a victim during childhood and adolescence of repeated sexual abuse over a prolonged period perpetrated by both his primary caretaker and by third parties. As is often the case, self-disclosure of abuse by borderline patients tends to occur a bit later in the course of treatment, after a degree of trust has been established with the therapist. It is also typical of such cases that the process of disclosure is not only a function of increasing willingness to reveal embarrassing events, but also a function of gradually increasing recall of these events, which have often been repressed. Often the process of disclosing abuse will be facilitated by a skilled therapist who is aware of the relationship between a history of childhood sexual abuse and adult Borderline Personality Disorder and is willing to address the issue of sexual abuse directly.

The DSM-IV-TR Criteria for Borderline Personality Disorder

The DSM-IV-TR states that "the essential feature of Borderline Personality Disorder is a pervasive pattern of instability of interpersonal relationships, self-image, and affects, and marked impulsivity that begins by early adulthood and is present in a variety of contexts" (APA 2000, 706). The DSM description continues by pointing out that individuals with Borderline Personality Disorder make frantic efforts to avoid real or imagined abandonment. These efforts may take a variety of forms, including extreme efforts to comply with every wish of one's adult attachment figure, threats of self-harm or suicide in the event of being abandoned, or preemptive denigration and abandonment of the attachment figure, in order to be the partner who leaves rather than the partner who is left. The latter pattern characterized John's adolescent relationships with same-sex friends as well as his adult relationships with women.

The DSM-IV-TR lists nine defining criteria for Borderline Personality Disorder, five of which must be present in order to justify assigning this diagnosis:

(1) frantic efforts to avoid real or imagined abandonment. Note: Do not include suicidal or self-mutilating behavior covered in Criterion 5.
(2) a pattern of unstable and intense interpersonal relationships characterized by alternating between extremes of idealization
(3) identity disturbance: marked and persistently unstable self-image or sense of self
(4) impulsivity in at least two areas that are potentially self-damaging (e.g., spending, sex, substance abuse, reckless driving, binge eating). Note: Do not include suicidal or self-mutilating behavior covered in Criterion 5.
(5) recurrent suicidal behavior, gestures, or threats, or self-mutilating behavior
(6) affective instability due to a marked reactivity of mood (e.g., intense episodic dysphoria, irritability, or anxiety lasting a few hours and only rarely more than a few days)
(7) chronic feelings of emptiness
(8) inappropriate, intense anger or difficulty controlling anger (e.g., frequent displays of temper, constant anger, recurrent physical fights)
(9) transient, stress-related paranoid ideation or severe dissociative symptoms (APA 2000, 710).

In order to be diagnosed with Borderline Personality Disorder an individual must meet five of these criteria. However, some individuals who have experienced childhood abuse of various forms meet fewer than five of these criteria. For this reason, the following chapters in this volume (chapters 5–9) consider some of these criteria individually. We emphasize further that the clinician working with patients who complain or of otherwise manifest any combination of these symptoms should be open to the possibility that there is a history of childhood abuse.

Evidence of the Relationship between Childhood Abuse and Borderline Personality Disorder

Considerable empirical data is available to support the contention that abuse during childhood and adolescence, particularly sexual abuse, is associated with the emergence of Borderline Personality Disorder during adulthood. The majority of studies pertinent to this issue have compared groups of patients diagnosed as having Borderline Personality Disorder to various comparison groups with respect to self-reports of childhood experiences elicited in structured interviews. Links, Steiner, Offord and associates (1988) compared eighty-eight inpatients diagnosed as suffering from Borderline Personality Disorder to forty-two inpatients who had borderline traits but were not diagnosed with Borderline Personality Disorder. The investigators interviewed the patients with respect to various aspects of their childhood experiences, including a history of various forms of childhood abuse perpetrated by caretakers and others. The results of this study indicated that the patients with the diagnosis of Borderline Personality Disorder were significantly more likely than the comparison group patients to report that they had been sexually abused by a caretaker. They were also significantly more likely than comparison group subjects to report that they had been physically abused by a caretaker, and to report that they had been separated from their primary caretaker for a period of three months or more.

Zanarini, Gunderson, Marino and colleagues (1989b) compared fifty outpatients diagnosed as having Borderline Personality Disorder to fifty-five outpatients with other DSM Axis II disorders. They found that patients in the borderline group were significantly more likely than patients with other Axis II disorders to report that they had been sexually abused by a caretaker before the age of eighteen. They also found that patients in the borderline group were significantly more likely than comparison group subjects to report that they had been abused verbally by a caretaker. Zanarini and her associates also compared the borderline patients to patients who met the DSM-III criteria for antisocial personality disorder. They found that the borderline group were significantly more likely than the antisocial personality group to report that they had been separated from their primary caregiver for a period of at least one month prior to the age of six years.

Herman, Perry, and van der Kolk (1989) compared twenty-one outpatients diagnosed with Borderline Personality Disorder to a mixed comparison group of thirty-four outpatients that contained eleven patients with borderline traits and twenty-three patients diagnosed with some other Axis II disorder. A significantly higher proportion of the borderline group reported being sexually abused before the age of nineteen. The borderline group and the comparison group did not differ significantly with respect to whether or not they reported a history of being physically abused as children.

Orgata, Silk, and Goodrich (1990) compared twenty-four inpatients diagnosed with Borderline Personality Disorder to eighteen depressed inpatients. They found that patients in the borderline group were significantly more likely than those in the depressed group to report that they had been sexually abused during childhood and/or adolescence. The two groups did not differ significantly with respect to self-reported physical abuse or with respect to self-reported neglect. More than half of the borderline group (53 percent) reported that they had been abused sexually by more than one perpetrator. Specifically, five of the borderline patients reported being abused by their father, one by their mother, seven by a sibling, six by another relative, and twelve by a nonrelative.

Ludolph, Westen, Misle and associates (1990) compared twenty-seven female adolescent inpatients who had been diagnosed with Borderline Personality Disorder to a comparison group of twenty-three female adolescent inpatients with mixed psychiatric disorders. The investigators found that the patients in the borderline group were significantly more likely than those in the comparison group to report a history of childhood sexual abuse. Eight of the patients in the borderline group reported that they had been abused by their fathers; two by their mothers; and eleven by others. The patients in the borderline group indicated that the sexual abuse began between the ages of six and ten.

Taken together, these studies clearly indicate that a history of childhood sexual abuse is associated with the emergence of Borderline Personality Disorder. The evidence of a relationship between childhood physical abuse and BPD is not as consistent. These findings have been widely interpreted as suggesting that sexual abuse is the primary cause of borderline pathology, both in scholarly publications (Herman and van der Kolk 1987; Perry, Herman, van der Kolk et al. 1990), and particularly in works aimed at the general public (e.g., Bass and Davis 1994; Blume 1990). However, the available evidence does not support the position that there is a direct one-to-one causal relationship between childhood sexual abuse and Borderline Personality Disorder. Rather, the relationship between CSA and BPD appears to be complex, mediated by both the parameters of the sexual abuse and frequently co-occurring pathogenic conditions in the home environment. In addition, given the similarity noted above between aspects of anxious/ambivalent attachment and aspects of Borderline Personality Disorder, it has been hypothesized that adult attachment mediates the relationship between childhood abuse and adult borderline pathology. This argument suggests that abuse causes the child to feel worthless and intensely insecure regarding the availability of attachment figures, and these disturbances in identity and object relations lead in turn to the frantic efforts of borderlines to avoid abandonment. The following sections of this chapter consider these complicating factors.

Parameters of Childhood Sexual Abuse

Paris and Zweig-Frank (1997) reviewed the literature on a wide variety of traumatic events that can occur during childhood, and they concluded that most of the studies indicated that single negative events "do not on the whole have long-term psychological sequelae in adulthood" (15). With specific reference to the relationship between the trauma of childhood sexual abuse and the development of BPD in adulthood, they concluded that the literature showed that "a history of CSA is associated with a number of phenomena also characteristic of borderline patients: unstable mood, suicide attempts, substance abuse, and sexual revictimization" (16). However, they also concluded that "fewer than a quarter of those with a CSA history have any demonstrable long-term sequelae" (16). They suggested that the development of adult sequelae might be a function of the specific nature of the abuse, and therefore they determined to study the parameters of childhood sexual abuse in relation to the emergence of BPD in adulthood.

These investigators compared a sample of seventy-eight female outpatients who had been diagnosed with BPD to a sample of seventy-two female outpatients who had been diagnosed with some other personality disorder. They administered a semistructured interview to obtain histories of childhood sexual abuse and its parameters, physical abuse and its parameters, and separation or loss. The interview format consisted of a broad range of questions regarding various aspects of childhood development in which the items concerned with abuse are embedded.

Childhood sexual abuse was defined as unwanted sexual contact, ranging from fondling to sexual intercourse, that occurred prior to the respondent's sixteenth birthday and was perpetrated either by a family member or by a non–family member who was five or more years older than the victim. A history of CSA was noted dichotomously. When abuse was indicated, separate

72 ~ Chapter Four

questions were asked about the parameters of the abuse. These included the relationship of the victim to the perpetrator(s), the frequency of occurrence of abuse (using a five-point scale with response options ranging from "single incident" to "very often"), the duration of the time interval over which the abuse occurred, the age of the victim at the time the abuse began, and the nature of the abuse. The latter was scored as a series of dichotomies, according to whether or not the victim reported the occurrence of each of four categories of sexual acts: fondling, genital fondling, oral sex, and penetration. In addition, the interview elicited reports of the use of force in the commission of the abuse, whether or not the victim had the ability to disclose the abuse at the time that it occurred, and the success of attempts to get help. These variables were similarly scored dichotomously.

The investigators also queried and recorded physical abuse perpetrated by a caretaker. They scored for separation or loss if there was any "death or permanent separation from a parent any time in the first 16 years of life" (1997, 19). Finally, the investigators administered the Parental Bonding Index (PBI), which yielded four scale scores measuring the participants' perceptions of the extent to which each of their parents was (1) affectionate toward them and (2) controlling.

A univariate chi-square test indicated that patients in the BPD group were significantly more likely than those in the comparison group to report a history of sexual abuse. Whereas 70.7 percent of the BPD group reported a history of sexual abuse; only 45.8 percent of the non-BPD group reported such a history. Univariate tests also indicated that the BPD and non-BPD groups did not differ significantly with respect to the proportion of participants who reported being sexually abused by father, mother, stepfather, stepmother, or any caretaker. The BPD participants, however, were significantly more likely to report abuse by a sibling (14.1 percent of the BPD group vs. 4.2 percent of the non-BPD group); by some other relative (24.4 percent of the BPD group vs. 8.3 percent of the non-BPD group); and by a nonrelative known to the family (34.6 percent of the BPD group vs. 15.3 percent of the non-BPD group). In addition, the BPD participants were more likely to report that they had been abused by multiple perpetrators (37.2 percent of the BPD group vs. 13.9 percent of the non-BPD group).

The BPD group and the comparison group did not differ significantly with respect to the frequency of abuse reported, the duration of the abuse, or the age of the victim at the onset of abuse. The two groups differed significantly with respect to only one form of sexual abuse—sex acts involving penetration (32.7 percent of the BPD group vs. 6.1 percent of the non-BPD group). The two groups did not differ significantly with respect to the use of force by the perpetrator, the ability to disclose the abuse at the time, or the efficacy of attempts to get help.

In univariate analyses, a significant difference was observed between the BPD and non-BPD groups with respect to the proportion of respondents reporting a history of physical abuse by a caretaker (73.1 percent among the BPD group vs. 52.8 percent among the non-BPD group). The two groups did not differ significantly with respect to the proportion who reported a separation from or loss of a parent before the age of sixteen. This proportion was substantial in both groups (51.3 percent of the BPD group vs. 45.8 percent for the non-BPD group). Of the four scores derived from the Parental Bonding Index, the two groups differed only with respect to affection shown by mother. The BPD group had a lower score on this scale.

In addition to the univariate comparisons noted above, the investigators ran a logistic regression to predict group membership (BPD vs. non-BPD) from overall sexual abuse, physical abuse by a caretaker, the four PBI scales, and separation or loss before the age of sixteen. The only significant predictor in this regression analysis was sexual abuse (beta = .47, $p < .02$). The other two predictors that had been significant in the univariate analyses (physical abuse and maternal affection) did not make significant contributions to the prediction of BPD when included with CSA.

Paris and Zweig-Frank (1997) interpreted these findings as supporting "the large number of studies showing that histories of CSA are particularly common in patients with BPD" (23). However, they also noted that the overlap between the BPD and non-BPD groups was substantial. They emphasized that not all their borderline patients reported abuse, and that many of their non-borderline patients did report abuse. The investigators interpreted the results of the logistic regression analysis as indicating that "a history of CSA discriminated borderline from non–borderline personality disorders more than the other psychological factors measured here" (24). They also interpreted the significance of the parameters of multiple perpetrators and abuse involving penetration as consistent with the hypothesis that the traumatic effects of childhood sexual abuse can lead to the development of BPD. However, they pointed out that the parameters of multiple perpetrators and abuse involving penetration were reported by only a minority of the borderline patients. For this reason, they concluded that

> there may be a subgroup of patients with BPD in which CSA plays a particularly important role. In that subgroup of patients (about a quarter of our sample), severe CSA discriminated borderline from nonborderline patients more strongly. However, in the majority of BPD cases, CSA either lacked the

parameters of severity (penetration and multiple perpetrators) or was absent. (1997, 25)

These findings support our contention that the severity of the childhood trauma may determine whether the adult survivor will simply manifest the characteristics of insecure, anxious/ambivalent attachment, or whether full-blown Borderline Personality Disorder will result. Thus therapists working with patients who may be borderline must carefully assess the objective parameters and the subjective meanings of the childhood abuse that these patients may have experienced. They must be sensitive to possible indications of physical and sexual abuse, yet they cannot assume that such abuse occurred. Therapists must adopt a stance that encourages patients to recall and disclose all aspects of their childhood and adolescent experiences, without leading patients toward a preconceived conclusion.

Other Pathogenic Factors in the Childhood Environment

Other investigators have focused their attention on aspects of the childhood environment other than sexual abuse that may lead to the development of borderline pathology in adulthood or interact with various forms of sexual abuse to produce BPD. Zanarini and colleagues (1997) reported the results of a carefully designed study aimed at evaluating the relative importance of a variety of pathological childhood experiences in the etiology of Borderline Personality Disorder. These investigators compared a sample of seventy-eight inpatients diagnosed as having BPD with thirty-seven inpatients diagnosed with some other Axis II disorder. These patients were assessed for pathological childhood experiences using the Revised Childhood Experiences Questionnaire (CEQ-R), a semistructured interview that elicits data on various forms of abuse and neglect. The CEQ-R assesses abuse perpetrated by full-time caretakers, including physical abuse, sexual abuse, emotional abuse, and verbal abuse. It also assesses various forms of neglect on the part of caretakers, including physical neglect, emotional withdrawal, inconsistent treatment, denial of feelings, the lack of a real relationship, the parentification of the child, and the failure to provide protection. In addition, the CEQ-R assesses noncaretaker sexual abuse. Finally, the CEQ-R assesses separations from full-time caretakers that lasted one month or more.

When the two groups were compared with respect to the proportion of individuals in each group who indicated that they had experienced each of the various forms of abuse, significant differences were obtained with respect to physical abuse by a caretaker, sexual abuse by caretaker and/or noncaretaker, emotional withdrawal by caretaker, and perceived lack of a real relationship with caretaker. In each case the proportion of participants reporting the specific form of abuse was higher among the BPD group than among the comparison group. However, the BPD and comparison group subjects did not differ significantly with respect to reports of early childhood separations from caretakers.

The investigators compared participants who reported having been sexually abused to those who did not on self-reports of the other categories of abuse. These bivariate comparisons indicated that participants who reported sexual abuse were significantly more likely than those who did not to report emotional abuse by the caretaker, physical abuse by the caretaker, emotional withdrawal, and failure to provide protection. Moreover, "sexual abuse almost always occurred in conjunction with at least one other type of abuse and/or neglect" (1997, 34).

Finally, Zanarini and her colleagues (1997) carried out a logistic regression which indicated that the diagnosis of Borderline Personality Disorder was associated significantly to five factors: (1) being female; (2) sexual abuse by a male caretaker; (3) sexual abuse by a male noncaretaker; (4) emotional withdrawal by a male caretaker; and (5) lack of a real relationship with a female caretaker.

Based on these results, Zanarini and colleagues (1997) concluded that "childhood experiences of both abuse and neglect were basically ubiquitous for our borderline patients" (36), and that "childhood experiences of both abuse and neglect were significantly more common among borderline patients than among control subjects" (37). These findings are consistent with the results of earlier studies. They also concluded that sexually abused patients are more likely than non–sexually abused patients to come from chaotic environments. Therefore sexual abuse does not occur in a vacuum but in a context of ongoing experiences of abuse and neglect. Thus, when all types of pathological childhood experiences are considered together, sexual abuse is certainly an important factor in the etiology of BPD, but other factors, including various forms of neglect by caretakers of both genders, also appear to play an important role.

Zanarini and her colleagues (1997) pointed out that no study to date, including their own study, has indicated that all BPD patients have been sexually abused; and no study to date has indicated that all patients who have been sexually abused are borderline. Therefore childhood sexual abuse is neither necessary nor sufficient for the development of BPD. They concluded that

For about half of our borderline patients, childhood sexual abuse appears to be an important etiological factor. However, this abuse usually seems to be embedded in an atmosphere of general chaos and biparental neglect. For the other half of our patients, other forms of abuse (i.e., emotional abuse, verbal abuse, and physical abuse), in conjunction with various forms of neglect, probably play a more central etiological role. (1997, 42)

This conclusion suggests the potential utility of several different conceptualizations of the etiology of Borderline Personality Disorder. The role of sexual abuse in the emergence of borderline pathology would seem to indicate that BPD is closely related to posttraumatic stress syndrome and dissociative disorders. On the other hand, when one considers the fact that not all borderlines appear to have been sexually abused, one might conclude that some other mechanism may be involved in the development of borderline pathology. Given the relationships observed between borderline pathology and history of emotional withdrawal and neglect, one is led to conceptualize an alternative (or co-occurring) path to borderline pathology resulting from failures on the part of the primary caregiver to provide the secure holding environment required for the development of stable object constancy and secure attachment. In chapter 3 we considered the relationship between various forms of childhood abuse and insecure attachment. Here we suggest that neglect and emotional withdrawal may lead to attachment disorders that may in turn be associated with the development of certain features of BPD, primarily those involving fear of abandonment and unstable interpersonal relationships. This path may operate separately from or in conjunction with the path that leads from the trauma of physical and sexual abuse to other characteristics of severe borderline pathology, including the more directly self-destructive aspects of substance abuse, risky sexual behavior, self-mutilation, and suicidality. The intervening role of attachment in the relationship between childhood abuse and borderline pathology is considered in the next section of this chapter.

Childhood Abuse, Attachment Disorders, and Borderline Personality Disorder

Salzman, Salzman, and Wolfson (1997) noted that the literature supporting the relationship between childhood sexual abuse and the emergence of BPD clearly reveals that a history of sexual abuse, especially repeated abuse with multiple perpetrators, emerges almost invariably within the context of a dysfunctional home environment. Salzman and her associates cited references to home environments characterized by several different pathogenic conditions, including (1) parental neglect (Paris and Frank 1989); (2) alcoholism and/or affective instability among family members (Links, Boiago, Huxley et al. 1990); and (3) "family chaos" and "disrupted attachments" (Ludolph, Westen, Misle et al. 1990). Salzman and associates also pointed out that two studies had been designed to compare the relative strength of the effects of physical and sexual abuse per se to the effects of a family climate of emotional violence and impaired attachments (Ludolph et al. 1990; Zanarini et al. 1989a). These two studies both reported "a stronger association between impaired family attachment, emotional violence, or neglect, and BPD than with specific traumata of physical or sexual abuse" (Salzman et al. 1997, 71). Finally, Salzman and colleagues referred to five separate studies (Briere and Zaidi 1989; Gunderson and Sabo 1993; Links et al. 1990; Shearer, Peters, Quaytman et al. 1990; Westen et al. 1990) which had concluded specifically that "childhood sexual abuse may be predictive of specific features of severely symptomatic borderline personality functioning, while not necessarily providing a comprehensive or general understanding of the etiology of this disorder" (1997, 72). Based on this these prior studies, Salzman and her colleagues designed two studies to test the hypothesis that insecure attachment to one's maternal caregiver is related more strongly than specific occurrences of physical and/or sexual abuse to the development of BPD across the whole spectrum of that disorder.

In their first study Salzman and associates (1997) administered the Adolescent Attachment Interview (Salzman 1988, 1990) to 101 female college students. This instrument allowed the investigators to classify each participant with respect to attachment, using the five-category classification: secure, avoidant, ambivalent, secure/avoidant, and secure/ambivalent. Based on this classification, the investigators selected forty-one respondents in an approximation of stratified random sampling. The authors noted that these forty-one subjects were "chosen deliberately to provide approximately equal numbers in each of the five attachment classifications" (1997, 74). The actual attachment group frequencies were as follows: secure (n = 10); avoidant (n = 7); ambivalent (n = 11); secure/avoidant (n = 7); and secure/ambivalent (n = 6). Each respondent was interviewed to ascertain the presence of borderline pathology and recalled aspects of the home environment.

Of the forty-one participants, nine were classified as meeting the criteria for BPD, and one additional participant was classified as manifesting a borderline trait. Thirty-one of the forty-one participants had no diagnosis. Diagnosis of BPD was related strongly to attachment classification. None of the participants who were classified as securely attached were diagnosed as BPD; and nine of the eleven participants (81.8 percent) who were classified as ambivalently attached were also diagnosed as BPD. The authors noted that the major overlap between the ambivalent attachment classification and BPD reflected primarily "the more angry, impulsive, emotionally labile form of the disorder" (1997, 75). The authors noted that prominent among the characteristics that led to the BPD diagnosis within this group were extreme interpersonal difficulties, intense, unmanageable attacks of anxiety or anger, rejection sensitivity, and unstable self-experience. The authors also reported that the nine participants who were classified as ambivalent and diagnosed as BPD reported numerous explicit examples of inconsistent maternal behavior that vacillated between love and hate. The hallmark of this behavior was "the intensity and unpredictability of the mothers' attacks on the daughters' self-esteem" (1997, 76). The authors concluded that these mothers were unable to provide steady, nurturant caregiving. The mothers' responses to the daughters' need for nurturance appeared to fluctuate as a function of the mothers' moods.

Salzman and associates (1997) interpreted these findings within an object relations context, noting that the ambivalent attachment experiences of these nine women "stirred up intense frustrations and object hunger in this group of young women" (78). The investigators reported that the subjective reports of these nine women made it clear that their mothers were "simultaneously intense and oblivious to the child's needs" (78), and they suggested that "this particular combination of experiences that predisposes daughters to a more 'hysterical' presentation—that is, impulsive, acting-out—presentation of borderline pathology symptoms to a more withdrawn or 'schizoid' presentation" (78). They also noted that within the ambivalent attachment group only two reports of rape and no other reports of physical or sexual abuse. One of the two women who had been raped had also attempted suicide. The authors interpreted this datum as supporting the idea that abuse history is related to the severity of borderline pathology.

While this conclusion is logical, one might also note that the absence of physical and sexual abuse in the majority of the BPD group provides an explanation for the general lack of the most serious borderline symptoms within the group, including aggressive acting-out behaviors, risky behaviors such as substance abuse and promiscuous sexual activity, and self-mutilation. In fact, it appears that the results of the study by Salzman and her colleagues (1997) is consistent with the view that specific traumatic experiences involving physical and sexual abuse, particularly repeated abuse, may explain the more severe self-destructive manifestations of BPD, whereas insecure attachment resulting from neglect and/or emotional abuse may explain the failure of the borderline to maintain stable relationships, emotional equilibrium, and positive self-concept.

Salzman and her associates reported the results of a second study involving thirty-one adult volunteer subjects, all of whom displayed some of the symptoms of BPD. These subjects were recruited through a newspaper advertisement soliciting volunteers to participate in a study of the effectiveness of a pharmacological treatment for individuals who had mild to moderate symptoms of BPD. Attachment classification was ascertained through the use of the adult attachment interview, administered independently by three clinicians. Unanimous agreement among the three clinicians with respect to attachment classification was required to retain a participant in the study. Initial screening interviews were used to determine whether each participant met the DSM-III-R criteria for Borderline Personality Disorder. The initial interview was also used to ascertain history of physical and or sexual abuse. Those respondents who met these criteria were further screened using the Structured Clinical Interview for DSM-III-R Personality Disorders (SCID-II) (Spitzer, Williams, and Gibbon 1987) and the Revised Diagnostic Interview for Borderlines (DIB-R) (Zanarini et al. 1989b). In order to be diagnosed as having full BPD, the participant had to fall into one of two groups: (1) scoring 5 or above on the BPD section of the SCID-II and 7 or above on the DIB-R; or (2) scoring 4 or above on the BPD section of the SCID-II and 8 or above on the DIB-R. In addition, the investigators applied specific criteria to "ensure that this was a mildly to moderately symptomatic sample, albeit with clearly defined borderline pathology" (1997, 80). Specifically, they excluded individuals manifesting self-destructive behavior and individuals with recent hospitalizations for suicide.

One of the thirty-one participants had to be excluded because the three clinicians could not reach unanimous agreement with respect to her attachment classification. The remaining thirty distributed as follows: secure (2); ambivalent (5); avoidant (12); secure/avoidant (9); and secure ambivalent (2). Four of the five ambivalent participants met the criteria for full BPD, as did eight of the twelve avoidant participants. The women in the ambivalent BPD group were similar to those described in the first study. They recalled their mothers as very much present, but rarely attuned to their daughter's needs. These daughters reported a gnawing and rarely satisfied emotional hunger.

In contrast to these ambivalent women, the avoidant BPD group recalled being on their own most of the time, with a mother who was either emotionally spent or otherwise unable to offer comfort or nurturance. These women were often either first-born or last-born children, and they recalled their mothers being constantly tied up with siblings, preoccupied by marital difficulties, or simply not being there when needed. These women did not persist in trying to engage with their mothers. Instead, they realized that mother would not be there to soothe, protect, or understand them, and they withdrew. Often they concluded that it was their own inability to express emotional needs that explained their own failure to develop satisfactory attachments.

Of the thirty-one participants in study 2, all of whom displayed borderline pathology, only six (19.4 percent) reported a history of physical and/or sexual abuse. Of these six, two reported both physical and sexual abuse, one reported physical abuse alone, and three reported sexual abuse alone. The proportion of participants reporting physical and sexual abuse in this sample is substantially smaller than the corresponding proportions in other studies of the relationship between childhood abuse and BPD (Herman et al. 1989; Orgata et al. 1990). Salzman and her colleagues (1997) noted that the proportion of participants in their study who were physically and/or sexually abused "more nearly resembles figures estimating abuse frequencies in nonclinical populations" (87). This finding may be interpreted in the light of the method through which the sample was selected for study 2, which drew on outpatients and sought individuals who were mildly to moderately symptomatic, specifically excluding individuals with a history of self-mutilation or a recent hospitalization for suicide attempt. These findings are consistent with the view that individuals who have histories of physical and/or sexual abuse, particularly sexual abuse that is repeated and involves penetration, are those most likely to manifest severe borderline pathology, including self-destructive behaviors.

Conclusion

The literature indicates that borderline pathology is quite variable in severity, with the mildest manifestations including social withdrawal, fear of abandonment, and a pattern of unstable interpersonal relationships. These diagnostic criteria can be explained by the impact of inconsistent or neglectful early attachment relationships, which lead to insecure adult attachment. In the case of inconsistent early relationships in which the primary attachment figure vacillates between loving and hateful behavior, the child is likely to develop ambivalent attachment as an adult. This pattern would be expected in cases of long-term emotional abuse and extreme verbal abuse.

In the case of early relationships involving physical abuse and sexual abuse, particularly repeated and severe abuse taking place over a prolonged period of time, the more severe manifestations of Borderline Personality Disorder are likely to emerge. These include impulsive behaviors in areas that are likely to be self-destructive, including risky sex, substance abuse, reckless and/or drunk driving, impulsive spending, and binge eating. Also included among the indicators of more extreme borderline pathology are the self-destructive behaviors of self-mutilation and suicide attempts.

Additional sequelae of childhood physical and sexual abuse that manifest as symptoms of severe borderline pathology include extreme affective instability (such as intense episodic depression), intense inappropriate anger that may lead to temper tantrums or actual physical confrontations, and dissociative symptoms.

These conclusions provide considerable guidance for the clinician working with clients who display some combination of the symptoms of Borderline Personality Disorder. Where the client complains of unstable interpersonal relationships and fear of abandonment, the clinician should be alerted to probe for inadequate early attachment relationships and less severe forms of childhood abuse that might result in insecure adult attachment patterns. However, where more extreme manifestations of borderline pathology are present, particularly self-destructive behaviors, the clinician should be particularly vigilant for indications of severe traumatic childhood experiences associated with severe physical and/or sexual abuse.

CHAPTER FIVE

~

Childhood Abuse
and Eating Disorders

Carol: A Case of Bulimia

Carol was a twenty-eight-year-old single female who sought treatment for bulimia at an upscale wellness center in New England. Carol enrolled in a two-week intensive residential program designed for eating-disordered women. This program employed a cognitive–behavioral approach to eating disorders, and the initial two-week residential program was followed by long-term aftercare carried out through weekly individual therapy sessions near home, monthly weekend visits to the wellness center, and a twenty-four-hour a day phone support line.

Carol reported that she had been binge eating for about ten years, since starting college. At first she did not regard bingeing and purging as a problem. The behavior began as an occasional binge-eating episode with friends on weekends, generally on Saturday nights after dates. There was a substantial degree of acceptance of these binges among her dorm mates. It was a way to eat ice cream and cookies and not get fat. However, over time the bingeing behavior had grown increasingly more frequent and extreme. Carol stated that for the past year or so she felt that her bingeing and purging had gotten totally out of control. She said that when she decided to seek help, she was bingeing eight to ten times each week. These binges occurred after work each day and several times a day on the weekends.

Carol was a partner in a medium-size regional public relations/advertising firm. She had taken an entry-level position at this firm immediately after completing college. She had attended a large private university in Boston. Although her family was quite wealthy and could easily afford to pay for college, Carol had nevertheless won an athletic scholarship for soccer and volleyball. She reported that she had always been a "pretty good" student as well. Carol was bright, attractive, and hardworking. She had risen rapidly in the firm and reported a high six-figure income. She was not overweight. In fact, she was in very good shape, which she attributed to her strict workout routine. She dressed stylishly and expensively, even during her stay at the informal wellness center, which was as much a spa and resort as a treatment facility. Carol said that she was single and lived alone. However, she reported that she had an active social life, dating several men regularly and socializing extensively with clients and business associates. She said that she attended numerous sporting events and music concerts. She also indicated that she was sexually active. In fact, the exact words she used at first to describe her sex life were "very active."

On a typical workday, Carol drove to work early, picking up coffee and a bagel or roll on the way. She was generally at her desk by 8:30. She worked all morning and went to the gym to exercise each day around noon. She said that she engaged in strenuous aerobic activity and also lifted weights. Her workouts lasted approximately an hour and a half each day. After her workout she generally drank large amounts of water and/or diet soda. She reported that she typically ate nothing for the rest of the afternoon but had several cups of coffee and/or diet sodas to "keep her energy up." Carol generally worked hard till 6:30 or 7:00 each night. On the way home from work, Carol invariably stopped at McDonald's, Kentucky Fried Chicken, or some other fast food restaurant, where she purchased a large quantity of take-out food. If she stopped for fried chicken, she bought a whole bucket, along with side dishes and rolls. If she went to a burger place, she bought several of the big ones with the biggest container of fries they had. Carol also stopped at a convenience store where she purchased additional junk food like corn chips, candy, and ice cream.

Carol said that she normally planned her evening so that she could take a shower and change to sweat clothes when she got home, then curl up in front of the TV and eat. She said that she would eat until she became uncomfortably full, at which point she would vomit. On some days, however, Carol could not wait to eat until after she showered and changed. Sometimes she would start her binge in the car before she got home. She said that she did not know why she waited till she got home on some days and not on others. She said the eating in the car just seemed to happen, without her making a conscious decision to begin to eat. Regardless of when and where she started to eat, Carol said that during her binges she would feel totally out of control. She said that in a way she enjoyed the eating, at least when she began to eat. However, she also said that as she continued to eat she often lost track of what she was doing. She said she was scarcely aware of what was going on until she got to the point where she began to feel physically sick. It was as if she didn't even remember eating, but rather only remembered the feeling of being so full that she had to throw up. After purging, she would drink large quantities of water and throw up again. She said that this second round of vomiting made her feel "clean." She said that after this second purging she was able to relax, and by this point she was typically very tired. Carol said she generally watched the news and went to sleep around 11:30 or midnight. However, she reported that on most of these nights she fell asleep feeling ashamed and guilty, thinking that her life was "fucked up" and she was "some kind of pervert."

On typical weekend days, Carol would also binge eat and purge in the morning. She would get up and go out for coffee and doughnuts. Sometimes she would go to a bakery and get fresh bread and pastries. She would eat these sweets until she thought that she "was ready to burst," then purge, shower, get dressed, and go out. Then she would go out to the gym for a long workout, after which she would do her errands. If she would not be going out at night, she brought back food in the afternoon and repeated the weekday bingeing and purging routine.

These "typical" days were interspersed with other days when Carol dated or engaged in social activities associated with business. Evening business entertainment occurred on an average of once or twice a week and usually involved having dinner with clients. She dated at least one night each weekend. She had several regular boyfriends, but she described these relationships as "very casual" and "with no strings." Carol was not involved in any committed heterosexual relationship, nor did she have a close female confidant. Carol said that her dates generally involved dinner and attending a game, a show, or a concert. Some dates were spent in a local sports bar drinking beer and watching a sporting event, if the game of the day was taking place out of town.

Carol described eating in restaurants as extremely challenging. She said that she was constantly tempted to overeat, and that she was also tempted to drink too much alcohol. She said that she could usually control these urges, but sometimes she could not. She reported that she purged in restaurant rest rooms quite frequently. She explained that this kept her from feeling ill when she overate, and also kept her from getting drunk when she had too much to drink. She said that she was generally successful in hiding this behavior from the friends and clients with whom she was socializing, but she also confessed that several of the people at her office and at least one of her male friends had questioned her about whether she was "all right." She found these inquiries humiliating, and said that embarrassment had been a major factor in her decision to seek treatment.

Carol said that she often brought a boyfriend home to spend the night, and she reported a bit sheepishly that she also occasionally engaged in a "one-night stand" with a client or someone she met while involved in business entertainment. Carol said that when she had a man staying over she was typically not tempted to binge or purge. She also said that on those occasions not purging allowed her to become intoxicated, which was "good for sex." However, most often, on the morning after having a man stay over, Carol arranged her schedule so that she would be able to "get him on his way" fairly early in the day. She said that it made her uncomfortable to have a guy hanging around her house all morning, "taking up my space and keeping me from getting the house cleaned up and organized." Carol said that after a boyfriend had gone she would typically binge, purge, shower, and head off to the gym to work out.

Carol's treatment at the wellness center was focused on modifying the binge eating and purging behavior. This type of treatment is aimed at identifying the triggers to bingeing behavior and on developing and practicing alternative behaviors that she could use to avoid bingeing. The therapists at the center did not emphasize aspects of Carol's personal history that might explain the etiology of her eating disorder. Further, they did not go to great lengths to explore the other troubling aspects of Carol's self-reported presenting problem, including the possibility that she was engaging in risky sexual behavior, the possibility of an alcohol use disorder, or the possibility of an attachment disorder that seemed to preclude the establishment of a long-term committed heterosexual relationship.

However, the therapist that Carol saw on a weekly basis near her home was more open to the exploration of these issues. This therapist was aware that bulimia was frequently associated with a history of childhood sexual and physical abuse, and she believed that this relationship could be causal. Carol's therapist also recognized also that other self-destructive behaviors, including potentially risky sex and substance use disorders, were similarly associated with childhood abuse. Accordingly, Carol's therapist not only guided and monitored Carol's compliance with the cognitive behavioral intervention for bulimia but also encouraged Carol to explore her feelings regarding diverse aspects of her life, and to disclose her memories regarding her family life during childhood and adolescence.

Carol was quite forthcoming with regard to her family life as a child and adolescent, which she categorized as "extremely fucked up." Carol was the eldest of three children, all girls. She described her mother as cold and emotionally withholding, yet at the same time extremely demanding. Her mother constantly pushed Carol to excel in both the athletic and the academic arenas. Carol felt that her mother was frustrated with the way her own life had turned out and that she had tried mightily to live through her daughters. Although her mother was bright and had attended a prestigious women's college, she had gotten married during her last year of school and had never pursued a career of her own. She married a well-connected young man who had earned an MBA and had immediately taken over the management of a fairly large family-owned manufacturing company. Carol's father was driven to prove that he was more than just the fortunate heir to a profitable business. Accordingly, he worked tirelessly to expand the business, opening overseas manufacturing plants and taking the company public. He was frequently away on business trips for extended periods.

Carol's mother felt neglected by her husband. She thought that he looked down on her and was having affairs around the world. She complained bitterly of her husband's faults to everyone who would listen, including her children. She began to drink too much, and she had several affairs of her own, one of which was with Carol's prep school soccer coach. She became intermittently cold toward her husband when he was at home, and she did not go out of her way to keep her own extramarital affairs discreet.

Carol's mom was so focused on her own misery that she was unable to offer warmth or emotional support to Carol or her younger daughters. Furthermore, she was so focused on her own lack of accomplishment that she relentlessly insisted that her daughters excel physically and mentally. She told them that through their own accomplishments they would be able to have lives that did not involve depending on a man. She carefully monitored their diet, exercise, and study routines. She was hypervigilant with respect to their eating habits, forbidding sweets and strictly limiting the consumption of other food. She insisted that Carol participate in varsity sports in school, and she also insisted that Carol enroll in summer skills development programs to ensure that she would become very good at these sports.

Carol's dad was also miserable. He was a workaholic who received little or no positive feedback for his efforts from his parents or his wife. He was indignant over the fact that his wife resented rather than appreciated all his hard work, and he was frustrated by her lack of warmth and affection. He too began to drink and attempted to find warmth in his daughters, who attempted to make up for their mom's coldness in any way they could. The family system dynamics were ripe for incest, which began when Carol was fifteen. She remembered the details of her first incestuous encounter very well. Her father had returned from a long overseas trip in time to attend an important soccer game with Carol's mom. Carol had performed well, and her team won. After the game Carol said that she had "really tried hard" to show her dad how good she had become. This comment angered her mother, who felt that Carol's father had no right to be doted on in this manner, since he was never around to do the things that needed to be done to make sure that Carol would become the soccer player that she was. Carol's mom made a special point to severely criticize the one or two bad plays that Carol had made, which Carol found more hurtful than her mom's usual critiques. Then her mom disappeared, going off with Carol's coach and telling everyone not to bother to wait for her for dinner.

Carol's dad was humiliated and began to cry. When they returned home he began to drink. At dinner, he drank more, and he gave a glass of wine to Carol to toast her great game. Carol remembers that by the end of dinner he was alternately crying and laughing, and she remembers blaming it all on her mom. She remembers trying to help her dad get up to go to bed, but ending up in his study because she was not sure he could make it up the stairs. She remembers trying to comfort him, drinking more wine, and then having sex with him. In relating this incident, she stressed that it was she rather than her father who initiated the sexual activity. She also recalled that she enjoyed the sex very much, even though it was somewhat painful at first. She also recalled that she did not feel guilty about it immediately, but did later. Her immediate emotional reactions were sexual satisfaction, the feeling that she had somehow eased her father's pain, and the sense that she had in some way "made up for" and "gotten even" with her mother. Carol said that she felt she had eased her father's pain, because he fell asleep right after having sex, and for the first time since she had known him he appeared to be in a peaceful state of mind. Carol also said that she felt as if she had successfully turned all of her mother's perfectionism against her by satisfying her father as her mother could not, and by receiving attention from her father that her mother had not.

Carol had several other incestuous encounters with her father, but in fairly short order he cut off the sexual relationship. He told her that it was wrong, that he had been weak, and that they could not continue to have sex. He said that he realized that she meant well, and he told her that it was not her fault, but his, because he was her father and he was an adult. Carol said that at this point she did feel somewhat guilty, but at the same time she felt extremely powerful, like she had this beautiful body and this gift of sexual healing. She said that her feelings toward her mother continued to be dominated by resentment, but she said that she also felt just a tinge of gratitude, because she believed that her mother had been right to insist that she work hard to perfect her body and mind.

After losing her virginity with her father, Carol began to have sexual relations with boys her own age. When her father ended the incestuous relationship, Carol seduced her soccer coach. She said that she was attracted to him because he was older, because he had done a lot to help her improve herself, because he was in really good physical shape, and because it would be still another way of telling her mother, "fuck you." At the point in her life when Carol entered treatment at the wellness center, she said that she still had a warm and caring relationship with her father, although she didn't see him a great deal, since they are both so wrapped up in their respective careers. She indicated that she has only a cold and formal relationship with her mother, for whom she has little affection and less respect. Carol also reported that her mother and father are still married, although they pretty much "do their own things."

Carol made good progress in her treatment for bulimia. She diligently performed the various homework assignments that are associated with the cognitive behavioral approach to the treatment of eating disorders. Basically, Carol worked as hard at defeating her bulimia as she had worked at school, soccer, and her career in public relations. Within a few months she had greatly reduced the frequency and intensity of her bingeing and purging. She reported that this success made her feel much better about herself, and she also reported that she greatly appreciated the positive feedback that she received for her success, both from the therapists at the wellness center and from her regular therapist at home. Carol remains in therapy working on these issues.

Child Abuse and Eating Disorders

Carol's bulimia illustrates the relationship between childhood emotional, sexual, and/or physical abuse and the development of eating disorders in adolescence or adulthood. Carol's abuse experience did not begin with the initiation of the incestuous relationship with her father when she was fifteen. Carol's abuse history began early in childhood in the form of emotional abuse on the part of her primary caretaker, her mother. Carol's mother did not provide a warm and nurturing emotional environment for her. She set unattainable standards and criticized her daughter when these standards were not met. Thus Carol experienced multiple forms of abuse, over a considerable period of time, at the hands of several different perpetrators. As we shall see in the literature reviewed in the following section, bulimia is most likely to occur among those who experience several forms of childhood abuse.

Carol's history also illustrates another common aspect of eating disordered pathology among those with a history of childhood abuse—that the eating disorder frequently occurs in conjunction with other serious psychological symptoms. Carol had attachment issues characterized by an extreme pattern of avoidant attachment, which limited her heterosexual relationships to uncommitted sexual liaisons. In the context of these relationships, Carol engaged in risky behavior in the form of multiple sexual partners, casual sex with relative strangers, and having sex while intoxicated.

Carol said that she had been helped in her battle with bulimia by insights she derived from discussing her childhood and adolescent experiences. This work helped her understand her mother's role in establishing Carol's perfectionism, as well as her pathological need to obtain soothing and sensual gratification from food and sex. It had become pretty clear to her why she could not trust men but only used them as objects for her gratification. This case illustrates the potential synergistic effects of cognitive behavioral treatment and dynamic treatment in the case of women with eating disorders and histories of abuse.

Evidence of the Relationship between Childhood Abuse and Subsequent Eating Disorders

A large body of evidence suggests a relationship between childhood abuse, particularly sexual abuse, and eating disorders experienced during adolescence and adulthood. Several studies have indicated that adolescent females who have been diagnosed with an eating disorder are disproportionately likely to report a history of childhood sexual abuse (Ackard, Neumark-Sztainer, Hannan, French, and Story 2001; Chandy, Blum, and Resnick 1996b; French, Story, Downes, Resnick, and Blum 1995; Moyer, DiPietro, Berkowitz, and Stunkard 1997; Perkins and Luster 1999; Wonderlich et al. 2001). Other studies have shown that adult women with eating disorders are characterized by high rates of childhood sexual abuse (Conners and Morse 1993; Hall, Tice, Beresford, Wooley, and Hall 1989; Kearney-Cooke 1988; Oppenheimer, Howells, Palmer, and Chaloner 1985; Root and Fallon 1988; Wonderlich, Breverton, Jocic, Dansky, and Abbott 1997). Vanderlinden, Vandereycken, van Dyck, and Vertommen (1993) reported that bulimic women in particular tended to report histories of childhood sexual abuse.

On the other hand, several studies comparing samples of women with eating disorders to samples of women with other mental health diagnoses have indicated no significant differences with respect to the incidence of self-reported histories of childhood abuse (Finn, Hartmann, Leon, and Lawson 1986; Steiger and Zanko 1990). However, these same studies did report that both eating disordered patients and patients with other mental health diagnoses were more likely to have histories of childhood abuse than were non-diagnosed community controls. These findings have been interpreted as suggesting that childhood abuse is associated with suboptimal adult mental health in general, rather than associated specifically with eating disorders (Herman 1992b).

Some evidence suggests that experiencing multiple forms of childhood abuse is likely to be associated with subsequent eating disorders. Rorty, Yager, and Rossotto (1994) compared forty patients with bulimia to forty matched controls in regard to retrospective reports of childhood sexual abuse, physical abuse, and emotional abuse. They found that the two groups of women were not differentiated significantly by childhood sexual abuse history alone. However, the two groups were differentiated significantly by a combination of childhood sexual abuse with another form of childhood abuse. Similarly, based on a study of ninth- and twelfth-grade boys and girls, Neumark-Sztainer, Story, Hannan, Beuhring, and Resnick (2000) reported that the incidence of eating disorders was highest among those who reported experiencing both physical and sexual abuse than it was among those who experienced only one form of abuse. Of those reporting histories of both sexual abuse and physical abuse, 23.8 percent of the girls and 30.4 percent of the boys had an eating disorder. In contrast, among those reporting sexual abuse only, 16.1 percent of the girls and 22.1 percent of the boys had an eating disorder. Among those reporting physical abuse only, 16.4 percent of the girls and 9.3 percent of the boys had an eating disorder.

A recent large sample study suggests that the likelihood of developing an eating disorder is greater in the presence of multiple forms of sexual abuse (Ackard and Neumark-Sztainer 2003). These investigators examined the responses of 81,247 ninth- and twelfth-grade students in Minnesota public schools who completed the Minnesota Student Survey, an anonymous self-report measure developed by the Minnesota Department of Children, Families, and Learning. This survey included items assessing (1) history of sexual abuse committed by a family member ("Has any older or stronger member of your family ever touched you sexually against your wishes or had you touch them sexually?"); (2) sexual abuse committed by an adult outside the family ("Has any adult or older person outside the family ever touched you sexually against your wishes or forced you to touch them sexually?"); and (3) sexual abuse by a date ("Have you ever been the victim of a date rape?").

The survey assessed binge eating with the question, "During the last twelve months, have you ever eaten so much in a short period of time that you felt out of control (binge eating)?" The survey also asked respondents to indicate whether in the past twelve months they had engaged in each of a series of weight control behaviors, including "fast or skip meals," "use diet pills or speed," "vomit (throw up) on purpose after eating," and "use laxatives." In addition to these measures of eating disordered behaviors, the survey contained scales measuring self-esteem and emotional well-being, and items measuring suicide attempts and suicidal ideation.

The results of the survey indicated that 2.5 percent of the girls (n = 1,005) and 0.5 percent of the boys (n = 198) reported being abused sexually by a family member; 6.1 percent of the girls (n = 2,440) and 1.7 percent of the boys (n = 676) reported being abused sexually by a nonfamily adult; and 2.2 percent of the girls (n = 889) and 1.6 percent of the boys (n = 629) reported sexual abuse on a date. In addition, 3.8 percent of the girls (n = 1,537) and 2.3 percent of the boys (n = 907) reported experiencing two or more of the three forms of sexual abuse. Among both boys and girls, in comparison to respondents who reported no history of sexual abuse, experiencing either a single form of sexual abuse or multiple forms of sexual abuse was associated with an increased likelihood of binge eating, fasting or skipping meals, taking diet pills, vomiting, and taking laxatives. In each category of eating disordered behavior, the proportion of respondents who endorsed the behavior was greatest among respondents who reported multiple forms of sexual abuse. Sexual abuse history was also related significantly to low self-esteem, poor emotional well-being, and suicidal thoughts and or attempts.

This study was limited by its cross-sectional design, which precludes any definitive conclusion that sexual abuse has a causal relationship to eating disordered behaviors. Particular characteristics of some young people possibly make them susceptible to sexual abuse as well as prone to developing an eating disorder. Nevertheless, the study does clearly establish relationships between several different forms of childhood sexual abuse and several different forms of eating disordered behavior.

There is ongoing debate among those researching eating disorders as to whether the existing research actually justifies the conclusion that a causal relationship exists between various forms and combinations of childhood abuse and various eating disorders. Several studies have argued that existing studies do not provide definitive proof of a causal relationship (Coovert, Kinder, and Thompson 1989; Pope and Hudson 1992; Stice 2001). For example, Stice (2001) emphasized that despite the many cross-sectional retrospective studies demonstrating a relationship between a history of childhood abuse and eating disorders experienced in adolescence and adulthood, no prospective studies have demonstrated that childhood abuse is a risk factor for eating disorders. Stice argued that "theorists have suggested that childhood sexual abuse is a risk factor for eating pathology" (Fairburn et al. 1998). However, childhood sexual abuse has not emerged as a significant predictor of bulimic pathology in prospective research (Vogeltanz-Holm et al. 2000; Stice 2001, 59).

Based on his analysis of the existing literature, Stice referred to the putative causal relationships between child abuse and eating disorders as "clinical myths" that are "perpetuated, despite the lack of rigorous scientific evidence" (2001, 59). Although we (JAT and ORS) absolutely concur with Stice's assessment of the current empirical data as failing to provide definitive proof of the causal relationship between childhood abuse and eating disorders, we feel that his use of the term "clinical myths" is unfortunate. Too much theoretical evidence and too much clinical experience suggests the existence of such relationships to conclude that they are nonexistent, simply because they have not been demonstrated formally with rigorous empirical studies to this point. We do, however, concur with Stice that there is a pressing need "to evaluate putative etiologic risk factors in methodologically sound studies" (2001, 59).

The following section considers various eating disorders that have been linked through clinical observation and/or correlational association in cross-sectional studies to histories of childhood abuse.

Eating Disorders Linked to Childhood Abuse

The eating disorders that have been linked to childhood abuse include bulimia, anorexia, and compulsive overeating. In her book on female survivors of incest, Blume (1990) suggested that the trauma of incest is most likely to lead to eating disorders in women, because "rigid social expectations define women through their appearance," and because "a person with no outside source of gratification and control can still manipulate her food intake" (151). Blume also asked the rhetorical question, "Which of the manifestations of a disturbed relationship with food might a survivor develop?" (151), and she responded that each eating disorder takes care of a different need.

Bulimia

Bulimia nervosa is characterized by "binge eating and inappropriate compensatory methods to prevent weight gain" (American Psychiatric Association 2000, 589). A second defining characteristic is that "the self-evaluation of individuals with Bulimia Nervosa is excessively influenced by body shape and weight" (2000, 589). The DSM-IV-TR specifies that to qualify for this diagnosis the binge eating and the inappropriate compensatory behaviors must occur, on average, at least twice a week for three months. However, many bulimics binge and purge more frequently.

A binge is defined as eating in a discrete period of time (usually less than two hours) an amount of food that is definitely larger than most individuals would eat under similar circumstances. An episode of binge eating need not occur entirely in a single setting. For example, an individual may begin to binge in a restaurant and then continue to binge at home. Therefore, on those occasions when Carol began eating while driving home from a fast food restaurant and then continued to eat upon returning home, each episode consisted a single binge. The foods consumed during a binge may be sweet, high-calorie foods such as ice cream, doughnuts, candy, or cake. However, binge eating is determined more by the large quantity of food consumed than by the types of food consumed. The DSM-IV-TR states that bulimics eat more at a sitting than other individuals, but the proportions of the total food intake that consist of proteins, fats, and carbohydrates tend to be similar. Thus Carol's consumption of fried chicken and burgers in addition to salty snacks and ice cream is consistent with the definition of bulimia.

The DSM-IV-TR states that bulimics are typically ashamed of their eating and purging behaviors and attempt to conceal their symptoms. It states further that binge eating usually occurs in secrecy, or at least as inconspicuously as possible. For the same reason, binge eating is often characterized by rapid consumption. The embarrassment associated with bingeing and purging was illustrated in Carol's case, since she was motivated to seek treatment primarily by the embarrassment associated with inquiries from friends who noticed or suspected the bulimic behaviors. However, Carol's bingeing was actually initiated in college as a group social activity among dorm mates. There is a substantial degree of acceptance of bingeing and purging among young women who are intensely concerned with maintaining an acceptably low body weight, and sometimes women who go off to college are initiated into bingeing and purging through the influence of peers.

A key characteristic of bingeing is the sense of being out of control. Bingers sometimes describe their eating behavior as frenzied; and they often report that they are unable to stop eating once a binge has begun. They may eat to the point that they are uncomfortably or even painfully full. Bingers also describe a dissociated aspect of the binge experience, as if they are observing themselves from outside their bodies. Another characteristic of binges is that they tend to be triggered by stressful events and/or negative mood states. They also tend to occur when the individual is fatigued. The bingeing tends to reduce dysphoria temporarily, but is typically followed by negative feelings of guilt and self-recrimination.

The other key characteristic of bulimia nervosa is the use of diverse inappropriate compensatory behaviors to avoid weight gain resulting from binge eating. The most common of these methods is vomiting following an episode of binge eating. The DSM-IV-TR states that "purging is employed by 80 percent to 90 percent of the individuals with Bulimia Nervosa who present for treatment at eating disorders clinics" (2000, 590). The effects of purging include the immediate relief of painful feelings of fullness, as well as relief from the fear of gaining weight. Initially bulimics tend to induce vomiting by sticking their fingers down their throat to stimulate the gag reflex. Less frequently, they may consume ipecac in order to vomit. Over time, however, bulimics typically become very good at inducing vomiting. They often become able to vomit at will.

Other compensatory behaviors employed by bulimics to avoid weight gain include the misuse of laxatives and/or diuretics, enemas, diet pills, fasting for a day or more following a binge, and exercising excessively. The DSM-IV-TR estimates that approximately one-third of bulimics misuse laxatives. Those who misuse laxatives typically also purge as well. Many bulimics employ multiple inappropriate compensatory behaviors to avoid weight gain. Exercise is considered excessive when it significantly interferes with other important activities, when it is done at inappropriate times or in inappropriate settings, and/or when it is continued despite injury.

Blume (1990) noted that those who are not very familiar with bulimia may not recognize that it is a serious condition. Unlike individuals with anorexia nervosa, those with bulimia nervosa "do not waste away; rather, they appear to be the perfect image of womanhood. Often they are very attractive, successful women" (152). However, bulimia can lead to a variety of serious medical problems ranging from electrolyte imbalances that may result in irregular heartbeat to a ruptured esophagus that is associated with repeated vomiting. Malnutrition may also occur, and "with malnutrition comes dulled mental, sensory, and emotional functioning" (153). Furthermore, Blume pointed out that vomiting after eating is not the painless form of weight control that many women believe it to be when they first hear of it. In some bulimic women, the urge to vomit becomes so strong that they may vomit fifty to seventy times per day. Vomiting may result in the loss of dental enamel and the concomitant increase in dental cavities.

In addition, the DSM-IV-TR indicates that individuals with bulimia nervosa are likely to manifest mood disorders such as Dysthymic Disorder or Major Depressive Disorder, and they are also likely to exhibit low self-esteem. In most cases mood disturbances begin at the same time that the bulimia begins, but in some cases the mood disturbance precedes the development of bulimia. Dysthymic disorders frequently remit following effective treatment which reduces the frequency of bingeing and purging. Also frequently found in conjunction with bulimia are anxiety disorders and substance abuse. The DSM-IV-TR states that approximately 30 percent of bulimics abuse alcohol and/or stimulant diet pills.

Blume (1990) argued that bulimia may be the direct result of a history of incest. She speculated that the "original guilt and shame that accompanies incest" is numbed by bingeing, which gives a temporary "illusion of control over emotions and anxieties" (153). However, after the "high" of the binge comes the violent elimination of the food, which Blume describes as "vomited like a poison" (153). Blume argued that the experience of purging "symbolizes the experience of the incest survivor, whose guts are filled with poison, self-hate, and deep rage—all of which she feels the drive to purge herself of" (153).

However, following the purging, the bulimic experiences deep feelings of guilt and shame. Blume conceptualized the feelings experienced following purging as a substitute for the original guilt and shame that accompanies incest. Blume also suggested that purging helps the bulimic remain beautifully thin, which contributes to the bulimic's "quest for perfection" (153).

Anorexia

Individuals with histories of childhood abuse are also at increased risk for developing anorexia nervosa. The DSM-IV-TR describes the essential feature of anorexia nervosa as follows: "the individual refuses to maintain a minimally normal body weight, is intensely afraid of gaining weight, and exhibits a significant disturbance in the perception of the shape or size of his or her body" (American Psychiatric Association 2000, 583). Postmenarcheal females with this disorder are amenorrheic. The threshold minimum weight required for the diagnosis of anorexia nervosa is 85 percent of the weight that is considered to be normal for an individual of a given age and height. These normal weights are in turn obtained from Metropolitan Life Insurance actuarial tables.

Typically, the low weight that defines anorexia is achieved through restriction of food intake. Often individuals in the process of developing anorexia begin by excluding from their diets certain categories of food perceived to be particularly fattening, but most anorexics eventually end up with a very restricted diet. Some anorexics also engage in vomiting, the misuse of laxatives and diuretics, the use of stimulants, and excessive exercise to reduce their weight. The DSM-IV-TR describes two subtypes of anorexics, the restricting type and the binge-eating-purging type. Restricting anorexics achieve weight loss through dieting and exercise, whereas the binge-eating-purging type purge, or misuse laxatives, diuretics, stimulants, or enemas to achieve weight loss. Anorexics in the latter category may not binge eat but nevertheless purge after consuming small amounts of food. The distinction between the binge-eating-purging type of anorexia and bulimia is that the anorexic falls below the minimum weight criterion, whereas the bulimic does not.

Anorexics seek to lose weight because they greatly fear becoming fat, but this fear does not subside as they lose weight. The anorexic has a distorted and inaccurate perception of her body weight and shape. Some anorexics continue to feel that they are fat in an overall sense, even after their weight has fallen to critically low levels. Others recognize that they are in fact generally thin, but they continue to diet nevertheless, because they feel that a particular part or parts of their bodies are too fat. Anorexics typically experience a sense of pride in the self-discipline that they display in restricting food intake. They tend to regard any weight gain as an indication of lack of self-control. Individuals suffering from anorexia nervosa often exhibit obsessive-compulsive tendencies, both related to and unrelated to food. Some anorexics hoard food but do not consume it.

Blume (1990) noted that anorexia nervosa is a serious disease. Some anorexics starve themselves to death. Others die from heart attacks when they begin to regain weight. Anorexia results in the loss of secondary sex characteristics, including breasts, pubic hair, and menses. Blume suggested that incest survivors may become anorectic in an unconscious effort to avoid being sexual. They have experienced sex not as gratifying, but as abuse, violence, and subjugation. Therefore,

> The incest survivor protects herself through the building of walls that substitute for the power she cannot exercise. In the case of the anorexic, perhaps that wall is the façade of the child: on some level, looking childlike may seem the key to dissuade others from being sexual with her. (152)

In her book on mother–daughter incest, Ogilvie (2004) argued similarly that anorexia is at once a means of controlling one's body and avoiding sexual attention:

> For many mother–daughter incest survivors, food may become a focus, a means of control, and a way not to be sexual. To the anorexic, staying thin

and wearing baggy clothes hides her womanliness, her sexuality, her body. It may help her to take the stance that no one is going to take charge of her body as had been done to her in childhood. She may want to send the message that nobody is home, that a vault is built around her feelings.

The guilt and self-hatred that survivors of childhood abuse often feel has been cited as a factor in the etiology of anorexia. Davis (1991) suggested that adult survivors of childhood sexual abuse "believe that the abuse was their fault, that they're not worth much, and that somehow they're different than other people" (18). Survivors feel there is something bad, wrong, or dirty at their core. Davis argued that the sense of self-loathing that survivors feel is often hidden but extremely deep. She argued further that this self-hate may be expressed in two quite different ways: (1) The survivor may attempt to be perfect on the outside to compensate for bad feelings on the inside and/or (2) the survivor acts out self-destructive feelings through self-injurious behaviors. Anorexia, with its potentially fatal outcome, is one such self-injurious set of behaviors. Blume (1990) made this point directly, arguing that anorexia is "a pure expression of anger turned inward" (152).

Although most of the literature on anorexia focuses on women, we note that it does occur among males, albeit less frequently than among females. Abraham and Llewellyn-Jones (2001) reported that "Anorexia nervosa occurs in males fifteen times less frequently than in females" (141). Most males with anorexia nervosa spend hours each day exercising. Like female anorexics, males are obsessed about food and body image. Abraham and Llewellyn-Jones reported that male anorexics "may become personal trainers or work in the food industry" (141). These authors also noted that male anorexics are even more likely than female anorexics to have concurrent problems such as obsessive-compulsive disorder, substance use disorders, and personality disorders. Men who develop anorexia nervosa may also binge eat.

Compulsive Overeating

Obesity is not included as an eating disorder in the DSM-IV-TR because simple obesity has not been reliably "associated with a psychological or behavioral syndrome" (American Psychiatric Association 2000, 583). There are many reasons other than psychological ones as to why an individual can be overweight. In many individuals, obesity is thought to be based primarily on medical issues (e.g., genetic, metabolic). The DSM-IV-TR allows for the recognition of those situations where obesity is thought to be at least in part psychologically based by instructing clinicians to note the presence of "psychological factors affecting a medical condition."

However, investigators concerned with the relationship between child abuse and eating disorders typically include compulsive overeating among the possible sequelae of child abuse. For example, in her description of victims of mother–daughter incest, Ogilvie (2004) argued that "to the overeater, food is a comfort, a means of escape, a disconnection from the pain, a way to fill that huge hole in the soul. Her world consists of fear, shame, and hopelessness. When bingeing, food is the anesthetic. It removes her from the situation" (75). Similarly, in her description of female incest survivors, Blume (1990) suggested that "food can serve as a substitute for friendship and nurturing, as a comfort or a reward, as an activity when one is bored, or a replacement for love and attention that were lacking during childhood. It can numb feelings or cause a high" (154).

Blume differentiated between simple overeating and the compulsive overeating that is occasionally found among survivors of childhood abuse. Compulsive overeating may involve either bingeing or steady overeating, but it functions "to achieve a high or an altered emotional state" (154). Blume pointed out that compulsive overeaters often react to sugar in extreme ways. They may get high, get "dopey," or become irritable; but they all experience mood changes. Thus the overeating has the effect of anesthetizing anger, anxiety, or pain. Blume argued that in this way compulsive overeating, like other forms of addiction, functions to distort feelings. She pointed out further that many compulsive overeaters are also alcoholics.

Blume described compulsive overeaters as frequently hiding or hoarding food (as an alcoholic may have a secret stash of liquor). She said that they turn to food when they are confronted with an unmanageable situation or when unpleasant feelings arise. They do not appear to eat because they are enjoying the eating itself, but rather because of the effect that the eating has on their mood. Thus Blume described one compulsive overeater as often finding herself "in front of the refrigerator at three o'clock in the morning without any awareness of how she got there, shoving food into her mouth as fast as she could, yet tasting none of it" (155). This patient indicated that she felt powerless to stop the process and hated herself for it. Blume emphasized that not all women who eat too much are as psychologically impaired as the compulsive overeater. "It is the way the food is used, the way feelings are mismanaged, and the alteration of attitudes that distinguishes this problem from a weight problem" (155). Thus the clinician working with an overweight client needs to assess for this unique mood altering aspect of the client's overeating behavior that defines compulsive overeating. When this aspect of the client's experience is discovered, further efforts to assess for possible childhood abuse would appear to be warranted.

Etiological Models Explaining the Relationship between Childhood Abuse and Eating Disorders

Several recent studies have posited and empirically evaluated theoretical models developed to explain the association between childhood abuse and subsequent eating disorders. These models focus on sexual abuse, and they suggest that the relationships between childhood abuse and disturbed eating may be explained and mediated by the effects of two categories of variables: (1) shame regarding one's body and body disparagement and (2) dissociation.

Bodily Shame and Body Disparagement

Petrie and Tripp (2001) noted that several studies (including Conners and Morse 1993; Schaaf and McCanne 1994; Wonderlich et al. 1997) had reported a connection between childhood sexual abuse and eating disorders experienced during adolescence and/or adulthood, but none of these studies had considered "the possible pathways through which sexual abuse may increase women's risk of developing these disorders" (17). Instead, these studies simply demonstrate that women with histories of sexual abuse manifest a higher prevalence of eating disorders than women without such histories. Petrie and Tripp argued that what was missing in previous research was "a test of a theoretical pathway linking these two constructs" (17).

In order to provide such a test, Petrie and Tripp (2001) turned to the theoretical model proposed by Kearney-Cook and Striegel-Moore (1994). This model suggested that the experience of being abused sexually leads to intense feelings of shame surrounding one's body, which in turn lead to "body disparagement." The latter term was defined as "the diffuse experience of body degradation or body loathing endured by the sexually abused individual" (306). Petrie and Tripp elaborated the body disparagement construct by suggesting that it "encompasses both affective and attitudinal components toward one's body as well as the subjective evaluation of body shape and appearance" (2001, 18). Kearney-Cook and Striegel-Moore (1994) suggested further that the greater the body disparagement, the greater the likelihood of developing eating disordered attitudes and behaviors.

Petrie and Tripp (2001) used a series of survey questionnaires and self-report diagnostic instruments to a sample of 330 female undergraduates at a large southwestern university. They administered a sexual abuse history questionnaire to assess history of sexual abuse, which they defined as both unwanted attempts and actual contact or touching of one's sexual parts before and after the age of fourteen. This questionnaire was structured to provide indications of the severity of the abuse reported (attempts, touching, and penetration), the age at the onset of the abuse, the duration of the abuse, and the frequency of specific abuse occurrences. For the purpose of testing the proposed causal model, respondents were grouped into three categories, representing (1) no history of sexual abuse; (2) history of abuse before the age of fourteen; and (3) history of abuse after the age of fourteen. In classifying respondents into these three categories, only relatively "severe" abuse was counted as sexual abuse. Petrie and Tripp (2001) defined severe abuse as "unwanted touching, forced touching of the perpetrator's sex organs, and/or forced sexual intercourse" (20).

Bodily shame and guilt was measured by a six-item self-report questionnaire developed specifically for this study. The Shame Scale asked participants to indicate the extent to which they agreed with statements such as "I feel ashamed of my body or some part of it." and "I feel ashamed about exposing specific body parts." Body disparagement was measured by several scales. The Appearance Evaluation subscale of the Multidimensional Body-Self Relations Questionnaire (MBSRQ) was used to measure the respondent's overall satisfaction with her body. The Body Shape Questionnaire (BSQ) was used to assess the respondent's concerns regarding her body size and shape. The Body Parts Satisfaction Scale (BPSS) was used to measure the participant's dissatisfaction with specific parts of her body.

Disordered eating was measured by the fifty-item Questionnaire for Eating Disorder Diagnosis (Q-EDD). This questionnaire was used to group participants into one of three groups: (1) asymptomatic (no eating disorder symptoms); (2) symptomatic (having some eating disorder symptoms but not meeting DSM-IV criteria for an eating disorder); and (3) eating disordered (meeting DSM-IV diagnostic criteria). The eating disordered category includes six subgroups, represented by anorexia, bulimia, and four eating disorders not otherwise specified (EDNOS) (subthreshold bulimia, menstruating anorexia, nonbingeing bulimia, and binge eating disorder).

The results of the study indicated that 60 percent of the sample (n = 178) reported experiencing sexual abuse. Seventy of the respondents reported being abused sexually before the age of fourteen. Twenty-five respondents (7.6 percent) were classified as eating disordered according to DSM-IV criteria; 240 respondents (72.7 percent) were categorized as symptomatic; and 65 (19.7 percent) were classified as asymptomatic.

A path analysis indicated that the causal model specified by Kearney-Cooke and Striegel-Moore (1994) fit the data well. History of sexual abuse was related directly and positively to bodily shame, accounting for 8 percent of the variance in shame. There was also a direct and positive relationship between bodily shame and body disparagement, with shame accounting for

73 percent of the variance in disparagement. Finally, a direct and positive relationship was found between body disparagement and disordered eating, with body disparagement accounting for 70 percent of the variance in eating disorders. Petrie and Tripp (2001) interpreted these findings as confirming that women reporting sexual abuse do experience feelings of shame and guilt; that women who feel ashamed and guilty about their bodies also tend to experience higher levels of body degradation and loathing; and that women who disparage their bodies tend to report increased levels of eating disorder symptomatology.

Petrie and Tripp (2001) acknowledged that the design of their study is still cross-sectional in nature. The use of path analysis to test a "causal model" does not change the fact that the data were all gathered at one point in time. Therefore the correct interpretation of the findings is that they are *consistent with* the theory that childhood abuse leads to shame, that shame leads to body disparagement, and that body disparagement leads to eating disordered behavior. However, the findings do not prove that this is in fact the etiology of eating disorders. Nevertheless, the study is useful in presenting a plausible theoretical explanation of the nature of the relationship between child sexual abuse and subsequent eating disorders, and it demonstrates correlations among variables that are consistent with this explanation.

Dissociation

Another variable that has been posited as explaining the relationship between childhood sexual abuse and subsequent disordered eating behavior is dissociation. This explanation suggests that "individuals with histories of child sexual abuse may engage in eating disorder behaviors in an effort to anesthetize the psychological distress regarding their victimization histories" (Korte, Horton, and Fallon 1998, 55). Dissociation has been described as a pattern of numbing or dulling negative or distressing thoughts and feelings which can be used as a coping mechanism for an individual who is experiencing or has experienced trauma (Root and Fallon 1989). This numbing is achieved by "interfering with the normal storage, retrieval, and integration of thoughts, feelings, sensations, and memories" (Putnam 1993, 40). Thus individuals who have experienced childhood sexual abuse and have not worked through the trauma may find ways to dissociate from these experiences (Root and Fallon 1989). Korte, Horton, and Fallon (1998) suggested that "abusing food may be a temporary way to avoid feelings that come about from a victimization experience" (55). Root (1991) argued that starving, bingeing, and vomiting are addictive and can become a dissociative coping mechanism.

Everill, Waller, and Macdonald (1995) offered a slightly different explanation of the role that dissociation may play in the relationship between childhood sexual abuse and adult bulimia. These investigators suggested that dissociation arises as a consequence of early traumatic experiences such as childhood sexual abuse, and that once individuals begin to use dissociation in this manner, they may then continue to use it to deal with subsequent stressful events. Everill and colleagues argued that an individual who tends to overeat in order to self-soothe under stress may ordinarily be constrained from doing so by the awareness of the negative long-term consequences of overeating, including weight gain, guilt, and self-hatred. However, if this individual dissociates, these constraints are removed, and she or he is free to initiate binge eating. This explanation of the role of dissociation places less emphasis on the continuing need of the survivor of child sexual abuse to anesthetize painful feelings associated with the abuse. The operative role of dissociation that is posited is to free the individual from the normal constraints which would inhibit the self-destructive bingeing behavior, thus allowing the individual to obtain some gratification.

The logic of a mediating role for dissociation in the relationship between child sexual abuse and the subsequent emergence of bulimia is compelling, but empirical support for this causal pathway is scant. Korte, Horton, and Graybill (1998) investigated the relationship in a sample of 391 college students, including 219 females and 173 males. These investigators obtained retrospective self-reports of child sexual abuse using a modified version of the Finkelhor Questionnaire (Finkelhor 1979). Child sexual abuse was defined as sexual experience involving contact (e.g., fondling, intercourse) between (1) a child twelve or under and an adult eighteen years of age or older; (2) a child twelve or under and another child or adolescent at least five years older than the victim; (3) an adolescent aged thirteen to sixteen and an adult at least ten years older; or (4) a situation in which a child or adolescent endured a nonconsensual sexual experience in which force or coercion was used by a perpetrator of any age.

Bulimic behavior was measured by scores on the Bulimia Test-Revised (BULIT-R) (Thelen, Farmer, Wonderlich, and Smith 1991). This test contains a twenty-eight-item scale measuring the severity of bulimic behaviors. The theoretical range of scores on this scale is from 28 to 140, and scores above 85 have been interpreted as indicating clinically relevant bulimic tendencies. Dissociation was measured by the dissociation subscale of the forty-item Trauma Symptom Checklist (TSC-40; Elliott and Briere 1992).

Results indicated that 16.6 percent of the total sample (n = 65 participants) reported histories of child sexual abuse. Among females, 21.6 percent (n = 47) reported being sexually abused; and among males 10.4 percent (n = 18) reported being abused. Thirty-seven of the participants (9.4 percent) reported clinically relevant levels of bulimic behavior. As expected, individuals who had histories of child sexual abuse scored significantly higher than those who did not on the dissociation subscale of the TSC. Also as expected, individuals with clinically relevant levels of bulimic behavior scored significantly higher than those not reporting such levels of bulimic behavior on the dissociation subscale. However, the interactive effect on TSC-40 dissociation subscale scores of history of CSA and clinically relevant levels of bulimic behavior was not significant. The latter finding was interpreted as failing to provide support for the view that dissociation mediates the relationship between CSA and bulimia.

However, the study also yielded unexpected results with respect to the simple bivariate relationship between CSA and bulimic symptoms. When scores on the BULIT-R were broken down by history of child sexual abuse, no significant difference was observed. In fact, only seven participants who reported histories of childhood sexual abuse had BULIT-R scores above the cutoff of 85 used to define clinically relevant bulimic behavior. Thus the findings of the study run counter to previously and subsequently reported studies that do indicate a significant relationship between history of CSA and the subsequent emergence of bulimia (Hall, Tice, Beresford, Wooley, and Hall 1989; Miller, McCluskey-Fawcett, and Irving 1993; Moyer, DiPietro, Berkowitz, and Stunkard 1997; Perkins and Luster 1999; Root and Fallon 1988; Vanderlinden, Vandereycken, van Dyck, and Vertommen 1993; Waller 1992). This is crucial to the interpretation of the results obtained with respect to dissociation, for two reasons. First, it would be extremely unlikely that dissociation would emerge as a significant mediator of a relationship which is nonsignificant to begin with. Second, the lack of a significant relationship between history of CSA and subsequent bulimic symptoms in this study, compared to the significant relationships frequently reported in other studies, suggests that the nonclinical undergraduate sample employed by Korte, Horton, and Graybill (1998) may not be representative of the relationships under study. The authors acknowledge this possibility. They stated that their sample may be "more homogeneous than the general population and less distressed than a clinical population," and they suggested that "those reporting a history of child sexual abuse or bulimic tendencies in college samples are at least doing well enough to function in college" (61).

Given these methodological limitations, the results of this study should probably be interpreted as neither supporting nor rebutting the theoretical argument that CSA promotes dissociation, which in turn facilitates the emergence of bulimic behavior. Korte and her associates (1998) cautioned that the lack of substantial overlap between history of CSA and bulimic symptoms that they observed "suggest that clinicians should clearly not 'jump to conclusions' about child sexual abuse when they have a client with bulimic behaviors" (61). Strictly speaking, this statement is probably good advice, because a clinician should not jump to conclusions regarding the possible etiology of any individual pathology without adequate information gathering and clinical hypothesis testing. However, the findings of this study should not in any way be viewed as excusing the clinician from assessing for history of CSA in the case of a patient with serious bulimic symptoms.

Another study containing data relevant to the possible mediating role of dissociation in the relationship between CSA and bulimia was reported by Rodriguez-Srednicki (2001). This study was designed to explore the relationships between history of CSA and various forms of self-destructive behavior, as well as the possible mediating effects on these relationships of dissociation. The study employed a survey of 441 female students recruited at nine different colleges in the greater New York metropolitan area.

The survey included a self-report measure of history of CSA. CSA was defined in the survey as "any sexual behavior that occurs between a child under the age of sixteen and any person at least five years older than the victim." Sexual behavior was in turn defined as including both "sexual contact (e.g., fondling, intercourse, sodomy) and noncontact forms of sexual behavior (e.g., exhibitionism, requests for sex, lewd or lascivious jokes)" (Rodriguez-Srednicki 2001, 80). Respondents were asked to read this definition and to respond yes or no to whether they had experienced such abuse. The survey also included the Binge Eating Scale (BES; Gormally, Black, Daston, and Rardin 1982), which measures the severity of binge eating behavior. The survey contained two measures of dissociation, the Dissociative Experiences Scale (DES; Bernstein and Putnam 1986), and the dissociation subscale of the Trauma Symptom Checklist (TSC; Briere 1992b).

The results indicated that 175 of the responding women (39.7 percent) reported that they had experienced child sexual abuse as it was defined in the survey. As expected, those who did report a history of CSA scored significantly higher than those who did not on the Binge Eating Scale. The sexually abused respondents also scored significantly higher than the nonabused respondents on each of the two measures of dissociation. Scores on the binge eating scale were related significantly (but weakly) to scores on the DES ($r = .13, p < .01$), but they were not related significantly to scores on the TSC Dissociation subscale ($r = .07, p < .05$). A multiple regression mediation analysis (Baron and Kenny 1986) suggested that the dissociation measures were not significant mediators of the relationship between history of CSA and binge eating.

The results of this study are limited by the same factors that limit the results of the study by Korte and her colleagues (1998) reported above. The sample was undergraduates, a nonclinical group which may not be characterized by particularly severe symptoms of bulimia and may not be highly prone to dissociative symptoms. In addition, the definition of CSA employed in this study was fairly loose, including noncontact forms of abuse. On the other hand, parallel analyses reported in this study with respect to self-destructive behaviors other than binge eating did indicate significant mediation due to dissociation. These other categories of self-destructive behavior included use of illegal drugs, frequency of getting drunk using alcohol, risky sex, and suicide attempts. Therefore, there must have been sufficient variability within the sample with respect to both binge eating symptoms and dissociation to make it feasible to obtain significant findings. Nevertheless, one suspects that the use of clinical samples including individuals with serious bulimic symptoms might yield different findings.

Conclusion

An extensive body of empirical research employing cross-sectional designs has indicated that childhood abuse, including physical abuse, sexual abuse, and emotional abuse, tends to be associated with the development of various forms of eating disorders later in life. Several theoretical explanations have been offered for this association, including explanations involving shame and guilt, body image disturbances, and dissociation. Clinicians working with eating disordered clients widely endorse the view that a history of childhood abuse may contribute to the development of eating disorders, and it is now standard operating procedure for clinicians to assess for abuse history. Anecdotal evidence such as the case of Carol described in this chapter suggests that the exploration of abuse experiences can help clients with eating disorders to understand aspects of their dysfunctional attitudes and behaviors.

Unquestionably, a great deal more research is needed to definitively prove a causal link between childhood abuse and adult eating disorders. In particular, prospective longitudinal research is required. Based on current data alone, however, clinicians working with clients who have eating disorders are advised to cautiously explore childhood experiences and conditions that existed in the family of origin.

~

CHAPTER SIX

Childhood Abuse and Adult Substance Use Disorders

Lora: A Case of Substance Use Disorder

A community court gave seventeen-year-old Lora the option of entering a residential substance abuse treatment program for adolescents or serving a six-month sentence in a juvenile correctional facility. Lora had been charged with prostitution, attempted robbery, resisting arrest, and assaulting a police officer. On the night of her arrest, police officers observed an altercation outside a car between Lora and a middle-aged man. The man was getting the worst of the struggle. When the officers broke up the fight, they found the man's wallet in Lora's bag. He claimed that she had accosted him as he was getting into his car and asked him for a dollar, and when he took out his wallet to give her the money she had grabbed it from him. Lora claimed that he had agreed to pay her $50 for oral sex but then refused to pay when he failed to have an orgasm. She said that she was only "collecting what's mine." The officers decided to arrest them both. When the female officer told Lora she was being arrested, Lora went ballistic. She jumped on the officer and began to hit her. Lora tried to scratch and bite her as well. The male officer in the pair managed to restrain Lora long enough for his partner to handcuff Lora, and they loaded her into the back of their car. They called for backup to take the man to jail, because they were afraid to put him in the same car as Lora. It was clear to the officers that Lora was intoxicated, and they found a bottle of cognac and small quantities of marijuana and crack cocaine in her bag.

Lora was evaluated immediately by the social worker on duty at the community court facility, who concluded that Lora's most serious problems were alcohol abuse (DSM-IV-TR 305.00) and cocaine abuse (DSM-IV-TR 305.60). The social worker also ascertained that Lora had run away from an abusive home situation and was alternately living on the street or with an aunt and her boyfriend. For this reason, a residential substance abuse program for adolescents was recommended. After a consultation involving an assistant district attorney, a public defender, the social worker, and the judge, Lora was presented with the option of drug treatment or jail. With some difficulty, the public defender managed to convince Lora that the treatment option was preferable, since successful participation in treatment would result in the dismissal of the charges and allow her to avoid having a criminal record.

The clinicians at the treatment facility to which Lora was sent assessed all new patients for history of childhood abuse of various forms, since individuals with substance dependence and substance abuse diagnoses frequently have histories of childhood physical, sexual, and/or emotional abuse. The successful treatment of an individual with both a substance use problem and a history of childhood abuse requires that both issues be addressed simultaneously.

When Lora arrived at the treatment center, she was sullen and uncommunicative, and she steadfastly denied having a substance abuse problem. However, she turned around quickly. She expressed relief at having a clean and safe place to sleep, three meals a day, and free access to a shower. She made friends with several of the other residents and began to interact in group. Once she became engaged in the community, Lora freely discussed both her substance abuse history and the abuse she experienced during her childhood and adolescence. She indicated that her mother was an alcoholic and a cocaine addict who had lived with a series of men. Lora described her mother as promiscuous, often engaging in sexual activity with a number of men. Lora indicated that her earliest memories were scenes of her mother engaging in various sexual activities with these men. Lora said that her mother often accepted drugs or money from her sexual partners, and she indicated that some of the men who lived with her mother were "more like pimps than real boyfriends." Lora said that her mom was alternately loving and punitive toward her, depending on whether she was using drugs and the status of her relationship with her current male partner. When things went badly with the men, her mother became verbally and physically abusive toward Lora. At these times she often referred to Lora as her "accident" and slapped her, pinched her, or pulled her hair for any number of real or imagined minor misbehaviors.

Lora was first abused sexually by one of her mother's live-in boyfriends, David, beginning when she was eight. Lora recalled that before the sexual activity began, David was always solicitous of her feelings and he often hugged and kissed her in an affectionate way that she liked. One day when her mom was out he gave her a big hug and said that he loved her very much. When she hugged him back, he began to fondle her genital area. Lora said that she pulled back and felt confused and frightened. David reassured her by saying that he loved her mommy and that it made her mommy happy when he touched her that way, and now that Lora was getting bigger he wanted to love her and make her happy too. He did not continue with his sexual advances that day, but subsequently he took advantage of the times that they were alone to gradually further his advances and at the same time convince Lora that he was teaching her the things that big people did to give each other pleasure and to show each other how much they loved each other. He told her that every young woman had a special man like him to teach her these things, and he told her that she should never tell anyone because it wouldn't be special if it wasn't a secret between the two of them. He also told her that her mother in particular could never know, because "mommies want their daughters to stay little," and her mother might be upset if she knew that Lora was becoming a grown woman.

Over the course of several months, David extended his sexual advances to performing oral sex on Lora, masturbating her and digitally penetrating her vagina, and having her masturbate him and perform fellatio on him. However, Lora said that they never had genital intercourse. David was alternately loving and vaguely threatening. He brought her presents and he told her she was special. He told her that she was very beautiful and that men would always love her and be good to her. David also gave her alcohol, which he said was another good thing that came with getting bigger. Lora said that she really liked the alcohol. She explained that she came to enjoy both the attention David gave her and the sexual activity. However, at the same time on some level she felt that it was "all wrong." In the midst of these conflicting emotions, Lora said that the alcohol helped her to calm down and "not to feel guilty" about the things that they were doing.

This abuse continued for nearly three years, until Lora's mom broke up with David and he moved out of the house. Lora said that she was upset when David left because he gave her things and made her feel good about herself, and because she had come to enjoy the sexual activity. In fact, Lora said that when David left she wondered if she had disappointed him or failed to satisfy him sexually. Lora also said that she was afraid of her mother and felt that when David left she lost a protector. Lora said that as far as she knew her mother had never become aware of the sexual activity between her and David.

Lora's mom had a new man living in the house promptly after David left, and Lora said that within a few weeks of his moving in she had "seduced him." Lora was very clear in retrospect that from the time John moved into the house, she had gone out of her way to be seductive. Although she was only eleven at that time, she had already begun to develop breasts, and she could tell right away that John was attracted to her. One afternoon when her mom was away, Lora went to the refrigerator and brought out two beers. At first John said that she shouldn't be drinking, but when he realized that she wanted to seduce him he didn't hesitate to take advantage of the situation. This was the first time that Lora had genital intercourse. She said that she didn't like the sex with John as much as she had enjoyed the sexual activity with David. However, she said that it made her feel powerful to know that she could seduce him. She also said that it made her feel like she was on an equal footing with her mom, and she felt vaguely like she was getting even with her mom for her past abuses.

After the first sexual experience with John, however, he demanded sex regularly, "almost every time they were alone," and he wasn't as gentle, as flattering, as generous, or as solicitous as David had been. Lora complied, but more because she felt that she had to than because she wanted to. She began to use alcohol regularly in an effort to make their sexual encounters more pleasurable and less guilt producing. The abuse with John lasted only a few months, because Lora's mom threw him out of the house. Lora said that she thought her mom realized that there was something going on between her and John. Lora remembered that she had overheard them have a big fight and that her mom had told him to keep his hands off Lora. However, Lora's mom never asked her directly whether any sexual activity had taken place between them. After John left, Lora's mom kept on having men over and having sex with them without making any particular effort to be discreet, but she didn't have a man move in with them for a long time.

Over the years that Lora's mom was living with David and then with John, Lora was in elementary school. Although she was very bright and never had any trouble keeping up with schoolwork, Lora had some serious social issues. She was "different" from the other kids her age. Her dress was prematurely sexual and she behaved in a seductive manner toward male classmates, who responded by labeling her as "weird." Lora came to regard her precocious sexuality as a matter of pride. She alluded to her sexual activities with the other girls in her class, and she bragged about using alcohol. On a few occasions one teacher or another would express an interest in her welfare, but Lora regarded any expressions of concern with suspicion. She would never allow any of her teachers to establish a close relationship with her. Although there were many times when she felt like she hated her mother at home, Lora felt the need to defend her mother to strangers.

When Lora entered junior high school at age twelve, she met a fourteen-year-old girl with a similar history of physical, emotional, and sexual abuse, and a similar pattern of substance abuse. They became best friends immediately. Cathy introduced Lora to her circle of friends, who were the "druggies" in the school. For the first time Lora did not feel like an outsider. Now she had a group with whom she could identify and hang out. She began drinking more, both in and out of school, and she began using marijuana on a regular basis and cocaine on occasion. She and Cathy engaged in promiscuous sexual activity, primarily oral sex, with the boys in this social circle. At this time Lora felt accepted and regarded her sexuality as her primary social asset. She said it made her feel powerful to know that the boys wanted to be with her. Over the course of junior high school, Lora's school performance began to slip, yet remarkably she managed to do enough to remain on grade level until ninth grade.

When Lora was fifteen years old and in ninth grade, she and Cathy began to skip school. They spent time at Cathy's house, where they both drank and had sex with several adult men who periodically stayed there. They also began hanging out in a local social club, where they learned to extract money and drugs from the older male patrons in exchange for sexual favors. When Lora's mom became aware of the truancy, she attempted to force Lora to give up Cathy and her other friends and to get back into attending school regularly. This precipitated a major confrontation as Lora told her mother that she wasn't doing anything that her mother didn't do. Lora's mom smacked her, and a physical altercation ensued that ended with Lora packing up her things and walking out. She took her stuff to her aunt's house, and she slept there most nights on the couch. Other nights she stayed with Cathy. Some nights the two of them stayed out all night on the street or went home with guys. Lora and her friend stopped going to school altogether. Lora and Cathy hung out together, using a great deal of alcohol and pot and cocaine, and hooking to make money. This pattern had been going on for about two years at the time of Lora's arrest and subsequent referral to substance abuse treatment.

History of Child Abuse and Substance Abuse

Lora's history of physical, emotional, and sexual abuse and her substance abuse issues illustrates several pathways that are cited most frequently to explain the association between child abuse and subsequent substance abuse

(Blume 1990; Evans and Sullivan 1995). First, children are more likely to be abused when one or both of their parents has a substance use disorder, and children are also more likely to develop a substance use disorder when their parents have such a disorder. The association between parental substance abuse and child abuse is due to the lowering of normal inhibitions and social restraints that accompanies the use of alcohol and drugs. The association between parental substance abuse and substance abuse by children is due to both genetic predisposition and environmental factors, including the social modeling of substance use and the ready availability of substances to be abused. Lora was probably genetically vulnerable for a substance use disorder. Her mother was certainly dependent on both alcohol and cocaine, and her absent father may well have been a substance abuser as well. Furthermore, Lora's mother clearly viewed the use of alcohol and cocaine as rewarding and desirable behaviors; most of the time alcohol and other drugs were in the house and readily available for anyone to use.

A second path linking a history of childhood abuse to subsequent substance abuse has to do with the anxiety and pain experienced by the child victim. Alcohol can be used to anesthetize both actual physical pain and negative affect. It can also be used to dull feelings of guilt. In the case of Lora, her first abuser introduced alcohol to her as a reward for her sexual behavior. Because he was someone whose attention she desired, both the sexual activity itself and the alcohol had secondary reward components. It has also been suggested that the use of substances can give rise to a sense of excitement in the experience of an abused child, who may feel disconnected from the self or "dead" inside (Blume 1990, 157).

A third link between childhood abuse and later substance abuse is social. Children who are being abused tend to feel different from other children. They are lonely and alienated, and they tend to satisfy their need to belong by identifying with and adopting the values and habits of other alienated individuals whom they find in bars or doing drugs at home or school. It is not surprising that Lora connected with her friend Cathy, since it was the first time she found someone who shared significant aspects of her personal experience. It is not surprising either that Lora felt at home with the substance-using crowd at school. For the first time she felt accepted.

Finally, the connection between childhood abuse and subsequent substance use disorders is strengthened by the tendency of those who abuse substances to experience further trauma in daily living. They are prone to angry outbursts and confrontations, altercations, and run-ins with authority. Their continuing substance abuse is likely to result in social isolation, and substance abuse also renders them vulnerable to physical, emotional, and sexual

revictimization. Unrelenting exposure to negative life experiences may lead to or exacerbate feelings of hopelessness and depression. These negative affective reactions may lead to further abuse of substances, in a vicious cycle of trauma and substance abuse.

Evidence of the Relationship between Childhood Abuse and Subsequent Substance Abuse

Several distinct bodies of empirical research support the existence of relationships between childhood physical, emotional, and sexual abuse and the emergence of subsequent substance use disorders. These studies may be grouped according to the population being studied, and on the basis of the nature of the childhood abuse examined. With respect to population, the studies may be grouped, first, with respect to the gender of the population studied. Most reports have focused on either females or males, but not both. Much more research has been reported on females than on males. Second, the studies may be grouped with respect to the nature of the population studied. Some studies have focused on persons in treatment for substance abuse; some have compared individuals in treatment for substance abuse disorders to individuals in treatment for other psychiatric diagnoses; and still other studies have focused on samples drawn from the general (nonclinical) population.

Women in Treatment for Substance Use Disorders
Mullen and Fleming (1998) pointed out that the first set of studies supporting the relationship between childhood abuse and subsequent substance abuse were reports on populations of clients who were in treatment for substance use disorders. These studies showed that disproportionately large numbers of these clients reported histories of childhood abuse, particularly childhood sexual abuse. Most of these studies focused on women in treatment for substance abuse (Cohen and Densen-Gerber 1988; Hagan 1988; Kovach 1983; Miller, Downs, Gondoli, and Keil 1987; Miller, Downs, and Testa 1993; Miller, Moeller, and Kaufman 1987; Rohsenow, Corbett, and Devine 1988; Sterne, Schaefer, and Evans 1983; Yandow 1989).

Fergusson and Mullen (1999) pointed out that these studies are limited by the fact that the rates of self-reported childhood sexual abuse found in these studies vary greatly, calling into question the actual strength of the association between child sexual abuse and subsequent substance abuse. Ladwig and Anderson (1989) found that only 20 percent of their sample of females in treatment for substance abuse reported a history of child sexual abuse, but Covington and Cohen (1984) found that 74 percent of their sample reported a history of childhood sexual abuse. Nevertheless, a review of twelve studies conducted prior to 1995 concluded that women in treatment for substance abuse tended to report histories of childhood sexual abuse significantly more frequently than women in the general population (Fleming 1997).

A further limitation pertaining to many of these studies is the possibility that both the childhood sexual abuse and the substance use disorder could result from factors that were not examined. For example, parental substance abuse might account for a substantial portion of the variability in both self-reported childhood sexual abuse and subsequent substance use disorders among women with such histories. This limitation does not pertain in the case of the study reported by Miller and associates (1993) which showed that the relationship between treatment for substance use disorders as an adult and self-reported childhood sexual abuse persisted, even after controlling statistically for the effects of demographic characteristics and parental alcohol abuse disorders. In addition, even if the relationship between treatment for substance use disorders and childhood sexual abuse could be explained by other factors, this would not alter the implication of the relationship that clinicians working with women in treatment for substance use disorders should routinely assess for history of childhood abuse.

Women Receiving Mental Health Treatment

Wilsnack, Vogeltanz, Klassen, and Harris (1997) pointed out that a second body of literature focused on adult women receiving mental health treatment. These studies assessed both self-reported history of childhood sexual abuse and history of substance use disorders (Briere and Runtz 1987; Brown and Anderson 1991; Goodwin, Cheeves, and Connell 1990; Pribor and Dinwiddie 1992). All but one of these studies indicated that mental health patients who reported a history of childhood sexual abuse were significantly more likely than those who did not to also report past or current substance use disorders. One study employing slightly different methods yielded contradictory findings (Hussey and Singer 1993). This was a study of female adolescents who were inpatients. The results indicated that those inpatients who were being treated for alcohol abuse did not differ from those inpatients who were being treated for other psychiatric diagnoses with respect to self-reported history of child sexual abuse. This study differed from the others in this group in that the participants were adolescents, and the alcohol use disorder they had was sufficiently serious that they were involved in inpatient treatment. Their inpatient status may indicate particularly serious or long-standing alcohol use disorders. Their inpatient status may also indicate the presence of other psychosocial factors that indicate the advisability of removing the child from the home to an inpatient setting, rather than re-ferring the child to an outpatient treatment program.

Furthermore, some of the adolescent inpatients being treated for diagnoses other than substance use disorders may have been diagnosed as depressed, or they may have been admitted for eating disorders or other self-destructive be-havioral problems. But these diagnoses have also been shown to be related to history of childhood sexual abuse. This could explain why the rate of self-re-ported history of CSA was elevated in the group not being treated for alco-hol abuse. On balance, it seems fair to conclude that the weight of available empirical evidence does suggest that among adult women who are inpatients, those being treated for alcohol abuse are more likely to report a history of child sexual abuse than those who are being treated for some other psychi-atric disorder.

Women in the General (Nonclinical) Population
All of the studies described in the two foregoing sections are concerned with clinic samples. Therefore, the findings of these studies do not apply to the general population of women. However, a growing number of empirical stud-ies have examined the relationship between childhood abuse and subsequent substance abuse within nonclinical samples (Burnam, Stein, Golding et al. 1988; Bushnell, Wells, and Oakley-Browne 1992; Fergusson, Lynskey, and Horwood 1996; Mullen, Martin, Anderson, Romans, and Herbison 1993; Pe-ters 1988; Rodriguez-Srednicki 2001; Scott 1992; Stein, Golding, Siegel, Burnam, and Sorenson 1988; Wilsnack, Vogeltanz, Klassen, and Harris 1997; Winfield, George, Swartz, and Blazer 1990). These studies all reported sig-nificant relationships between a history of child sexual abuse and subsequent substance use disorders in women, and all have reported that these relation-ships persist even after controlling statistically for possible confounding vari-ables (Fergusson and Mullen 1999). More specifically, three of these demon-strated a significant relationship between the severity of the childhood sexual abuse reported and the likelihood of developing a substance abuse dis-order (Fergusson et al. 1996; Mullen et al. 1993; Peters 1988).

Noteworthy among these studies of CSA and substance abuse among women in the general population is the study reported by Wilsnack and her colleagues (1997), which employed a large sample representative of the na-tional population of women. These investigators reported on data drawn from a sample of 1,099 women, drawn and weighted statistically so as to rep-resent "the non-institutionalized U.S. female population age 21 and older" (266). The data were collected during ninety-minute personal interviews that were conducted in the respondents' homes by trained interviewers from the National Opinion Research Center. The survey included detailed questions on child sexual abuse, alcohol consumption, the adverse consequences of alcohol consumption, and other drug use.

The questions concerned with childhood sexual abuse asked about respondents' exposure before the age of eighteen to each of eight specific sexual acts: (1) exposure of the respondents' genitals; (2) exhibitionism (by the perpetrator); (3) touching/fondling; (4) sexual kissing; (5) oral–genital contact (receives); (6) oral–genital contact (performs); (7) anal intercourse; and (8) vaginal intercourse. Respondents were not asked whether they had been sexually abused, so the subjectivity associated with the respondent's individual definition of sexual abuse was eliminated. The interview did not contain queries about sexually provocative verbal remarks or sexual propositions or solicitations. An affirmative response with respect to any of the eight categories of sexual activity was followed up with queries on the number of individuals involved in the sexual activity, the relationship of the person or persons involved to the respondent, the age of the respondent and the others involved at the time that category of sexual activity first occurred, and the respondent's feelings about the experience at the time that it occurred.

The investigators subsequently defined childhood sexual abuse as (1) any intrafamilial sexual activity before the age of eighteen that was unwanted by the respondent or involved a family member five or more years older than the respondent and (2) any extrafamilial sexual activity that occurred before age eighteen that was unwanted, or any extrafamilial sexual activity that occurred before the respondent was thirteen and involved another person five or more years older than the respondent. According to this definition, the authors reported that 21.4 percent of their sample had experienced childhood sexual abuse.

The survey questions connected with alcohol use included measures of (1) the frequency of heavy episodic drinking (six or more drinks in a day) during the past twelve months; (2) the frequency of intoxication over the same period; (3) the number of problematic consequences of drinking that occurred in the last year; and (4) the number of alcohol dependence symptoms experienced. Problematic consequences of alcohol use included driving while feeling intoxicated, starting fights with family members or others, damage to work, drinking-related home accidents and problems with children, and complaints from spouse or partners regarding one's substance use. Respondents were asked about five common symptoms of alcohol dependence, including memory lapses while drinking, morning drinking, rapid drinking, inability to stop drinking before becoming intoxicated, and inability to stop or reduce alcohol consumption over time.

Measures of use of substances other than alcohol included self-reports of lifetime use of three categories of drugs: (1) prescription psychoactive drugs, including tranquilizers, sleeping pills, and painkillers; (2) illegal drugs, including marijuana, cocaine, heroin, and hallucinogens; and (3) over-the-counter psychoactive drugs, including nonprescription painkillers, tranquilizers, sleeping aids, diet pills, and cough medicine. Questions on prescription drugs and illegal drugs asked whether respondents had used each category of drug more than five times in their lives; and questions on over-the-counter drugs asked whether they had ever used the drug "every day or almost every day for more than two weeks at a time" (269). The survey instrument also included brief measures of depression, anxiety, sexual dysfunction, and precocious onset of sexual activity.

Logistic regression analyses indicated that respondents with histories of childhood sexual abuse differed from those without such histories in that the abused sample scored significantly higher on the frequency of intoxication during the last year, the number of problem consequences of alcohol use that were experienced, and the number of symptoms of alcohol dependence experienced. In addition, the sexually abused women were significantly more likely than the nonabused women to report problematic use of psychoactive prescription drugs and use of illegal drugs. These differences remained significant after controlling statistically for the effects of demographic variables. In addition, the women reporting histories of childhood sexual abuse were more likely than the nonabused group to report having experienced at least one episode of clinically significant depression; and the women reporting CSA were more likely than those not reporting CSA to have engaged in precocious sexual activity.

Child Abuse and Subsequent Substance Use Disorders among Men

Existing research on the relationships between various forms of childhood abuse and subsequent substance use disorders among men is not nearly as extensive as the corresponding research on women. However, what research there is suggests that the magnitude of these relationships may be substantial (Bachman, Moggi, and Stirnemann-Lewis 1994; Chandy, Blum, and Resnick 1996b; Collings 1995; Dimock 1988; Freeman-Longo 1986; Harrison, Edwall, Hoffman, and Worthen 1990; Hernandez, Lodico, and DiClemente 1993; Olson 1990; Peters and Range 1995; Urquiza and Capra 1990). For example, a study of male veterans who were being treated for substance use disorders reported by Triffleman, Marmar, Delucchi, and Ronfeldt (1995) indicated that 77 percent of the sample had been exposed to severe childhood trauma. This study also showed that the men who reported the most serious childhood abuse also had the most serious substance use disorders, in that they were also the most likely to be diagnosed as dependent upon multiple substances.

Physical Abuse and Subsequent Substance Use Disorders
Studies of the relationship between childhood abuse and subsequent substance use disorders among men have tended to focus more on the sequelae of physical abuse than have the corresponding studies of women. However, the literature suggests that physical abuse is associated with subsequent substance use disorders among both men and women (Briere and Elliott 2003; Carlson 1991; Dube, Anda, Felitti, Edwards, and Croft 2002; Hendricks-Matthews 1993; Kunitz, Levy, McCloskey, and Gabriel 1998; Langeland and Hartgers 1998; Malinosky-Rummell and Hansen 1993). Pagliaro and Pagliaro (1996) reported that the parental use of corporal punishment on adolescents is related to the subsequent development of alcohol abuse and dependence. This report is significant in view of the finding reported by Straus and Kantor (1994) that more than half of a large national sample of adults in the United States recalled being administered corporal punishment during their teen years.

Furthermore, several investigators have suggested that a history of childhood physical abuse may actually be associated more closely with substance use disorders than history of childhood sexual abuse (Brown and Anderson 1991; Evans and Sullivan 1995; Sanders and Giolas 1991; Zanarini and Gunderson 1987). In addition, a number of recent studies strongly suggest that a combination of physical abuse, sexual abuse, and/or other forms of childhood abuse or other adverse experiences is most likely to be related to subsequent substance use disorders (Bensley, van Eenwyk and Simmons 2000; Dong, Anda, Felitti, Dube, Williamson et al. 2004; Dube, Anda, Felitti, Croft, Edwards, and Giles 2001; Dube et al. 2002; Dube, Felitti, Dong, Chapman, Giles, and Anda 2003; Liebschutz, Savetsky, Saitz, Horton, Lloyd-Travaglini, and Samet 2002; Tam, Zlotnick, and Robertson 2003).

Multiple Forms of Childhood Abuse
and Subsequent Substance Use Disorders
Dube and her associates (2002) surveyed 17,337 adults who visited the Kaiser Permanente Health Appraisal Clinic in San Diego. These investigators sought to determine the relationships between self-reported indicators of adult alcohol abuse and two sets of predictors: (1) parental alcoholism and (2) a set of eight "adverse childhood experiences" (713) which occurred before the age of nineteen. These adverse childhood experiences (ACEs) included

verbal abuse, physical abuse, sexual abuse, having a battered mother, exposure to substance abuse in the household, mental illness in the household, parental separation or divorce, and having a household member who was incarcerated.

The measures of alcohol abuse included a self-report measure of "heavy drinking," which asked whether the respondent had consumed "at least fourteen drinks per week during any ten-year period from age nineteen to the present" (717). Alcohol abuse was defined as a yes response to the question, "Have you ever had a problem with your use of alcohol?" (717). Alcoholism was defined similarly as a yes response to the question, "Have you ever considered yourself an alcoholic?" Finally, respondents were asked whether they had ever been married to someone or lived with someone who was a problem drinker or an alcoholic.

The questions measuring the ACEs were drawn from several different sources, including the Conflict Tactics Scale (CTS; Straus and Gelles 1990). Verbal abuse was measured by two questions from the CTS: (1) "How often did a parent, stepparent, or adult living in your home swear at you, insult you, or put you down?" and (2) "How often did a parent, stepparent, or adult living in your home threaten to hit you or throw something at you, but didn't do it?" Responses to these (and other) questions drawn from the CTS were made on a five-point Likert-type response scale with the following options: "never," "once or twice," "sometimes," "often," and "very often." A respondent was coded affirmatively for verbal abuse if he or she selected the "often" or "very often" response option for either of these two questions.

Physical abuse was measured by the following questions from the CTS: "Sometimes parents or other adults hurt children. While you were growing up, that is, in your first eighteen years of life, how often did a parent, stepparent, or adult living in your home: (1) push, grab, slap, or throw something at you? or (2) hit you so hard that you had marks or were injured?" A respondent was coded affirmatively for physical abuse if his or her response was "often" or "very often" to the first question, or if his or her response was "sometimes," "often," or "very often" to the second question.

Sexual abuse was assessed by four questions drawn from Wyatt (1985). The query read as follows: "Some people, while they were growing up in their first eighteen years of life, had a sexual experience with an adult or someone at least five years older than themselves. These experiences may have involved a relative, family friend, or stranger. During the first eighteen years of life, did an adult, relative, family friend, or stranger ever (1) touch or fondle your body in a sexual way, (2) have you touch their body in a sexual way, (3) attempt to have any type of sexual intercourse with you (oral, anal, or vaginal), or (4) actually have any type of sexual intercourse with you (oral, anal, or vaginal)?" A yes response to any one of these four questions led to the respondent being coded affirmatively for childhood sexual abuse.

Dube and her colleagues (2002) used four questions from the CTS to define childhood exposure to a battered mother. This section of the survey read as follows: "Sometimes physical blows occur between parents. While you were growing up in your first eighteen years of life, how often did your father (or stepfather) or mother's boyfriend do any of these things to your mother (or stepmother)? (1) push, grab, slap, or throw something at her, (2) kick, bite, hit her with a fist, or hit her with something hard, (3) repeatedly hit her over at least a few minutes, or (4) threaten her with a knife or gun, or use a knife or gun to hurt her." Respondents were coded affirmatively for exposure to a battered mother if they selected a response of "sometimes," "often," or "very often" to either of the first two questions, or if they selected any response other than "never" to either of the last two questions. The investigators did not include any measure of domestic violence involving a female perpetrator and male victim.

The adverse childhood event (ACE) representing the presence of substance abuse in the household was defined in this study as separate from parental alcoholism, which the investigators viewed as a separate variable. The ACE classification for household substance use was based on two questions, based on Schoenborn (1995). The first question asked whether the respondent, during his or her first eighteen years, had lived with someone other than a parent who was a problem drinker or alcoholic; the second question asked whether the respondent had lived with anyone at all, including a parent, who used "street drugs." An affirmative response to either of these questions resulted in the respondent being coded affirmatively for household substance abuse.

Mental illness in the household was ascertained by a single question, which asked whether or not during the respondent's childhood anyone in the household was depressed or mentally ill or had attempted suicide. Parental separation or divorce was similarly measured by a single question: "Were your parents ever separated or divorced?" The ACE on incarceration of a household member during the respondent's childhood was similarly ascertained by the answer to a yes/no question.

Questions on whether the respondent's mother or father was an alcoholic were used to classify respondents into one of two groups—those with and without a history of alcoholism in one or both parents. The analyses of the relationships between the ACEs and the respondent's own behavior with respect to alcohol were then carried out separately for respondents who did and did not report parental alcoholism.

The results indicated that 24 percent of the responding women and 18 percent of the responding men reported that at least one parent was an alcoholic. As expected, having at least one parent who was an alcoholic was related significantly to self-reported heavy drinking, alcohol abuse, alcoholism, and marrying or living with an alcoholic. Among both the respondents who had an alcoholic parent and the respondents who did not have an alcoholic parent, each of the individual ACEs was related significantly to each of the four indicators of adult alcohol problems.

Furthermore, within each of the two groups formed on the basis of parental alcoholism, there was a strong relationship between the number of ACEs reported and each of the four indicators of adult alcohol problems. Among respondents with one or more alcoholic parents who also reported at least four of the ACEs, the proportion who reported that they drank heavily was 24.2 percent, and the proportion who reported that they had alcohol-related problems was 30.7 percent. Among respondents who did not report a history of parental alcoholism, the proportion who classified themselves as alcoholics was four times greater among those who reported four or more ACEs than it was among those who reported zero ACEs. And among respondents who did report that one or both parents were alcoholics, the proportion who classified themselves as alcoholics was three times greater with four or more ACEs, as opposed to none. Further analyses indicated that the relationships between the number of ACEs reported and the indicators of adult alcohol problems were similar for female and male respondents.

The authors emphasized the importance of their large sample size, particularly with reference to the conclusions that they could draw regarding males. They noted that "most prior studies that investigated the influence of childhood abuse on the risk of alcoholism have tended to focus on women [and] those studies that included men often had insufficient information for adequate study of these associations among males" (2002, 724). Their study indicated "a strong association between the eight individual ACEs and alcohol misuse and abuse among men" (724), and they argued further that "assessment of the associations of childhood sexual and physical abuse and related exposures, both individually and cumulatively, among men is critical since alcohol use and abuse is substantially greater among men" (724).

We need to learn more about the "cumulative" impact of various forms of abuse and other adverse childhood experiences because the various forms of abuse and family dysfunction tend to occur in combination. This aspect of childhood abuse has been illustrated recently in the study reported by Dong and associates (2004). These investigators argued that no summary analysis of the interrelationships among multiple forms of childhood abuse and household dysfunction had been reported, and that "a full exploration of the interrelationships is critical to understanding the long-term effects of adverse childhood experiences" (45). This is because investigators who study only one or two of these childhood exposures "are likely to miss the apparent negative effects of co-occurring traumatic or stressful experiences [and] when such co-occurrence is ignored, researchers and clinicians may hold the implicit assumption that the meaning of the presence of one type of childhood adversity is the same in all cases whether or not others are present" (45).

Dong and her colleagues (2004) surveyed 8,629 adult members of the Kaiser Permanente health plan. The survey asked respondents to report on ten ACEs, including emotional, physical, and sexual abuse, emotional and physical neglect, witnessing domestic violence, parental marital discord, and living with substance abusing, mentally ill, or criminal household members. Eight of these ACEs were measured in exactly same manner that they were measured in the study by Dube and associates (2002) described above, except that substance abuse within the household included one's parents as well as other relatives and nonrelatives. The two additional ACEs included in the study by Dong and colleagues (2004) were emotional and physical neglect.

Emotional neglect was measured by a five-item scale drawn from the Childhood Trauma Questionnaire (CTQ) (Bernstein, Fink, Handelsman, Foote, Lovejoy et al. 1994): (1) "There was someone in my family who helped me feel important or special." (2) "I felt loved." (3) "People in my family looked out for each other." (4) "People in my family felt close to each other." (5) "My family was a source of strength and support." These five statements were rated on a 5-point Likert-type scale having response options ranging from 1, signifying "never true," to 5, signifying "very often true." The ratings were reverse coded and summed to obtain an emotional neglect score having a theoretical range from 5 through 25. Respondents scoring 15 or higher were coded affirmatively for emotional neglect.

Physical neglect was measured by a five-item scale containing the following statements: (1) "I didn't have enough to eat." (2) "I knew there was someone there to take care of me and protect me." (3) "My parents were too drunk or too high to take care of me." (4) "I had to wear dirty clothes." (5) "There was someone to take me to the doctor if I needed it." These items were rated by respondents using the same 5-point Likert-type scale. Items 2 and 5 were reverse-coded and the items were summed to obtain a physical neglect score ranging from 5 through 25. Respondents scoring 10 or higher on this scale were coded affirmatively for physical neglect.

Logistic regression analyses were employed to determine whether the presence of each category of ACE was associated significantly with the risk of having the other types of ACEs, after controlling for the effects of demo-graphic variables including gender, race, and level of education. The preva-lence of each of the ten categories of ACEs in the sample ranged from 6 per-cent reporting that a family member was incarcerated to 28.2 percent reporting exposure to substance abuse in the household. Among persons re-porting one category of ACE during childhood, 86.5 percent reported at least one additional ACE, and 38.5 percent reported four or more additional ACEs. These proportions are substantially higher than one would expect if the ACEs were independent of one another.

When individuals reporting one category of ACE were compared to per-sons not reporting that experience, the odds ratio of having at least one of the other nine ACEs ranged from 2.0 to 17.7. For example, the prevalence of reporting physical abuse was 80.5 percent among persons who reported emotional abuse, compared to 20.1 percent among persons who had not, yielding an adjusted odds ratio of 17.7. The corresponding odds ratios were significant for every one of the ten ACE categories.

Thus the various forms of childhood abuse and other adverse childhood events tend to be found in conjunction with each other, and it is important to attempt to understand the effects of various combinations of these ACEs on adult outcomes. This conclusion applies to substance use disorders as well as other adult outcomes of abuse. This aspect of multiple forms of abuse is dis-cussed in this chapter because substance use disorders have been the focus of most of the studies that have considered the interrelatedness of multiple forms of childhood abuse.

Definitions of Substance Abuse and Dependence

As we have seen in several of the studies described above, investigators have employed diverse measures of substance abuse, ranging from crude di-chotomies to efforts aimed at assessing the severity of the abuse. The DSM-IV-TR (American Psychiatric Association 2000) distinguishes first between substance abuse and substance dependence in general terms, irrespective of the particular substance(s) involved. Then additional specifiers are added to reflect the unique characteristics of particular substances.

Substance Abuse
According to the DSM-IV-TR, the "essential feature of Substance Abuse is a maladaptive pattern of substance use manifested by recurrent and signifi-cant adverse consequences related to the repeated use of substances" (APA 2000, 198). The substance-related problem must have occurred repeatedly

during the same twelve-month period, and it must have led to clinically significant impairment or distress, as indicated by one or more of the following: (1) recurrent substance use resulting in a failure to fulfill major role obligations at work, school, or home (e.g., substance-related absences or poor work performance; substance-related absences, suspensions, or expulsions from school; neglect of children or household); (2) recurrent substance use in situations in which the substance use is physically hazardous (e.g., driving an automobile or operating machinery when impaired by substance use); (3) recurrent substance-related legal problems (e.g., arrests for substance-related disorderly conduct; and (4) continued substance use despite having persistent or recurrent social or interpersonal problems caused or exacerbated by the effects of the substance (e.g., arguments with one's spouse concerned with the consequences of intoxication or physical fights while intoxicated).

Substance Dependence
Substance dependence is characterized by "a cluster of cognitive, behavioral, and physiological symptoms indicating that the individual continues use of the substance despite significant substance-related problems" (APA 2000, 192). This feature of substance dependence is similar to the fourth criterion of substance abuse described above. However, substance dependence is differentiated from substance abuse by the compulsive quality of the substance use, which may reflect the development of tolerance for the substance and the development of withdrawal symptoms when the use of the substance is discontinued. The criteria for the diagnosis of substance dependence include a maladaptive pattern of substance use, leading to clinically significant impairment or distress, as indicated by the occurrence within the same twelve-month period of *three or more* of the following: (1) tolerance, as defined by either (a) a need for markedly increased amounts of the substance to achieve intoxication or the desired effect or (b) markedly diminished effect with continued use of the same amount of the substance; (2) withdrawal, as manifested by either (a) the onset of withdrawal symptoms when the drug is not taken or (b) the use of the substance or a closely related substance is continued to avoid or relieve withdrawal symptoms; (3) the substance is often taken in larger amounts or over a longer period of time than was intended; (4) there is a persistent desire and/or unsuccessful efforts to cut down or control substance use; (5) a great deal of time is spent in activities required to obtain the substance, use the substance, or recover from the effects of using the substance; (6) important social, occupational, or recreational activities are given up or reduced because of substance use; (7) the use of the substance is continued

despite knowledge of having a persistent or recurrent physical or psycho-logical problem that has been caused or exacerbated by the substance.

Note that since three of the seven criteria listed above are required to as-sign a diagnosis of substance dependence, it is possible to assign the diagno-sis without detecting evidence of either tolerance or withdrawal. For this rea-son, a diagnosis of substance dependence is made along with a specification as to whether or not physiological dependence is present. The diagnosis of substance dependence with physiological dependence is made when the pa-tient manifests tolerance and/or withdrawal; and the diagnosis of substance dependence without physiological dependence is made when there is no ev-idence of either tolerance or withdrawal. In the case of substance depen-dence without physiological dependence, the substance dependence is char-acterized by a pattern of compulsive use of the substance, as indicated by three or more of criteria 3 through 7 listed above.

Etiological Models Explaining the Relationship between Childhood Abuse and Substance Use Disorders

Lora's case illustrated several of the many plausible explanations for the ob-served relationship between childhood abuse and subsequent substance use disorders. There is the frequent involvement of parental substance abuse, which has both genetic and environmental components. There is the simple fact of emotional and/or physical pain, which leads to efforts to self-medicate through the use of alcohol or other anesthetizing substances. There is the somewhat more complex extension of the role of pain embodied in the idea of Posttraumatic Stress Disorder and its continuing relationship to substance abuse. There is the impact of the victim's attempt to deal with abuse through the defense of dissociation, the tendency of the victim to continue to utilize this defense during periods of stress encountered later in life, and the associ-ation between dissociation and substance abuse. There are also social link-ages. Childhood abuse is associated with insecure attachment, which is in turn associated with poor social adjustment, including both isolation and hostility. Social adjustment difficulties may ultimately be reflected in identi-fication with outcast groups, including those who engage in substance abuse.

In discussing these various linkages, it is important to establish at the out-set that the etiological models discussed are not mutually exclusive. On the contrary, these linkages are most productively viewed as co-occurring and mu-tually supporting. We know that children who experience one form of abuse are likely to experience other forms of abuse as well. We know that adult vic-tims of childhood abuse do not tend to experience a single psychosocial adjustment problem, but rather are likely to experience multiple symptoms. It appears to follow logically that the pathways connecting childhood abuse with adult adjustment problems will co-occur and reinforce each other. This conclusion may be one of the primary inferences drawn from the research reviewed earlier in this chapter indicating a relationship between the number and severity of ACEs a child experiences and the number and severity of the adjustment difficulties that child is likely to experience later in life.

It is organizationally convenient and heuristically useful to discuss separately the several etiological models aimed at explaining the relationship between childhood abuse and subsequent substance use disorders. However, in considering these models, the reader is urged to remain aware that more than one of these processes may be relevant to any case. Indeed, understanding the relationships among and additive effects of multiple forms of abuse and multiple pathways to substance abuse and other adult adjustment disorders is the principal challenge that confronts both clinicians and researchers involved in seeking to understand the impact of childhood abuse.

Parental Substance Abuse
A substantial amount of research demonstrates that substance abusing parents are more likely to abuse their children than non–substance abusing parents (Conners, Bradley, Mansell, Liu, Roberts et al. 2004; Elliot 1994; Famularo, Kinscherff, and Fenton 1992; Famularo, Stone, Barnum, and Wharton 1986; Murphy, Jellinek, Quinn, Smith, Poitrast, and Goshko 1991; Seagull 1997; Wolfner and Gelles 1993; Yama, Fogas, Teegarden, and Hastings 1993). Other research demonstrates that the children of substance abusing parents are more likely than other children to develop substance abuse problems of their own (Rowe 1989; Pagliaro and Pagliaro 1996; Rubio-Stipec, Bird, Canino, Bravo, and Alegria 1991; Schinke, Botvin, and Orlandi 1991; Woodside, Coughey, and Cohen 1993). Thus one could argue that the relationship between a history of childhood abuse and subsequent substance abuse disorders is at least in part the result of the substance abuse of the parent.

Pagliaro and Pagliaro (1996) have argued that the increased risk of substance use disorders among the children of substance abusers "appears to be mediated through biological (e.g., genetic predisposition), psychological (e.g., 'pro-use' attitudes), and sociological (e.g., socially learned behavior) variables" (150). The largest body of research concerns the genetic relationship. The pathways differentially labeled "psychological" and "sociological" by the Pagliaros might be combined into the overarching category of environmental, so as to highlight more clearly the difference between the roles nature and nurture play in the etiology of substance abuse.

However, there is no good reason to distinguish between the effect of parental attitude toward substance use and the effect of social learning that may result from observing parents actually abuse alcohol or other drugs. McDermott (1984) compared the impact of socially learned behavior to the impact of parental attitude on the likelihood of a child developing a substance use disorder later in life. He found that both the child's observation of the parent's own substance abuse and the parent's expression of favorable attitude toward the use of intoxicating substances predicted subsequent substance use disorders in children. However, the parental attitude variable was a stronger predictor of subsequent substance abuse by the child than was the observation of actual substance abuse by the parents. The importance of both modeling and parental attitudes toward the use of intoxicants is indicated by the following quotation of an adolescent heroin user, taken from transcribed patient treatment session notes:

> I was around 13 or 14 and the old lady was firing it [heroin], "Hey if you're gonna be doing that in front of me, give me some or I'll go do it by myself." She said, "Okay, if you're gonna fix, do it around here, then if you OD [overdose] I can get you to the hospital." It was accepted around my house. Accepted to get high. I think there are a lot of other kids like that out there in the same position. Their parents don't give a shit one way or the other. (Pagliaro and Pagliaro 1996, 150)

The literature on the genetic connection between parental alcoholism and substance abuse disorders among children is also clear. Several studies have shown that the sons of alcoholic fathers are at increased likelihood of abusing substances, even after the effects of environmental influences are controlled (Frick, Lahey, Loeber, Stouthamer-Loeber, Christ et al. 1992; Gabel and Shindledecker 1993).

One study that considered the role of both genetic and environmental factors in the link between parental alcoholism and subsequent child substance use disorders concluded that the genetic link was the stronger of the two. Prescott and Kendler (1999) studied heritability of alcohol abuse among 3,516 male twins from male–male pairs born in Virginia between 1940 and 1974. These investigators found that the concordance rate for alcoholism between identical twins was significantly higher than that for fraternal twins, supporting the genetic link. They reported that more than half of the variability in the likelihood that an individual would develop alcoholism at some point in his lifetime was attributable to genetic factors. A smaller but still significant proportion of the variability in the likelihood of becoming an alcoholic was attributable to environmental factors not shared by the individual members of the twin dyads. Environmental factors shared by the members of twin dyads did not explain significant variability in alcoholism. Prescott and Kendler concluded that "genetic factors played a major role in the development of alcoholism among males, with similar influence for alcohol abuse and alcohol dependence . . . in this population-based sample, environmental factors shared by family members appear to have had little influence on the development of alcoholism in males" (1999, 40).

These findings suggest that parental alcoholism and the genetic predisposition of the child of an alcoholic to subsequent substance use disorders may explain part of the relationship between various forms of childhood abuse and subsequent substance use disorders. Certainly clinicians working with substance abusing clients should routinely assess for both history of various forms of child abuse and parental substance abuse. Clinicians should assess the client's perceptions of the relationship between parental substance abuse and dimensions of child abuse. Clinicians should elicit data on the parameters of parental substance abuse, including the substances used, the frequency and duration of substance use, and the impact of substance use on parenting behavior. Clinicians should also determine the extent to which the substance-abusing client was exposed to messages signifying acceptance of substance use, as well as the extent to which the client was exposed to adults modeling substance use behavior.

The Self-Medication Hypothesis

A long-standing, durable, and appealingly straightforward theory that has been employed to explain the relationship between history of child abuse and subsequent substance use disorder is the self-medication hypothesis, popularized by Khantzian (1985, 1997, 2004). This application of the self-medication hypothesis states that child abuse is painful and that the victims of various forms of child abuse tend to resort to the use of addictive substances to help them deal with the pain. Once the victim begins to use substances to cope with pain, the addiction process sets in. The victim gradually develops tolerance for the substance(s) being used to cope with pain, so he or she uses progressively more. The individual may also begin to develop withdrawal symptoms. In this regard, Khantzian (2005) acknowledged that tolerance and physical dependence are more commonly associated with advanced phases of addictive disease, but he asserted that "early in the course of addiction to a substance an individual can develop more subtle signs of physical tolerance and withdrawal" (1). Thus, following the termination of the childhood abuse, the victim may continue the substance use, and the disease process may continue its downhill course.

According to Khantzian (2004), "the main implication of the self-medication hypothesis is that "in the majority of cases suffering leads to substance use disorders and not the other way around" (588). In addition, Khantzian explicitly asserted that the hypothesis applies to both alcohol abuse and dependence and dependence on heroin and cocaine (Khantzian 2004).

Posttraumatic Stress Disorder and Substance Abuse
The application of the self-medication hypothesis to the relationship between childhood abuse and subsequent substance use disorders has a more complex variant, which specifies that trauma experienced during childhood leads to the development of Posttraumatic Stress Disorder (PTSD), and the victim turns to the use of anesthetizing chemicals to control the symptoms of PTSD (Lisak and Miller 2003). These symptoms, which will be considered in detail in the next chapter of this book, may be summarized briefly as including high levels of anxiety, particularly in conjunction with stimuli which evoke memories of abuse (Goodwin 1996). Victims of childhood abuse who develop PTSD are also characterized by a pervasive sense of sadness and shame (Gelinas 1983; Goodwin 1985, 1988, 1989, 1993; Herman 1981).

These symptoms of PTSD persist after the traumatic childhood abuse experiences have come to an end. Therefore, the victim may employ substances not only at the time of the abuse, to anesthetize the pain of the ongoing abuse, but also after the termination of the abuse, to manage the symptoms of PTSD that continue to affect the victim over time. The use of addictive substances for either of these purposes has the effect of initiating the addiction process and increasing the likelihood of being diagnosed with a substance abuse disorder later on in life.

Empirical evidence supporting the causal path leading from childhood abuse to PTSD to substance abuse disorders has been provided by Kilpatrick, Acierno, Saunders, Resnick, Best et al. (2000). These investigators collected data from a national sample of 4,023 adolescents of both genders between the ages of twelve and seventeen. They assessed history of trauma in the form of physical assault, sexual assault, and witnessing violence. They also assessed abuse of alcohol and other drugs in the respondent's family of origin. They assessed PTSD using an instrument designed and used previously by Resnick, Kilpatrick, Dansky, Saunders, and Best (1993); and they assessed substance use disorders using a structured clinical interview. Kilpatrick and her colleagues (2000) found that PTSD, alcohol abuse/dependence, and marijuana abuse/dependence were all predicted by each of the trauma history variables, as well as by familial alcohol abuse/dependence and familial abuse of/dependence on other drugs. Data obtained with respect to the self-reported age of onset of victimization experiences and substance use disorders suggested victimization increases the risk of substance use disorders, rather than substance use increasing the risk of victimization.

Stewart and Conrod (2003) reviewed the empirical data relevant to the co-morbidity of PTSD and SUD, and they concluded that trauma exposure leads to increased rates of SUDs, "because trauma results in PTSD symptoms, which patients attempt to self-medicate through drinking and drug misuse" (41). In support of this conclusion, Stewart and Conrod cited the findings reported by Epstein, Saunders, Kilpatrick, and Resnick (1998), who examined the mediating role of PTSD symptoms in explaining the relationship between childhood sexual abuse and alcohol problems in adulthood. These investigators studied a sample of nearly 3,000 adult women, each of whom was interviewed regarding childhood sexual abuse history, as well as lifetime experience with PTSD symptoms and alcohol abuse symptoms. The investigators found that alcohol abuse was greater among sexual abuse victims who developed symptoms of PTSD than among sexual abuse victims who did not develop these symptoms. Path analysis indicated a significant pathway between childhood sexual abuse and PTSD symptoms, as well as a significant pathway from PTSD symptoms to alcohol abuse symptoms. Multiple regression mediation analysis indicated that the relationship between childhood sexual abuse and adult alcohol abuse was completely mediated by PTSD symptoms.

Other empirical data supporting the role of PTSD symptoms in mediating the relationship between trauma history and the development of an SUD include reports that among adults with co-morbid PTSD and SUD, substance abuse tends to be situation specific. That is, substance abuse tends to occur most frequently in contexts that have been associated in the past with the substance's tension-reducing effects (Stewart, Conrod, Samoluk, Pihl, and Doninger 2000; Sharkansky, Brief, Peirce, Meehan, and Mannix 1999). Studies also suggest that adults with co-morbid PTSD and SUD tend to report that they use substances in response to anxiety sensitivity, which is defined as fear of anxiety-related situations (Peterson and Reiss 1992; Stewart, Samoluk, and MacDonald 1999; Taylor, Koch, and McNally 1992). Stewart et al. (2000) reported that among adult women with co-morbid PTSD and SUD, anxiety sensitivity mediated observed relationships between PTSD symptoms and situation-specific heavy drinking in negative contexts.

Hysterical Symptoms, Dissociation, and Alexithymia

Another explanation of the relationship between childhood abuse and the subsequent development of substance abuse disorders involves the psychological defenses employed by victims of abuse to wall off traumatic experiences and memories of these experiences. These include the primitive defenses of denial, isolation of affect, and splitting, which are ultimately reflected in the emergence of hysterical symptoms (Goodwin, Zouhar, and Begman 1989), dissociative symptoms (Coons, Bowman, and Pellows 1989; Fergusson and Mullen 1999; Goodwin et al. 1989; Kluft 1985; Putnam 1985; Rodriguez-Srednicki 2001; Spiegel 1994; Steinberg 1995), and alexithymia (Krystal 1982; Scher and Twaite 1999).

Evans and Sullivan (1995) proposed that the relationship between childhood abuse (specifically sexual abuse) and subsequent substance abuse is explained and mediated by dissociation. They argued that sexually abused children tend to disengage from their painful reality by dissociating, and that the pattern of dissociation developed during childhood persists into adolescence and adulthood. They argued further that "if survivors are using psychic numbing to detach from their feelings, alcohol and other drugs can aid them in their effort to numb the pain" (1995, 188). Thus they conceptualize the substance abuse as ancillary to the dissociation. Both dissociation and substance abuse are seen as insulating the victim from painful affect, and the substance abuse is viewed as augmenting the anesthetizing effect of dissociation. However, they also proposed that "the use of chemicals not only mimics but also promotes further dissociation: it intensifies the customary use of 'checking out' in order to cope for those survivors who effectively disengage from reality via dissociation" (76).

Rodriguez-Srednicki (2001) studied the relationships among childhood sexual abuse, dissociation, and a series of self-destructive behaviors, including drug use, alcohol abuse, binge eating, self-mutilation, risky sex, and suicidal tendencies. The design of this study was described in chapter 5 on eating disorders (see above, p. 81). The results of this study of female college students that were obtained with respect to binge eating were different from the results obtained with respect to substance use disorders. Respondents reporting histories of child sexual abuse were more likely to manifest binge eating, more likely to abuse illicit drugs, and more likely to abuse alcohol. However, whereas dissociation did not mediate the relationship between child sexual abuse and binge eating, dissociation did mediate the relationships between child sexual abuse and each of the two measures of substance abuse.

The mediating role of dissociation in the relationship between CSA and each of the two substance abuse variables was demonstrated through multiple regression mediation analysis. For each of the two substance abuse variables, the regression of substance abuse on self-reported history of CSA was significant. However, when scores on the dissociation subscale of the Trauma Symptom Checklist (TSC) were added to the regressions at step two, dissociation was a significant predictor of substance abuse, while self-reported history of CSA fell to nonsignificance. These findings may be interpreted as indicating that victims of CSA tend to employ both dissociation and intoxicating substances to help anesthetize the pain associated with the abuse and memories of the abuse. In addition, one could hypothesize that a victim of abuse might be tempted to self-medicate with drugs, but be constrained from doing so under normal circumstances due to fear of adverse health consequences and/or social disapproval of the use of alcohol and other drugs. In a dissociated state, however, the same victim might be freed from these constraints, allowing the self-medication to take place. In either case, the findings of this study strongly suggest that clinicians working with substance abusing clients should be certain to assess for childhood abuse and for dissociative tendencies.

Scher and Twaite (1999) reported a study of the relationship between self-reported history of CSA and alexithymia among a sample of 137 recovering substance abusers who were participating in outpatient substance abuse treatment programs. Alexithymia is a multidimensional construct characterized by difficulty in identifying and characterizing one's feelings, difficulty in distinguishing between feelings and bodily sensations, an impoverished fantasy life, and speech and thought that are concrete and tied closely to external events (Sifneos 1973, 1975). Krystal (1982) suggested that alexithymia develops in response to extreme trauma. He argued that alexithymia serves much the same function as dissociation—to protect the individual from experiencing painful affect. Scher and Twaite administered the Toronto Alexithymia Scale (TAS) (Taylor, Bagby, Ryan, and Parker 1990; Taylor, Ryan, and Bagby 1985) to participants. History of CSA was ascertained from clinic records and verified by respondent self-report.

Scher and Twaite (1999) reported that respondents who indicated a history of childhood sexual abuse (n = 68) scored significantly higher on the TAS than respondents who reported no such history (n = 68). Within the abused group, measured alexithymic symptomatology was significant to several parameters of the abuse. TAS scores were correlated positively with the reported duration of the sexual abuse. TAS scores were significantly higher when the perpetrator of the abuse was a father or stepfather and when the abuse involved oral, anal, or vaginal penetration. In addition, TAS scores were higher when the abuse first occurred after the victim was twelve. The authors' general conclusion was that "the development of alexithymic symptoms may represent another defense victims may employ to insulate themselves from painful affect, along with dissociative symptoms and substance abuse, which have been shown previously to characterize adult survivors of child sexual abuse" (1999, 26). The authors also suggested that therapists working with substance abusing populations should routinely assess for both alexithymia and history of childhood sexual abuse, as well as the parameters of the abuse that occurred.

Social Isolation and Hostility

Still another explanation of the relationship between various forms of childhood abuse and subsequent substance use disorders posits a role for the mediating effects of social isolation and hostility. We have already considered the impact that childhood abuse is likely to have on the development of a sense of self and on adult attachment relationships (see chapter 3, above). As noted earlier in this chapter, children who are abused tend to feel "different" from other children and frequently have difficulty in forming and maintaining satisfying social relationships. These children, like Lora in our case study, may gravitate toward marginal groups using alcohol and other drugs.

Volkan (1994) presented a formal theory of object relations and substance abuse. This theory has three primary hypotheses: (1) People who have satisfactory object relations will not feel the need to compulsively use substances of abuse, even those that are highly addictive. (2) People who have poor object relations, inadequate ego identity development, narcissistic disturbances, and introjective depression are likely to initiate the use of addicting substances as reactivated transitional objects and to continue to use these substances compulsively. (3) People who continue to abuse substances compulsively will exacerbate ego disturbances. Eventually they will develop schizoid pathology, and in the end they will become likely candidates for suicide.

Applied to the situation of an abused child, Volkan's theory suggests that deficits in early object relations and the internalization of punitive and frustrating parental objects lead to drug use, which provides a temporary regressive experience of a primary good object. The use of drugs also masks the introjected bad objects and the associated feelings of self-criticism and worthlessness. However, as the effects of the substance wear off, the feelings associated with the bad objects representations return, and now they are even stronger as a result of having been repressed. This prompts the victim to use even more of the substance to control dysphoria, initiating an upwardly spiraling cycle of negative affect and substance abuse. Furthermore, Volkan argued that because bad object representations carry tremendous aggressive energy, they constantly threaten to surface and overpower the ego. This eventuality would be reflected in aggressive and possibly violent behavior.

The latter assertion has been supported by Lisak and Miller (2003), who described the "cycle of violence" that characterizes the relationship between childhood trauma and the later perpetration of interpersonal violence. These investigators concluded that researchers "have amassed considerable evidence indicating that individuals who suffer childhood victimization are at an increased risk for perpetuating interpersonal violence later in life" (Lisak and Miller 2003, 79). They noted that much of this research has been carried out using samples of convicted felons.

For example, Weeks and Widom (1998) studied 301 male convicts, administering a detailed questionnaire containing multiple measures of childhood physical abuse, sexual abuse, and neglect. Weeks and Widom found that more than two-thirds of the men in their sample reported histories of childhood victimization, most commonly physical abuse. In a similar study, Dutton and Hart (1992) reported that 41 percent of their sample of 604 convicted felons had experienced "serious childhood abuse." Moreover, the rate of violent acts among felons who had been abused as children was more than twice the corresponding rate among felons who did not report being abused.

Conclusion

Individuals who are abused as children are at increased risk for developing substance use disorders. The more severe the abuse, the more forms the abuse takes, and the more other adverse childhood events the child experiences, the greater the risk of subsequent substance abuse. A number of theoretical explanations have been offered for the relationship between child abuse and subsequent substance abuse. These include the genetic contributions of the abusive parents, who are frequently themselves substance abusers. They also include environmental factors, including adult models of substance use behavior and positive attitudes toward substance use.

Other hypotheses regarding the relationship between childhood abuse and subsequent substance use disorders include the self-medication hypothesis, which states that victims use drugs to anesthetize the pain associated with the abuse; the use of the drugs for this purpose expands to more general abuse and dependence through the addictive nature of the drugs. A related hypothesis states that childhood trauma leads to Posttraumatic Stress Disorder, and that individuals with the symptoms of PTSD, such as anxiety and depression, use drugs to cope with these symptoms. Other related hypotheses state that victims use dissociation and alexithymia to defend against the trauma of abuse, and the use of these defenses predisposes the victim to substance use and abuse.

Childhood abuse and subsequent Substance Use Disorder may also be related through the attachment patterns and object relations that tend to develop when the child is abused instead of nurtured. Abuse may lead to insecure attachment, which in turn is associated with poor social relations and the sense of being an outcast. This may lead the victim to identify with other outcasts, including the bar-going, drug-taking crowd. The internalization of bad object representations derived from abusive parents may also lead victims to use substances to control dysphoria. The internalization of bad object representations may also create anger and hostility that may be reflected in violent behavior.

Clinicians working with substance abusing clients must always assess for history of childhood abuse. They should also assess for the client's own perceptions of history of self-medication. Clinicians should assess for symptoms of PTSD, including dissociation and alexithymia. Careful consideration should be given to adult attachment patterns and the client's social adjustment. Clinicians should assess for aggressive and violent behavior. Furthermore, clinicians should ascertain the client's perceptions of the relationships among these factors.

CHAPTER SEVEN

~

Childhood Abuse and Adult Sexual Dysfunction

Case Studies of Sexual Dysfunction

Childhood abuse (and particularly childhood sexual abuse) is associated with a broad range of adult sexual issues, ranging from a complete lack of interest in sex to compulsive participation in risky promiscuous sex with multiple partners and strangers. Some victims of childhood sexual abuse are anorgasmic. Others can achieve orgasms only when they are intoxicated or only through the use of pornography involving sadomasochistic or abusive sexual behavior. Some victims of childhood sexual abuse become prostitutes. Some are subject to revictimization, which may involve being a repeated victim of sexual assault or may take the form of repeatedly becoming involved in abusive relationships. To capture the variety of negative sexual outcomes associated with childhood abuse, we present several case studies.

Ambivalence about Sex

Gail was twenty-eight years old when she and her husband Mark sought sex therapy. They had been married for five years. They came because of an incident that occurred several days before. While having sex, Gail was suddenly overcome with anger toward Mark. She was unable to control herself, and she pushed him away and hit him several times with her fists before he could restrain her and get her to calm down. Gail felt horrible about what she had done because she loved Mark and felt that he did not deserve to be treated that way. Mark was flabbergasted by the incident,

137

since he had always felt that they had a loving emotional relationship as well as a good sexual relationship.

When they talked about what had happened, Gail disclosed to Mark for the first time that she never felt really comfortable with sex. She said that she often had a visceral negative reaction to being touched in a sexual manner, and that she generally dreaded Mark's advances. Gail also admitted that she almost never had an orgasm during sex, although she often pretended to. She said that on the rare occasions when she did have an orgasm, she had almost always been "at least a little bit intoxicated." In the absence of any disinhibiting chemicals, however, Gail said that she was not sexually responsive and typically found sex to be "uncomfortable bordering on painful."

Nevertheless, Gail tried hard to please Mark. She kept herself in good physical shape and often dressed provocatively. It was important to her that Mark desired her and spoke well of her to their friends. Gail said that sometimes when they were out together she would feel sexually turned on and would kiss Mark passionately and fondle him in a manner indicating she was sexually attracted to him. When they were at home, however, Gail was never turned on. When Mark made sexual advances, Gail said she felt satisfied that he wanted her but annoyed that he had to have her. Nevertheless, she rarely turned Mark down when he wanted to have sex and always asked what he would like her to do to please him, and was always willing to fulfill his requests. Because of her desire to please him, Mark had always been satisfied with their sexual relationship.

After Gail confided these feelings to Mark, he felt terrible that he had not picked up on Gail's ambivalence. He said that in retrospect he had noticed that Gail never expressed her sexual needs to him or asked him to do anything in particular that she found exciting or particularly pleasurable. However, he had been fooled into thinking that she was having orgasms most of the time, and he said that he had assumed that she was satisfied. He said that he had attributed her failure to initiate sex and her failure to express her desires to feminine shyness. He said that in retrospect he felt he should have tried harder to get Gail to tell him what she wanted him to do, because if he had pushed her on this point she might have told him sooner that she really wasn't sexually excited.

When asked why she reacted with such anger recently, Gail said that the anger "suddenly just seemed to come from somewhere deep inside." Gail said that she often felt angry during and after sex with Mark, and that this anger was related to her own inability to be sexually satisfied, coupled with a feeling of resentment toward Mark because he could. She knew it wasn't fair of her to think this way, but she resented Mark because pleasing him without being satisfied herself made her feel "sort of like used and degraded." Gail also said that there was a particular way that Mark sometimes touched her nipples that she found especially intrusive and abhorrent. She said that when she hit Mark that night she had been feeling generally angry about being used and having to "perform" for him, and that then Mark had touched her breast in just that way. The two feelings coming together were just too much for her to contain, and she struck out.

Mark and Gail continued in sex therapy together, and the therapist recommended that Gail also begin individual therapy. It was several months into her individual treatment that Gail remembered and disclosed to her therapist the fact that she had been a victim of incest perpetrated by her father for several years. As she remembered more and more of the details of that abuse, she recalled that her father had fondled her nipples, that she had from time to time found this very exciting, and that as the incestuous relationship progressed she had come to feel immense guilt over the fact that she was turned on by this touching.

Compulsive and Addictive Sex

John was a thirty-eight-year-old bachelor who joined a self-help peer support group for victims of child sexual abuse. John joined the group after a longtime male friend of his commented that John had "slept with every woman he had ever met and became friends with none of them." This comment struck home. John was approaching midlife and was panicking over the possibility that he might never marry, settle down, and have children, "like normal guys do." John was a successful investment banker with an MBA from Harvard and was earning big bucks. He was good-looking and worked hard to stay in shape. He was also accomplished in diverse areas, from gourmet cooking to current events to fly fishing. He was extremely attractive to women, and he was extremely attracted to women.

In spite of his many accomplishments, if you asked John what he did best, he would respond without hesitation, "make love." John fancied himself the answer to a woman's prayer for a man with who could make intelligent conversation, cook a romantic dinner, give her a long sensual massage, and satisfy her every sexual fantasy. John had been a high achiever all his life. He had worked hard and excelled in every area of life: academics, sports, business, and women. He often quipped to his male friends that "anyone can work hard, but only a few of us can get the job done."

John attributed some of his high achievement motivation to his family background, which also involved several forms of abuse. John's parents had divorced when he was a baby, and his father had more or less dropped out of his life. His mother was an alcoholic who tended to ignore him and never expressed love for him or praised his achievements. He was frequently in the care of baby-sitters, and when he was twelve he was seduced by a seventeen-year-old baby-sitter. This was immensely gratifying to John, for two reasons. First, the baby-sitter told him that she loved him and that she had the "best sex of her life" with him. Second, when he told his male friends at school what had happened he became a bit of a folk hero. John and this baby-sitter had sex a number of times over a period of about six months, and then she went away to college.

John's next baby-sitter was a friend of the first, and John quickly seduced her. In retrospect it was not clear to John whether he had been recommended as a sexual partner to the second baby-sitter by the first baby-sitter, or whether he simply assumed that older girls who baby-sit are available to be seduced. In any case, the second baby-sitter also gave John a great deal of positive feedback on his sexual prowess, and he began to think of himself, more than anything else, as a lover. The second baby-sitter came around for about a year, at which point she too went off to college. By then John didn't need a baby-sitter any longer. He was almost fourteen and he began to date.

John dated mostly older girls when he was in high school, because "the older ones wanted to have sex." He also seduced several adult women who lived in his neighborhood. He said that he was always aware of which women were looking to have sex, and he always accommodated them. The problem was that all of these relationships were purely sexual in nature, and none lasted very long. The women were interested in having good sex with a handsome young man who aimed to please and could get the job done, and John was interested in being desired and told how good he was. None of these relationships had any potential for long-term growth. John said that he never thought of himself as being emotionally intimate with his lovers, and he certainly did not think of sex as an expression of love. He said that for him making love was always more of an art form, something like making the perfect cast when fly-fishing.

When John went to college, he began to perfect the supporting elements of his repertoire of seduction. He said that he learned to cook when he heard that women liked it. For the same reason he learned about wine, politics, literature, and the arts. He was driven by the idea of making himself as attractive as possible, because it was in the approval of his lovers that John found his identity. John was very clear that what he loved most about sex was having the power to satisfy a woman and at the same time leave her wanting more. He said that when he made love he never allowed himself to have an orgasm before his partner had "at least one." When he described sexual encounters, seemed to take on the perspective of his partner, describing in great detail such details as her vocalizations during sex and the power of her vaginal contractions when she reached orgasm.

Although on one level John's motivations and behavior could be viewed as having positive benefits for him and his lovers, on another level his motivations and behavior were clearly dysfunctional. For one thing, John never said no. Since he was so attractive, he was frequently approached by women. But John seemed to regard a friendly greeting from a woman as a cue to automatically activate his seduction repertoire. He regarded any invitation as a mandate for a command performance. He reported that he frequently was sleeping with several different women at a time. He stated that he once made love to three different women in a twenty-four-hour period. On several occasions he met a woman at a party or a bar and could not be certain whether or not they had already had sex. Moreover, he acknowledged that the most frequent reason why his relationships ended was that the women realized that he had no interest in a committed, monogamous relationship.

After John's male friend pointed out that John had reached the age of thirty-three without ever establishing a truly intimate relationship with a woman, John began to do some research on relationship issues. He learned enough about child abuse to know that his mother had abused him emotionally, and enough to realize that what had gone on between him and his babysitters was not simply "every young boy's wildest fantasy," but a form of child sexual abuse that had the power to disrupt the development of a healthy sexual self-concept. Therefore, when John's friend suggested that he seek help, John sought out a support group for survivors of child sexual abuse. When John introduced himself to the group, the first thing they told him was that it would be unacceptable for him to sleep with any of the women in the group.

Trading in Sex

Tracy was forty-two when she entered individual psychotherapy with a psychologist in private practice in an upscale suburb of New York. Her presenting complaint was that "my life is a sham and I am nothing but a high-class whore." She stated that she was in her "second marriage of convenience," and that this time her husband was "even richer and even less exciting than my first husband." She said that she wished that she had the courage to get out of this marriage, but she did not. She depended on her husband to support her opulent lifestyle, which included a large estate in Westchester and vacation homes in Aspen and Costa Rica.

Tracy was strikingly attractive. She came to her first therapy appointment dressed for tennis but meticulously made up. Her therapist made a comment to the effect that it was a beautiful day to be outside. Tracy's responded was that it was her job as a "trophy wife" to be fit and attractive. She went on to say without further prompting that she had always been attractive, even as a child, and had learned early in life that you could get whatever you wanted from men in exchange for being sexy. Tracy immediately told her therapist that she had been adopted by a wealthy family at birth, and that she became the victim of incest at the hands of her adoptive father.

Tracy reported that her earliest memory was of her father fondling her, and she said that his sexual abuse had continued throughout her childhood, progressing to oral sex and eventually to genital intercourse by the time she was twelve. Tracy said that her father was always solicitous of her feelings, reassuring her that what they were doing was right and that he loved her for it even more than he would otherwise. He also told her that her mother was "not nice" to him, and that that was why they had no children and they had to adopt Tracy. He gave Tracy the implicit idea that she owed it to him to accept his sexual advances, because this was the reason she had been adopted.

During their incestuous encounters, her father was always gentle. She said that he never threatened or forced her to do anything, but instead bribed her with his affection and with expensive gifts and special favors that he tied directly to their sexual activities. Her father was particularly lavish in his praise and gifts when Tracy was spontaneously affectionate with him. He also specifically asked her whether she liked the different things he did, and he went out of his way to make sure that his sexual behavior was gratifying to her. Tracy acknowledged deriving pleasure from her father's sexual attentions, although she was aware that what they were doing was not normal, and she felt guilty about it.

Tracy quickly learned to be seductive with boys and adult males other than her adopted father. During elementary school and junior high school she would hug and kiss the boys, and she would often ask them what they would give her for a kiss, or what they would like to do if they were alone together. Many times her teachers mentioned that she was "extremely affectionate," and a few times they even commented that it might be better if she did not behave quite so affectionately. However, she was attending expensive private schools, and great care was taken not to address this issue in too confrontational a manner. In high school Tracy was routinely seductive with her male instructors, and she disclosed having sexual relationships with two of them. She also had sexual relationships with several boys in her school, as well as with a counselor at summer camp. Although Tracy had all the material possessions she could possibly want, she regularly tied her sexual favors to some form of payment, whether help doing schoolwork, special privileges, or special consideration in work evaluations.

Tracy reported that her seductive behavior with others infuriated her father, which made her want to be even more seductive with others. One summer she even got her father to pay for a trip to Europe for her and her mom, on the basis of the threat that if she returned to camp that summer she would renew her sexual relationship with the counselor there. In order to make this threat, of course, Tracy had to reveal to her dad that she had been having sex with the counselor. He was beside himself when he heard this, but she made him shut up by indirectly threatening to disclose their relationship to her mother, who, she claimed, was unaware of it.

Tracy's pattern of seduction continued through college, where she had affairs with students, professors, and older men. In her senior year she met a man fourteen years her senior who owned a large manufacturing company that he had inherited from his father. She laughingly told her therapist that it was "love at first sight" when she realized that this man made her father "look like he was poor." She was married within six months, much to the chagrin of her parents. She joked that she traded in the Jeep Grand Cherokee that her father had given her for graduation from prep school for a Porsche. She also backtracked in her story to clarify the meaning of "love at first sight." She told the therapist that of course she never really loved her husband, although she did think of him as a nice person.

Tracy settled into a life of opulence with her new husband and willingly complied with his requests for sex, understanding that this was part of the bargain. Even though her husband was far from her ideal lover, she nevertheless achieved orgasms regularly. She said the sex with him was best described as "tolerable bordering on acceptable." Although she and her husband had not discussed children, Tracy became pregnant soon after they married. She told her therapist that she regarded her pregnancy as an "insurance policy on the security of the relationship." When her daughter was born and for several years thereafter, Tracy and her husband were reasonably happy, focusing on their common interest in raising their child. Tracy and her husband continued to have sex, but she made certain that she did not become pregnant again. Although she loved her daughter very much, she saw no need to have more children. She said that she was afraid that additional children would make her look older, and she said that she did not want to dedicate so much time to kids that she was deprived of having a good time. Of course, her childrearing responsibilities were eased considerably by the fact that she had a full-time nanny, a full-time housekeeper, and a part-time chef.

Tracy's first marriage ended because she could not remain faithful to her husband. She said that she had spent a lifetime being seductive with men, and she did not know how to be a faithful wife. She said that it was always exciting to her to have men flirt with her, and if the man was attractive, there was a very good chance she would become involved sexually. She had her first affair with her personal trainer when her daughter was four, and she had a number of other brief affairs over the next few years, until she and her husband divorced after nine years of marriage. Her husband initiated the discussion on divorce. He was aware of her infidelities and he said that he felt used. He had also begun a sexual relationship with another woman, whom he was convinced really loved him. The divorce was amicable and left Tracy secure financially. Money was not an issue for her ex-husband, and he was anxious to minimize the impact of the split on their daughter.

Tracy said that she never understood how she could be out of control with men who turned her on, and at the same time so in control when it came to men with money. Then she amended her "out of control" remark to make it clear that she was never out of control in the sense that she would ever marry a man who was not rich. Lovers who had no money were for entertainment only.

Tracy said that she enjoyed being divorced and single for a time, but she realized that this status was inconvenient when it came to participation in some of the grander society events that she had always enjoyed. Therefore Tracy consciously set about finding a new husband. She noted that at the age of thirty-one, with a ten-year-old daughter, she had fewer choices than she did when she was just finishing college. However, she also noted that she had moved into a higher social class as a result of her first marriage, and she said that even though the targets were fewer, many had great value. After examining the available options for about a year and a half, Tracy found the CEO of a large electronics corporation who was in the process of getting divorced. Once she had decided that he would be an appropriate husband, seducing him was "trivial." She noted that at that time she was still a knockout, and she also indicated that she was completely aware of how emotionally needy this man would be at that point in his life.

When Tracy came to therapy, she was still married to her second husband. She described him as "average looking" and "totally wrapped up in his work." She said that he was "away a lot" and found sports and golf more interesting than their relationship. Unlike her first husband, this second husband seemed to regard their marriage as a convenience, much as she did. He had two children from his first marriage and wanted no more. He came and went as he pleased, and he gave Tracy whatever she wanted to keep her happy while he was doing his thing. There were times when they would not see each other for days. He was rather demanding, however, when he wanted to be with her. If he wanted to go somewhere requiring a spouse, he made the plans and expected her to report for duty. If he wanted sex, he expected the same. Tracy said that she understood that this was reasonable enough, given the freedom that she had most of the time to indulge herself. However, on another level she felt used. She said that the quid pro quo of their relationship was just a little but "too up front." As her marriage moved into its tenth year, she said that she felt more and more like she was being paid a retainer to be available for sex and available to look beautiful at necessary social engagements. In short, she felt like a "high-class hooker."

This feeling was exacerbated by two developments. First, Tracy's daughter, now twenty, became engaged. When Tracy met her daughter's fiancé, she realized that they had a relationship that was qualitatively different from anything she herself had ever known. The couple planned to attend medical school together, and they planned a career working with the World Health Organization. They were young, idealistic, and in love. He did not come from a wealthy family, and Tracy's daughter didn't care. Tracy said that seeing the nature of their love and their sense of purpose in life hit her "like a brick" and made her realize how much she had missed in her own life. Second, during a rare heart-to-heart talk with her daughter, Tracy learned that her daughter was aware of her affairs and those of Tracy's second husband. Her daughter did not bring these things up to hurt Tracy or condemn her behavior but to explain why she had chosen her fiancé. She said that she wanted a committed, monogamous relationship with a man she truly loved and respected. This revelation added to Tracy's sense that she had used her sexuality as a commodity to exchange for security and material rewards. At that point, Tracy felt the need to explain herself to her daughter, and she told her the story of how she had been abused by her adoptive father. Tracy's daughter said that she loved her mom very much and she understood how difficult it must have been to be treated that way. She also suggested that the time had come for Tracy to see a therapist in an effort to sort things out. That conversation took place just before Tracy entered therapy.

Reliance on Abusive Pornography

Brian was a thirty-eight-year-old man who entered sex therapy when he began to experience erectile dysfunction when having sex with his wife of twelve years, Jane. He explained that they had previously enjoyed what he considered a very satisfactory sex life. He said that over the years they had engaged in a wide variety of mutually satisfying sexual activities. Typically he would bring his wife to orgasm through a combination of oral stimulation of her clitoris and digital stimulation of her G spot. She would then guide his penis into her vagina and bring him to climax with pelvic thrusting. Recently, however, Brian said that he seemed to be "short-circuiting" in the middle of their lovemaking. He said that he would become very excited while performing oral sex on his wife, particularly when she was obviously turned on. As long as he was stimulating her, he would have a strong erection. Once she came and he inserted his penis in her vagina, however, he would begin to lose his erection. Sometimes he would have a weak orgasm before his penis became too soft to allow him to thrust inside of her; and sometimes he would lose his erection completely and just stop. He explained that it was like he "just lost interest" right in the middle of sex. He said that this was very upsetting to his wife, who expressed the fear that he didn't love her anymore and even asked whether he was having an affair. Brian said that his wife tried to help the situation by altering their routine, initiating sexual activity, and doing her best to stimulate him manually and orally. Brian said that this worked pretty well at first, but with rare exception now any time he penetrated her vaginally with his penis, he would lose his erection and fail to have an orgasm.

When questioned about the things that really turned him on, Brian sheepishly disclosed to his sex therapist that even though he typically experienced erectile dysfunction with his wife, he always had strong erections and powerful orgasms when he viewed pornographic videos and masturbated. He had purchased his first such video about a year before he began experiencing sexual dysfunction with his wife, and he recognized that there had been a relationship between the increasing frequency of his use of pornography and the decrease in his sexual functioning with his wife. On further questioning, Brian revealed that he was not particularly turned on by standard pornographic videos of men and women engaging in various forms of sex. What turned him on were pornographic videos involving themes of bondage and forced sex. He particularly liked videos in which a woman was abducted and bound, then tormented by being tickled unmercifully, gently spanked, and having a vibrator applied to stimulate her clitoris and vagina.

Brian explained that he did not like videos in which it appeared that anyone was actually being harmed, but the thought of having a woman completely at his mercy drove him crazy. He explained that he was turned on by the idea that he could make a reluctant stranger experience the orgasm of her life by assuming complete control of her sexual responses. He said that his ultimate fantasy was that a voluptuous woman would be tied up in such a way that he would have free reign to stimulate any of her erogenous zones in any way that he knew would turn her on. He believed that under these conditions he would be able to discover exactly the right combination of stimulations, the combination that would overcome her frustration with being tied up and her anger over being violated, so that eventually it would be impossible for her to keep herself from having an incredible climax. He fantasized further that after she climaxed, the woman would beg him to never let her go, but instead take permanent charge of her body and her orgasmic response.

Brian's therapist was aware of the relationship between childhood sexual abuse and the predilection for abusive pornography, and she carefully assessed for a history of abuse. Although Brian did not immediately disclose his abusive experiences, he did acknowledge that he sometimes had dreams of having sex with his mother. These dreams involved both oral and genital sexual relations, and on occasion the dreams involved spankings and various forms of bondage. In time Brian was able disclose that he had in fact been abused sexually by his mother as a young child, and that he had become involved in an incestuous sexual relationship with his mother around the time he started junior high school. The first abuse he could recall occurred when he was very young and involved fondling his penis during baths and when putting him to bed. He also recalled having his mother bathe with him, from the time he was a baby right through elementary school. He said that one time when she was naked in the bathtub with him he got an erection. He said that he did not think this was the first time he had ever had an erection, but it was the first time he could specifically remember having one. He recalled that on that occasion his mother had told him that he was growing up to be a big strong man, while at the same time she reached out to hold his penis and give it a gentle squeeze. When she did that Brian got very excited and let out a loud gasp, at which point his mother gave him a smack on his behind and told him that he needed to be quiet. Brian remembered that his mother often went out of her way to see him naked, even after he became sexually mature. One of her favorite devices for getting him naked was to have him take down his pants to be spanked. He said that he knew the spankings were just a pretense, because most often his alleged misbehavior was completely fictitious, and because his mother spanked him so gently that it was not the least bit painful, but rather sexually stimulating.

Brian recalled that their incestuous sexual relationship had begun on one of these occasions when his mother was giving him a spanking for some misbehavior that Brian was certain he had not committed. He said that his mother had him stand naked in front of her, and that she was spanking him on his buttocks very lightly with her right hand, while at the same time she was fondling his penis with her left hand. When he got an erection, she pulled him toward her and performed oral sex on him while alternately caressing and gently slapping his behind. When he ejaculated, his mother was delighted and praised him to no end, saying that someday he would make some woman very happy.

Then his mother told him that she was going to make it her business to show him what to do to please a woman. Over time, she showed him how to perform oral sex on her and how to stimulate her G spot. Whenever she had an orgasm, she would praise him and tell him how strong and handsome he was. She would say that she was teaching him to be a great lover and that some lucky lady would owe her a great debt of gratitude some day. Brian said that from time to time he raised a mild protest regarding these "lessons," asking if other mothers did these things with their sons. His mother responded that only the best mothers who really loved their sons took the time to teach them how to make love. Brian said that the incestuous relationship continued well into junior high school, and that his mother ended it suddenly when he told her that he had sex with a girl from his school. Brian said that when he told her that he had sex with the girl, his mother asked him to tell her exactly what they had done and whether the girl had enjoyed it. Although Brian was very uncomfortable answering these questions, he did answer them. When he told her that he thought the girl had enjoyed it very much, his mother said, "Great. Then I've taught you well." Brian said that she sounded more like a coach than like a mother. From that point on, she never again sought to "spank" him or make any other gesture leading to sexual relations. Brian said that he felt as if he had been graduated from a school for sex, and that his mother was the headmistress,

Brian also said that other than having an incestuous sexual relationship with her son, his mother was "pretty normal." She was a single mother who had never been married, and Brian was her only child. She had a good job as a manager in a chemical distributorship. Brian said that she drank a bit and liked to "party" with her girlfriends, but he did not think she had a problem with substance abuse. Brian said that throughout his childhood and adolescence, including the period when she was having sex with Brian, his mother always had one or more boyfriends who were her own age. Brian said that as far as he could tell, his mother had normal sexual relations with these men.

Revictimization

April was a twenty-four-year-old woman who was referred to a support group for battered women by police officers who responded to a neighbor's complaint about a domestic disturbance in April's apartment. The neighbors had heard April arguing with her boyfriend and they heard her screaming at him to stop. They were afraid that he was beating her, so they called 911. By the time the police arrived the disturbance was over and the boyfriend had left. However, the officers sat with April and had her tell them what had happened.

She told them that her boyfriend had gotten drunk and wanted to have sex. She had responded that she wasn't interested in having sex with a drunk and told him to sleep it off. But this only made him angry. He accused her of never being affectionate with him and demanded proof that she loved in the form of compliance with his demands for sex. When April realized how angry he was, she tried to calm him down by apologizing for not being affectionate enough and promising to make love after he sobered up. But he became even angrier and assaulted her, slapping her in the face, throwing her down on the couch, and forcing her to have sex with him. When he had finished, April looked at him and told him that he should really be proud of himself because had just raped her. At that point he was filled with remorse and tried to apologize, but she told him to "just get out" of her apartment and leave her alone. He left reluctantly, telling her that he loved her and that he would call her when she was feeling better.

April told the police officers that she wasn't interested in pressing charges, but she didn't want to see him again. The officers said that she didn't need to make any decisions about pressing charges at that moment, and they told her that she could get a restraining order to keep him away from her. They also told her that she needed to get into a support group for battered women that was run by a social worker they knew, so that she could learn how to prevent things like this from happening in the future.

April came to the group and told the other members that the boyfriend who assaulted her had a pattern of being alternately loving and then verbally and physically abusive toward her. She said that she had wanted to get out of the relationship for some time, but every time she tried to break up with him he would cry and tell her that he loved her and he couldn't live without her. He said that if she really did leave him he might do something crazy, like maybe kill her first and then kill himself. Between his declarations of love and his threats, the boyfriend had always managed to keep April from ending their relationship, at least until the night that the police came and told her about the group. The group leader and the other women in the group validated April's desire to get rid of this boyfriend. They also supported her for being strong and refusing to take him back, as she had done before.

Eventually April revealed that this was not the first time she had been involved in an abusive relationship, nor was the rape the first time she had been sexually assaulted. She told the other women in the group that she had a boyfriend in high school who mistreated her, and that she wasn't able to end the relationship until she went away to college. She also told the group that she had been the victim of date rape on two different occasions, once during college and once the summer after she graduated. She said that she wasn't very good at picking men and was "even worse at saying no."

April also told the group that there had been a number of times when she had sex with a man when she really didn't want to, simply because it was easier to just go ahead and have sex than it was to disappoint the man or hurt his feelings. She said that it always seemed easier to have sex than to explain why she didn't want to. The most recent example of failing to say no occurred with her forty-year-old boss at work. April said that she got the sense that he was attracted to her and didn't want hurt his feelings by rejecting him. So she tried hard to be nice to him and make him think that she found him attractive. What's interesting about this encounter is that after they had sex, her boss apologized to her for being inappropriate and promised that it would not happen again, no matter how provocatively she behaved. It turned out that her boss actually felt as if he had been seduced by her, rather than the other way around.

April also disclosed to the women in the group that she had been the victim of incest perpetrated by her father. She said that she had never been able to say no to him, and that somehow she thought that made it harder for her to say no to other men as well. She also said that she had a vague sense of obligation when it came to sex, as if she owed it to a man to have sex if he wanted, unless there was some really good reason for turning him down. Needless to say, all these issues were confronted in the group, both by the social worker who was leading the group and by the other members of the group.

Childhood Abuse and
Subsequent Sexual Adjustment Difficulties

The foregoing case examples illustrate the broad range of sexual adjustment difficulties that have been linked to childhood abuse. There is ample evidence, based on both anecdotal clinical observations and large sample empirical studies, supporting the existence of a relationship between childhood abuse and subsequent sexual adjustment difficulties. In this section of the chapter this evidence will be reviewed. The section has been organized under the following six headings, corresponding to different types of sexual adjustment difficulties: (1) lack of interest in sex or ambivalence regarding sex; (2) premature and/or promiscuous sexual activity; (3) sexual addiction/compulsivity and related risky sexual behavior; (4) engaging in prostitution or otherwise using sex as a commodity or in a manipulative manner; (5) inability to achieve sexual gratification except through the use of violent or abusive pornography or engaging in sadomasochistic behavior or fantasy; and (6) sexual revictimization. Within each of these categories of sexual adjustment difficulties, the scope and nature of the difficulties will be described; evidence of the relationship of the difficulties to childhood abuse will be presented; and theories explaining the relationship will be considered.

Lack of Interest or Ambivalence Regarding Sex

Engel (1989) described a series of specific problems that fall within the general category of lack of interest in sex or ambivalence regarding sex, which also includes lack of sexual desire and inhibition of sexual feelings. This includes the inability to enjoy sex and the inability to have an orgasm. It may include refraining from sex altogether or having sex only to accommodate the needs of one's partner. Also included in this category are specific dysfunctions such as erectile dysfunction in men and vaginismus in women. Another problem that falls into this category is discomfort with being touched on particular parts of the body or in a particular manner. Suddenly experiencing fear and/or anger during sex, like Gail in the case study above, is another manifestation of ambivalence regarding sex.

Elliot (1994) described the sexual adjustment difficulties experienced by a group of ten adults (two men and eight women) who were abused as children and/or adolescents. The experiences of these victims are described briefly to provide an idea of the diversity of the abuse they experienced and the diversity of sexual adjustment difficulties they experienced. One of the males stated that his mother was physically and emotionally abusive to him throughout his childhood, while his father was "emotionally neglectful and psychologically absent" (17). At the age of eight this boy was molested by two unrelated adolescent girls from the neighborhood, who fondled him and performed oral sex on him. The second male in this group of victims was "sexually abused by his mother at the instigation of his father, who was intermittently psychotic and who also sexually and physically abused his son" (18). The abuse perpetrated by the mother on her son included bondage, mutual sexual fondling, reciprocal oral sex, reciprocal administration of enemas, and sexual penetration with objects. The mother performed these sexual behaviors on her son in response to coercion by her husband, who also abused her physically and sexually. In addition, the boy was forced to have vaginal intercourse with his mother and with his older sister while his father watched. This abuse began before the boy reached the age of five and lasted until he was fourteen, when the abuse was disclosed and he was removed from the home.

The first female victim in the group was the older sister of the second boy. She was abused by her mother in the same manner her brother had been abused, with bondage, mutual sexual fondling, reciprocal oral sex, reciprocal administration of enemas, and sexual penetration with other objects. In addition, both of the siblings were forced to watch their parents having sexual intercourse with each other. The sister was subjected to vaginal intercourse performed by her father as well as by her brother. Sometimes her mother witnessed these sex acts. The abuse experienced by this girl also began before she was five and continued until she was sixteen, when the abuse was disclosed and she and her brother were both removed from the home.

Two other female victims in the group were abused by mothers under coercion by fathers. In each case the abuse began before the child was five years old, and in each the abuse consisted of fondling by the mother at the father's direction, as well as sex acts performed on the victims by their fathers while their mothers were forced to watch. One of these two female victims also indicated that her mother had been physically and emotionally abusive.

Three female victims reported being initially abused by mothers coerced by their husbands to perform sexual acts on their daughters. These sex acts included genital fondling and penetration of the vaginal and anal openings with objects. In these cases the mothers continued to abuse their daughters independently without being coerced. These three victims were also physically and emotionally abused by their mothers and sexually abused by their fathers. In each case, the abuse began before the age of five. In each of these cases as well, the sexual abuse by the mother was discontinued by the age of six or seven, but the physical and emotional abuse continued until the victims were much older.

One female victim described a pattern of abuse that began when her father instigated abuse that was carried out by her mother following his directions. Over time the mother carried out sexual abuse independently and even instigated her father's participation in the abuse. In this case the sexual abuse perpetrated by the mother included bondage, genital fondling, oral sex, penetration with objects, sexual contacts with animals, and being forced to witness her parents engaging in sexual relations. Initially her father modeled all of the abusive behaviors and directed her mother to perform them. In addition, the girl was subjected to anal and vaginal intercourse by her father, and she was impregnated by him. The physical and sexual abuse carried out by her mother lasted until mid-adolescence. The physical and emotional abuse perpetrated by both parents, as well as the sexual abuse perpetrated by her father, persisted into the victim's adulthood.

Another female victim reported that she was physically neglected by her mother during her early childhood. From the age of five she was subjected to daily enemas, allegedly to relieve constipation. These enemas continued until the girl went away to college, and they even continued when the girl came home from college on holidays. She even reported that her mother found it necessary to administer one final enema to her daughter on her daughter's wedding day. This victim also reported that from the time she reached preadolescence, her mother would expose her to adult sexual relations by leaving doors open so that her daughter would observe her having sex with various boyfriends. This victim described the experience of observing her mother's sexual encounters as embarrassing, but she did not categorize it in her mind as abuse. She said that she assumed that doors were left open in other homes as well. She did not recognize this behavior as abuse until she was into her thirties.

The final female victim in Elliot's group had been sexually abused by her sister, who was five years older than she. The victim was also emotionally abused by her mother, who constantly belittled her and told her that she was incompetent. Given the emotional abuse perpetrated by the mother, the victim turned to her older sister for some validation and nurturance, but instead she received both sexual and emotional abuse. Her sister forced her into fondling the sister's breasts and sucking her nipples. The older sister would masturbate while the victim fondled her. When the younger sister objected, the older sister threatened to go to the mother and tell her that it was really the younger sister had initiated the sexual behavior. The victim believed that she would be punished severely if her older sister carried out this threat, so she continued to comply with her older sister's demands.

Of these ten victims, all but one reported sexual adjustment difficulties and/or difficulties with close relationships in general. Elliot reported that three of the eight female victims never married. One of these victims who never married reported that she was a lesbian. She said that she felt comfortable with her sexuality, but she also reported that she was never able to tolerate a long-term relationship with a female partner, despite her desire to have such a relationship. Two others among the female victims married men who abused them physically, emotionally, and/or sexually. In one of these cases the abusive husband also sexually abused their daughter. Two of the female victims married men who were not abusive and had children with these husbands, but both of these women divorced soon after having children. The last female victim entered into a marriage of convenience which lasted only a few months after the wedding. One of the two male victims in Elliot's sample was briefly married, but his wife divorced him after learning that he had sexually abused the child of a friend. This male victim also had a significant substance abuse problem.

Each of the women in Elliot's group who had been married reported a history of difficulty becoming sexually aroused and difficulty having orgasms. Two of the women who never married reported that they had avoided sexual relationships entirely as adults. While this data is anecdotal in nature and the number of cases described by Elliot (1994) is small, the fact that all but one of these victims reported sexual adjustment difficulties certainly supports the idea of a relationship between childhood abuse of various kinds and adult sexual difficulties. In addition, the problems reported were in general serious problems rather than minor adjustment difficulties.

Browne and Finkelhor (1986) reviewed the extensive empirical literature on the relationship between childhood abuse and adult sexual adjustment difficulties. They concluded that both clinical studies and nonclinical studies based on community samples supported the view that childhood abuse is associated with adult sexual adjustment difficulties. Meiselman (1978) reported that adult female victims of incest who were receiving treatment at a mental health clinic almost universally reported sexual adjustment difficulty since their childhood victimization. Meiselman reported that 87 percent of her sample of incest victims were classified as having had a "serious" problem with sexual adjustment. In contrast, among women being treated at the same clinic who had not been sexually victimized as children, only 20 percent reported any form of adult sexual adjustment problem. In a similar study employing a somewhat more stringent definition of sexual adjustment difficulty, Herman (1981) found that 55 percent of clinic patients with a history of incest reported later sexual problems. Langmade (1983) compared a group of women incest victims in therapy to a matched group of female therapy patients who reported no history of sexual abuse. Langmade reported that the women in the incest victim grouped scored higher than the women in the comparison group on self-report measures of anxiety surrounding sex, sexual guilt, and dissatisfaction with sexual relationships. Briere (1984) reported that among women attending a mental health clinic, 45 percent of those who had been sexually abused as children reported sexual adjustment difficulties in adulthood, compared to just 15 percent of women attending the same clinic who did not report abuse. In addition, Briere found that in comparison to the controls, significantly more of the women who reported a history of childhood sexual abuse complained of a diminished, inadequate, or nonexistent sex drive.

Studies of nonclinical samples have also tended to support the relationship between child abuse and adult sexual adjustment difficulties. For example, Courtois (1979) reported that among her large nonclinical sample of women, 80 percent of those who reported that they had experienced incest during childhood also reported that they were unable to relax and enjoy sexual activity. The women in the sample who reported histories of incest were also more likely than those without a history of childhood sexual abuse to report that they either (1) avoided or abstained from sex or (2) experienced a compulsive desire to have sex. Finkelhor and associates (Finkelhor 1979, 1984; Finkelhor and Baron 1986) developed a measure of sexual self-esteem and administered the measure to a large sample of college students. He reported that students with histories of childhood sexual abuse had significantly lower scores on the sexual self-esteem measure than students who did not report such histories. Finkelhor, Hotaling, Lewis, and Smith (1989) reported that women from a community sample who reported childhood sexual abuse involving intercourse were significantly less likely than women reporting no history of abuse to report that they were satisfied with their sexual relationships as adults.

Mullen, Martin, Anderson, Romans, and Herbison (1994) surveyed and interviewed a community sample of 2,250 women in New Zealand. The survey contained questions ascertaining history of childhood abuse as well as items concerned with the respondent's adult sexual behavior and adjustment. Mullen and his associates found that women who reported a history of childhood sexual abuse were more than twice as likely as those who reported none to indicate current sexual adjustment difficulties (47 percent of the abused group versus 28 percent of the nonabused group). Moreover, among the subset of abused women who reported childhood sexual abuse involving penetration, 70 percent reported current sexual adjustment problems.

The reasons most frequently mentioned in the literature to explain the relationship between childhood abuse and adult sexual adjustment disorders are concerned with fears and false beliefs about sexuality that developed as a result of the abuse. Thus Bass and Davis (1994) argued that:

> When children are sexually abused, their natural sexual capacity is stolen. You were introduced to sex on an adult's timetable, according to an adult's needs. You never had a chance to experience your own desires from the inside. Sexual arousal became linked to feelings of shame, disgust, pain, and humiliation.

Pleasure became tainted as well. And desire (the abuser's desire) was dangerous, an out-of-control force used to hurt you. (41)

This explanation is perfectly reasonable. If one's first experience with sex is
a source of shame, it is natural to experience shame in connection with sex
later in life, thus inhibiting normal sexual arousal. If one's first experience
with sex is terrifying and painful, it is only natural to fear sex from that point
on and to avoid sex whenever possible. Moreover, if one's first experience
with a sexual partner is with someone who intimidates and hurts us, it is understandable that anger engendered by the perpetrator of the sexual abuse
that occurred during one's childhood could resurface uncontrollably and be
visited on a loving partner later on in life.

In his book on sexually abused men, Gartner (1999) quoted a male victim
to illustrate the connection between the shame associated with child sexual
abuse and later inhibition of the normal sexual response. Victor, who was
abused by his father, stated that "all pleasure is bad. Do you know why? It's
bad that my father is touching my penis. His touching my penis gives me
pleasure. Therefore, it's bad to have pleasure" (1999, 200). Gartner observed
that as a result of this association, "many sexually abused men feel ambivalent about being sexual at all" (1999, 201). Gartner also pointed out that sexual dysfunction is common among these men, including "lowered or excessive sexual desire, sexual aversion erectile disorder, inhibited orgasm, and
premature ejaculation" (1999, 201).

Bass and Davis (1994) suggested that the dysfunctional learning that may
result from childhood sexual abuse may focus on particular sensory experiences that evoke negative emotional responses. For example, "if your softball
coach pinched your breasts in the locker room after every game, you may not
want your lover touching your breast today" (250). In this context the reader
may recall that in the first case study presented in this chapter, Gail's anger
boiled over during sex when Mark touched her nipples in a manner that reminded her of how her abusive father had touched her.

On the other hand, negative emotional responses to the sexual advances
of a partner may be very broad, comprising a generalized fear reaction. Maltz
(2001) argued that "survivors may come to believe that sex is always physically and emotionally hurtful. Sexual abuse can be painful if it is violent and
sadistic. But even when it's gentle, abuse leaves survivors with the pain of
feeling betrayed and used by the offender" (2001, 87). Maltz observed that
sexual abuse can hurt for many different reasons. In violent sexual abuse, offenders use sex as a way to express anger. Some sexual abuse involves sadistic practices such a physical restraint, force, torture, and bodily mutilation

that cause the victim pain. In addition, forced sex and abusive intercourse and penetration inhibit muscle relaxation and lubrication in females. For these reasons sexual abuse is often physically painful, and survivors may not distinguish between sex in general and abusive sex that is violent, sadistic, premature, or forced. Therefore survivors of childhood sexual abuse may end up fearing sex in general. Furthermore, even if the abuse is not physically painful, it is likely to be emotionally painful because it involves psychological betrayal and loss.

Thus Bass and Davis suggested that "as an abused child, your sexual feelings were wired directly into fear. Every time you felt aroused, you also felt afraid. Now you can't become aroused without fear" (1994, 265). Obviously the fear of sexual arousal that is derived from the evoked memories of fear experienced during abusive sexual encounters in childhood would be expected to inhibit one's natural sexual response. However, the problem is compounded by an additional fear, namely, the victim's fear of the possible outcomes of the anger that is evoked by the memories of abuse. The adult victim may fear what he or she might do as a result of these angry feelings that arise during sex. Victims like Gail may fail to become sexually aroused because they are afraid that if passion causes them to lose control, they may harm their partner. Thus Bass and Davis quoted a victim of childhood sexual abuse as stating that

> There's some kind of connection between passion and anger for me. As soon as I start feeling passionate, somehow anger gets involved, and I get afraid of being aggressive in a hurtful way. So often when I start feeling passionate, I shut right down, because I'm afraid of hurting my partner. (1994, 165)

Another aspect of childhood physical and sexual abuse that is relevant in the context of fear of sex is the lack of control experienced by the victim. Because victims of child sexual abuse were clearly unable to control the abusive sexual experiences, many victims end up believing that sex in general means losing control. However, their abusive sexual experiences were painful and terrifying. Therefore victims also tend to be terrified by the prospect of losing control during sex. For this reason some survivors may be able to perform sexually only when they initiate the sexual activity, since initiating the sexual activity makes them feel in control. Other victims have a need to control the parameters of the sexual encounter, that is, to determine when to have sex, where to have sex, and what positions to use when having sex. Still other victims fear the loss of control they associate with passion as so threatening that they never allow themselves to become sexually aroused.

Premature Sexuality and Promiscuity

The second category of sexual adjustment disorders includes premature sexuality and promiscuous sexual behavior. The assessment of premature sexuality is generally based on the age at which the individual first engages in consensual intercourse. Promiscuity generally refers to having sex very frequently and to having sex with multiple partners. There is no consensus in the literature regarding the age at which the initiation of sexual activity moves from "premature" to "appropriate," nor is there any consensus on how often one must have sex or how many sexual partners one must have in order to be appropriately described as promiscuous. These are clearly subjective decisions, and they are probably too sensitive to be discussed casually or speculated on in academic forums. Characteristic of the reluctance of academics to make judgments regarding the parameters of appropriate sexual behavior is the following nonjudgmental comment, made by a speaker at a professional conference on sexuality: "Nonmonogamous sex is not necessarily bad, but it is often not fully intimate" (Glaser 1998).

However, there is ample literature suggesting that individuals who have been sexually abused as children tend to describe themselves as sexually active at a younger age and more sexually active in general than nonabused individuals. Men and women who have histories of childhood sexual abuse tend to report that their earliest consensual intercourse occurred at an earlier age than individuals who have not been sexually abused (Fergusson, Horwood, and Lynskey 1997; Hernandez, Lodico, and DiClemente 1993; Raj, Silverman, and Amaro 2000). Individuals who were sexually abused as children are more likely than nonabused females to report being sexually active during adolescence (Hernandez, Lodico, and DiClemente 1993; Stock, Bell, Boyer, and Connell 1997). The literature suggests that individuals with a history of childhood sexual abuse are more likely than those without such a history to characterize themselves as promiscuous (De Young 1982; Herman 1981). The literature also suggests that individuals who have histories of childhood sexual abuse (and/or physical abuse) tend to report having a greater number of sexual partners both as adolescents (Cavaiola and Schiff 1988; Fergusson et al. 1997; Luster and Small 1997; Roosa and Tein 1997; Sansonnet-Hayden, Haley, Marriage, and Fine 1987) and as adults (Courtois 1979, 1988; Laumann, Gagnon, Michael, and Michaels 1994; Seidner and Calhoun 1984; Meston, Heiman, and Trapnell 1999). For example, Luster and Small (1997) reported that female adolescents who reported being sexually abused also reported having three times as many sexual partners as their nonabused peers.

In commenting on some of the earlier studies noted in the foregoing paragraph, Browne and Finklehor (1986) drew an interesting distinction between describing oneself as promiscuous and reporting the actual number of sexual partners that one had over a specified period of time. They illustrated this distinction by reference to the study of female undergraduates reported by Fromuth (1983). In this study, participants reporting a history of child sexual abuse were significantly more likely than those not reporting abuse to describe themselves as "promiscuous." However, the abused and nonabused groups in this study did not differ significantly in terms of the actual number of sexual partners they reported. These contrasting findings prompted Browne and Finklehor (1986) to speculate that "the promiscuity of sexual abuse victims may be more a function of their negative self-attributions . . . than their actual sexual behavior" (71). On the other hand, we hasten to add that several of the other studies alluded to in the previous paragraph did find significant differences between individuals with and without histories of childhood abuse in terms of the actual numbers of sexual partners reported.

The literature concerned with the relationship between childhood abuse and promiscuity tends to attribute the association to the survivor's need for closeness and nurturance. Children who are victims of sexual abuse may assume that the only way they can be comforted and nurtured is through sex. Herman (1981) reported that 35 percent of the incest victims in her sample described themselves as promiscuous, and she observed that these women seemed to have a "repertoire of sexually stylized behavior" (40) that they used to get attention and affection. In their study of women survivors of child sexual abuse, Bass and Davis (1994) described the survivor's faulty association of nurturance with sex as follows:

> When you want closeness, intimacy, or communication, when you want to feel you are loved and cared for, when you're unhappy, disappointed, or angry, you ask for sex instead. It makes sense that survivors who received all their attention sexually as children now sexualize even nonsexual needs. (269)

Gartner (1999) offers a similar explanation for promiscuity observed among male victims of childhood sexual abuse:

> A child whose sexuality has been compromised by early abuse and eroticized relationships learns that sexuality and seduction constitute his interpersonal currency. Having learned that his sexuality is valuable to others, he may make it the basis for his self-esteem. If that happens, sexuality permeates all his interpersonal encounters. In addition, interpersonal closeness often becomes eroticized because sex is the only way for the man to feel intimate (or seemingly intimate). (202)

Maltz (2001) posited an additional path through which childhood abuse may be linked to adolescent and/or adult promiscuity. This path is based on the control issue. The survivor of childhood abuse who associates sex with loss of control may react in two very different ways. As we saw in the foregoing section on lack of interest and/or ambivalence regarding sex, the survivor may so fear the loss of control that he or she shuts down normal sexual responsiveness. But Maltz suggested that an alternative response to the idea that sex is uncontrollable is simply to "give in to it," by inviting or initiating sexual activity on the slightest hint of attraction or by routinely responding positively to the advances of a potential partner, even a stranger.

Sexual Addiction/Compulsivity
Gold and Seifer (2002) focused on sexual addiction/compulsion (SAC), along with the risky sexual behaviors that are manifestations of this condition. SAC is distinct from promiscuity. Thus Gold and Seifer (2002) pointed out that SAC is not the same as "nymphomania or Don Juanism," since the diagnosis is not made solely on the basis of frequency of sexual activity. Rather, "the defining characteristic of SAC is that it consists of sexual behavior over which the individual does not experience a sense of control, and which consequently repeatedly creates social, occupational, or legal problems for her or him" (65). Moreover, particularly among individuals with SAC who have histories of childhood sexual abuse, the sexual activity associated with SAC often occurs during dissociative states.

Gold and Seifer noted that "most of the existing knowledge base on SAC is derived almost exclusively from clinical observation" (63). Gold and Heffner (1998) reported that there is very little hard empirical research on SAC, despite the fact that a sizable network of institutions and organizations related to the treatment of SAC has been in existence for a number of years. Gold and Seifer noted that because of the lack of empirical research relevant to the validity of the diagnosis, SAC is not explicitly recognized in the DSM-IV. They also noted that what little literature is available on SAC does not overlap much with the literature on childhood abuse, so that there is "very little literature that explicitly addresses the possible relationship between these two areas" (2002, 64). This represents another distinction between simple promiscuity and SAC, for as we saw above, a great deal of literature supports the relationship between childhood abuse and subsequent premature or promiscuous sexual behavior.

Researchers have variously argued that SAC is an addiction (Carnes 1983), a compulsion (Allers, Benjack, White, and Rousey 1993; Fischer 1995; McCarthy 1994), or an impulse control disorder (Levin and Troiden

1988). Gold and Seifer suggested that the reason for this controversy is that SAC may be construed as meeting certain of the diagnostic criteria that define each of these disorders. For example, sexual addiction/compulsion looks like an addiction because it has many of the characteristics that define substance dependence, including the need to engage in increasing amounts of sexual activity to obtain the desired effect (i.e., tolerance), the likelihood that the victim will make repeated efforts to curtail his or her sexual activity, and the likelihood that the victim will sacrifice other areas of living in order to engage in sexual activity (Goodman 1992, 1993). SAC resembles an obsessive-compulsive disorder because sexual addicts are often obsessively preoccupied with thoughts of sex, because sex has the effect of temporarily reducing anxiety, and because the sexual behavior in which the subject engages may be ego dystonic (Butts 1992; Coleman 1992). Finally, SAC resembles an impulse control disorder, such as compulsive gambling, because it has many of the characteristics of a substance abuse disorder but there is no substance involved (Barth and Kinder 1987).

Gold and Seifer argued that "when one considers the relatively extensive spectrum of problems that have been associated with a background of CSA, it is striking how relatively little literature has addressed the impact of CSA on adult sexual functioning" (2002, 61). They suggested that the scant attention paid to adult sexual adjustment difficulties was probably the result of the many other pressing and even life-threatening problems presented by survivors of childhood sexual abuse who enter treatment. They pointed out that

> Often clients with a CSA history present with a number of grave difficulties, such as intense and frequent distress, self-injury and other forms of self-destructive behavior, and severe dissociation that disrupts the capacity to maintain a sense of continuity and focus on the here and now. In comparison to problems of this magnitude, developing a gratifying sex life is likely to be a relatively trivial concern, particularly if one assumes that the impact CSA most often has on sexual behavior is avoidance. (62)

However, Gold and Seifer (2002) pointed out that sexual addiction/compulsion is in fact characterized by participation in risky and impulsive sexual behavior that may have severe negative consequences. These behaviors include anonymous sexual encounters with strangers picked up on the street or other public places, solicitation of prostitutes, engaging in sexual activities under the influence of alcohol or some other disinhibiting chemical, engaging in unprotected sex, and spending hours at a time as well as large sums of money at strip clubs or pornographic websites (Briere and Elliott 1994; Browning and Laumann 1997; Cavaiola and Schiff 1988; Courtois 1988; Dimock 1988; Dodge, Reece, Cole, and Sandfort 2004; Fergusson et al. 1997; Walser and Kern 1996).

It also appears that the frequency of at-risk sexual behaviors displayed by survivors of CSA with a sexual addiction is related positively to the severity of the sexual abuse that was experienced. Cinq-Mars, Wright, Cyr, and Mc-Duff (2003) surveyed and interviewed 125 adolescent girls, twelve through seventeen years old, who had a history of childhood sexual abuse confirmed by youth protection services or a qualified licensed professional. These researchers measured the parameters of the sexual abuse experienced by the girls, using the Sexual Abuse History Questionnaire (Theriault, Cyr, and Cinq-Mars 1997), administered in the form of structured interview. This questionnaire assesses types of abuse experienced, frequency and duration of abuse, the relationship of the victim to the perpetrator(s), whether or not the victim disclosed the abuse, and the response to disclosure. The investigators also measured various forms of family adversity, using the Inventory of Family Problems (Theriault, Cyr, and Cinq-Mars 1997). This instrument assessed financial difficulties, verbal abuse or physical violence from parents toward children, and abusive and/or violent interactions between the parents. Finally the girls completed a nineteen-item questionnaire measuring at-risk sexual behavior. This questionnaire included items measuring age at the time of first consensual sexual activity, number of voluntary sexual partners during the respondent's lifetime and during the past year, frequency of condom use, and the number and outcome of any pregnancies.

The results of the study by Cinq-Mars and her associates (2003) indicated that the likelihood that an adolescent in their sample of survivors of childhood sexual abuse would report being sexually active at the time of the study was related positively to her having experienced sexual abuse involving penetration, having been abused by more than one perpetrator, and having experienced sexual abuse involving coercion. An index score representing the severity of childhood sexual abuse was related positively to being sexually active, having multiple consensual sexual partners, and irregularity of condom use.

The costs associated with the at-risk sexual behaviors manifested by individuals who have a sexual addiction problem include the loss of one's primary relationship when the behavior is discovered, the possibility of contracting AIDS or some other sexually transmitted disease, and the expenditure of so much time and money on sex that it threatens one's employment and financial security. These considerations led Gold and Seifer (2002) to conclude that the consequences of SAC can be just as severe as the consequences of other adjustment disorders that have been linked to childhood abuse, including eating disorders, substance abuse disorders, and self-mutilation.

A number of different theories have been advanced to explain the relationship between childhood abuse and addictive and risky sexual behavior. Mayall and Gold (1995) cited learned helplessness associated with the experience of being abused that renders the survivor unable to say no to the sexual advances of a potential partner. They also suggested that the reinforcement received from the perpetrator of the abuse in exchange for compliance with sexual demands leads the victim of abuse to define his or her self-worth through sexuality, so that every new sexual conquest represents a validation of the self. Timms and Connors (1992) argued that the experience of sexual abuse results in a blurring of sexual boundaries that may also lead to increased sexual activity.

Gartner (1999) emphasized the role of dissociation in the relationship between childhood sexual abuse and compulsive sexual activity. He argued that victims of childhood sexual abuse frequently learn to defend themselves from the abusive experience through the mechanism of dissociation, and that

> compulsive sexual activity can be a compelling way to soothe the unregulated affect that emerges when dissociation breaks down. In common with other compulsive dissociative adaptations to trauma, such as gambling, overeating, and various addictions, sexually compulsive behavior is a dissociative solution to the problem of managing anxiety. (1999, 165)

Schwartz, Galperin, and Masters (1995a,b) explained that the dissociative defenses often employed by victims of childhood abuse tend to leave the victim feeling depersonalized, numb, and empty. Addictions can help such victims experience highs that make them feel they are still alive but also "numb them out" when they think about the abuse they experienced or feel uncomfortable or disturbing impulses, such as the impulse toward self-destructive behavior.

Thus addictive behaviors such as compulsive sexual and risky behavior may appear on the surface to represent nothing more than poor impulse control, yet paradoxically these compulsive behaviors may serve to control manifestations of other impulses which are potentially even more dangerous, at least in the short term, such as self-mutilation and suicide attempts. Further, as noted by Spiegel (1990), compulsive sexual behavior not only offers physical discharge in and of itself, but also has the added force for a survivor of being very close to the original traumatizing behavior. When engaging in compulsive sexual behavior, the behavior itself becomes the focus of the survivor's attention, allowing a self-hypnotic dissociative trance to take control of the consciousness.

The role of dissociation in sexual addiction/compulsivity is supported by a study reported by Bancroft and Vukadinovic (2004). These investigators interviewed thirty-one "sex addicts," including patients at the Kinsey Institute Sexual Health Clinic (n = 11) or persons recruited at a Sex Addicts Anonymous (SAA) group (n = 22). Of these thirty-nine participants, fourteen (45 percent) spontaneously "described a state of mind during their acting out which could be regarded as a form of dissociation from reality." These findings are all the more striking in view of the authors' acknowledgment that "we had not anticipated this pattern, and therefore, did not include any appropriate trait measure of dissociative tendency" (235). It seems likely that dissociative tendencies would have been manifested even more strongly had a measure such as the Dissociative Experiences Scale been included in the study.

Gartner also discussed the "biological underpinning of how sexual compulsivity soothes anxiety" (1999, 165). He noted that during hyperarousal such as that which occurs during episodes of abuse, the body releases opioids to tranquilize itself and assuage pain. Gartner described this stress-induced analgesia as "compellingly seductive." He argued that the bodily change is powerfully reinforcing, so that the individual is motivated to experience it again and again. Therefore the victim may be motivated to repeat the sexual behavior that first gave rise to the production and release of these self-soothing chemicals. Because the secretion of the opioids was initially the result of traumatic sexual activity, the survivor may become compulsively sexual as a means of recreating those tranquilizing effects. In short, "engaging in compulsive sex thus allows a man to reexperience directly the biochemical means his body used to calm his anxiety when the abuse first occurred" (166).

Gartner argued that both the release of opioids and the hypnotic focusing on the sexual behavior are self-soothing, helping the survivor regulate the unmanageable affect that may be triggered by superficially innocuous cues that remind the survivor of the abusive experiences. However, he also noted that unpredictable situations may contain triggers that suddenly lead to unmanageably high levels of sexual arousal. These triggers may lead in turn to greater dissociation, and the concomitant inability to monitor the safety of one's sexual activity. This may place the survivor at risk for harm.

In support of the role of dissociation in mediating the relationship between childhood abuse and subsequent compulsive sexual behavior, Gold and Seifer (2002) observed that the sexually abused clients they treated for sexual addiction/compulsivity (SAC) "often had poor recall of even recent instances of SAC and described a subjective state of being in a daze, truncated awareness, and absence of agency during SAC episodes" (59). Gold and Seifer explained that when SAC clients begin to discuss their compulsive sexual behaviors in treatment, they often realize that they have been completely unaware of important aspects of these behaviors.

For example, they described a female client in her early thirties who had been sexually molested by an adult male baby-sitter and by her brother during childhood. When this woman entered treatment, she stated that she frequently engaged in sex with strangers, and she said that she did so because she found these encounters intensely pleasurable. However, when she discussed specific instances of such liaisons in turn, she invariably described each incident as "disappointing, ungratifying, humiliating, or even physically painful" (2002, 68). Frequently her descriptions of the sexual encounters ended with a complaint that men were generally sexually inept and interested only in their own pleasure. The discrepancy between this client's global assumption that she engaged in compulsive sexual behavior because she liked it and her description of the frustrating quality of the actual encounters suggests that during these encounters she had distanced herself from the awareness of what she was actually experiencing.

The failure of an SAC client to recognize that he was not deriving gratification from his compulsive sexual behavior is also illustrated by Gold and Seifer (2002) in their description of a man in his mid-twenties who had been sexually abused as a child by a female friend of his mother. He came to treatment in an effort to break a compulsive pattern of drinking and watching dancers at strip clubs. He reported that he would spend up to eight hours at a time engaged in this activity, wasting substantial amounts of time and money. He said that he had tried to cut back on the activity but failed. In the course of discussing these activities, this client realized for the first time that he never obtained any actual sexual gratification from this activity. He never purchased lap dances from the dancers. He never touched the dancers at all. Furthermore, after leaving the club he would go home and fall asleep, without masturbating or having sex with his wife. The lack of awareness of the nongratifying nature of this behavior again suggests a dissociative disconnection.

Perhaps the most convincing clinical case evidence of the dissociative quality of compulsive sexual behavior is found in the case reported by Gold and Seifer of a woman in her late twenties who worked as a dancer at a strip club. As a child she had been molested by her father. When she entered treatment, she insisted that she enjoyed her job and found it sexually exciting to have men watch her dance naked. However, after several months of therapy, she had an epiphany. While performing one night, she said that she suddenly "came to" and became intensely aware of the way the men were staring at her, and she was "horrified." Following this revelation she immediately stopped working at strip clubs.

The explanation of the relationship between childhood abuse and SAC as mediated by dissociation parallels a similar explanation of the relationship between childhood abuse and eating disorders (see above, chapter 5) and a similar explanation of the relationship between childhood abuse and the self-destructive behaviors of self-mutilation and suicide attempts (see chapter 8 below). In each case the dissociation is seen as disinhibiting the survivor from engaging in a self-destructive behavior that he or she might otherwise avoid on the basis of social proscription or the clear knowledge of the negative consequences of the behavior.

Prostitution or Otherwise Using Sex as a Commodity

This category of sexual adjustment difficulty comprises prostitution and related activities in the sex industry, including stripping and working in the pornography industry. These activities are socially stigmatized and often legally proscribed. This category also contains individuals like Tracy, described earlier in this chapter, who came into treatment viewing herself as "nothing more than a high-class whore" because she had consciously and purposefully used her sexuality to get wealthy men to marry her and provide for her material needs. Tracy's sexual behavior is perfectly legal. Moreover, her attitude toward using sex for profit in this manner is regarded by many as socially acceptable, as manifested in such folk sayings as, It is just as easy to fall in love with an investment banker as it is to fall in love with a carpenter. Nevertheless, there is a negative connotation associated with such behavior, as manifested in terms like "gold digger" and "gigolo," and this orientation toward sex appears to represent a sexual adjustment disorder when it is ego dystonic, as it was with Tracy. In her case, it was sufficiently distressing that it became the primary motivation for her seeking treatment.

There is a substantial body of empirical literature that supports the relationship between childhood abuse, particularly sexual abuse, and prostitution (Blumberg 1978; Chu 1992; James and Meyerding 1977; Silbert and Pines 1981; Spencer 1978; van der Kolk 1989; Vander Mey and Neff 1982; Widom and Ames 1994). These are largely retrospective studies of prostitutes that show a much higher than expected incidence of child sexual abuse among prostitutes, both male and female, both adolescent and adult. In addition, Ross, Anderson, Heber, and Norton (1990) found that among a sample of exotic dancers there was also a much higher incidence of self-reported childhood sexual abuse than among the general population of women.

Typical of these studies is that reported by Silbert and Pines (1981), who interviewed two hundred females who were either current or former prostitutes in the San Francisco Bay area. These participants ranged in age from ten to forty-six, with a mean of twenty-two. The authors reported that 60 percent of the respondents who were still engaged in prostitution were sixteen or under, and that many were ten, eleven, twelve, and thirteen years old. Seventy-eight percent reported that they had started prostitution as juveniles. Sixty percent of the respondents reported that they had been sexually abused as juveniles (sixteen or under).

Most of those who reported being sexually abused had been abused at ages far younger than sixteen. The mean age of the first victimization was ten years old. The average duration of abuse was twenty months. Two-thirds of the victims reported that they had been abused by father figures. However, most of the respondents reported that they had been abused by more than one person: 33 percent were abused by their natural fathers; 30 percent by a stepfather or a foster father; 4 percent by their mother's common law husband; 28 percent by a brother; 17 percent by an uncle; 15 percent by some other relative; and 31 percent by friends of the family, neighbors, and/or acquaintances. Only 10 percent reported being molested by strangers.

In 82 percent of the cases of abuse, some sort of force was used. In 25 percent of the cases, physical force was used; in 23 percent emotional force in the form of promises or threats was employed. In one-third of the cases, both physical and emotional coercion were involved. There were an average of four acts of force involved in each case of child sexual abuse. In 91 percent of the cases, the respondent reported that nothing could be done to prevent the abuse. Seventy percent of the respondents stated that they believed that the abuse was involved in their decision to become a prostitute. In addition, the relationship between being abused and becoming a prostitute was supported by the finding that 96 percent of the juvenile prostitutes in the study were runaways. These participants typically indicated that they had run away from home because they were being abused sexually and/or because they were experiencing physical or emotional abuse. Having run away from home, they were confronted with the need to obtain food and shelter, making them vulnerable to be recruited into prostitution by pimps. The authors recommended that an important step in reducing the likelihood that these girls will become prostitutes would be to place outreach workers at bus terminals and other places where runaways gather, so that they can be directed to alternative modes of survival.

Spatz and Widom (1994) reported the results of a study that employed a prospective cohorts design that compared a sample of children who had been sexually abused before the age of eleven to a matched control sample who had not been abused. These groups were compared on subsequent arrests, and the results showed that a significantly larger proportion of the sexually abused group were subsequently arrested for prostitution either as adolescents or as adults. Interestingly, this study did not indicate that running away from home was a significant mediator of the relationship between childhood sexual abuse and subsequent prostitution. In addition, the study indicated that children who had been physically abused but not sexually abused were less likely than children who had been sexually abused but not physically abused to be arrested subsequently for prostitution. On the other hand, the children who had been physically abused but not sexually abused were significantly more likely than the children who had been sexually abused but not physically abused to be arrested for other sex crimes, such as sexual assault.

In addition to the role of running away from home in mediating the relationship between childhood abuse and subsequent prostitution, investigators have proposed several different causal pathways. Finkelhor and Browne (1985) referred to a learning process of traumatic sexualization which occurs "when a child is repeatedly rewarded by an offender for sexual behavior that is inappropriate to his or her level of development . . . through the exchange of affection, attention, privileges, and gifts for sexual behavior, so that a child learns to use sexual behavior as a strategy for manipulating others to satisfy a variety of developmentally appropriate needs" (531). These needs include the need for nurturance and the need for closeness, as well the need for physical care and comforting. The idea of learning that sex is a commodity that one may exchange for the satisfaction of other needs clearly creates a predisposition toward prostitution as well as a predisposition toward the kind of gold digging behavior displayed by Tracy.

Maltz (2001) pointed out that our culture reinforces the view that sex is a commodity that can be exchanged for attention, love, power, and security. She referred to phrases in the popular lexicon such as "*losing* your virginity," "*getting* laid," and "*giving* sex" as reflecting and contributing to the general view that sex is "something to obtain, a skill to possess, or a commodity to sell to others" (89). She argued that in this frame of mind people are reduced to sexual objects, and sex becomes no more than acts of physical stimulation and release. She also suggested that it is within this frame of mind that prostitution and pornography thrive. Maltz also provided a case example that illustrates perfectly that aspect of traumatic sexualization that results in viewing sex as a commodity. Maltz quoted a teenage survivor of father–daughter incest describing her experience:

When I was a girl my father would take me shopping. He'd point out a dress or a pair of shoes and ask me if I wanted them. When I'd say yes, he'd tell me if I did this and this and this with him sexually, he'd get me the things. Or he'd tell me if I did one sex act he'd give me such and such an amount of money, and if I did another sex act or let him take pictures of me, he'd give me more. (89)

In this example, the exchange of a sex act for a specific commodity or a specific amount of money is completely transparent, and the case illustrates how an incestuous father can teach his daughter to be a prostitute. Maltz also noted, however, that abuse survivors who think of sex as a commodity may not become prostitutes but gold diggers like Tracy. Maltz argued that

When sex is learned as a commodity, the pull to continue thinking of sex this way can be strong. Survivors may fear that without this view, they would suffer economically, feel bankrupt, or be deprived. A survivor who has thought of sex as a payoff for financial support from a partner may worry that she will be destitute if she begins to change her view of sex. (2001, 89–90)

Maltz also argued that in the commodity view, sex can also be seen as a payoff for love or faithfulness. The survivor may think, "I have to give it to him or he'll want to get it elsewhere" (90). The survivor may feel that her partner will leave her if she stops being sexual. This viewpoint also relates to the sexual adjustment difficulty of promiscuity discussed above. Thus Maltz described a twenty-year-old male survivor of childhood sexual abuse who believed that every woman he dated expected sex from him and would be angry with him if he did not make a pass at them. She noted that whenever sex is seen as a commodity, it can feel more like a job that needs to be performed than an activity we engage in because it is satisfying and pleasurable.

Several modified versions of the traumagenic sexualization paradigm have also been used to explain the relationship between childhood sexual abuse and prostitution. One such variant involves the likelihood that the victim will develop a poor self-concept as a result of being sexually abused. Thus Bass and Davis (1994) argued that the victim may come to believe that sex is all that he or she is good for. This negative self-concept facilitates the victim's entrance into the socially proscribed and stigmatized profession of prostitution. Blume (1990), viewing the process of traumagenic sexualization from a radical feminist perspective, noted that the survivor may simply come to the conclusion that since I must provide sex anyway, I "might as well get paid for it" (181).

Still another explanation for the relationship between child abuse and prostitution involves the idea that the prostitute has ostensible control over the terms of his or her sexual exchanges. This element of control was clearly absent in the childhood sexual abuse experiences. Therefore, becoming a prostitute may be viewed as an effort to gain mastery over an area of life that was previously completely out of control (Chu 1992; Sandberg, Lynn, and Green 1994; van der Kolk 1989). Sandberg and his associates argued that "as a prostitute, the abuse victim will continually reenact the abuse scenario, and on some level take charge of, control, or alter the situation and/or her reaction to it. For instance, rather than being forced to have intercourse with a perpetrator, the prostitute is in charge of administering sex" (1994, 248–49). However, Sandberg and his colleagues also pointed out that this sense of control is largely illusory, since prostitutes are frequently taken advantage of, cheated, or physically abused by their customers.

In summary, prostitution may be seen as bringing together many of the dysfunctional lessons taught by childhood sexual abuse, as well as neurotic needs engendered by that abuse: these include the idea that sex is a commodity, the idea that the victim is good for nothing except to be a sexual object, and the need to repeat the abusive situation in an effort to gain mastery over sexuality that the survivor perceives as out of control. Prostitution is also a high-risk behavior. As such it may be viewed as serving the survivor's need to overcome prevailing negative affect by seeking the adrenaline rush associated with danger.

Reliance on Sadomasochistic Pornography, Fantasy, or Behavior for Sexual Gratification

Some victims of childhood sexual abuse are incapable of experiencing sexual gratification except through participating in sadomasochistic sexual practices, observing abusive pornography, or engaging in abusive fantasies. Although there is not a large volume of empirical data on the relationship between childhood sexual abuse and either participation in sadomasochistic sexual practices or the use of abusive pornography or fantasy, there is a good deal of anecdotal material (Bass and Davis 1994; Gartner 1999; Maltz 2001; Mullen and Fleming 1998) and some empirical evidence (Nordling, Sandnabba, and Santtila 2000). In the latter study, investigators surveyed 164 male and 22 female practitioners of sadomasochistic sex, recruited at two sadomasochistically oriented clubs in Finland. The survey included measures of sexual abuse history as well as measures of psychological health and social adjustment. The results indicated that the proportion of respondents in the sample who reported histories of childhood sexual abuse was significantly greater than the corresponding proportion within the general Finnish population. Results also indicated that the respondents who did indicate histories of childhood sexual abuse were more poorly adjusted so-cially than the nonabused respondents, more likely than the other respon-dents to have attempted suicide, and more likely to have sought profes-sional psychological assistance.

Bass and Davis (1994) explained the connection between childhood sex-ual abuse and reliance on abusive sexual stimulation as follows:

> The context in which we first experience sex affects us deeply. Often there is a kind of imprinting in which whatever is going on at the time becomes wo-ven together. So if you experienced violation, humiliation, and fear at the same time as you experienced arousal and pleasurable genital feelings, these el-ements twisted together, leaving you with emotional and physical legacies that link pleasure with pain, love with humiliation, desire with an imbalance of power. Shame, secrecy, danger, and the forbidden feel thrilling. (273)

Because of the early pairing of sexual pleasure with the negative physical and emotional aspects of abuse, some abuse survivors are not able to become sex-ually aroused or experience orgasm in the absence of stimuli that mimic or recreate some aspect of the abuse. Thus Bass and Davis described an incest survivor who could climax only if she imagined her father's face, and a vic-tim who had been molested by a neighbor who could reach orgasm only if she was stimulated in exactly the same manner as she had been by that perpe-trator as a child. Similarly, if one were physically coerced or restrained dur-ing childhood sexual abuse, it may be impossible for that person to become sexually aroused as an adult unless he or she is bound or beaten.

In his book on male victims of sexual abuse, Gartner (1999) noted that "two different gay men have told me that every man they knew who (like themselves) was deeply involved in bondage and other sadomasochistic prac-tices had been sexually or otherwise abused during childhood" (220). Gart-ner also noted that sadistic fantasies that are not acted out are also common among victims of childhood sexual abuse. He described the case of a male pa-tient who had recurring fantasies of tying men up and either tickling them until they screamed or bringing them nearly to orgasm but not allowing the orgasm to take place. Gartner indicated that until this patient began treat-ment he had never made the connection between these fantasies and his own experiences with sexual abuse. That patient eventually disclosed that his own grandparents had tickled him mercilessly as part of a sexual game they played. The patient also revealed that when his father abused him, he kept himself from reaching orgasm in order to frustrate his father. It is no ac-cident that there are pornographic videos that feature the tickling of persons who are restrained, or that pornographic videos involving themes of bondage frequently involve the dominant "master" or "mistress" stimulating a submissive "slave," but not allowing the slave to achieve an orgasm until being given permission to do so by the dominant protagonist.

The issue of control is obviously a crucial element of sadomasochistic sexual practices as well as abusive pornography and fantasy. Thus Maltz (2001) noted that "some survivors cling to abusive fantasies because these fantasies offer opportunities for them to feel in absolute control of sex" (174). The survivor may design sexual scenarios that incorporate exactly the elements of the abuse they experienced that have become eroticized for them. Moreover, with the vast array of pornographic materials that are available, survivors may purchase books or videos that similarly incorporate these elements. Using fantasy and/or programmed pornographic materials to create exactly the combination of stimuli that the survivor finds most arousing can give the survivor a sense of control that can compensate for the feelings of helplessness that were experienced during the childhood abuse. This sense of control is augmented when the subject of the fantasy or pornography is itself control, as in videos with themes of bondage. Maltz (2001) quoted a survivor who explained her use of abusive fantasy as follows:

> Abusive fantasies have helped me feel the power and control that I didn't have when I was being abused. While this worked in the short run, now that I feel better about myself, I want to experience more in sex. I can't do it as long as I keep spacing out into these kinds of fantasies. (174)

Maltz (2001) also noted that the use of abusive fantasies and pornography has the effect of recreating and reinforcing the original abuse experience. For this reason, in order to achieve sexual healing, many survivors realize that they must curtail these behaviors. This enables them to move away from the sexual abuse dynamics of the past and begin to learn new and healthy forms of sexual expression, such as pleasurable sensations and loving thoughts in the context of sexual contact with a caring partner.

Revictimization

The final category of unsatisfactory adult sexual adjustment considered here is the tendency of victims of childhood abuse to be "revictimized" later. The most common scenario for revictimization involves women with histories of childhood sexual abuse having an elevated risk of becoming victims of sexual assault in adulthood. However, revictimization is often defined as including forms of abuse other than rape and attempted rape. Thus

Messman-Moore and Long (2000) noted that "revictimization may occur in the form of unwanted sexual contact, physical abuse, and psychological maltreatment" (489).

Noll, Horowitz, Bonanno, Trickett, and Putnam (2003) explicitly included becoming the victim of domestic violence as a manifestation of revictimization. These authors also pointed out that "definitions of revictimization have varied with some studies limiting outcome variables to rape, other studies broadening the definition to include physical assault or any criminal victimization, and still others including self-harm as a type of revictimization" (2003, 1453). Sandberg et al.(1994) included becoming a prostitute as a manifestation of revictimization. This would appear to make some sense, in view of the fact that prostitutes are frequently coerced into this activity by their pimps, as well as the fact that prostitutes are frequently coerced by their clients into performing sex acts that they do not wish to perform. Several investigators have suggested that victims of childhood sexual abuse are more likely than other patients to experience therapist–patient sexual exploitation and that this is also a form of revictimization (Kluft 1989, 1990a,b; Pope and Bouhoutsos 1986; Sandberg et al.1994).

Noll and her colleagues (2003) offered a good commonsense definition of revictimization that includes both sexual and physical abuse perpetrated on the survivor by others but excludes self-harm:

The current study distinguishes self-harm and revictimization as separate but related behaviors. We operationally define victimization (either sexual or physical) as harm perpetrated by an outside source that serves as a reenactment of the initial abuse. Self-harm, on the other hand, implies a direct [harm] inflicted by the survivor herself and represents a certain internalization of the trauma. Therefore, self-harm is not considered a category of revictimization but will be studied as a separate and distinct phenomenon. (2003, 1453–54)

According to this definition, a victim of child sexual abuse who becomes a prostitute because she is physically coerced or threatened by a pimp or performs an unwanted sex act because she is coerced or threatened by a client would be viewed as revictimized, but a prostitute who voluntarily exchanges sex for money on her own terms would be viewed as engaging in a form of self-harm.

There is ample evidence of the relationship between childhood sexual abuse and revictimization in the form of sexual assault and abuse. Russell (1986) studied a community sample of 960 women, 28 percent of whom reported being sexually abused before the age of fourteen. She found that

60 percent of these women also reported being raped or experiencing attempted rape on one or more occasion after the age of fourteen. The corresponding proportion among respondents who did not report a history of childhood sexual abuse was 35 percent. Briere and Runtz (1987) studied 152 adult women who sought treatment at a community counseling center, 44 percent of whom reported a history of childhood sexual victimization. They found that the women with histories of CSA were more than twice as likely as those without histories of CSA to report that they had been raped as adults. A number of other studies have indicated that women with a history of CSA are at a significantly increased risk for adult sexual victimization, compared to women who do not report histories of CSA (Arata 1999a,b; Arata and Lindeman, 2002; Collins 1998; Fergusson, Horwood, and Lynskey 1997; Fromuth 1986; Gidycz, Coble, Latham, and Layman 1993; Gorcey, Santiago, and McCall-Perez 1986; Himelein 1995; Kessler and Bieschke 1999; Koss and Dinero 1989; Krahe, Scheinberger-Olwig, Waizenhofer, and Kolpin 1999; Mayall and Gold 1995; Urquiza and Goodlin-Jones 1994; Wyatt, Guthrie, and Notgrass 1992; Wyatt, Newcomb, and Riederle 1993). Based on reviews of the literature, Polusny and Follette (1995) and Messman and Long (1996) each concluded that the revictimization hypothesis had received consistent support in a wide range of studies using community, college, and clinical samples. Other studies have employed samples of rape victims (Ellis, Atkeson, and Calhoun 1982; Miller, Moeler, Kaufman, DiVasto, Pathak, and Christy 1978; Russell 1984). These studies indicated that the proportion of adult rape victims who report histories of childhood sexual abuse is higher than the corresponding proportion in the general population of women.

A more limited body of literature supports the relationship between childhood sexual abuse and adult physical abuse. For example, in their study of adult women at a community counseling center described above, Briere and Runtz (1987) found that the CSA victims were not only more likely than non-CSA victims to be sexually assaulted, but were also more than twice as likely as nonvictims to report being battered as adults. Other empirical studies indicating a relationship between CSA and adult physical abuse have been reported by Finkelhor and Yllo (1983) and by Walker and Browne (1985). Messman-Moore and Long (2000) concluded that the few studies that had been reported relevant to this relationship indicated that between 27 percent and 49 percent of survivors of CSA experienced physical abuse as adults. Several investigators have suggested that victims of CSA may be more likely to be emotionally abused as adults than nonvictims (Okun 1986; Tolman 1989). This connection is suggested on the basis of the premise that verbal abuse often precedes and/or accompanies physical abuse, particularly in the context of domestic violence. However, Messman-Moore and Long (2000) noted that "to date no studies regarding this form of revictimization [emotional abuse] are available with CSAS" (491).

In response to the lack of available empirical data with respect to the relationship between CSA and subsequent emotional abuse, Messman-Moore and Long (2000) conducted a retrospective survey study of 648 female college students. The participants were described as young (mean age = 19.7 years, SD = 3.4), single (92.1 percent never married), Caucasian (83.3 percent), and largely middle class. The participants completed the Life Experiences Questionnaire (LEQ) (Long 1999), which was used to screen for CSA. A modified version of the Sexual Experiences Survey (SES) (Koss and Gidycz 1985) was used to assess adult unwanted sexual contact. The Conflicts Tactics Scale (CTS) (Straus 1979) was used to assess the presence and extent of intimate violence among dating partners and spouses. Finally, the Psychological Maltreatment of Women Inventory (PMWI) (Tolman 1989) was used to assess psychological abuse.

Of all respondents, 127 (20.1 percent) reported a history of CSA, while 506 did not. Fifteen participants did not provide enough information to be classified accurately with respect to history of CSA, and these women were dropped from the analysis. With respect to sexual revictimization, the results of the study indicated that the group reporting a history of CSA were significantly more likely than the non-abused group to report unwanted fondling with an acquaintance due to a misuse of authority (e.g., by a professor), unwanted oral–genital contact with an acquaintance due to alcohol or drug use, unwanted sexual intercourse with an acquaintance due to misuse of authority, and unwanted sexual intercourse with an acquaintance due to the use of physical force (e.g., date rape). In addition, the women reporting a history of CSA were significantly more likely than the nonabused women to report unwanted intercourse by a stranger due to misuse of authority. With respect to revictimization in the form of physical abuse, the study indicated that women reporting a history of CSA were significantly more likely than women not reporting a history of CSA to have experienced both minor physical violence and severe physical violence. And with respect to revictimization in the form of emotional abuse, the respondents reporting a history of CSA were significantly more likely than the nonabused group to report instances of emotional–verbal abuse, and more likely as well to report acts of dominance–isolation. Thus the results reported by Messman-Moore and Long (2000) support the relationship between childhood sexual abuse and revictimization in the form of sexual abuse, physical abuse, and emotional abuse.

A wide range of theories have been offered to explain the relationship between childhood abuse and subsequent revictimization. Some are intuitively obvious commonsense explanations; others are more complex. Some of them have been alluded to previously in connection with other adult sexual adjustment disorders, and others are specific to the problem of revictimization. The various theories are not mutually exclusive, and several of the theoretical processes described may well be at work in a single case of revictimization.

Messman and Long (1996) and Classen, Field, Koopman, Nevill-Manning, and Spiegel (2001) presented summaries of several of the more popular and time-tested theories used to explain the relationship between CSA and subsequent revictimization. These include (1) the possibility that childhood sexual abuse leads to such low self-esteem on the part of victims that they feel their mistreatment is deserved (Jehu and Gazan 1983; Walker 1981, 1984); (2) the role of learned maladaptive attitudes and behaviors, such as victims' idea that they only have value as a sexual object, or the view that sex is a commodity to be exchanged for affection, nurturance, or material reward (Jehu and Gazan 1983; Wheeler and Berliner 1988); (3) making poor relationship choices, such as choosing partners who share characteristics with their childhood abuser(s), having a substance abuse problem, being a control freak, or being predisposed to employ verbal abuse or physical violence (Herman and Hirschman 1981; Tsai and Wagner 1978; van der Kolk 1989); (4) denial (Walker 1984); and (5) learned helplessness (Peterson and Seligman 1983; Walker 1984; Walker and Browne 1985).

Some of these explanations have been fine-tuned over time and related to more comprehensive theories of development. For example, Sandberg, Lynn and Green (1994) noted that the role of low self-esteem in fostering revictimization can also be stated in terms of object relations theory (Fairbairn 1954; Cashdan 1988; Masterson and Klein 1989). This theory focuses on how the developing child creates mental representations of self and others. The theory suggests that through the psychological mechanism of "introjection," the child "comes to view him- or herself in the same way that he or she is treated by significant others" (Sandberg et al. 1994, 249). This means that a child who is subjected to severe abuse will form a negative view of the self. In addition, because the child must depend on the parent for survival, it would be very threatening for a child victim of sexual or physical abuse to think of the parent as bad or evil. Therefore, the child is likely to blame himself or herself for the abuse, concluding that he or she in fact deserves to be treated that way. Over time, this negative view of the self will lead the survivor of child abuse to reenact the perpetrator–victim dynamic with others. Thus Gelinas (1983) noted that survivors will tend to allow, or even elicit, abusive interchanges with others. Through the mechanism of projective identification, victims tend to recreate the abusive relationship. Because they view themselves as bad and worthy of punishment, they tend to act in ways that are likely to lead to mistreatment. For the same reasons the survivor may attempt to punish the bad part of the self through self-mutilation (Buchele 1993; Gelinas 1983).

Classen and her colleagues (2001) expanded upon the link between CSA and revictimization involving poor relationship choices. These investigators observed that "one of the consequences of having been sexually abused in childhood is the development of aberrant relationship models that in turn lead to interpersonal difficulties" (497). They explored the role of relationship difficulties in a sample of 52 adult female survivors of childhood sexual abuse who were diagnosed with post-traumatic stress disorder. The participants completed the Sexual Experiences Survey (SES) (Koss and Gidycz 1985) as a measure of sexual revictimization, and they completed the Inventory of Interpersonal Problems (IIP) (Horowitz, Rosenberg, Baer, Ureno, and Villasenor 1988) as a measure of interpersonal adjustment difficulties. The IIP yielded subscale scores for eight different interpersonal problems.

Classen et al. (2001) reported that seventeen of the fifty-two women who participated had experienced sexual revictimization during the six months preceding the study. Of the seventeen, sixteen had experienced sexual coercion, and one had experienced an attempted rape. When members of the revictimized group were compared to the other women in the sample, significant differences were observed with respect to three of the eight subscales. The revictimized group scored higher than the nonrevictimized group on social avoidance, nonassertiveness, and on the overly nurturant subscale. The authors observed that "the interpersonal problems of being overly nurturant and having difficulty in being assertive paints the picture of an individual who places the needs and concerns of others before her own [and] has a hard time saying no" (503–4). The authors also suggested that "as a result of their social avoidance, these women may have fewer appropriate and protective social contacts, or they may be perceived as more vulnerable and thus become targets of exploitative men" (504).

The theme of learned helplessness is implicit in theme of powerlessness contained in the theory of the traumagenic dynamics of child sexual abuse advanced by Finkelhor and Browne (1985). They argued that powerlessness or disempowerment results from the process of child sexual abuse,

> in which the child's will, desires, and sense of efficacy are continually contravened. Many aspects of the sexual abuse experience contribute to this

dynamic. We theorize that a basic kind of powerlessness occurs in sexual abuse when a child's territory and body are repeatedly invaded against the child's will. This is exacerbated by whatever coercion and manipulation the offender may impose as part of the abuse process. Powerlessness is then reinforced when children feel fear, are unable to make adults understand or believe what is happening, or realize how conditions of dependency have trapped them in the situation. (532)

The powerlessness that is instilled in the child victim persists through adolescence and into adulthood and renders the survivor incapable of responding appropriately to threatening situations. Thus Briere (1992a) argued that childhood maltreatment encourages passivity, helplessness, and dependency. It teaches the victim to tolerate and accept violence in interpersonal relationships. In short, childhood abuse teaches victims to be subordinate to perpetrators of subsequent sexual, physical, and emotional abuse.

In the discussion of prostitution presented earlier in this chapter, we argued that a link between CSA and subsequent prostitution lies in the survivor's attempt to gain mastery over the sexual victimization experience by reenacting it under circumstances where he or she can exert the control which was conspicuously missing in the abusive childhood encounter. Several investigators have argued that the "repetition compulsion" is similarly involved in revictimization in general (Chu 1992; van der Kolk 1989). Freud (1954) argued that individuals repress memories of early traumatic experiences, and these repressed memories lead the victim to reenact the experiences in the present, in an effort to integrate these experiences. He suggested that "the patient is obliged . . . to repeat as a current experience what is repressed, instead of recollecting it as a fragment of the past" (1954, 18). Sandberg and associates (1994) concluded that until the survivor has "worked through" the original trauma, "repressed elements will continue to compel him or her to repeat the experience, despite the harm it may cause" (248). Moreover, because the process occurs at the unconscious level, the person is unaware of the connection between the initial traumatic experience and current life situations. This explains why many individuals who are repeatedly victimized as adults do not connect this outcome to their history of child abuse until they have begun treatment.

Another theoretical link between CSA and revictimization that is not intuitively obvious is the information processing hypothesis advanced by Horowitz (1975), who based his theory on Piaget's concept of assimilation and accommodation, the cognitive processes through which new information is integrated into preexisting cognitive schemas. Horowitz argued that active memory has an intrinsic tendency to engage in repetition, and memories of a stressful stimulus will continue to be processed until cognitive processing has been completed. Thus until early experiences involving sexual or physical abuse have been integrated into the victim's cognitive schema, the defense of repression will break down from time to time, and the victim will experience intrusive memories of these events. Horowitz also hypothesized that the repetition compulsion functions at the emotional and behavioral level as well. For this reason, survivors may also experience emotional flooding in the form of panic attacks or crying spells, or they may engage in "behavioral reenactments" of the traumatic events. Several investigators have suggested that sexual revictimization is a specific form of behavioral reenactment (Chu 1992; Gelinas 1983; van der Kolk 1989).

Dissociation has been suggested as a link between CSA and subsequent revictimization (Noll et al. 2003). Dissociative processes, ranging from simple daydreaming to the extreme diagnosis of Dissociative Identity Disorder (formerly multiple personality disorder) have been shown to be particularly characteristic of victims of childhood sexual abuse (Chu and Dill 1990; Putnam 1997, 2000). Dissociative processes have also been shown to occur more frequently among victims of multiple sexual assaults than among the general population (Putnam, Helmers, Horowitz, and Trickett 1995; van der Kolk et al. 1991; Zlotnick, Begin, Shea, Pearlstein, Simpson, and Costello 1994).

Zlotnick and colleagues (1994) argued that dissociation is initially useful to the victim of child sexual abuse because it provides a defense against the negative affect associated with the victimization. However, individuals who learn to dissociate when abused as children tend to continue to use this defense as adults. This is problematic because it may increase their vulnerability to revictimization. Thus Noll and her colleagues argued that "by blocking or distorting threatening material from entering conscious awareness, individuals may be less able to process danger cues and may be less likely to experience the anticipatory anxiety that normally signals the presence of danger" (2003, 1455). Furthermore, when a victim dissociates from a trauma at the time of its occurrence, the memories of the event are likely to be fragmented and incomplete, leaving the victim unable to learn from the traumatic event and increasing the likelihood of an ineffective or dysfunctional response to future threats (Chu 1992; Irwin 1999).

Finally, Posttraumatic Stress Disorder has been proposed as a link between CSA and adult revictimization (Arata 1999b,c; Noll et al. 2003). PTSD is a distinct diagnostic category, and its relationship to various forms of childhood abuse is considered in some detail in chapter 9 of this volume. However, in relation to revictimization, we note simply that adult survivors of CSA are more likely than adults with no history of CSA to be diagnosed with PTSD (Deblinger, McLeer, Atkins, Ralphe, and Foa 1989; Lindberg and Distad 1985; McLeer, Deblinger, Atkins, Foa, and Ralphe 1988; Rowan and Foy 1993; Rowan, Rodriguez, and Ryan 1991; Saunders, Arata, and Kilpatrick 1990) and that several of the symptoms of PTSD appear to increase the likelihood of revictimization (Arata 1999c; Ellis, Atkeson, and Calhoun 1982; Miller et al. 1978).

Among the symptoms of PTSD listed in the DSM-IV-TR that might be construed as increasing the likelihood of revictimization are persistent avoidance of stimuli associated with the trauma and persistent symptoms of increased arousal, including concentration problems, distractibility, sleep disruption, and exaggerated startle response (American Psychiatric Association 2000). Noll and her associates (2003) noted that "a victim who is experiencing avoidant symptoms may be prone to making inaccurate or uninformed decisions regarding potential danger because of the fact that the trauma has been denied, minimized, or otherwise not fully integrated" (1455). Similarly, sleep disruption and hyperarousal could interfere with the survivor's ability to recognize and respond appropriately to danger cues in the environment. Consistent with the idea that these aspects of PTSD may increase the likelihood of revictimization are the results of studies indicating that adult survivors of CSA who have experienced revictimization reported significantly more symptoms of PTSD than survivors who report no revictimization (Arata 1999c; Sandberg, Matorin, and Lynn 1999).

~

CHAPTER EIGHT

Childhood Abuse and Adult Self-destructive Behavior

Case Studies in Self-destructive Behavior

Self-destructive behavior is conceptualized in different ways. It is most often defined narrowly as including self-mutilation and suicidal tendencies. However, it is sometimes defined more broadly as comprising such diverse behaviors as (1) extreme risk-taking behavior, including reckless driving, speeding, drunk driving, and/or "accident proneness"; (2) compulsive and risky sexual activities; (3) bulimia and other eating disorders; (4) acute and severe compulsive substance abuse; and (4) other self-defeating activities such as compulsive excessive spending, compulsive gambling, and self-sabotage in personal and professional relationships. In addition, the hallmark symptoms of self-mutilation and suicidal behavior are sometimes circumscribed in nature, but at other times they occur in conjunction with a broad array of other serious symptoms. Self-destructive behavior often begins during adolescence and runs its course by early adulthood, but in other cases it continues for a lifetime. Self-destructive behavior is more common among women, but the most extreme form of self-destructive behavior, the successfully completed suicide attempt, is more common among men. Due to the diverse nature of the definition and manifestations of self-destructive behavior, we present several different case studies to introduce this topic.

An Adolescent Who Self-mutilates

Sandy is a fourteen-year-old ninth grader. She was referred for treatment by a school counselor who felt she was depressed and had received information from a classmate that Sandy was cutting herself with a razor blade. Although Sandy had not initiated treatment, she was quite receptive to entering treatment when her counselor suggested it to her. In her first session with her therapist, she acknowledged being depressed and cutting herself. She said she felt bad about herself most of the time. She said she was anxious about the future, with no plans for a career and no vision of life as an adult. She said she was uncomfortably anxious much of the time and chronically sad. Sandy said that contrary to what one might expect, cutting herself was not extremely painful but made her feel better.

Sandy said that while she was engaging in self-cutting she felt virtually nothing. Instead, she said that she focused on carrying out the cutting in a careful and precise manner. She said this extreme care was necessary to avoid injuring herself so seriously as to require medical attention, thus revealing her secret self-mutilating behavior. Sandy said that because of her intense mental focus during the cutting, she was able to temporarily stop thinking the negative thoughts about herself that otherwise obsessed her thinking. She also said that after she had cut herself she would feel some pain, but this feeling was overwhelmed by a sense of tension reduction.

Sandy articulated the sense that she was always in pain without being able to figure out why and always afraid that something bad would happen to her. She said that when she cut herself it was like she had a reason for feeling the pain, and a sense that the damage had been done. Therefore, she could relax for a time. But this effect of the self-cutting did not last very long, and when her anxieties began to build again the awareness of how sick the self-mutilation really was made her feel even worse.

During her treatment, some of the reasons why Sandy felt bad about herself emerged. Sandy indicated that her parents had been highly critical of her for as long as she could remember. She said that they were bitter, dissatisfied individuals who seemed uncomfortable with themselves, with each other, and most of all with her. Sandy said she never heard them express affection toward each other, and they never said they loved her. In fact, they never said anything good about her. Sandy said that when they weren't ignoring her, they were criticizing her. She reported that they constantly criticized her mode of dressing, her choice of friends, and her taste in music and movies. She was especially hurt by her mother's tendency to criticize her in front of other people, including family members and even strangers.

Sandy's father was physically as well as emotionally abusive toward her. Her father disciplined her by hitting her with his fists and shoving her into the wall. This emotional and physical abuse led her to experience negative thoughts about herself, including thoughts that she was unattractive, untalented, and undesirable. She reported that cutting herself with a razor blade allowed her to interrupt these negative thoughts. She said that cutting herself produced a feeling that was almost like "being high." She also said that seeing her own blood helped convince her that she was "a real person" who was "really here."

Sandy also engaged in other self-injurious behaviors, including pulling out clumps of her hair, scratching herself until her skin was raw and bleeding, and burning herself with cigarettes. However, her preferred mode of self-injury was cutting. She explained that she would always cut herself in the same place on her wrist, and that she would cut just deep enough to bleed but not require stitches. In this way, she thought that she could keep her self-cutting a secret. However, a friend in school saw the cuts and scars on Sandy's wrist and told a counselor about them.

Sandy told her therapist that sometimes she wished she could go to sleep and not wake up. However, she had never actually considered how to kill herself. In addition, none of her self-mutilating behaviors were in any way life threatening, and she did not report engaging in any other risky or self-destructive behaviors. Her therapist felt that Sandy was not a suicide risk.

Self-destructive Behavior Maintained into Midlife

A different pattern of self-destructive behavior is apparent in Alice, a forty-two-year-old woman who engaged in various forms of self-destructive behavior and experienced a broad range of other psychological symptoms for as long as she could remember. Alice participated in various mutual self-help support groups for victims of childhood abuse after she became aware of the existence of such groups during college. She had also been in individual psychotherapy and was hospitalized on three occasions for depression.

Alice's psychological symptoms over the years included chronic depression as well as severe depressive episodes, eating disorders (both bulimia and restricting anorexia, at different points in her life), chronic social anxiety, agoraphobia, self-mutilation (mainly self-cutting but also self-burning), and sexual dysfunction. Alice indicated that she had experienced several periods of severe depression and had made several suicide attempts that she described as "serious." Alice is aware of the difference between suicidal gestures and serious efforts to kill herself, because she explicitly stated that her self-mutilating behaviors were not attempted suicides, but rather instrumental efforts aimed at coping with extreme negative affect. During her first hospitalization Alice was diagnosed as having borderline personality. Various physicians had prescribed a range of medications to alleviate depression and anxiety, but Alice reported that these had been largely ineffective. She currently describes herself as "still very depressed" but "getting by," with the continuing support of her therapist, the peers in her support group, and her husband.

Alice was married to the same man for over twenty years, and they had one daughter who was in college. She reported that she loved her husband and considered him a "very good man," but she never had a rewarding sex life. Alice married her husband because he was kind and undemanding rather than handsome, exciting, or irresistible. She described him as the first man with whom she had felt any sense of comfort. She indicated that she had sex with her husband when he wanted to, but she was generally indifferent and anorgasmic. In fact, Alice noted feeling uncomfortable when touched at all, even by him, and feeling relieved when the sex was over. Alice explained that she occasionally felt aroused by his touch, but then feelings of excitement were overwhelmed by guilt. She also explained that as much as she wanted to please her husband, she always felt resentment after sex. She felt she was taken advantage of or used in some way. Alice indicated that in spite of her years in treatment she had never discussed sex with her husband.

The many symptoms reported over the years and currently by Alice appeared to be associated with an extensive history of childhood sexual abuse, emotional abuse, and neglect perpetrated primarily by her mother, but to some extent by her father as well. She described her parents' marriage as loveless and unhappy, but not characterized by excessive amounts of arguing or any obvious domestic violence. Her parents had married in their mid-thirties, and Alice was their only child. Alice's father was an international marketing executive and traveled constantly. Alice reported an impression that theirs was a marriage of convenience, based on her father's need to present a facade of a traditional family life and her mother's need to avoid becoming an old maid.

Alice reported that her mother had abused her sexually and emotionally. From her first recollection, Alice and her mother slept in the same bed whenever her father was away from home, which was most of the time. Alice recalled being fondled and receiving oral sex from her mother as far back as she could remember. She also remembered her mother putting her fingers and various objects in her vagina. Her mother coerced her into touching her mother's breasts and genitals and eventually into performing oral sex on her mother. If Alice refused to do as she was told or indicated that she did not enjoy what was happening, her mother would say that Alice didn't love her and would lock Alice up in her room for days at a time with nothing to eat and only water to drink. Alice said that she hated being locked up the most. She said that being ignored and neglected in this way was worse than being abused. Alice said that eventually she came to accept the sexual intimacies with her mother as the price that she had to pay to be recognized and cared for. Alice said that her mother continued to sleep in the same bed with her until she left for college. In addition to sleeping in the same bed throughout her childhood and adolescence, Alice also reported that her mother insisted that they bathe together and clean each other's genital areas.

Alice felt isolated and separated from her peers during elementary school and high school. She was not certain exactly when she became completely aware that the sexual activity between her and her mother was inappropriate and socially proscribed, but she knew that she felt uncomfortable with it from her earliest recollection. As far back as she could remember, her mother had told her that this behavior was their secret, and that she should never tell her father or anyone else about it. In addition, Alice was always kept somewhat isolated from the world outside the family. She was never allowed to have friends stay over or to go along with friends on their family outings. Her mom picked Alice up after school each day and brought her straight back to their house. Once during high school Alice attempted to disclose her situation to a female teacher with whom she felt some connection, but the teacher avoided the subject and even suggested that children Alice's age sometimes imagined things that didn't really happen. After that, Alice did not attempt to reveal her history of abuse to anyone until she was in college, when she learned of the existence of the self-help peer support group for victims of childhood abuse.

Alice resented her father for never being at home, for never showing her that he cared for her, and for not knowing what her mother was doing to her. Alice said that there were times when she believed that he must have known what was going on and that he simply ignored it because it was convenient for him. She didn't know for sure, however, because she never had the courage to confront either her mother or her father about the abuse, despite the frequent encouragement of her peers and various therapists to do so. Today, at midlife, in spite of a stable marriage and peer and professional support and therapy, Alice remains dissatisfied, unhappy, and in pain.

Self-destructive Behavior Defined

The self-destructive behavior we focus on in the present chapter includes self-mutilation and suicidal behavior. Several other forms of self-destructive activity that are frequently included in a broad conceptualization of self-destructive behavior include eating disorders, substance abuse, compulsive and risky sexual behavior, and sexual revictimization. These have been considered separately in previous chapters, for several reasons. For example, Bratton (1999) argued that even though some professionals lump eating disorders and substance abuse under the broad category of adult self-abuse, "there is too much evidence that substance addictions are separate diseases" (110). Bratton argued that "alcohol and drug dependencies and eating disorders need to be addressed as primary problems once they have taken hold in a life. Any recovery work from childhood abuse will be blocked if substance abuse continues unchecked" (111).

Here we consider self-mutilation and suicidal tendencies. Dubo, Zanarini, Lewis, and Williams (1997) noted that "both self-mutilation and manipulative suicidal behavior are pathognomonic symptoms of borderline personality disorder" (107). However, neither self-mutilation nor suicidal tendencies is uniquely associated with a borderline diagnosis. Moreover, the literature is clear that self-injurious behavior and suicide attempts are conceptually distinct. Thus van der Kolk, Perry, and Herman (1991) pointed out that self-injurious behavior is "quite distinct from suicide attempts in intent, lethality, age at onset, sex ratio, and interpersonal meaning" (1665).

Paivio and McCulloch (2004) described self-injurious behavior as "intentional non-lethal self-injury, among non-psychotic and non-developmentally disordered individuals [that] includes behaviors such as head banging, hair pulling, scratching, burning, and cutting self" (340). They pointed out that self-cutting is the most frequent form of self-injurious behavior. Paivio and McCulloch also noted that repetitive self-injury is a defining feature of Borderline Personality Disorder, but they pointed out that self-injurious behavior is also a correlate of a number of other psychological disturbances, including depression, obsessive-compulsive disorder, Posttraumatic Stress Disorder, eating disorders, and substance abuse. Thus self-injurious behavior tends to characterize those with Borderline Personality Disorder, but it may appear among individuals with differing diagnoses as well.

The typical self-mutilator is a female adolescent or young adult who is single, intelligent, and comes from a middle-class or upper-class family (Darche 1990; Favazza and Conterio 1988). The self-injurious behavior typically begins during adolescence, and it often stops after ten to fifteen years (Favazza and Rosenthal 1993; van der Kolk et al. 1991). In contrast, suicidal behavior is more common after midlife, and during the midlife period completed suicides are more common among males than among females (Favazza and Conterio 1988).

Self-injurious behavior and suicidal behavior also differ in their impact on affect. Dubo and her colleagues (1997) noted that "unlike suicidal behavior, self-mutilation is associated with relief from intolerable affects, such as despair, anxiety, rage, loneliness, and self-hatred" (108). Self-mutilation has also been described as alleviating feelings of depersonalization (Favazza 1989). These dysphoric affects are often precipitated by a crisis in personal relationships involving real or perceived rejection or abandonment. Leibenluft, Gardner, and Cowdry (1987) argued that in the context of rejection or abandonment, self-mutilation, unlike suicidal acts, can serve as a means of communicating to others a state of internal distress that cannot be put into words.

Childhood Abuse and Self-destructive Behaviors

Despite the differences between self-injurious behavior and suicidal behavior in terms of the groups primarily affected, the typical course of symptoms, the affective outcomes of the behaviors, and psychological meaning of the behaviors, a substantial body of empirical data leaves little doubt that both these forms of self-destructive behavior are associated with childhood trauma. Several studies have shown that abused children tend to display self-destructive behavior patterns immediately. Other studies have shown that self-destructive behaviors experienced during childhood are associated with the emergence of self-destructive behaviors subsequent to the abuse, either during adolescence or later in adulthood.

Children

With respect to early manifestations of self-destructive behavior, several empirical studies have reported relationships between early physical abuse, sexual abuse, and/ or neglect and the emergence of both self-injury and suicidal tendencies during childhood. Based on a study of a group of children who had been physically and sexually abused, Green (1978) reported significantly elevated rates of self-destructive behaviors including head banging, biting, burning, and cutting. Rosenthal and Rosenthal (1984) studied a group of sixteen children between the ages of two and five who had been victims of abuse and neglect. They found that these children displayed elevated levels of both self-injurious and suicidal behavior. These findings are consistent with primate research, which has indicated that disruptions in maternal caretaking are associated with self-mutilation. Mineka and Suomi (1978) reported that when young rhesus monkeys were separated from their mothers, they tended to bite themselves and bang their heads.

Adolescents

Numerous studies have indicated that a history of childhood physical and sexual abuse is related to both self-injurious behavior and suicidal behavior among adolescents. Several studies have indicated that the experience of prior or concurrent physical abuse is related to suicidal ideation and behavior among adolescents. Grossman, Milligan, and Deyo (1991) reported a significant relationship between self-reported physical abuse and suicidal phenomena among Navajo adolescents. Jones (1992) reported a significant relationship among adolescents between the self-reported frequency of being hit by an adult in the family that made them bleed or left a bruise and the self-reported frequency of suicidal thoughts, plans, and attempts. Wagman Borowsky, Resnick, Ireland, and Blum (1999) studied physical abuse and suicidal tendencies among Native American adolescents. They found that being physically abused, either by a family member or anyone else, was related significantly to frequency of suicide attempts. These authors also reported that this relationship pertained to both female and male participants.

Several studies have also supported the relationship between history of childhood sexual abuse and suicidal phenomena among adolescent populations (Beautrais 2000; Bensley, Van Eenwyk, Spieker, and Schoder 1999; Buddeberg, Buddeberg, Gnam, Schmid, and Christen 1996; Fergusson, Horwood, and Lynskey 1996; Grossman et al. 1991; Martin 1996; Martin, Bergen, Richardson, Roeger, and Allison 2004; Rey Gex, Narring, Ferron, and Michaud 1998; Wagman Borowsky et al. 1999). Bensley and associates (1999) reported that adolescents' self-reports of (intrafamilial) sexual abuse and/or (extrafamilial) sexual molestation were related significantly to their self-reports of the "most serious suicidal phenomena" they had experienced. Response options with respect to the latter variable comprised a four-point Likert-type scale, as follows: (1) suicidal thoughts; (2) suicidal plans; (3) noninjurious suicide attempt(s); and (4) injurious suicide attempt(s). Bensley and colleagues found that adolescents with a history of sexual abuse or molestation tended to report significantly more serious suicidal phenomena than those who did not report such a history. Respondents who reported experiencing both intrafamilial sexual abuse and extrafamilial molestation were most likely to report a history of injurious suicide attempts. This finding is in line with the general tendency alluded to in the chapter on substance abuse above, for more extensive patterns of childhood abuse and a larger number of adverse childhood experiences tend to be associated with more serious subsequent pathology.

Martin and colleagues (2004) surveyed 2,485 adolescents from twenty-seven Australian schools. The average age of the respondents was fourteen years. The survey asked respondents to indicate if they had ever been sexually abused and if so, by whom. The survey also asked those who reported a history of sexual abuse to rate their current level of distress in regard to the abuse. The survey assessed suicidal tendencies with a series of questions that covered thinking about suicide, making plans to commit suicide without carrying them out, making threats of suicide to others, and actually attempting suicide. The survey also measured depressive symptoms (using the Center for Epidemiological Studies Depression Scale), hopelessness (using the Beck Hopelessness Scale), and global family functioning (using the family assessment device general functioning subscale).

Female respondents were more likely to report histories of sexual abuse than males (5.4 percent of females versus 2.0 percent of males). Respondents who reported a history of sexual abuse were significantly more likely than those not reporting abuse to report to have (1) thought about killing themselves (73 percent of the abused group versus 25 percent of nonsexually abused group); (2) made plans to kill themselves (55 percent of the abused group versus 12 percent of the nonsexually abused group); (3) threatened to kill themselves (45 percent of the abused group versus 9 percent of the nonsexually abused group); and (4) actually attempted to kill themselves (24 percent of the abused group versus 5 percent of the nonsexually abused group). Among males, these relationships continued to be significant after controlling for depression, hopelessness, and family dysfunction. Among females, the relationships between sexual abuse and these indicators of suicidal tendencies were mediated by depression, hopelessness, and family dysfunction.

In addition, Martin and his associates found that respondents' reports of the subjective distress they experienced in relation to the sexual abuse experience were related significantly to several suicidal tendencies indicators. Sexually abused girls who reported current high levels of distress over sexual abuse they had experienced were three times more likely than nonabused girls to report experiencing suicidal thoughts or making suicide plans. Sexually abused boys who reported current high levels of distress over their abuse experience were ten times more likely than nonsexually abused boys to report suicidal thoughts or plans, and they were fifteen times more likely to report actual suicide attempts. These investigators concluded that "a history of sexual abuse should alert clinicians . . . to greatly increased risks of suicidal behavior and attempts in boys, even in the absence of depression and hopelessness" (2004, 491).

Oates (2004) reviewed the results of several recent studies of the relationship between child sexual abuse and suicidal tendencies among adolescents. Oates concluded that the literature clearly supported the conclusion that sexual abuse is a risk factor for suicidal behavior among adolescents. Oates concluded further that "the risk appears to be a cumulative one with other factors such as ongoing distress about the abuse, family dysfunction and other adverse life events all contributing" (488). Oates recommended that practitioners who see adolescents with clinical or emotional problems should routinely inquire about sexual abuse history and suicidal thoughts and behaviors. He also recommended that clinicians work to alleviate family dysfunction and symptoms of dysphoria among adolescent patients.

Also based on a review of the recent literature, Evans, Hawton, and Rodham (2005) concluded that "there is a clear link between different types of abuse and suicidal phenomena occurring during childhood and adolescence" (54). However, Evans and her colleagues cautioned that abuse is but one of several factors that may contribute to suicidal behaviors in adolescents. The other etiological factors they named included "psychiatric disorder, some personality traits and coping styles, emotional and socio-economic deprivation, interpersonal problems, social isolation, media influence and the availability of methods for self-harm" (55).

There is some data suggesting that a history of various forms of abuse is associated not only with increased suicidal tendencies among adolescents but also increased self-injurious behavior (Martin et al. 2004; Ludolph, Westen, and Misle 1990). The study by Westen and associates (1990) employed an adolescent psychiatric inpatient sample, including borderline and nonborderline patients. This study found a significant relationship between self-reported history of childhood sexual abuse and scores on the impulse section of the Diagnostic Interview for Borderlines (DIB) (Gunderson, Kolb, and Austin 1981). This scale measures self-mutilation as well as manipulative suicide attempts. Westen and colleagues did not find a significant relationship between history of childhood sexual abuse and life-threatening suicide attempts.

The study reported by Martin and associates (2004) described above employed a community sample of adolescents. The investigators assessed not only indicators of suicidal tendencies but also deliberate self-injury. They found that adolescents who had been sexually abused were significantly more likely than non–sexually abused adolescents to deliberately injure themselves (54 percent of the sexually abused group versus 17 percent of the non–sexually abused group).

College Students

Several studies have focused on the relationships between various forms of childhood abuse and various forms of self-destructive behavior among populations of young adults attending college (Bryant and Range 1995; Paivio and

McCulloch 2004; Peters and Range 1995; Rodriguez-Srednicki 2001; Stepakoff 1998). The study reported by Rodriguez-Srednicki (2001), referred to above in the contexts of binge eating, substance abuse, and risky sexual behavior, also examined self-mutilation and suicidal tendencies in a sample of female college students. Rodriguez-Srednicki reported that the women in her sample who reported a history of childhood sexual abuse (n = 175) did not differ significantly from those who did not (n = 266) on a one-item self-report rating of frequency self-mutilation during the previous year. However, the two groups did differ significantly with respect to mean number of self-reported suicide attempts during the previous year. The group reporting a history of sexual abuse was significantly higher with respect to suicide attempts.

Paivio and McCulloch (2004) studied various forms of childhood abuse and self-injurious behavior among a sample of 100 female undergraduates. They measured childhood abuse using the Childhood Trauma Questionnaire (CTQ) (Bernstein and Fink 1998). The CTQ is a twenty-eight-item questionnaire that yields subscale scores for five forms of childhood abuse, including: (1) emotional abuse (e.g., People in my family said hurtful and insulting things to me); (2) physical abuse (e.g., I was punished with a belt, board, cord, or some other hard object); (3) sexual abuse (e.g., Someone tried to touch me in a sexual way or make me touch them); (4) emotional neglect (e.g., People in my family felt close to each other); and (5) physical neglect (e.g., I had enough to eat). Paivio and McCulloch measured self-injurious behavior with the Self-Injurious Behaviors Questionnaire (SIBQ). This is a six-item questionnaire. Respondents use a four-point Likert-type scale to rate the lifetime frequency with which they had engaged in each of the following forms of self-injurious behavior: cutting, burning, head banging, scratching, hair pulling, and punching. These are the most common forms of self-injurious behavior (Osuch, Noll, and Putnam 1999). Response options in each case range from "never" to "often/many times."

Paivio and McCulloch (2004) reported that 41 percent of their sample indicated engaging in at least one form of deliberate self-injurious behavior. Most of those who reported one such behavior reported other forms of self-injury as well. Self-cutting was the form of self-injury reported most frequently. Moreover, Paivio and McCulloch reported significant positive correlations between each of the five forms of childhood abuse measured by the CTQ and the overall score for self-injurious behavior derived from the SIBQ. These correlations ranged in magnitude from .25 to .37. These findings provide strong support for the relationship between history of childhood abuse and self-mutilation among college women. The difference between the findings reported by Rodriguez-Srednicki (2001) and those reported by Paivio and McCulloch (2004) with respect to self-injury may well result from the more reliable measure of self-injurious behavior employed in the latter study.

Adults

Numerous studies link various forms of childhood abuse to both suicidal behavior and self-injurious behavior among adults in diverse populations.

Clinical Samples

Many of these studies have employed psychiatric patient samples (Bryer, Nelson, Miller, and Krol 1987; Links, Boiago, and Huxley 1990; Russ, Shearin, and Clarkin 1993; van der Kolk, Perry, and Herman 1991). Bryer and associates (1987) found that among a sample of sixty-six adult female inpatients, those reporting a history of childhood sexual abuse were not only more likely to be diagnosed as borderline than those not reporting childhood sexual abuse, but also exhibited more suicidal behavior. Links et al. (1990) studied eighty-eight inpatients diagnosed with Borderline Personality Disorder. They found that the BPD patients who reported a history of childhood sexual abuse were more likely than those who did not report childhood sexual abuse to display self-mutilation and other self-damaging behavior.

Van der Kolk, Perry, and Herman (1991) studied seventy-four women between the ages of eighteen and thirty-nine who had been diagnosed with one or more DSM-III personality disorders, including Borderline Personality Disorder, Antisocial Personality Disorder, Schizotypal Personality Disorder, and Bipolar II Disorder. Van der Kolk and his colleagues found that a history of childhood physical and sexual abuse predicted both self-injurious behavior and suicide attempts.

Abuse history was assessed by administering the Traumatic Antecedents Questionnaire (TAQ) (Herman, Perry, and van der Kolk 1989). The TAQ is a hundred-item semistructured questionnaire that assesses both history of various forms of abuse and history of disruptions in parental care. The TAQ includes questions about primary caretakers as well as other important relationships in childhood and adolescence. It assesses physical and sexual abuse, the presence of domestic violence in the home, substance abuse within the family, and patterns of family discipline and conflict resolution. The TAQ assesses disruptions in parental care in four distinct areas: physical neglect, emotional neglect, family chaos, and separations from primary caregivers. Each of these four types of disrupted parental care was assessed at each of three points in the life span: 0–6 years, 7–12 years, and 13–18 years.

Van der Kolk and his colleagues obtained data on self-destructive ideas and behavior during intake, using the Impulse Anger Checklist (Perry and

Cooper 1986). This measure included a rating for suicidal ideation and counts of the number of reported suicide attempts, episodes of skin cutting, head banging, and self-burning. The Impulse Anger Checklist also included counts of participants' reports of the number of episodes of risky behavior they had engaged in, as well as the number of occurrences of eating disordered behaviors. The latter maladaptive behaviors are sometimes grouped with self-mutilation and suicidal behaviors under the overall heading of self-destructive behavior.

The results of this study indicated that thirty-nine of the seventy participants assessed at intake (56 percent) had made one or more suicide attempts. Both history of childhood neglect and history of childhood sexual abuse were significant predictors of suicidal behavior. Self-cutting was reported by twenty-eight of the participants (40 percent). Self-cutting was predicted by history of childhood physical abuse, history of childhood sexual abuse, history of childhood neglect, history of family chaos, and history of parental separations. The frequency of occurrence of other forms of self-injurious behavior, including self-burning, was related significantly to neglect and family chaos.

Ystgaard, Hestetun, Loeb, and Mehlum (2004) studied seventy-four women and men who were admitted consecutively to a general hospital after a suicide attempt. As part of the admission process, these patients were interviewed regarding prior suicide attempts and self-mutilation. The Childhood Experience of Care and Abuse (CECA) interview schedule was used to assess childhood sexual abuse, physical abuse, neglect, antipathy from parents, loss of parents, and severe discord in the family before the age of eighteen. The investigators found that within this sample the proportion of patients reporting each form of childhood abuse assessed was elevated. The proportion reporting "severe" sexual abuse was 35 percent and the proportion reporting "severe" physical abuse was 18 percent. The proportion reporting neglect was 27 percent and the proportion reporting parental antipathy was 34 percent. Loss of a caregiver was reported by 37 percent of the sample, and exposure to family violence was reported by 31 percent. Both physical and sexual abuse were independently associated with repeated suicide attempts, even after controlling for the effects of other adverse childhood factors. A history of physical and/or sexual abuse was most likely among patients who reported both self-mutilation and repeated suicide attempts.

Community Samples

There is ample research demonstrating the relationship between childhood abuse and self-destructive behavior in populations of adults drawn from the community (Bagley and Ramsey 1986; Boudewyn and Liem 1995; Brown, Cohen, Johnson, and Smailes 1999; Molnar, Berkman, and Buka 2001; Romans, Martin, Anderson, Herbison, Mullen, and Phil 1995; Silverman, Reinherz, and Giaconia 1996).

Etiological Models Explaining the Relationship between Child Abuse and Self-destructive Behavior

Our review of the literature revealed a minimum of four different theoretical explanations that have been proposed to explain the relationship between childhood abuse and subsequent self-destructive behavior. These involve (1) self-hatred and self-punishment; (2) dissociation and the failure of embodiment; (3) the neurobiological models; and (4) the emotion regulation model. The following sections consider these different models in turn.

Self-hatred and Self-punishment

The most venerable and most straightforward theory explaining the link between childhood abuse and self-destructive behavior, developed primarily in the context of childhood sexual abuse, suggests that victims tend to feel self-hatred, which is often translated into self-punishment in the form of self-mutilation or other self-destructive behaviors (Knittle and Tuana 1980; MacFarlane and Waterman 1986; Summit 1983). Knittle and Tuana (1980) described self-mutilation as a form of anger turned inward. In the extreme this anger may lead to suicidal tendencies (Bess and Janssen 1982; Vander Mey and Neff 1982).

Shapiro (1987) suggested that victims of childhood sexual abuse feel self-hatred because they blame themselves for their bad behavior; they harm themselves physically in order to punish themselves for their transgressions. They feel intense anger because of the abuse they experience, but they are unable to physically strike out against their powerful abuser. Thus they are left with no place toward which to direct their anger except toward themselves. Self-cutting is perhaps the form of self-destructive activity that most clearly manifests anger toward the self. Van der Kolk, Perry, and Herman (1991) reported that victims of childhood sexual abuse were more likely to engage in this behavior than were victims of other forms of childhood abuse. They also reported that self-cutting tended to be more severe to the extent that the sexual abuse began at an earlier age.

Shengold (1979) suggested another reason why sexually abused children must blame themselves for the abuse they experience. The abused child cannot blame the abusing parent because the child depends on the abuser:

If the very parent who abuses and is experienced as *bad* must be turned to for relief of the distress that the parent has caused, then the child must, out of desperate need, register the parent—delusionally—as good. Only the mental image of a good parent can help the child deal with the terrifying intensity of fear and rage that is the effect of the tormenting experiences. The alternative—the maintenance of the overwhelming stimulation and the bad parental imago—means annihilation of identity, of the feeling of self. So the bad has to be registered as good. This is a mind-splitting or a mind fragmenting operation. (Shengold 1979, 536)

But if the child must cling to the belief that the parent is good, then she or he cannot blame the offending parent for the abuse. This leads to the victim blaming herself and even trying to make amends to the abusing parent. Often this takes the form of compliance with the sexual demands of the abusing parent. Compliance may exacerbate the tendency toward self-blame, particularly if any aspect of the sexual abuse is experienced as gratifying.

Summit (1983) referred to this dynamic of self-blame as the Child Sexual Abuse Accommodation Syndrome. He pointed out that abusing parents often take advantage of this syndrome by rewarding sexual compliance. Rewards may take the form of attention, in the sense that the victim receives affection and praise in the context of the sexual activity. Rewards may also take the form of tangible gifts. Such bribes may reinforce the victim's guilt feelings and leave her or him feeling like a prostitute. The abuser typically also demands that the abuse be kept secret, threatening that disclosure would destroy the family, cause the victim's mother to experience great pain, or perhaps lead the abuser to turn his attention to one of the victim's siblings. Compliance with the demand for secrecy adds further to the victim's tendency toward self-blame. Summit described the dilemma of the victim as follows:

In the classic role reversal of child abuse, the child is given the power to destroy the family and the responsibility to keep it together. The child, *not the parent*, must mobilize the altruism and self-control to insure the survival of the others. The child, in short, must secretly assume many of the role functions of the mother. There is an inevitable splitting of conventional moral values. Maintaining a lie to keep the secret is the ultimate value, while telling the truth would be the greatest sin. A child thus victimized will appear to accept or seek sexual contact without complaint. (1983, 185)

Presented with the dilemma of reconciling the painful reality of abuse with the need to protect the abuser and the family, victims employ diverse coping strategies. They may dissociate or develop altered states of consciousness to distance themselves from the pain. They may develop alexithymia. In extreme cases, they may develop Dissociative Identity Disorder. In the event that multiple personalities develop, the victim may use one persona to deal with helplessness and suffering, another to express badness and rage, and still another to express compassion and love. While these coping strategies are adaptive at the time of the abuse, they lay the foundation for subsequent pathology. Furthermore,

> If the child cannot create a psychic economy to reconcile continuing outrage, the intolerance of helplessness and the increasing feeling of rage will seek active expression. For a girl this often leads to self-destruction and reinforcement of self-hate; self-mutilation, suicidal behavior, promiscuous sexual activity and repeated runaways are typical. She may learn to exploit the father for privileges, favors, and material rewards, reinforcing her self-punishing image as "whore" in the process. . . . Ultimately the child tends to believe that she is so rotten that she was never worth caring for. (1983, 185)

Summit argued that the male victim of sexual abuse is more likely than the female to turn his rage outward in an aggressive and antisocial manner. The male is likely to be even more intolerant of his helplessness than the female, and he is more likely to rationalize that he is exploiting the relationship for his own benefit. However, the end result will still include self-blame and guilt.

Miller (1994) also focused on the victim's anger and on gender differences in the manner in which anger is handled. She argued from a feminist perspective that women are socialized to internalize anger, whereas men are typically taught to express anger outwardly. She stated that "men act out [and] women act out by acting in" (6). Miller suggested that some women with a history of severe abuse who feel unable to express their rage outwardly become trapped in a cycle in which they continuously reenact what happened to them as children by inflicting harm on themselves.

Finkelhor and Browne (1985) pointed out other social dynamics that frequently exacerbate the tendency of the victim of child sexual abuse to blame the self and experience feelings of badness, shame, and guilt. For example, society tends to stigmatize victims of sexual assault and sexual abuse, and this stigmatization extends to child sexual abuse. "Stigmatization is also reinforced by attitudes that the victim hears from other persons in the family or community" (533). Finkelhor and Browne argued that stigmatization may grow out of the child's prior knowledge or sense that the activity is considered deviant and taboo, as well as the child's fear that she or he may be viewed as at least partially responsible for the sexual activity. This knowledge is likely to reinforce the child's tendency to keep the abuse secret, thus contributing to the guilt that the victim already feels for allowing the abuse to take place.

If the child does disclose the abuse, stigmatization may be further exacerbated by the shocked reaction of those to whom the disclosure is made. These people may not respond to the victim by reassuring her that she was not to blame. They may believe that the abuse did in fact occur, but they may also blame the child for what happened. Alternatively, they may assume that the abuse never occurred, and that the victim is lying and maliciously attempting to cause trouble for the alleged abuser or for the entire family. In either case, the effect is to foster the continuation of the victim's self-blame, as well as the concomitant tendency to punish the self through various forms of self-destructive behavior.

Even though the etiological model linking child abuse to self-destructive behavior has been developed primarily within the context of childhood sexual abuse, some of the elements of this theoretical model apply to other forms of child abuse and neglect as well. For example, physical abuse at the hands of a parent represents another experience in which the child is likely to try to maintain a positive image of the parent on whom he depends, and likely to do so by assuming that he somehow deserves the abuse he has received. Neglect and emotional abuse may similarly cause the child to develop an extremely negative self-concept, self-hatred, and the feeling that he deserves pain and punishment. Thus clinicians working with patients who have displayed a tendency toward self-destructive behavior should assess for various forms of childhood abuse and, further, for self-blame, feelings of guilt and shame, lack of self-worth, and a sense that one somehow deserves physical and emotional pain.

Dissociation and the Reformulation of Embodiment

Van der Kolk and Kadish (1987) explained the relationship between childhood sexual abuse and self-mutilation by suggesting that the experience of sexual abuse leads to the development of self-protective mechanisms such as dissociation, depersonalization, emotional disconnection, and physical analgesia. These self-protective mechanisms serve to defend the victim from the physical and psychic pain associated with the specific acts of abuse, but they also leave the victim feeling generally unreal, detached, and numb. Self-mutilation may then develop as a form of self-stimulation, a means through which the victim can once again feel real and alive. Thus Favazza and Conterio (1988) characterized self-injurious behavior as a "purposeful if morbid act of self-help" (288).

Dissociation can also be used to explain the relationship between childhood abuse of various kinds and subsequent suicidal tendencies. A victim of childhood abuse may blame himself for the abuse, feel that he is worthless or evil, and believe that he deserves to be punished or even killed. However, the same social prohibitions that might cause a victim to feel guilt regarding childhood sexual experiences might also constrain that victim from actually attempting to commit suicide. During a dissociative episode, however, the victim may be freed from the normal constraining effects of social prohibitions regarding suicide. Steinberg (1995) noted that the most extreme form of dissociation is Dissociative Identity Disorder (DID), formerly known as multiple personality disorder. The most extreme form of self-destructive behavior is suicide. Fine (1990) even suggested that in a patient with several different alter personalities, one alter personality may think that he or she can kill another alter by means of a suicide attempt, without killing himself as well.

Thus there appears to be a twofold role for dissociation in the emergence of self-destructive behaviors: (1) the self-destructive behaviors may be thought of as providing relief from the numbed state that accompanies continuing dissociation and (2) current dissociation can free the individual from the normal cognitive constraints which would be expected to inhibit the self-destructive behavior. In this regard, one might speculate that survivors who engage in self-cutting may well be in a dissociated state when they do so. This would explain why they report feeling no pain until after the cutting incident is terminated; and it would also explain why they are not constrained from engaging in a behavior that is obviously viewed as abhorrent by society. It is also possible that during the self-cutting the survivor is reliving abuse experiences, but now the victim has assumed control over the parameters of the abuse.

Young (1992) suggested an amplified role for dissociation in the emergence of self-destructive behavior in her discussion of "the problem of embodiment" (89). She began by noting that based on the accumulated reports of those who have been sexually abused, the progression of dissociative phenomena "seems to be from an involuntary, physical experience of dissociation suffered during a traumatic event or during an initial episode of ongoing abuse to the voluntary inducement of dissociative states through self-hypnosis" (92). Once dissociation has progressed to the point where it may be induced at will, the survivor may use it to reformulate the definition and conditions of his personal identity. Young explained that for most people under most circumstances, some of the events go on inside my body are experienced by me as essentially physical—part and parcel of having a body and being embodied, while other internal events, such as thinking, imagining, remembering, dreaming, etc., although physiological processes, are experienced by me as essentially nonphysical, somehow independent of my body and my sense of being embodied.

For the survivor of severe trauma, including the survivor of severe sexual abuse, a radical reformulation of the conditions of personal identity may be required. So, on the one hand, post-trauma, me and mine might not be defined as events that go on inside my body but rather as events that go on inside my head exclusively (where the head means either "mind" or not "inside my body"), such as thinking, imagining, speaking, and remembering (where those memories are emotionally neutral), etc. On the other hand, events which go on inside my body, which seem to be essentially physical and inescapably tied to embodiment such as sexual, sensuous, affective, or proprioceptive experiences, no longer have anything to do with me, they are not me. (93)

Young (1992) argued that such a reformulation of one's personal identity can give the survivor some measure of control over painful past events. The survivor can forget or wall off memories of traumatic events by consigning them to the body, while at the same time excluding all bodily sensations and intense affects from consciousness. However, this adaptation entails an enormous sacrifice, since it also "makes problematic experiencing the everyday pleasures, sensations, and comforts of human embodiment" (93). Such reformulated embodiment would also help to explain the anhedonia and sexual dysfunction that frequently characterize adult survivors of childhood sexual abuse. Moreover, if victims effect reformulations of their personal identity such that the body and all experiences inside the body are "not me," then what the outside world views as self-abuse, including self-mutilation and suicide attempts, is not experienced as self-abuse by the survivors. Having succeeded in making their bodily experiences and sensations part of the "not me," victims have placed themselves in a position where they can treat their bodies with the same callous disregard that their abusers demonstrated.

The Neurobiological Models
Several neurobiological models have been suggested to explain the association between childhood abuse and the subsequent emergence of self-destructive behavior. Kirmayer and Carroll (1987) noted that people who are exposed to repeated shocks and injuries gradually become physiologically less sensitive to pain. They also develop elevated levels of enkephalin, one of the painkillers that is produced naturally by the body. Abused children

may become habituated to these elevated enkephalin levels. However, as adults, in times of calm or isolation, enkephalin levels may drop, creating a virtual withdrawal condition, characterized by increased tension and dysphoria. For such individuals, self-mutilation may amount to an attempt to alleviate anxiety and elevate enkephalin levels. These self-mutilators would be increasing their sensitivity by injuring themselves. Kirmayer and Carroll noted that self-mutilators often report feelings of euphoria when they push the boundaries of acceptable behavior by cutting themselves and running the risk of getting caught. These investigators also noted that some individuals who cut themselves report that their self-injurious behavior makes them feel special and unique. If they did not cut themselves, they would be just like everyone else.

Van der Kolk and Greenburg (1987) hypothesized that self-destructive behavior may result from trauma-induced psychophysiological changes involving an increase in neuronal excitability in the limbic system that interferes with normal mechanisms of regulating affect and behavior. This view has received some support in research reported by Teicher, Ito, and Glod (1993), who found that individuals reporting histories of various forms of childhood abuse tended to manifest symptoms of limbic system dysfunction and EEG abnormalities. Teicher and colleagues also reported that early trauma may impact the laterality of the developing brain in such a way as to cause increased right hemisphere activity and reduced interhemispheric communication. They suggested that the greater reliance on right hemisphere activity among individuals who have been abused as children might contribute to the emergence of impulsive behaviors such as self-mutilation.

Some data suggests a role for the dopaminergic systems in the emergence of self-destructive behavior. Winchel and Stanley (1991) reported several case studies of patients for whom the administration of opiate antagonistic medications appeared to diminish self-destructive behavior. There have also been reports suggesting that serotonergic dysfunction may be associated with both self-mutilation and suicidal behavior (Simeon, Stanley, and Frances 1992; Winchel and Stanley 1992). However, based on a review of the literature on the neurobiology of self-destructive behavior, Dubo and her colleagues (1997) concluded that the empirical evidence for the efficacy of pharmacological treatments for self-injurious behavior is limited.

The Emotion Regulation Model

Several investigators have linked the emergence of self-destructive behavior to difficulties in emotional regulation that result from various forms of childhood abuse (van der Kolk and Fisler 1994; van der Kolk, Perry, and Herman

1991). These investigators suggested that experiences of abuse and neglect during childhood impair the development of the capacity for self-regulation of affective states, as well as the capacity for using interpersonal relationships to help regulate emotional states. Paivio and McCulloch (2004) suggested that there are several components to effective emotional regulation. First, as first proposed by Fridja (1986), for an individual who is confronted with an affectively laden situation, effective emotional regulation requires the ability to modulate emotional intensity to avoid being overwhelmed or shutting down. In addition, as posited by Gross (1999), the individual must be able to communicate his or her feelings and needs to others in order to elicit required interpersonal support.

It has been suggested that the key components of emotional regulation cannot develop in a vacuum. The development of these capabilities requires that primary caretakers monitor and respond appropriately to the child's emotional expressions (Gottman 1997; Sroufe 1995; Wheeler and Broad 1994). In short, children must be taught how to regulate their emotional experience and derive comfort from others. Abused and neglected children face a twofold problem in this regard, since experiences of abuse are likely to arouse intense negative emotions, and at the same time the abusing parents are likely to ignore or invalidate these feelings. Thus Paivio and McCulloch argued that

> These family environments therefore provide limited opportunities for children to learn about and express feelings appropriately, and limited support for coping with painful emotional experiences. Survivors of severe childhood trauma, without effective capacities for emotion regulation can experience intense disorganization in the face of current stress. This can precipitate impulsive or aggressive actions, including self-injurious behavior, in order to express emotional pain and distress. (2004, 341)

In short, abuse and neglect leave the victim in pain and inhibit the capacity to express painful affect appropriately and thereby derive support and solace from others. As a result, some victims employ self-mutilation in an effort to communicate their pain (Kench and Irwin 2000; van der Kolk et al. 1991).

Several studies support this theory of the etiology of self-destructive behaviors. Favazza and Rosenthal (1993) asked self-injuring patients to describe their motivations. They found that the patients almost always referred to efforts to cope with negative emotional states. Among the reasons given were the reduction of emotional numbness, distraction from emotional pain, the release of anger and tension, relief from feelings of loneliness and alienation, and eliciting emotional support or comforting. Soloman and Farrand

(1996) reported that self-injurious behavior tends to occur primarily among women who are incapable of expressing their emotional needs, and they concluded that the self-injurious behaviors had the effect of substituting manageable physical pain for unmanageable emotional pain. Osuch, Noll, and Putnam (1999) asked patients to rate a series of statements reflecting possible motivations for self-injurious behavior. When these ratings were factor analyzed, five of the six factors extracted were related to the regulation or communication of emotion.

~

CHAPTER NINE

Childhood Abuse and Posttraumatic Stress Disorders

PTSD and Complex PTSD

Note that the title of this chapter refers to Posttraumatic Stress Disorders in the plural. In this chapter we consider (1) Posttraumatic Stress Disorder (PTSD) as defined specifically by the diagnostic criteria listed for PTSD in the last several editions of the *Diagnostic and Statistical Manual of Mental Disorders* (e.g., DSM-III-R 1987; DSM-IV 1994; DSM-IV-TR 2000) and (2) "Complex Posttraumatic Stress Disorder," as proposed initially by Herman (1992a,b). The original PTSD diagnosis, now sometimes referred to as "simple PTSD" (Herman 1992a, 379), was first employed by Gelinas (1983) to explain the effects of childhood sexual abuse.

Herman (1992a,b, 1993) subsequently argued that the actual diagnostic criteria for PTSD applied specifically to the impact of circumscribed traumatic events, such as a single occurrence of rape, and she proposed the expanded concept of Complex Posttraumatic Stress Disorder to represent the symptoms that characterize victims with histories of "prolonged, repeated trauma [which] can occur only where a victim is in a state of captivity, unable to flee, and under the control of the perpetrator" (Herman 1992a, 377). The latter description applies perfectly to a child who is repeatedly abused by a parent or parent surrogate, either physically or sexually.

A Case of Complex PTSD

Claire was forty-five when she entered treatment. The precipitating events were her second divorce and what she described as the resulting realization that her life was a disaster. Claire was quite attractive. She was a bit overweight, but in a voluptuous way. She wore an expensive business suit that was appropriate but also sexy. She was stylishly coiffed and made up. Claire said that she and the husband who had just divorced her were both physicians. Claire was involved in oncology research and was a tenured professor at a major university medical school. Claire said that her second marriage had lasted less than two years, and that her ex-husband had divorced her because she had been unfaithful.

Then she amended that statement to add that it wasn't just her infidelity that had led to the divorce. Her ex-husband had also complained that he never felt as if she had really engaged in the marriage and connected with him. They had married after a rather brief courtship, and he didn't realize that Claire didn't share his idea about what marriage involves. He said that he had expected them to grow close and to share their innermost feelings and aspirations, but this never happened. He also said that he expected married people to pool their financial resources and obligations. This never happened either. He said that they had been more like housemates who had sex. He complained that she wasn't really interested in his professional life or his family, and he said that she was unable to share her feelings.

Claire said he was right about everything. She had been unfaithful, in fact, more than once, and infidelity had also caused her first divorce, which had occurred just after she finished medical school twenty years ago. She said that the funny thing about her being "chronically unfaithful" was that she didn't really think of herself as an unusually sexual person. Although she had numerous sexual partners over the course of her lifetime, she said that it wasn't like she ran around seducing men. She said that a man would approach her and she would simply comply. She said that "there must be something about her that just gives off a message to come and get me." Claire also said that some of the time she felt attracted to her lovers, and some of the time she didn't. Sometimes sex was pretty good, and sometimes it was more like "a kind of a formality that simply needed to be carried out."

Claire said that even when the sex was good, she never really felt any strong attachment to her lover, and this included her husbands and the men with whom she had lived. She said that once when she was around thirty she had been living with a man for about two months. One day they had a big fight, and she left the apartment for a bar frequented by medical personnel.

There she met and became sexually involved with a doctor whom she described as handsome, intelligent, and powerful. Claire spent that night at the home of the new lover, and the next day she moved in with him. She told her therapist that she picked up her things at her old apartment when she knew her former boyfriend would be at work, and she simply left him a note saying they were through.

Claire also agreed with her ex-husband that she was unable to share her feelings. She said that she felt no urge whatsoever to reveal how she was feeling to any other person. She didn't derive any comfort from telling someone her problems, nor did she derive much joy from sharing her successes and accomplishments. Claire also observed that a lot of the time she didn't feel very much at all, and she didn't see how she could share things that she wasn't feeling. However, at the time she entered treatment, Claire was rapidly becoming aware that things in her life were not right, and she was also beginning to recognize that she was chronically depressed.

Prior to seeking treatment, Claire had sat down at her computer and conducted a kind of a critical review of where she was in life. She brought her new therapist a list that contained the major conclusions of this review. It said that she was (1) smack dab in the middle of her life; (2) divorced; (3) without children; (4) without close friends of either sex; (5) moderately successful professionally but lacking any real sense that her work was either personally stimulating or meaningful; (6) drinking too much and doing too much cocaine; (7) intermittently bulimic; (8) constantly depressed; (9) lacking any meaningful interests or activities other than work; (10) not experiencing any moments of spontaneous happiness or joy; (11) prone to inappropriate outbursts of anger; and (12) out of control sexually.

Claire's therapist was familiar with the construct of complex PTSD and its relationship to prolonged exposure to childhood trauma, so he suspected that Claire had been the victim of severe childhood abuse or neglect. Over time, as their relationship grew, he was able to elicit her recollections of her childhood, and it was clear that she had in fact experienced multiple adverse childhood experiences involving neglect, abandonment, and repeated sexual and physical assault. Claire said that all she knew about her mother was what her father had told her, and it was not pretty. Claire's father described her mother as very beautiful but hopelessly screwed up. She was twenty-three when they met. She was a "hippie artist" in San Francisco, and he was a forty-one-year-old married physician with three kids who was in town for a medical conference. They had a torrid affair that involved the consumption of large quantities of drugs. In a few months Claire's father left his wife and his kids to live with Claire's mother. Claire was born within a year of her parents' first meeting. Six months later Claire's mom was killed in an automobile accident. She was drunk and using cocaine at the time.

Claire did not recall any events from the first four or five years of her life. Her father told her that he had raised her with the help of a housekeeper and various nannies. He told her that when she was seven, he remarried. His third wife, Jane, was closer to his own age. She was a nurse at the hospital where her father was working. He was forty-seven and she was thirty-eight when they married. She had three children from her first marriage, two boys age fourteen and sixteen, and a girl age thirteen. Claire and her dad and his new wife and her three kids all moved in together. Claire said that they had a big house in an affluent suburban community, but "they were not the Brady bunch."

Although it took her a long time to discuss it, Claire remembered the situation in the home quite well. She said that her father and his wife were both heavily involved with their work and were out of the house a lot. Her father's housekeeper took care of the house and looked after Claire. Jane's thirteen-year-old daughter was given the job of baby-sitting for Claire when her father and Jane were out and the housekeeper was not on duty. When her parents were home, they did quite a bit of socializing, and their parties always involved a substantial amount of drinking and drug use. Jane's three children were also involved in drug use. Jane's oldest son was a drug dealer with a rather substantial business. Claire said that neither her father nor Jane seemed to care that this boy was dealing drugs. In fact, she believes that they were occasionally his customers.

Claire reported experiencing various forms of abuse perpetrated by Jane's children, Jane herself, and friends of Jane's children. Jane's daughter thought that it was "cute" to give Claire alcohol and other drugs, and so Claire began using substances early in life. Jane's two sons both began to abuse Claire sexually within a few months of their all moving in together. This began with fondling but eventually involved oral and genital intercourse. Claire said that she was essentially at the disposal of her older stepbrother, who raped her regularly and made her perform oral sex on both him and his brother. Claire said that the older brother made the younger one hold her down while he raped her. Once the younger brother objected, and the older brother beat him until he complied. The older brother also used threats to force his younger brother to perform oral sex on Claire and have vaginal intercourse with her. Claire said the boys also occasionally abused their sister sexually, but not to the same extent as they abused Claire.

Claire said she was sure that her father and stepmother were aware that this abuse was going on, but they did nothing to stop it. They had to know. After all, they were medical people, and several times Claire was injured by the sexual assaults seriously enough as to require minor treatment in the form of topical anesthetics. Claire said that on one occasion she asked Jane to tell her son to stop, but Jane said that Claire must be doing something to encourage him, and if she wanted him to stop she herself would have to get him to stop. Jane also told Claire that she could not bring this up with her father because if she did there might be a big fight and her father could get hurt.

Claire said that eventually she just accepted the abuse when it came. She said that she could anticipate getting raped by what was going on in the house and by her older stepbrother's behavior. If her father and Jane were going to be out for the evening, her stepbrother would begin to touch her and talk about "partying" when they left. Sometimes she was able to make arrangements to be somewhere else in order to avoid the attack, but this didn't work very often. Once she arranged to spend the night at a friend's house, but that strategy backfired because it turned out that her friend's brother was also a friend of her stepbrother, and she ended up that night being raped by both her stepbrother and her friend's brother. Eventually Claire just accepted the fact that she would be raped on a given evening. Then she usually drank to make it easier to bear. Occasionally, especially when she had been drinking or using some other drug, Clair said that she would become excited and experience some pleasure in the sexual behavior. She recollected that this made her feel guilty and confirmed her stepmother's accusation that she must be doing something to bring it on herself.

When her older stepbrother went off to college, the most serious abuse stopped. The younger brother had a sense that what had been going on was not right, so he generally left her alone. He even told her that he felt just as good that his brother was away at college as she did. Even so, she and the younger brother did have sex in which she was a willing participant. Claire said that on these occasions she felt they were having sex to somehow pay tribute to the absent older brother, as if they were both somehow under his continuing spell. Claire remembered that when the older brother had left for college, he had told his younger brother to "take care of Claire for me."

As Claire grew older and moved into middle school, her sexualized behavior continued. She had sex with the first boy who made sexual advances toward her. This happened at the first party she ever attended, in seventh grade. From that point on, Claire never said no. She also continued her use of alcohol and other drugs through adolescence and into adulthood. She observed at one point during treatment that sex was generally perfunctory but could be good if she was stoned. Amazingly, while all this was taking place, Claire had what appeared to be a normal and productive life. She always did well in school, as did her stepsiblings. She went to college and medical school. Her drug use and promiscuity were generally accepted within the academic/medical culture as normative and perhaps even as signs that she was a modern liberated women. Therefore, for a long time, Claire was not aware that she had a "problem." It was not until her second divorce and her midlife recognition of her failure to establish any intimate relationships that Claire realized the extent of her dysfunction and sought help.

PTSD

The DSM has defined Posttraumatic Stress Disorder in terms of the development of a specific set of symptoms following exposure to a traumatic stressor. According to the DSM-IV-R, the traumatic stressor must involve the "direct personal experience of an event that involves actual or threatened death or serious injury, or other threat to one's physical integrity; or witnessing an event that involves death, injury, or a threat to the physical integrity of another person; or learning about unexpected or violent death, serious harm, or threat of death or injury experienced by a family member or other close associate" (APA 2000, 463). Further, the individual's response to the traumatic event must involve intense fear, helplessness, or horror (in children the response must involve disorganized or agitated behavior).

The characteristic symptoms resulting from exposure to such a traumatic event include persistent reexperiencing of the traumatic event, persistent avoidance of stimuli associated with the trauma and numbing of general responsiveness, and persistent symptoms of increased arousal. The traumatic event may be reexperienced in a variety of ways. The victim may experience recurrent and intrusive distressing memories of the traumatic event, including images, thoughts, or perceptions. In young children one may observe repetitive play in which themes or aspects of the trauma are expressed. The victim may experience distressing dreams concerned with the event, although children may experience nightmares with nonspecific or unrecognizable content. Victims may have the feeling that the traumatic event is actually recurring. This feeling may involve illusions, hallucinations, and dissociative flashback episodes. These perceptions may occur upon awakening. They may also occur when the victim is intoxicated. Victims may also experience intense psychological distress and/or marked physiological reactivity when they are exposed internally or externally to cues that symbolize or remind them of the traumatic event. The DSM-IV-TR specifies that a victim must reexperience the traumatic event in at least one of these ways in order to be given a diagnosis of PTSD.

The DSM-IV-TR lists seven different ways in which a victim may manifest avoidance of stimuli associated with the traumatic event and numbing of general responsiveness: (1) The victim may make conscious or unconscious efforts to avoid thoughts or feelings associated with the traumatic event, and conversations about the event. (2) The victim may also make conscious or unconscious efforts to avoid activities, places, or people that arouse recollections of the trauma. (3) The victim may be unable to recall an important aspect of the traumatic event. (4) The victim may experience marked reduction of interest in or participation in previously significant activities. In addition, victims sometimes report (5) feeling detached or estranged from others; (6) having a restricted range of affect, such as an inability to feel loving emotions; and (7) having a sense of a foreshortened future. The latter sense would include a failure to have an expectation that one will have a career, get married, have children, and/or live out a normal life span. The DSM-IV-TR specifies that a diagnosis of PTSD requires that the victim display at least three of these manifestations of avoidance or numbing.

The DSM-IV-TR lists five symptoms of increased arousal, at least two of which must be present to justify a diagnosis of PTSD. These include (1) sleep disturbances; (2) irritability or outbursts of anger; (3) difficulty concentrating; (4) hypervigilance; and (5) an exaggerated startle response.

Assigning the diagnosis of PTSD requires that the specified symptoms have persisted for at last one month and that "the disturbance causes clinically significant distress or impairment in social, occupational, or other important areas of functioning" (APA 2000, 468).

The Relationship of Childhood Abuse to PTSD

There is ample evidence that childhood abuse, including both physical and sexual abuse, is related to being diagnosed as having PTSD. The relationship pertains among victims who are still children or adolescents, as well as among victims of childhood abuse who have become adults. Rodriguez, Vande Kemp, and Foy (1998) provided a thorough critical review of the studies of the relationship between CSA and PTSD, the studies indicating a substantial overlap between history of CSA and history of CPA, and studies comparing the incidence of PTSD diagnoses among survivors of CSA, survivors of CPA, survivors of both CSA and CPA, and comparison samples not reporting any history of childhood abuse.

Posttraumatic Stress Disorder among Sexually Abused Children

Rodriguez and his associates (1998) observed that there were many studies that investigated the incidence of PTSD among sexually abused children. Nine studies were reviewed that reported PTSD rates in clinical samples of sexually abused children. In these studies the incidence of PTSD ranged from a low of 20.7 percent (Deblinger, McLeer, Atkins, Ralphe, and Foa 1989) to a high of 73.5 percent (Sadeh, Hayden, McGuire, Sachs, and Clivita 1994). The disparity in the reported rates of PTSD may be explained by differences in the definition of CSA, and in the measurement procedures employed to assess both CSA and PTSD. In an earlier review of the literature in this area, Rowan and Foy (1993) pointed out that differences in the definitions of CSA employed in these studies resulted in potential differences in the composition of the CSA samples that made it difficult to compare the rates of PTSD reported. On the other hand, in seven of these nine studies the proportion of sexually abused children experiencing PTSD that was reported fell between 40 percent and 50 percent. Thus the bulk of the empirical data suggests a substantial incidence of PTSD among children who have experienced sexual abuse.

Another issue in this research is the presence or absence of a comparison group of non–sexually abused children. Most of these studies did not employ such a group. Rodriguez and colleagues (1998) pointed out that the failure to employ nonabused control groups made it impossible to "definitively isolate CSA as an etiological agent in the development of PTSD in clinical populations of sexually abused children" (21). However, in three of the nine studies such a comparison group was used (Deblinger et al. 1989; McLeer, Deblinger, Henry, and Orvaschel 1992; Sadeh et al. 1994). In all three of these studies, the rate of occurrence of PTSD within the sexually abused sample exceeded the rate within the comparison sample. McLeer and associates (1994) reported a PTSD rate of 42.3 percent within their sexually abused sample, versus a rate of 8.7 percent within a sample of matched nonabused controls. Sadeh and colleagues (1994) reported a PTSD rate of 73.5 percent in their CSA sample, compared to a PTSD rate of just 7.1 percent among nonabused controls. In the study reported by Deblinger et al. (1989) the PTSD rate of 20.7 percent among the CSA group was not statistically different from the PTSD rate of 10.3 percent among the controls. However, both these proportions were relatively low, and Rodriguez and colleagues (1998) suggested that this may have been due to poor operationalization of the measurement of PTSD. Deblinger and colleagues (1989) employed a retrospective measure of PTSD based on clinical review of medical charts, and Rodriguez and colleagues (1998) pointed out that these charts "were completed at a time when many clinicians did not assess for PTSD in sexually abused children" (21).

Another issue associated with this body of research is the possible co-occurrence of forms of childhood trauma other than CSA. Rodriguez and associates (1998) noted that "the experience of other types of trauma in addition to CSA could potentiate CSA-related PTSD in CSA groups [and] the experience of other types of trauma in non–sexually abused 'controls' could elevate PTSD rates in control groups" (22). They therefore recommended that research on the relationship between CSA and PTSD should also assess childhood physical abuse, as well as exposure to interparental violence, community violence, serious accidents, and other traumatic experiences in both the CSA group and the comparison group.

On balance, however, Rodriguez and colleagues concluded that the "existing studies provide preliminary support for a PTSD prevalence rate in the 40–50 percent range for help-seeking sexually abused children." Furthermore, a number of studies have reported significant relationships between selected parameters of childhood sexual abuse and the severity of the PTSD symptoms observed in abused children (Kiser, Heston, Milsap, and Pruitt 1991; McLeer et al. 1994; Wolfe, Sas, and Wekerle 1994). These parameters included the duration of the abuse, the use of coercion, the nature of the sexual abuse (e.g., involving penetration or not), and the relationship of the perpetrator to the victim.

Posttraumatic Stress Disorder among Adults with Histories of Childhood Sexual Abuse

A substantial body of research also supports the existence of a relationship between a history of childhood sexual abuse and an adult diagnosis of PTSD (Albach and Everaerd 1992; Arata 1999c; Cameron 1994; Folette, Polusny, Bechtle, and Naugle 1996; Lawrence, Cozolino, and Foy 1995; Lindberg and Distad 1985; O'Neill and Gupta 1991; Rodriguez, Ryan, Rowan, and Foy 1991; Roesler and McKenzie 1994; Rowan, Foy, Rodriguez, and Ryan 1994; Saunders, Villeponteaux, Lipovsky, Kilpatrick, and Veronen 1992). Commenting on the studies in this group that had been completed at the time of their review article, Rodriguez and colleagues (1998) noted that the same methodological issues pertained in these studies as in the studies of the relationship of CSA to PTSD among children—questions regarding the definition and measurement of both CSA and PTSD, the utilization of nonabused comparison groups, and the assessment of additional forms of trauma experienced during childhood. These issues notwithstanding, Rodriguez and colleagues (1998) concluded that the available evidence did warrant the general conclusion that "a significant portion of adults who experienced CSA involving contact events, especially penetration, may suffer from PTSD at some point in their lives after the abuse" (27).

Based on a nonclinical sample of 131 female CSA survivors, Saunders and associates (1992) reported lifetime PTSD rates of 11.5 percent among survivors who experienced noncontact CSA only, 33.3 percent among survivors who experienced sexual contact not involving penetration, and 64.1 percent among survivors of CSA involving penetration. Based on an outpatient clinical sample of forty-seven adult survivors of CSA, Rowan and associates (1994) reported a current PTSD rate of 69 percent. Furthermore, based on a sample of 117 that included the forty-seven survivors in the study reported by Rowan and colleagues (1994), Rodriguez and colleagues (1991) reported a current rate of PTSD of 72 percent and a lifetime rate of PTSD of 86 percent. Other studies that have employed standardized measures of PTSD have also reported current rates of PTSD among survivors of CSA of 70 percent or more (Lawrence et al. 1995; O'Neill and Gupta 1991). Based on the findings of their study, Rowan and colleagues (1994) recommended that a diagnosis of PTSD should be considered whenever an adult survivor of CSA enters treatment. Based on their review of the literature, Rodriguez and colleagues (1998) concurred with this recommendation.

An important question requiring further investigation is the extent to which symptoms of PTSD experienced by adult survivors of CSA are the direct result of the childhood abuse, as opposed to the result of subsequent adolescent/adult revictimization experiences. Rodriguez and colleagues (1998) noted that Horowitz (1977) and Gelinas (1983) suggested that PTSD symptoms in survivors of CSA "wax and wane over the lifespan of the trauma survivor depending on the survivor's experience of triggering events" (29). For this reason, they recommended doing longitudinal studies of CSA survivors. These studies would assess for PTSD during childhood, adolescence, and adulthood in order to indicate the developmental course of PTSD across the lives of PTSD survivors.

Arata (1999c) added another important reason to carry out such longitudinal studies. She observed that "the time period between the childhood trauma and the assessment of symptoms makes it difficult to be certain that PTSD has resulted from the childhood trauma and not subsequent traumas, in particular, adult/adolescent revictimization" (49). Arata observed that several studies had shown that survivors of CSA are at elevated risk for adult revictimization (Mayall and Gold 1995; Wyatt, Guthrie, and Notgrass 1992), and she raised the question of the extent to which PTSD in adult survivors could be related to a cumulative history of sexual victimization. She also asked whether PTSD might not be just a consequence of CSA and/or adult revictimization, but might possibly contribute to the likelihood of adult revictimization.

To address these questions, Arata interviewed forty-one women with histories of CSA. These women ranged in age from nineteen to forty-seven, with a median age of twenty-four. The interviews assessed past and current diagnoses of PTSD. In addition, the participants completed self-report measures of both victimization histories and current PTSD symptoms. Arata found that among women who reported histories of CSA but no adolescent or adult sexual revictimization, 25 percent were assigned a PTSD diagnosis at some point during their lifetime. In contrast, among women who reported both a history of CSA and sexual revictimization during adolescence and/or adulthood, 36 percent had a lifetime PTSD diagnosis. This difference was statistically significant.

Arata (1999c) examined the onset of symptoms of PTSD, and she reported that 70 percent of those with a lifetime diagnosis of PTSD reported the onset of symptoms during childhood, following the child victimization, whereas 30 percent reported that their PTSD symptoms did not begin until adulthood. All the women who reported CSA only, with no adolescent or adult revictimization, reported that their PTSD symptoms had begun during childhood. Among the women who reported both CSA and subsequent revictimization, 63 percent reported that PTSD symptoms had begun during childhood, whereas 37 percent reported an adult onset of PTSD symptoms. These two proportions did not differ significantly, due to the relatively small numbers of women involved in the comparison (ten revictimized women with childhood onset of PTSD versus six revictimized women with adult onset). Arata concluded that "the lack of significance of this finding suggests that PTSD may be just as likely to be a consequence of repeated victimization [as a consequence of the initial childhood victimization]" (62). Arata also reported a nonsignificant trend among revictimized women for current symptoms to be related to both the frequency of the CSA and the severity of the adult victimization. She therefore suggested that if this study were to be replicated with a larger and more generalizable sample, it might support the theory that PTSD is additive, with components of both the child and adult victimization contributing to the emergence of PTSD symptoms.

Although prospective longitudinal research will be required to clarify the complex relationships among CSA, subsequent sexual revictimization, and the development of symptoms of PTSD, it is clear that these relationships exist. Rodriguez and associates (1998) concluded that the existing research "suggests that at least two-thirds of adult survivors seeking treatment may have experienced PTSD symptoms at some point during their lives" (34). For this reason, these investigators recommended that adult survivors of CSA in treatment, like children and adolescents who have been sexually abused, should always be assessed and treated as necessary for PTSD symptoms.

Child Sexual Abuse, Child Physical Abuse, and PTSD

Far less research has been reported focusing specifically on the relationship between childhood physical abuse (CPA) and PTSD than has been reported on the relationship between childhood sexual abuse (CSA) and PTSD. There is considerable evidence that (1) CPA is as at least as common as CSA, and (2) there is a substantial overlap between the two forms of abuse. Rodriguez and his colleagues (1998) observed that "nonclinical and clinical studies have reported that many sexually abused children also experience physical abuse in childhood" (35). For example, based on a nonclinical sample of 668 women drawn from a gynecologic practice, Moeller, Bachman, and Moeller (1993) reported that 19.8 percent reported a history of CSA and 25.2 percent reported a history of CPA. Moreover, 35.6 percent of the CSA group also reported CPA. Surrey, Swett, Michaels, and Levin (1990) studied an outpatient sample of 140 women. They found that 29 percent of this group reported histories of CSA and 31 percent reported histories of CPA, and that 70 percent of the CSA survivors also reported CPA. Other studies reviewed by Rodriguez and colleagues reported proportions of CSA survivors who also reported experiencing CPA ranging from 41 percent to 83 percent (Brown and Anderson 1991; Chu and Dill 1990; Kirby, Chu, and Dill 1993; Swett and Halpert 1993).

These figures reinforce the need to consider the individual and combined effects of various traumatic experiences in fostering the development of PTSD. In particular, these figures strongly suggest the need to differentiate between the effects on subsequent PTSD of CSA, the effects of CPA, and the effects of experiencing both CSA and CPA. Unfortunately, as pointed out by Rodriguez and colleagues (1998), several of the studies of the relationship between CSA and subsequent PTSD have included victims of both CSA and CPA within the CSA group, thus failing to eliminate the possibility that observed relationships between CSA and PTSD might in fact reflect not just the impact of CSA, but the additive and interactive effects of CPA as well (e.g., Sadeh et al. 1994; McClellan, Adams, Douglas, McCurry, and Storck 1995).

Only a few studies examined the prevalence of PTSD- or PTSD-related symptoms among samples reporting dual abuse (histories of both CSA and CPA) (Adam et al. 1992; Haviland, Sonne, and Woods 1995; Kiser et al. 1991; Wind and Silvern 1992). Furthermore, these studies have been inconsistent with respect to both the comparison groups employed and the operationalization of PTSD. Kiser and associates (1991) reported that within an outpatient sample of abused children, 70.8 percent of those who had experienced both CPA and CSA were diagnosed as having PTSD. In contrast, the PTSD rate was 55 percent among those who experienced either CSA or

CPA, but not both. Unfortunately, collapsing the abuse categories into one form of abuse only versus both does not permit a direct comparison of prevalence of PTSD among victims of CPA only and victims of CPA only. This issue was resolved by Adam, Everett, and O'Neal (1992) in a study of inpatient children. They reported that 43 percent of the children who had experienced CSA only were diagnosed as having PTSD, as were 20 percent of the children who had experienced CPA only, and 21 percent of the children who had experienced both. Why those children who experienced both CPA and CSA were less likely to be diagnosed as having PTSD than those who experienced CSA alone is unclear.

Haviland and associates (1995) studied a sample of thirty-seven adolescents in residential treatment who had histories of CPA, CSA, or both. Of these, seven (18.9 percent) had experienced CPA only; fourteen (37.8 percent) had experienced CSA only; and sixteen (43.2 percent) had experienced both CPA and CSA. These investigators reported that the adolescents in the dual abuse group and those in the CSA only group each had significantly higher scores on a global measure of PTSD symptoms than the adolescents in the CPA only group. Wind and Silvern (1992) studied a nonclinical sample of 259 women. They categorized these women into four groups, representing history of CPA only, history of CSA only, dual abuse, and no abuse history. They administered the Trauma Symptoms Checklist, a self-report measure that includes some PTSD symptoms. Wind and Silvern reported that TSC scores were significantly higher among the dual abuse group than among the other three groups. Thus the literature concerned with the relative impact of CPA, CSA, and dual abuse on PTSD among children, adolescents, and adults is inconclusive. Some studies suggest that dual abuse in childhood is more likely to be accompanied with current or subsequent PTSD than either CPA or CSA alone; and some appear to suggest that CSA alone or in conjunction with CPA is more likely to be associated with PTSD. The latter studies imply that CPA simply tends to occur in conjunction with CSA but does not have an independent role in the etiology of PTSD.

The latter conclusion appears to be supported by the results of a study reported by Pelcovitz, Kaplan, Goldenberg, Mandel, Lehane, and Guarrera (1994) comparing the PTSD rate in a sample of physically abused adolescents to the PTSD rate in a comparable sample of non–physically abused adolescents. These authors reported no significant difference between the CPA group and the no-CPA group on PTSD. Furthermore, the only participants among the CPA group who were classified as manifesting PTSD also had histories of childhood sexual abuse. This finding might also be interpreted as suggesting the irrelevance of CPA. However, given the relatively scant amount of research on the relationship of CPA to PTSD, as well as the methodological issues and the conflicting findings that characterize the existing research, it would be prudent to conclude that a great deal more research needs to be done to understand the nature of this relationship. The effects of the parameters of physical abuse need to be investigated, including age of onset, severity, frequency, duration, and relationship to the perpetrator(s). In addition, further research is required to determine the manner in which physical abuse adds to and/or interacts with the effects of other adverse childhood events.

Complex PTSD

One possible reason why efforts to understand the relationships between various forms of childhood abuse and PTSD have been somewhat frustrating lies in the contention that the diagnosis of PTSD as defined by the diagnostic criteria contained in the DSM-IV-TR is probably less relevant to individuals who have experienced repeated occurrences of childhood abuse over prolonged periods of time than it is to individuals who have experienced discrete traumatic events. Herman (1992a) suggested that the diagnostic formulation of PTSD is applicable primarily to circumscribed traumatic events such as combat, disaster, and rape, but less appropriate as a description of the effects of situations involving repeated traumatic events from which the victim is unable to flee. Herman argued that such situations are characteristic of "prisons, concentration camps, and slave labor camps," and may exist as well "in some religious cults, in brothels and other institutions of organized sexual exploitation, and in some families" (1992a, 377–78). Childhood physical and sexual abuse that takes place within the family system may conform to Herman's description: the abuse may be repeated many times over a substantial period of time, and in most cases the child cannot escape, at least not until he or she is old enough to run away from home.

Herman argued that the dimension of captivity creates a unique relationship of "coercive control" between a victim and a perpetrator. This relationship applies regardless of whether the captivity is effected through the use of physical force, as in the case of prisoners or hostages, or whether the captivity results from "a combination of physical, economic, social, and psychological means . . . as in the case of religious cult members, battered women, and abused children" (1992a, 378). Herman noted that clinicians who work with survivors of childhood abuse have suggested the need to expand the definition of simple PTSD to better fit the symptoms that are typically observed in these patients. Gelinas (1983) described these patients as manifesting a traumatic neurosis characterized by chronic depression, dissociative symptoms, substance abuse, impulsivity, self-mutilation, and suicidal tendencies. All these symptoms have been considered in previous chapters of this book. Similarly, in relation to incest victims, Goodwin (1988) described a "severe posttraumatic syndrome" which includes dissociative states such as fugue, ego fragmentation, affective and anxiety disorders, reenactment and revictimization, somatization, and suicidal tendencies.

Herman (1992a) pointed out that the experience of prolonged abuse fosters the development of a "prodigious array of psychiatric symptoms" (379) and predisposes the survivor to become a psychiatric patient. Herman cited the results of several studies that reported the proportion of psychiatric inpatient samples who reported histories of childhood abuse (Briere and Runtz 1987; Briere and Zaidi 1989; Bryer, Nelson, Miller, and Krol 1987; Carmen, Rieker, and Mills 1984; Jacobson and Richardson 1987). These reports indicated that between 40 percent and 70 percent of adult psychiatric patients are survivors of childhood abuse. Herman also argued that survivors of childhood abuse who do become psychiatric patients tend to display more severe symptoms than patients who are not survivors of childhood abuse. Thus Bryer and his associates (1987) reported that adult female inpatients who reported histories of CPA or CSA scored significantly higher than other patients on standardized measures of somatization, depression, anxiety, interpersonal sensitivity, paranoia, and psychoticism. Similarly, in a study of outpatients being treated at a crisis intervention center, Briere (1988) reported that survivors of childhood abuse were more likely than other patients to experience insomnia, sexual dysfunction, dissociation, anger, suicidal tendencies, self-mutilation, and substance abuse.

Herman argued that clinical observation of survivors of childhood abuse suggested the existence of

> three broad areas of disturbance which transcend simple PTSD. The first is *symptomatic*: the symptom picture in survivors of prolonged trauma often appears to be more complex, diffuse, and tenacious than in simple PTSD. The second is *characterological*: survivors of prolonged abuse develop characteristic personality changes, including deformations of relatedness and identity. The third area involves the survivor's *vulnerability to repeated harm*, both self-inflicted and at the hands of others. (1992a, 379; emphasis added)

These three areas of disturbance, which are present in complex PTSD but not included in the diagnostic criteria for simple PTSD, are considered in the following sections.

Symptomatic Disturbances

Herman identified three groups of symptoms which are not included in the definition of simple PTSD and are characteristic of survivors of prolonged abuse. These include somatic symptoms, dissociative symptoms, and affective symptoms.

Somatic Symptoms

Among the somatic symptoms regularly observed in survivors of prolonged abuse but not included among the symptoms of simple PTSD, Herman (1992a) listed tension headaches, gastrointestinal disturbances, and abdominal, back, and pelvic pain. Other somatic symptoms included in Herman's description of complex PTSD are tremors, choking sensations, and nausea.

Dissociative Symptoms

Herman pointed out that among survivors of prolonged childhood abuse, "dissociative capacities are developed to the extreme" (1992a, 381). In this context, she cited Shengold (1989), who described the "mind-fragmenting operations" employed by abused children in order to preserve the delusion that one's parents are good. Shengold argued that abused children establish isolated divisions of the mind in which incompatible and contradictory images of self and parents are kept separate from each other and never permitted to coalesce. Herman also cited research indicating that the most extreme form of dissociation, multiple personality disorder, is almost always associated with a childhood history of massive and prolonged abuse (Putnam 1989; Ross, Miller, and Reagor 1990).

Affective Symptoms

The affective symptoms named by Herman as particularly characteristic of survivors of prolonged trauma are depression and rage. She noted that protracted depression is reported as the most common finding in virtually all clinical studies of chronically traumatized people (e.g., Goldstein, van Kammen, and Shelly 1987; Herman 1981; Hilberman 1980; Kinzie, Boehnlein, and Leung 1990; Walker 1979). Herman also argued that

> Every aspect of the experience of prolonged trauma combines to aggravate depressive symptoms. The chronic hyperarousal and intrusive symptoms of PTSD fuse with vegetative symptoms of depression, producing what Niederland calls the "survivor triad" of insomnia, nightmares, and psychosomatic complaints. The dissociative symptoms of PTSD merge with the concentration difficulties of depression. The paralysis of initiative of chronic trauma combines with the

apathy and helplessness of depression. The disruptions in attachments of chronic trauma reinforce the isolation and withdrawal of depression. The de-based self image of chronic trauma fuels the guilty ruminations of depression. And the loss of faith suffered in chronic trauma merges with the hopelessness of depression. (1992a, 382)

Furthermore, Herman described victims of prolonged or repeated trauma as experiencing the emotion of "humiliated rage" which may be directed at the perpetrator and/or those who remained indifferent to the situation and failed to help. Thus the female victim of incest perpetrated by a father may be as angry with her mother as she is with her father. Later in life this rage may manifest itself in angry outbursts directed toward anyone who reminds the victim of the original objects of her anger. Herman argued that efforts to control outbursts of anger may result in social withdrawal and paralysis of initiative. In addition, the victim's rage may be internalized as self-hatred, which may exacerbate depression and/or find expression in self-destructive and suicidal behavior. Herman noted that "while major depression is frequently diagnosed in survivors of prolonged abuse, the connection with the trauma is frequently lost" (1992a, 382). She also cited Kinzie and associates (1990) who concluded that such patients are incompletely treated when the traumatic origins of intractable depression are not recognized.

Characterological Disturbances

The characterological sequelae of prolonged victimization described by Herman (1992a,b, 1993) include pathological changes in the victim's relationship to the world as well as pathological changes in the victim's identity. Relationship changes result from the perpetrator's efforts to establish control over the victim through the repeated use of psychological trauma. Herman (1992a) argued that perpetrators seek "to instill terror and helplessness, to destroy the victim's sense of self in relation to others, and to foster pathological attachment to the perpetrator" (383). These goals may be accomplished through the use of violence, but more frequently the perpetrator will use the threat of death or serious harm, either to the victim or to someone close to her. This may be a sibling, the nonoffending parent, or even the perpetrator. Herman (1992b) noted that in cases of chronic childhood abuse, perpetrators also direct violence or threats of violence toward pets. Fear is also increased by unpredictable outbursts of anger and inconsistent enforcement of trivial and capricious rules.

Herman (1992a) contended that in addition to instilling terror, perpetrators of prolonged victimization also seek to destroy the victim's sense of

220 ~ Chapter Nine

autonomy. In prisoner situations, this may be accomplished by deprivation of food, sleep, shelter, exercise, personal hygiene, and privacy. In the case of childhood physical and sexual abuse, the destruction of the victim's autonomy may be accomplished through control of the victim's body. In order to maximize his control over the victim, perpetrators of prolonged victimization will seek to isolate the victim from other relationships which might provide the victim with emotional or physical support. Isolation may be accomplished by limiting or prohibiting social contact and/or communication with peers or adults outside the immediate family. To the extent that the victim is isolated, she (or he) will tend to become increasingly dependent on the perpetrator, not only for survival and basic bodily needs but also for information and emotional sustenance. This accounts for the phenomenon of "traumatic bonding," which leads the victim to cling to the perpetrator. Herman (1992a) noted that traumatic bonding may occur in hostages, battered women (Dutton and Painter 1981; Graham, Rawlings, and Rimini 1988), and victims of chronic child abuse (Herman 1981; Van der Kolk 1987).

Another symptom characteristic of survivors of prolonged victimization is passivity or helplessness. It only seems logical that a victim who has surrendered all control to his or her perpetrator would lack any sense of initiative or self-efficacy. Herman argued that extended captivity or exposure to abuse "undermines or destroys the ordinary sense of a relatively safe sphere of initiative, in which there is some tolerance for trial and error. To the chronically traumatized person, any independent action is subordination, which carries with it the risk of dire punishment" (1992a, 384). Thus it is not surprising that Walker (1979) explicitly applied the concept of "learned helplessness" to explain the frequent failure of battered women to extricate themselves from their abusive situation, or that Van der Kolk (1987) applied the same paradigm to chronically abused children.

Herman argued that survivors of childhood abuse specifically "develop even more complex deformations of identity" (1992a, 386). This makes sense, since the child is experiencing prolonged victimization at the same time as he or she is establishing an ego identity. Herman suggested that the experience of abuse results in the development of a "malignant sense of the self as contaminated, guilty, and evil" (386). This negative view of the self is also related to the dissociative symptoms displayed by many victims of childhood abuse. Herman noted that disturbances in identity formation are also characteristic of patients with Borderline Personality Disorder and patients with multiple personality disorder (now referred to as Dissociative Identity Disorder). Patients in both of these two diagnostic groups tend to have histories of severe childhood abuse. Herman pointed out that the fragmentation of the self into dissociated alters is the central feature of multiple personality disorder, and she argued that BPD patients "lack the dissociative capacity to form fragmented alters [but] have similar difficulties in the formation of an integrated identity" (386). The connections drawn by Herman among these differing diagnostic categories support the notion that survivors of protracted childhood abuse are indeed characterized by a group of symptoms that have been scattered throughout the DSM-IV under various diagnostic categories, suggesting the need to recognize the existence of complex PTSD as a distinguishable constellation of symptoms associated with prolonged victimization.

Repetition of Harm: Self-injury and Revictimization
Herman suggested that severe trauma is associated with "repetitive phenomena" (1992a, 386). In the case of simple PTSD, these repetitive phenomena take the form of intrusive memories of the traumatic event, the experience of bodily sensations that make the survivors feel as if they are reliving the traumatic event, and behavioral reenactments of the event. In the case of victims of repeated abuse that occurs over time, however, additional repetitive phenomena appear. These additional phenomena include various forms of self-injury and revictimization. Herman noted that these additional repetitive phenomena "do not bear a direct relation to the original trauma; they are not simple reenactments or reliving experiences" (1992a, 386). She argued that self-injury and revictimization are more characterological in nature. Herman did not make the obvious observation that it is only logical that victims of a circumscribed traumatic event would experience repetitive phenomena associated with that specific event, whereas victims of repeated trauma over extended periods of time might well lose their focus on any one specific instance of abuse, particularly after learning to employ dissociative defenses to protect themselves from these experiences.

Herman (1992a) cited research indicating that self-mutilation is rarely observed following a single traumatic experience, but frequently observed following protracted childhood abuse (Briere 1988; van der Kolk et al. 1991). Research also indicates that self-mutilation is most likely to develop among survivors whose abuse began early in childhood (van der Kolk 1989). Herman cited studies indicating that women who are survivors of childhood sexual abuse and women who regularly witnessed domestic violence as children are significantly more likely than nonabused women to become victims of rape, battering, and sexual harassment as adults (Goodwin, McMarty, and DiVasto 1982; Hotaling and Sugarman 1986; Russell 1986).

One final repetitive phenomenon that sometimes occurs in survivors of childhood abuse is that the survivors of abuse subsequently become the

abusers of others. Several studies indicated that a history of prolonged childhood abuse is related significantly to becoming an abuser, particularly among
men (Herman 1988; Hotaling and Sugarman 1986). Burgess, Hartman, and
McCausland (1984) reported that children who had been exploited in a sex
and pornography ring for extended periods tended to adopt the belief systems
of their perpetrators and become exploitative toward others.

The relationships observed between repeated victimization that takes
place over prolonged periods of time and these symptoms identified by Herman that are not included among the criteria for simple PTSD have led a
number of investigators to propose that the concept of PTSD should be expanded to include a spectrum of disorders related to traumatic experience
(Brett 1992; Herman 1992a, 1993; Pelcovitz, van der Kolk, Roth, Mandel,
Kaplan, and Resnick 1997; van der Kolk 1996; van der Kolk, Pelcovitz, Roth,
Mandel, McFarlane, and Herman 1996; van der Kolk, Roth, Pelcovitz, and
Mandel 1993). These investigators recommended that the DSM-IV should
be revised to include a new diagnostic category that pertains specifically to
early traumatic stress emanating from interpersonal sources. This new post-
traumatic stress diagnostic category would be named Disorders of Extreme
Stress (DES) or Complex PTSD (CP).

Hall (1999) noted that the proponents of the DES diagnostic category argued that the long-term effects of early repeated trauma are not well integrated in the DSM, and that

> the DSM fragments the effects of trauma, thereby rendering them all but in-
> visible. Thus, somatic responses to trauma are placed under "Somatization Dis-
> order," alterations in consciousness under "Dissociative Disorders," intrusive
> symptoms into the current diagnosis of PTSD, and interpersonal relationship
> problems into "Borderline Personality Disorder." Current research, including
> field studies on PTSD completed for the DSM-IV calls into question the justi-
> fication for separating these symptom categories.(53)

Hall cited a number of studies indicating that the symptom groups referred
to in the above quotation tend to be found in conjunction with each other
among adult trauma survivors (e.g., Ford and Kidd 1998; Roth, Newman,
Pelcovitz, van der Kolk, and Mandel 1997; van der Kolk et al. 1996; Zlotnick and Pearlstein 1997; Zlotnick, Shea, Pearlstein, Simpson, Costello,
and Begin 1996; Zlotnick, Zakrisky, Shea, Costello, Begin, Pearlstein, and
Simpson 1996). Hall also cited studies indicating that the relationships
among these symptom categories tended to be strongest among individuals
who had experienced early interpersonal trauma (Pelcovitz et al. 1997; van
der Kolk et al. 1996).

The proponents of the Complex PTSD syndrome proposed that the DSM-IV should include the new diagnostic classification of "Disorders of Extreme Stress—Not Otherwise Specified" (DESNOS) to represent the symptoms that characterized victims of extreme stress who have sustained repeated and/or accumulated interpersonal trauma during childhood, such as sexual and physical abuse. The diagnostic criteria proposed for the DESNOS diagnosis included seven primary categories of symptoms: (1) alteration in regulation of affect/impulses; (2) alteration in regulation of attention and consciousness; (3) alteration in self-perception; (4) alteration in perception of the perpetrator; (5) alteration in relationships with others; (6) somatization; and (7) alteration in systems of meaning.

The DESNOS construct was operationalized by means of the Structured Interview for Disorders of Extreme Stress (SIDES) (Pelcovitz et al. 1997; van der Kolk and Pelcovitz 1999; Zlotnick and Pearlstein 1997). This measure allows the clinician to determine the lifetime occurrence and present level of severity of each of twenty-seven specific symptoms that are characteristic of complex PTSD. These symptoms fall within one of the seven symptom categories enumerated above. In the area of regulation of affect and impulses, the SIDES includes difficulties with (1) affect regulation; (2) modulation of anger; (3) self-destructive behaviors; (4) suicidal preoccupations; (5) difficulty modulating sexual involvement preoccupation; and (6) excessive risk taking. In the category of regulation of attention and consciousness, the SIDES includes (7) amnesia and (8) transient dissociative episodes and depersonalization. Alterations in self-reception contained in the SIDES include perceptions of (9) ineffectiveness; (10) permanent damage; (11) guilt and responsibility; (12) shame; (13) nobody can understand; and (14) minimizing the trauma. Alterations in the perception of the perpetrator include (15) adoption of distorted beliefs; (16) idealization of the perpetrator; and (17) preoccupation with hurting the perpetrator. Alterations in relationships to others include (18) inability to trust; (19) revictimization; and (20) victimizing others. Somatization includes (21) digestive difficulties; (22) chronic pain; (23) cardiopulmonary symptoms; (24) conversion symptoms; (25) and sexual symptoms. Alterations in systems of meaning highlighted in the SIDES include (26) foreshortened future and (27) the loss of previously sustained beliefs (van der Kolk and Pelcovitz 1999, 25–26). These symptoms appear to capture the description of the symptoms of complex PTSD described by Herman (1992a,b).

The task force responsible for producing the DSM-IV did not include the proposed DESNOS diagnostic category in the DSM-IV. It did address the issue, in a somewhat understated manner, in the section on (simple)

Posttraumatic Stress Disorder (section 309.81). The following passage is contained in that section, under the subsection "Associated descriptive features and mental disorders":

> The following associated constellation of symptoms may occur and are more commonly seen in association with an interpersonal stressor (e.g., childhood sexual or physical abuse, domestic battering, being taken hostage, incarceration as a prisoner of war or in a concentration camp, torture): impaired affect modulation; self-destructive and impulsive behavior; dissociative symptoms; somatic complaints; feelings of ineffectiveness, shame, despair, or hopelessness; feeling permanently damaged; a loss of previously sustained beliefs; hostility; social withdrawal; feeling constantly threatened; impaired relationships with others; or a change from the individual's previous personality characteristics. (APA, DSM-IV 1994, 425)

This description of the constellation of symptoms commonly seen in association with an interpersonal stressor remains substantially unchanged in the subsequent DSM-IV-TR, with the one exception that in the DSM-IV-TR the examples provided for "an interpersonal stressor" include only "childhood sexual or physical abuse [and] domestic battering" (APA 2000, 465). The additional examples of being taken hostage, being incarcerated as a prisoner of war or in a concentration camp, and being tortured have been eliminated.

This is a small but interesting deletion from the description of the constellation of symptoms that represents complex PTSD, because it appears to differentiate between abuse experienced at the hands of a significant other, as opposed to abuse experienced at the hands of a stranger. Of course, one can experience childhood sexual abuse in the form of molestation by a stranger as well as in the form of incest at the hands of a parent, but the quality of repeated and ongoing abuse envisioned in connection with the complex PTSD syndrome is really more characteristic of incest or prolonged physical abuse at the hands of a family member. The DSM-IV-TR description of this associated constellation of symptoms also continues to include domestic battering, which is similarly abuse suffered at the hands of an individual with whom the victim has a loving relationship (which in the ideal would involve a sense of trust and security). Therefore, the most recent description of the symptoms of complex PTSD would appear to emphasize the violation of trust associated with the abuse, as well as the trauma of the abuse itself.

Another possible distinction that has not been made in the DSM-IV-TR would focus on age at abuse. This distinction would differentiate between abuse that occurs during the victim's childhood and early adolescence, while the ego is still developing, and abuse that occurs after the victim has already developed an ego identity. Van der Kolk and Pelcovitz (1999) cited studies indicating that the impact of trauma on self-regulation, self-concept, and in-terpersonal functioning is most profound in younger victims, as well as when the source of the trauma is interpersonal (Cole and Putnam 1992; Pynoos 1993). We propose that one possible reason for the negative relationship that has been observed between the age at the onset of abuse and the severity of the symptoms of complex PTSD observed later in life is that the young child who is abused has no established sense of self in relation to others to resist the potential effects of victimization. Whereas adults who become victims of prolonged abuse must first be broken down in order to create a survivor who manifests the symptoms of complex PTSD, the perpetrator who repeatedly assaults a young child has a blank canvas on which he may leave his mark. (For readers interested in the effects of trauma experienced as an adult on the identity and ego processes, there is a good discussion in Wilson 2004).

The Relationship between Repeated and Prolonged Childhood Abuse and Complex PTSD

There is empirical evidence that repeated and prolonged childhood abuse is associated with the symptoms of complex PTSD among victimized children (Hall 1999; Praver 1996) and adult survivors (Roth et al. 1997; van der Kolk et al. 1996; Zlotnick et al. 1996). Praver (1996) administered a scale assess-ing the severity of complex PTSD symptoms to children age six to twelve in four groups: children who had been victims of intrafamilial abuse, children who had been victims of extrafamilial abuse, children who had been victims of both intrafamilial and extrafamilial abuse, and children who had not ex-perienced trauma. Praver found that the children in each of the three groups who had experienced abuse scored significantly higher than the children in the nonabused group on the total core for complex PTSD and on each of the six subscales of the measure. In addition, Praver reported that the children who had experienced both intrafamilial and extrafamilial abuse scored sig-nificantly higher than the children who had experienced intrafamilial abuse only on four of the six subscales; and they scored higher than the children who had experienced extrafamilial abuse only on five of the six subscales. These findings support the view that complex PTSD results from an accu-mulation of negative experiences, as opposed to simple PTSD, which repre-sents the victim's responses to circumscribed traumatic events.

Hall (1999) argued that if Complex PTSD/Disorders of Extreme Stress rep-resent the responses of the individual to repeated interpersonal traumagenic events, then one would expect to find a positive relationship between the amount of accumulated trauma and the severity of symptoms of Complex PTSD/Disorders of Extreme Stress (CP/DES). Hall studied the clinical records of one hundred sexually abused boys and girls between the ages of three and seven. These records were drawn from two child abuse treatment programs, one in Toronto (n = 60) and the other in Calgary (n = 40). Hall used records to determine whether each case had experienced, in addition to the validated sexual abuse, each of the following additional forms of abuse: (1) physical abuse, (2) physical neglect, (3) emotional abuse, and (4) exposure to family violence. A Cumulative Negative Events Index score ranging from 0 to 4 was generated by counting the number of additional forms of abuse that had been experienced.

Each case was also rated for symptoms of CP/DES using the framework of the SIDES (see above) adapted for children. The rating framework contained twenty-eight child symptom variables that composed the same seven symptom categories that are measured by the SIDES. The index for Alteration in the Regulation of Affect/Impulses had five items that measured (1) affect dysregulation, (2) problematic aggression, (3) developmentally inappropriate levels of masturbation and/or self-focused sexualized behavior, (4) sexual preoccupation, and (5) interpersonal sexual behavior. The index for Alteration in Regulation of Attention and Consciousness had three items, indicating (6) presence of amnesia with respect to some or all maltreatment experiences, (7) dissociation, and (8) other reexperiencing behaviors. The index for Alteration in Self-Perception had four items, assessing (9) shame and/or self-blame for one's own maltreatment, (10) lack of sense of self or shyness, (11) pseudomaturity, and (12) problematic self-esteem. The index for Alteration in the Perception of the Perpetrator contained two items, including (13) identification with the offender (i.e., wants to see the offender) and (14) distorted beliefs (e.g., inappropriate blaming of others for the abusive experiences. The index of Alteration in Relationships with Others had seven items, measuring (15) poor social skills, (16) lack of normal empathy, (17) problematic internalization of right and wrong, (18) problematic nonsexual boundaries, (19) poor relationships with peers, (20) problematic relationship with mother, and (21) inappropriate use of practical jokes and trickery at the expense of others. The somatization index contained four items, including (22) frequent illnesses, (23) problematic affect expression (i.e., alexithymia), (24) toileting/elimination problems, and (25) eating/digestive problems. Finally, the index of Alteration in Systems of Meaning contained three items, measuring (26) hopelessness, (27) lack of capacity for imaginary play, and (28) joylessness. A global CP/DES Index score was generated for each case by counting the number of DES symptoms out of twenty-eight that were mentioned in the completed case folder.

The results of the study confirmed the expected positive relationship between the overall number of types of negative events experienced and the global CP/DES score. The sexually abused children in the sample who experienced none of the other forms of abuse assessed had the lowest global CP/DES global symptom score, and the CP/DES group mean scores increased in a linear manner as the number of additional forms of abuse experienced increased from zero to four. Obviously this study is limited by the fact that the severity of the sexual abuse experienced was not measured, nor was the severity of the other forms of abuse assessed. In addition, there was no matched comparison group of nonabused children, and there were no children in the sample who had experienced other forms of abuse but not sexual abuse. Additional research is required in which each of the various forms of abuse can be assessed not simply in terms of whether it occurred, but also in terms of the specific nature of the abuse, the duration and frequency of the abuse, the age at first onset, and the relationship of the perpetrator(s) to the victim. It is also important to determine how the abuse was disclosed and the reactions of significant others to this disclosure. Each of the measures of abuse could then be compared not just to a global measure of CP/DES symptoms, but to each of the seven symptom categories composing the complex PTSD construct.

Nevertheless, the findings reported by Hall (1999) are clearly consistent with the notion that repeated, prolonged, and severe childhood abuse is associated with the symptoms represented by complex PTSD. Hall concluded that her findings and the results of other existing research suggested "the need to consider the additive effects of multiple forms of maltreatment when planning for treatment of abuse children and adults" (65). The need to assess various forms of adverse childhood events and the cumulative severity of childhood abuse has been the subject of substantial recent discussion in the literature (Culbertson and Willis 1998; Rosenberg and Rossman 1998; Shirk and Eltz 1998).

A number of empirical studies have reported significant relationships between various forms of childhood abuse and adult manifestations of the symptoms included in the CP/DES construct (Ford and Kidd 1998; Pelcovitz et al. 1997; Roth et al. 1997; van der Kolk et al. 1996; Zlotnick, Shea et al. 1996, Zlotnick et al. 1997).

Van der Kolk and colleagues (1996) employed the data from the DSM-IV-PTSD field trial research to compare adults in three different trauma history groups on several measures of symptoms included in the complex PTSD construct. The three groups were a group who reported histories of inter-personal trauma (physical and/or sexual abuse) with early onset (before the age of fourteen) (n = 148); a group who reported histories of interpersonal trauma (physical and/or sexual abuse) with later onset (after fourteen years old) (n = 87); and a group who reported trauma through exposure to a nat-ural disaster (n = 59). These three groups were compared on dichotomous self-report measures of seven symptoms included in the complex PTSD syn-drome, including dysfunctional affect modulation, unmodulated expression of anger, self-destructive behavior, suicidal behavior, unmodulated sexual behavior, dissociation, and somatization.

Results indicated that participants in the group reporting early onset of in-terpersonal trauma in the form of physical and/or sexual abuse were signifi-cantly more likely than participants from the group exposed to natural disas-ter to report experiencing each of the seven symptoms of complex PTSD. Participants in the late onset of interpersonal trauma group were also signif-icantly more likely than the participants from the group exposed to natural disaster to report four of the seven symptoms of complex PTSD, including dysfunctional affect modulation, unmodulated expression of anger, suicidal behavior, and somatization. Participants in the early and late onset of inter-personal trauma groups also differed significantly on self-reports on four of the complex PTSD symptoms. Those in the early onset group were signifi-cantly more likely than those in the late onset group to endorse unmodulated expression of anger, self-destructive behavior, suicidal behavior, and dissoci-ation. The authors concluded that the diagnosis of (simple) PTSD does not adequately describe the full extent of the suffering experienced by victims of interpersonal abuse, particularly when that abuse occurred relatively early. Reporting on the same set of data, Pelcovitz and colleagues (1997) also con-cluded that early interpersonal victimization gives rise to more complex adult psychopathology than later interpersonal victimization. Pelcovitz and associ-ates (1997) further asserted that exposure to a natural disaster tends to be as-sociated with the symptoms of "simple" PTSD, but does not seem to con-tribute to the emergence of dissociative symptoms, somatization, or problems with affect regulation.

In a further analysis of the DSM-IV-PTSD field trial data, Roth and col-leagues (1997) focused solely on participants who reported physical and/or sexual abuse during childhood. Roth and his associates classified all partic-ipants into one of three groups with respect to type of abuse (physical only, sexual only, or both). They found that women were more likely than men to be coded for lifetime diagnosis of complex PTSD, so they ran separate logistic regression analyses for female and male participants, attempting to predict the lifetime diagnosis of complex PTSD from the type of abuse history reported. They found that the lifetime diagnosis of complex PTSD occurred quite frequently among all three groups of abused females, but they also obtained a significant effect due to type of abuse on the likelihood of being diagnosed with complex PTSD. The diagnosis of complex PTSD was most common among women who had experienced both physical and sexual abuse, next most common among the women who experienced sexual abuse only, and least common among women who had experienced physical abuse only.

Zlotnick and associates (1997) compared a sample of seventy-four adult female survivors of childhood sexual abuse to a sample of thirty-four women who had not experienced sexual abuse during childhood on a series of measures of CP/DESNOS symptoms. They reported that the CSA survivors scored significantly higher than the non–sexually abused comparison subjects on symptoms of somatization, dissociation, hostility, anxiety, alexithymia, social dysfunction, maladaptive schemas, self-destructive behaviors, and adult sexual victimization. Their results also showed that ratings of the severity of these symptoms were all related to each other, indicating the existence of a complex of symptoms associated with history of CSA. The authors concluded that the results of the study supported the CP/DESNOS construct and its relationship to CSA.

Childhood Abuse and Vulnerability to Trauma Experienced in Adulthood

Another relationship that clinicians should be aware of is that between a history of childhood abuse and the likelihood of experiencing significant psychological difficulties in the aftermath of trauma that is experienced subsequently during adulthood. Here is a substantial body of literature indicating that a history of childhood physical abuse (CPA) and/or childhood sexual abuse (CSA) predisposes an individual to the development of stress disorders following the experience of a traumatic event as an adult (Alexander 1993; Elliot and Briere 1995; Koopman, Gore-Felton, Classen, Kim, and Spiegel 2001; McFarlane 1986, 1988, 1990; Rodriguez, Vande Kemp, and Foy 1998; Tremblay, Hebert, and Piche 2000; Twaite and Rodriguez-Srednicki 2004; van der Kolk and Fisler 1994; Yehuda 1998; Yehuda and McFarlane 1995). The stress disorders include both PTSD as defined in the DSM-IV-TR and Acute Stress Disorder (ASD), which involves "the development of characteristic anxiety, dissociative, and other symptoms that occur within one month after the exposure to an extreme traumatic stressor" (APA 2000, 469).

The types of stressors that are specified in the DSM-IV-TR as leading to ASD are the same as those specified as leading to PTSD: (1) experiencing or witnessing an event (or events) that involves actual or threatened death or serious injury, or a threat to the physical integrity of self or others, and (2) a response involving intense fear, helplessness, or horror. In ASD, however, symptoms emerge either while the individual is experiencing the trauma or within one month of experiencing the trauma. This is different from the diagnostic criteria defining PTSD, in that the diagnostic criteria for PTSD require that symptoms persist for more than one month. Therefore the diagnosis of PTSD cannot be made during the month following the trauma.

In addition, the actual symptoms that compose ASD differ from those specified for PTSD. The diagnosis of ASD requires that the trauma victim experience at least three of the following dissociative symptoms: (1) a subjective sense of numbing, detachment, or absence of emotional responsiveness; (2) a reduction in awareness of one's surroundings (being in a daze); (3) derealization; (4) depersonalization; and (5) dissociative amnesia. The diagnosis of ASD also requires that the event be persistently reexperienced in at least one of the following ways: (1) recurrent images; (2) thoughts; (3) dreams; (4) illusions; (5) flashback episodes; (6) a sense of reliving the experience; and (7) distress on exposure to reminders of the traumatic event. Like PTSD, the ASD diagnosis requires that the victim display marked avoidance of stimuli that may arouse recollections of the trauma, and marked symptoms of anxiety or increased arousal. Also like PTSD, the ASD diagnosis requires that the victim experience clinically significant distress or impairment in social, occupational or other important areas of functioning.

Twaite and Rodriguez-Srednicki (2004) surveyed a nonclinical sample of 284 adults from the New York metropolitan area regarding history of childhood physical abuse, childhood sexual abuse, and the nature of their exposure to the terrorist attack on the World Trade Center on September 11, 2001. The survey took place six months after the attack. We measured symptoms of PTSD following the terrorist attack using the revised Impact of Event Scale (IES-R) (Weiss and Marmar 1997). This scale measures the symptoms of PTSD resulting from a specific life event. The symptoms include intrusive symptoms (nightmares and intrusive thoughts, images, and feelings), avoidance symptoms, and symptoms of increased arousal (e.g., easy startle response, hypervigilance). We also measured adult attachment, using the Attachment Style Questionnaire (ASQ) (Feeney, Noller, and Hanrahan 1994) and dissociation, using the Dissociative Experiences Scale (DES) (Bernstein and Putnam 1986). The latter measures were included to assess the possibility that the relationship between history of childhood abuse and PTSD might be mediated by adult attachment and/or dissociation.

There were 156 females and 128 males in our sample. Of the females, 39 (25.0 percent) reported histories of childhood sexual abuse (CSA), and 30 (19.2 percent) reported histories of childhood physical abuse. Of the males, 21 (16.4 percent) reported histories of CSA, and 20 (15.6 percent) reported histories of CPA. Among the females, 39 (25.0 percent) reported witnessing the attack on television as it was occurring (hence without warning), whereas 117 (75 percent) reported witnessing the attack later, in replays shown on television. Among the males, the corresponding proportions were 19.5 percent live as it occurred versus 80.5 percent only later in replays.

The results of the study indicated that the severity of symptoms of PTSD reported six months after the attack were related significantly to both history of CSA and history of CPA. Children with histories of abuse had more severe symptoms. We interpreted these findings as indicating that the experience of childhood trauma predisposed the adults to respond to the traumatic event of the attack, experienced as an adult, with a posttraumatic stress reaction. The results also showed that the severity of symptoms of PTSD reported six months after the attack were related significantly to the nature of the participant's exposure to the attack. Those respondents who witnessed the attack live, as it happened, reported more severe symptoms than those who witnessed the attack only later, on taped replays. We suggested that this finding indicates that experiencing the traumatic event unexpectedly and without warning is more traumatic than viewing a replay of the event with forewarning. Finally, as we expected, attachment and dissociation were significant mediators of the relationships between the childhood abuse measures and the severity of PTSD symptoms. Among securely attached adults, CSA and CPA were less likely to be associated with severe PTSD symptoms than they were among adults with insecure adult attachment. Among adults with a greater tendency to employ dissociative defenses, CSA and CPA were more likely to be associated with severe PTSD symptoms than they were among adults reporting relatively low levels of dissociative processes.

We interpreted these findings in the light of several different theoretical formulations. As alluded to in the chapter on Attachment Disorders above, it has been argued that children who experience childhood physical and/or sexual abuse fail to develop the secure attachments that can buffer the impact of extreme stress experienced later in life (Browne and Finkelhor 1986; Finkelhor and Browne 1985; Herman 1992b; McFarlane 1986). Similarly, it has been argued that children who are abused learn to use dissociative defenses to protect themselves, and they tend to continue to use these same defenses as adults. However, the use of dissociative defenses when confronted with a traumatic event as an adult may limit the individual's ability to process that event, which may in turn leave the individual vulnerable to the subsequent emergence of intrusive images and feelings in the form of the dreams and flashbacks that characterize PTSD (Brown 1994; Irwin 1994; Spiegel and Cardena 1991; van der Kolk et al. 1996).

Koopman and her colleagues (2001) studied fifty-four women who had histories of childhood sexual abuse. These women were all in treatment for PTSD associated with the childhood abuse. To measure the symptoms of ASD experienced by these women, the investigators administered the Stanford Acute Stress Reaction Questionnaire to these participants (SASRQ) (Cardena, Classen, Koopman, and Spiegel 1996; Cardena, Koopman, Classen, Waelde, and Spiegel 1999). This instrument asks respondents to "recall the stressful events that occurred in your life during the PAST MONTH [and] briefly describe the one event that was most disturbing on the lines below" (Koopman et al. 1999, 88). After writing the brief description, respondents are asked to read each of thirty statements describing different symptoms of ASD. The respondents are asked to rate how frequently they have experienced each symptom since the event they described. They rate each statement on a six-point Likert-type response scale having response options that range from 0 (not experienced) to 5 (very often). Based on these ratings, the SASRQ yields both dichotomous scores and numerical subscale scores representing each of the five major symptoms of ASD included in the DSM-IV-TR: (1) dissociative symptoms; (2) symptoms of hyperarousal/anxiety; (3) avoidance of reminders of the stressful event; (4) reexperiencing the stressful event; and (5) social/occupational impairment.

The investigators used the responses to the SASRQ to determine whether each participant met all of the individual criteria for ASD described in the DSM-IV-TR, and to determine whether each participant met all the criteria required to be assigned the ASD diagnosis. In addition, the investigators used the participants' descriptions of the most stressful event they had experienced during the past month to decide whether or not the event described conformed to the description of a traumatic event as included as a criterion for assigning the ASD diagnosis—an event threatening the life or physical integrity of the respondent or someone close to the respondent. The authors reported that initial interrater agreement in making this judgment was 87 percent and that differences were resolved through discussion.

The results of this study indicated that "the majority of the sample met criteria for each particular ASD symptom: dissociation (59 percent); reexperiencing (87 percent); anxiety/hyperarousal (96 percent) avoidance (94 percent); and impairment (79 percent)" (1999, 90). In addition, twenty-four of the fifty-four participants (44 percent) met all the symptom criteria required by the DSM-IV-TR to be given a diagnosis of ASD. However, based on the judgments made regarding the nature of the most stressful event reported by the participants, only three of the twenty-four women who had all the symptoms required for the ASD diagnosis had actually experienced an event that qualified as a traumatic event as required by the DSM for assigning the ASD diagnosis. Thus these women with histories of childhood sexual abuse and diagnoses of PTSD were typically experiencing ASD symptoms in the absence of the recent traumatic event which was, theoretically, the source of these symptoms. Koopman and her colleagues (2001) interpreted this finding as suggesting that "women CSA survivors who are seeking treatment for sexual abuse may experience sensitization to relatively minor stressors such that they report acute stress responses in association with the minor stressor" (91).

It is important for clinicians to be aware of these relationships when working with adult survivors of childhood abuse. These clients may be particularly vulnerable to experiencing symptoms of PTSD and ASD following an adverse life experience, and it would appear that they may develop rather serious symptoms even after experiences that would not appear to qualify as truly traumatic. One would suspect that even a verbal insult or perceived slight could result in symptoms that the client might mention during treatment, and the clinician needs to understand that such symptoms do not represent overreactions for survivors of childhood abuse in the same way that they might for clients without childhood abuse histories.

Conclusion

The literature is clear that the diagnosis of PTSD represented in the diagnostic criteria contained in the DSM-IV-TR does not adequately represent the symptoms characteristically displayed by adult survivors of prolonged interpersonal abuse experienced during childhood in general and during early childhood in particular. The construct of complex PTSD encompasses the great majority of the symptoms that adult survivors of childhood abuse display. The fragmentation of these symptoms within the framework of the DMS over the past several decades has complicated the task of unraveling the complicated relationships between various forms of childhood abuse and the broad range of negative psychosocial outcomes which appear to flow from such abuse and present themselves during adulthood. One would hope that research in this area in the future would be certain to assess multiple forms of abuse and the parameters of such abuse, as well as other adverse childhood experiences and environmental conditions. It would appear that the additive and interactive effects of these diverse predictors of unfavorable outcomes must be taken into account to adequately explain adult symptoms. On the outcome side of the equation, one would hope that the awareness of the complex PTSD construct created by recent research, coupled with the inclusion within the DSM-IV-TR of the reference to the "associated constellation of symptoms" that represents complex PTSD, will encourage researchers to always assess for the entire range of complex PTSD symptoms that have been shown to be related to prolonged childhood physical and sexual abuse.

~

CHAPTER TEN

Assessment of Adult Survivors of Childhood Abuse

The foregoing chapters showed clearly that the various forms of child abuse occur frequently in our society, and that adults with histories of childhood abuse are likely to experience some or all of a broad range of serious psychosocial adjustment difficulties. In the last chapter, we saw that a childhood history involving repeated instances of abuse that take place over time is associated with a syndrome of symptoms that include both the symptoms of simple PTSD (intrusive experiences associated with the trauma, avoidance, and arousal) and the additional symptoms of complex PTSD (dissociative symptoms, relationship difficulties, revictimization, somatization, affect dysregulation, and disruptions in identity) (Herman 1992a).

The broad range of symptoms associated with childhood abuse would appear to support the recommendation made by Allen, Coyne, and Huntoon (1998) to employ an omnibus measure of psychopathology such as the Millon Multiaxial Clinical Inventory (MCMI) (Millon 1994) to assess the degree to which a given patient may be suffering from each of the many possible negative effects of childhood abuse. This recommendation is supported further by the results of several studies which indicated that specific symptom scales of the MCMI significantly differentiated groups of adults with and without histories of childhood abuse (Alexander 1993; Allen, Coyne, and Console 1998; Busby, Glenn, Steggell, and Adamson 1993; Ellason, Ross, and Fuchs 1995).

However, before recommending the routine administration of the MCMI and attempting to specify the patterns of MCMI subscale scores that are associated with histories of abuse, we need to step back and consider the circumstances that led Allen and colleagues (1998) to adopt the regular use of the MCMI to assess their patients, and to compare the purpose of evaluation in their clinical setting to the circumstances under which the average clinician comes into contact with an adult survivor of childhood abuse. Allen and his associates were "conducting inpatient evaluations of women referred to a tertiary-care setting for specialized treatment of trauma-related disorders" (1998, 277). Thus their evaluations were aimed at ascertaining the severity of symptoms experienced by women already known to be survivors of trauma. But this is not typically the case when a new patient appears at a mental health clinic or a private practitioner's office seeking treatment for a specific psychosocial adjustment problem.

Consider the various case studies that introduced the chapters of this book concerned with the various categories of adult symptoms that have been linked to childhood abuse. We described an individual entering therapy with the primary complaint that his same sex and opposite sex relationships are superficial and unrewarding, hoping that therapy would help him develop his social skills and form closer and more meaningful relationships with others. We described a man who was hospitalized following a suicidal gesture that was apparently associated with despondency over an impending divorce and the disruption of his relationship with his daughter. We described a bulimic woman who sought treatment at an upscale health and wellness center. We described an adolescent girl arrested for prostitution who was given the option of entering a residential drug treatment program or going to jail. We described several different individuals who presented for treatment with some form of sexual adjustment disorder. These included a woman who was profoundly ambivalent about sex, a male "sex addict," and an affluent woman involved in a midlife crisis who described herself as nothing more than a high-class whore. We described an adolescent and an adult female who engaged in self-mutilating behaviors. We described a forty-five-year-old woman who entered analysis following her second divorce, complaining that her life was a failure and complaining of a variety of symptoms including an inability to say no to unwanted sexual advances.

The point of these case studies is that adult patients who are survivors of childhood abuse rarely present themselves as such. Adult survivors may not even know that they experienced abuse. Even if they do remember negative experiences from childhood, they may not link them to the difficulties that led them to seek treatment. Therefore they may not automatically recognize that it is important to disclose these experiences to their therapist. To the contrary, they may be embarrassed by the nature of the abuse they experienced and may be reluctant to disclose the abuse, at least until they have developed a significant level of trust in their therapist.

Therefore, we have three objectives for clinicians reading this chapter: First, we want to make sure that clinicians who treat diverse patient populations will routinely keep the possibility in mind that a patient's isolated symptoms may result from childhood abuse. On the other hand, the symptoms may also have an altogether different etiology, so the clinician should not assume prematurely that childhood abuse is involved. However, the clinician should always be aware of the potential role of childhood abuse and strive to elicit data that is relevant to this possibility. Therefore, our second goal for this chapter is to help clinicians develop sensitive approaches that motivate and enable patients to become aware of and disclose possible early abusive experiences at their own pace, as they become comfortable in doing so.

Our final goal for this chapter comes into play if preliminary assessment does suggest that childhood trauma may be a factor in the emergence of current distress. In this case, we seek to acquaint clinicians with a battery of instruments and procedures that can be used at appropriate points during treatment to assess both the parameters of childhood trauma and the range and severity of current symptoms. Begin such assessment procedures after the patient has recognized the following: (1) that he or she did in fact experience abuse or other traumatic events in childhood; (2) that these traumatic experiences may be related to the difficulties that he or she is currently experiencing; (3) that he or she was not responsible for these traumatic experiences; and (4) that the therapist can be trusted with the knowledge of these experiences. In most instances, these conditions will not be achieved until some time has elapsed in treatment. Therefore, the assessment process should be regarded as interactive with and mutually reinforcing and guiding the treatment process.

Facilitating Disclosure

The patient who presents for treatment with one or more of the symptoms of complex PTSD may or may not be a survivor of childhood abuse. Consequently the approach we employ initially is appropriate for all patients. The primary goal of the initial stages of treatment is for the therapist to communicate his or her responsiveness to the needs and concerns of the patient. The therapist must recognize and respond candidly to the patient's concerns regarding the nature of therapy and the likelihood of achieving the patient's goals. The therapist must encourage the patient to express any apprehensions he or she may have regarding the process, including concerns regarding potentially painful aspects of treatment and confidentiality.

These principles are crucial in the case of childhood abuse survivors, many of whom have been trained by their abusers to be acquiescent and helpless. They are taught that their needs are inconsequential and that their only value lies in the gratification they provide for their abuser. Therefore, the therapist who communicates that he or she actually cares about the patient's needs and concerns and is responsive to them has already begun to reeducate the patient regarding his or her personal worth and self-efficacy. For the same reason, in establishing such treatment parameters as frequency and duration of sessions, it is important that decisions be made jointly. The patient who did not experience childhood abuse may regard collaborative decision making as normal procedure in establishing a professional relationship, but the childhood abuse survivor may be overwhelmed by the fact that someone in a position of authority actually cares about his or her input. Several investigators have noted the importance of collaboration in establishing the parameters of the treatment relationship as a crucial element in making the patient feel safe and secure (Courtois 1999; McCann and Pearlman 1990; Pearlman 2001; Pearlman and McCann 1994).

As the patient's sense of self-efficacy, security, and trust develops, the therapist can encourage the disclosure of childhood recollections by teaching the patient that the problems we experience as adults are often related to the experiences of childhood. This can be taught first as a general principle that is relevant for all clients. Later on, if available data do begin to point toward the possibility of a history of childhood abuse, the principle can be reiterated in the specific context of childhood abuse. Pearlman and McCann (1994) recommended that eliciting the patient's trauma history is a process that should take place gradually and continuously over the course of treatment. Pearlman (2001) stressed that it is crucial that the patient be in control of the disclosure process, with the therapist providing gentle encouragement while protecting the patient from becoming overwhelmed:

> Clients must control the pace of revealing what happened to them in the past. The therapist provides assistance by encouraging clients to talk about painful events if they are reluctant to do so yet are struggling with avoidance-related problems such as depression, emotional numbing, and somatization. Alternatively, the therapist will encourage clients to slow down if they are revealing so much so quickly that they become overwhelmed and experience increased symptoms such as intrusive imagery, flashbacks, and dissociation or attempts to cope with strong feelings through self-destructive behaviors. (211)

Assuming that the patient discloses information warranting the conclusion that childhood abuse has occurred, the therapist is advised to continue the process of assessment by identifying the nature and parameters of the abuse and the range and severity of abuse-related symptoms.

There are a great many assessment techniques and measures that are used clinically to facilitate this continuing assessment process. To the extent that the patient grows to trust the therapist, understand the possible relationships between past experiences and current symptoms, and recognize that he or she is responsible for neither the abuse nor the resulting symptoms, selected measures may be used as necessary and advisable to elicit data that might not be revealed spontaneously in regular treatment sessions. In most cases these assessments will not be administered at one time. This could be overwhelming to the patient. Rather, the therapist will employ the various assessment techniques and measures judiciously, gradually adding to the available database while demonstrating the utility of each additional piece of information to the patient through careful explanation and interpretation. In this process, the therapist will enlist the patient as a collaborator in developing an understanding of the events and experiences that have led the patient to his or her current condition. This process will further empower the patient. The therapist will teach the patient that understanding the source of one's current difficulties is an important step in rectifying them. Data obtained through the use of standardized assessment techniques and measures will be combined with data obtained through informal assessment to develop the most complete description possible of the patient's experiences and difficulties.

Assessment Techniques and Instruments

There are a variety of techniques and measures clinicians can use in obtaining a complete trauma history and a detailed assessment of the nature and severity of the symptoms the patient is experiencing. These techniques will be employed in conjunction with the verbal reports of patients that are elicited during regular treatment sessions. The use of standardized assessment procedures will call the attention of the therapist and the patient alike to areas of traumatic experience that might otherwise be overlooked, as well as to symptoms that the patient has not spontaneously identified as problem areas that need to be addressed in treatment. In this section we present some of the measures that are available. We indicate the advantages and disadvantages of each measure, including the psychometric characteristics of the instrument. These measures may also be used by individual clinicians in an informal manner. For example, the clinician may employ the items in an instrument as a checklist that he or she keeps in mind (or on a clipboard) when inquiring about abusive experiences, simply to make sure that all potentially relevant areas are assessed.

General Measures of Abuse and Trauma

Norris and Hamblen (2004) reviewed seven standardized self-report measures of the traumatic events that adult respondents have experienced over the course of their lifetimes. These scales include the Traumatic Stress Schedule (TSS) (Norris 1990); the Traumatic Events Questionnaire (TEQ) (Vrana and Lauterbach 1994); the Trauma History Questionnaire (THQ) (Green 1996); the Traumatic Life Events Questionnaire (TLEQ) (Kubany, Haynes, Leisen et al. 2000); the Stressful Life Events Screening Questionnaire (SLESQ) (Goodman, Corcoran, Turner, Yuan, and Green 1998); the Life Stressor Checklist (LSC-R) (Wolfe, Kimerling, Brown, Chrestman, and Levin 1996); and the Brief Trauma Questionnaire (BTQ) (Schnurr, Spiro, Vielhauer, Findler, and Hamblen 2002). These measures all assess a broad range of traumatic events across the entire life span. They are not limited to events that occurred during childhood, and they are not limited to events that would be classified as falling into the five major categories of childhood abuse that we designated in chapter 1 of this volume (i.e., physical abuse, sexual abuse, neglect, emotional abuse, and secondary abuse).

For example, the Trauma History Questionnaire (Green 1996) consists of a list of twenty-four traumatic events that the respondent may have experienced: (1) mugging; (2) robbery; (3) a home break-in when the respondent was at home; (4) a home break-in when the respondent is absent; (5) a serious accident; (6) a natural disaster that placed the respondent or loved ones in danger; (7) a disaster of human origin that placed the respondent or loved ones in danger; (8) toxin exposure; (9) other serious personal injury; (10) any other situation in which the respondent feared being killed or injured; (11) witnessing a serious injury or death; (12) handling or seeing dead bodies; (13) having a close friend or family member murdered or killed by a drunk driver; (14) having a spouse, romantic partner, or child die; (15) having a serious or life-threatening illness; (16) having someone close experience a serious or life-threatening illness, injury, or unexpected death; (17) combat; (18) forced intercourse, oral, or anal sex; (19) forced touching of one's private parts; (20) other unwanted sexual contact; (21) aggravated assault; (22) simple assault; (23) being beaten, spanked, or pushed hard enough to cause injury; and (24) any other extraordinarily stressful situation or event. Respondents indicate whether they have experienced each of the categories of trauma, how many times they have experienced each type, and their age at the time each traumatic event occurred.

We have seen that the effects of various types of adverse childhood events may be cumulative (Dong et al. 2004). This suggests that it would be desirable for the clinician to assess not only the five major categories of childhood abuse named in chapter 1, but other adverse childhood events as well. Therefore, it would not be a bad thing for the clinician to explore the various categories of trauma included in the THQ, through either the actual administration of this instrument or discussion during sessions. We have also seen that childhood trauma may potentiate reactions to traumatic events experienced during adulthood (Alexander 1993; Koopman et al. 2001; Twaite and Rodriguez-Srednicki 2004). Therefore, it is desirable to know about various traumas that patients may have experienced as adults, as well as those experienced during childhood. Since the THQ asks respondents to indicate their age at the time that each traumatic event occurred, it provides a measure of traumatic events experienced both during childhood and during adulthood.

Other instruments in this group employ separate questions to assess traumatic experiences that occurred during childhood and traumatic events experienced later in life. For example, the Traumatic Life Events Questionnaire (Kubany et al. 2000) assesses the respondent's history of experiencing each of twenty-three types of events, including (1) natural disaster; (2) motor vehicle accident involving injury or death; (3) other accident involving injury or death; (4) combat; (5) sudden or unexpected death of a close friend or a loved one due to accident, illness, suicide, or murder; (6) a loved one surviving a life-threatening illness, accident, or assault; (7) personal experience with a life-threatening illness; (8) being mugged or robbed by someone with a weapon; (9) being physically assaulted by an acquaintance or by a stranger; (10) witnessing someone being attacked or assaulted; (11) being threatened with death or bodily harm; (12) childhood physical abuse; (13) witnessing severe family violence; (14) physical abuse from an intimate partner; (15) childhood sexual touching by someone at least five years older (with probes for use of force and penetration); (16) childhood sexual touching by someone less than five years older (with probes for use of force and penetration); (17) adolescent unwanted sexual activity (with probes for use of force and penetration); (18) adult unwanted sexual activity (with probes for force and penetration); (19) sexual harassment; (20) stalking; (21) having a miscarriage (self or partner); (22) having an abortion (self or partner); and (23) other extremely disturbing or distressing experience. Items 12, 15, and 16 refer specifically to abuse occurring during childhood; and item 17 refers specifically to abuse occurring during adolescence.

Each of these surveys assesses both childhood and adult trauma, and having data with respect to any of the categories of adverse experiences included in either instrument could potentially prove useful to clinicians working with survivors of childhood abuse. However, neither of these instruments by itself would provide an adequate assessment of childhood abuse experiences. This is because the instruments are not focused specifically on childhood abuse, and they therefore omit or provide inadequate data on important categories of childhood abuse. For example, the THQ does not include items on emotional abuse, neglect, or secondary abuse (except in the case where a parent was seriously injured or died as a result of domestic violence). Similarly, the TLEQ does not include items assessing emotional abuse or neglect, though it does contain several categories of events that are relevant to the experience of secondary abuse.

For these reasons, the clinician working with patients who are survivors of childhood abuse will wish to employ measures that have been developed with specific reference to childhood abuse experiences. Of course, parts of these general measures of trauma and abuse may be useful to clinicians. Norris and Hamblen (2004) have provided their readers with a table indicating where these instruments can be obtained (96–98).

Measures of Childhood Abuse

Briere (2004) reviewed both the measures used to obtain adults' retrospective reports of the various types of abuse they experienced during childhood and their perceptions of the symptoms they are experiencing as adults. He stressed that "most instruments that evaluate traumatic events in adulthood either overlook childhood abuse or merely include it as one of many traumas that the participant can endorse" (549). He noted several scales that specifically examine childhood maltreatment history in adults, but he cautioned that these instruments "vary considerably in terms of the number of forms of abuse or neglect they assess and the amount of abuse-specific detail they offer" (549). Of the measures Briere reviewed, three appear to be the most relevant: the Child Maltreatment Interview Schedule (CMIS) (Briere 1992a); the Childhood Maltreatment Questionnaire (CMQ) (Demare 1993); and the Childhood Trauma Questionnaire (CTQ) (Bernstein and Fink 1998; Bernstein, Fink, Handelsman et al. 1994).

The Child Maltreatment Interview Schedule (CMIS) (Briere 1992a) is a forty-six-item measure of various forms of maltreatment occurring before the age of seventeen: parental physical unavailability, parental disorder and substance abuse history, parental psychological unavailability, psychological abuse, emotional abuse, sexual abuse, and physical abuse. Many of the items in the CMIS contain a large number of subquestions that elicit detailed data on such parameters of the abuse/neglect experience as frequency, severity, age of onset, and relationship of respondent to the perpe-trator. The majority of the items in the CMIS simply indicate the occur-rence and describe the parameters of a particular form of abuse or neglect. Therefore in general the items are not summed to form scale scores. For this reason, data on reliability are not reported. The exception to this general rule is the seven-item scale measuring psychological abuse, which was orig-inally developed by Briere and Runtz (1988; 1990) and is included as item 7 in the CMIS. This scale assesses the frequency of occurrence of the fol-lowing psychologically abusive behaviors on the part of parents, steppar-ents, or foster parents: (1) yell at you; (2) insult you; (3) criticize you; (4) try to make you feel guilty; (5) ridicule or humiliate you; (6) embarrass you in front of others; and (7) make you feel like you were a bad person. The authors of this psychological abuse scale reported internal consistency reliability coefficients for the scale ranging from .75 to .87.

There is also a short form of the CMIS that contains eleven items with numerous subquestions, including also the seven-item scale measuring psy-chological abuse. A copy of this unpublished short form may be downloaded from Dr. Briere's website (www.johnbriere.com).

The Childhood Maltreatment Questionnaire (CMQ) (Demare 1993) con-sists of three major components: the Psychological Maltreatment Ques-tionnaire (PMQ), the Physical Abuse Questionnaire (PAQ), and the Sex-ual Abuse Questionnaire (SAQ). The PMQ provides detailed data on twelve dimensions of psychological abuse and neglect. These dimensions are (1) rejecting; (2) degrading; (3) isolating; (4) corrupting; (5) denying emotional responsiveness; (6) exploiting (nonsexual); (7) verbal terrorism; (8) physical terrorism; (9) witness to violence; (10) unreliable and incon-sistent care; (11) controlling and stifling independence; and (12) physical neglect. Each PMQ item measures the frequency of occurrence of a specific maltreatment behavior falling into each of these areas.

The Childhood Trauma Questionnaire (CTQ) (Bernstein et al. 1994; Bern-stein and Fink 1998) began as a seventy-item self-report measure of the fre-quency and severity of childhood abuse experienced in each of six areas: (1) physical abuse; (2) sexual abuse: (3) emotional abuse; (4) physical neg-lect; (5) emotional neglect; and (6) related areas of family dysfunction, such as substance abuse. The items of the CTQ are statements that begin with the phrase, "When I was growing up . . . " and each statement is rated on a Likert-type scale having response options ranging from 0 (never true) to 5 (very often true). The items in the original CTQ did not employ terms like "abuse," "neglect," or "trauma," because the authors considered these terms subjective. In addition, the authors felt that these terms have an evaluative and stigmatizing quality that could arouse defensiveness and therefore might lead respondents to underreport abusive experiences (Bernstein et al. 1994).

The first validation study carried out on the CTQ employed a sample of 286 substance dependent patients (Bernstein et al. 1994). A principal components analysis of the responses of this sample yielded four meaningful factors: physical neglect, emotional neglect, physical and emotional abuse, and sexual abuse. Eleven items loaded .40 or above on the physical neglect factor (e.g., "There was enough food in the house for everyone"); sixteen items loaded .40 or above on emotional neglect (e.g., "People in my family didn't seem to know or care what I was doing"); twenty-three items loaded .40 or above on physical and emotional abuse (e.g., "I was punished with a belt, board, cord, or some other hard object," "People in my family said hurtful and insulting things to me"); and five items loaded .40 or above on sexual abuse (e.g., "Someone tried to touch me in a sexual way or make me touch them"). The internal consistency of these four empirically derived subscales were good to excellent (alpha coefficients ranged from .79 to .94). The authors also reported test-retest coefficients for a subsample of forty patients in the sample. The test-retest correlations ranged from .80 to .83 with an average interval of 3.6 months between testings.

A subsequent validity study employing adolescent inpatients (Bernstein, Ahluvalia, Pogge, and Handelsman 1997) indicated a similar factor structure for the CTQ, except that the factor representing physical and emotional abuse in the earlier study split into two factors representing physical abuse and emotional abuse separately. Paivio and Cramer (2004) administered the CTQ to a sample of 470 undergraduate students from a midwestern Canadian university. They obtained the same five-factor solution reported by Bernstein and his associates (1997).

There is also evidence that respondents' recollections of childhood abuse as measured by the CTQ are stable over time, even if the respondents are undergoing treatment aimed at remediating abuse-related symptoms. Paivio (2001) administered the CTQ and measures of symptom severity to thirty-three patients in therapy for symptoms related to childhood abuse. She reported that these patients demonstrated significant changes in every outcome area that was assessed. These included significant reductions in overall symptom distress, as measured by the Symptom Checklist-90-Revised (SCL) (Derogatis 1983), and significant reductions in the frequency of trauma-related intrusion and avoidance, as measured by the Impact of Event Scale (IES) (Horowitz 1986). In addition, the participants demonstrated significant reductions in scores on the Resolution Scale (RS) (Singh 1994), which measures the degree to which respondents are troubled by negative feelings (e.g., anger, sadness, guilt, shame) or unmet needs with respect to a specific other person. In spite of the reductions in symptoms experienced by this group, their self-reports of childhood abuse made using the CTQ did not change. The mean scores of the sample on the CTQ factors did not change significantly, and test-retest reliability correlations ranged from .62 to .92, with a median of .86. Thus it is clear that the CTQ is an excellent instrument to use with survivors of childhood abuse who have sought treatment, since data obtained on the nature and parameters of childhood abuse using the CTQ will remain relevant as treatment proceeds.

In addition, Bernstein and his colleagues have developed and validated a brief screening version of the CTQ (Bernstein and Fink 1998; Bernstein, Stein, Newcomb et al. 2003). The short form of the Childhood Trauma Questionnaire consists of twenty-five items plus three validity items. Five items compose each of the five CTQ subscales. Unlike the items in the original seventy-item CTQ, some of the items in the twenty-five-item form use terms like "abused." The CTQ manual states that "because the self-report format may be less invasive than face-to-face interviews and help promote feelings of privacy, it may increase the likelihood of disclosure" (Bernstein and Fink 1998, 2). The authors indicated that the CTQ can be administered in both clinical and nonclinical settings and can be administered individually or in groups. They argued that "when given at intake or early in treatment, the CTQ quickly identifies individuals with histories of childhood trauma so that appropriate treatment can be provided" (1998, 3). They maintained that the CTQ provides a quantitative measure of childhood trauma that allows for a more precise characterization of the severity of traumatic experiences. They also stated that when the CTQ is used in conjunction with other available data, it can help the clinician identify individuals who are at risk for trauma-related symptoms and problems such as PTSD, suicide attempts, and sexual dysfunction. Finally, Bernstein and Fink (1998) noted that the administration of the CTQ can serve as a means of initiating a dialogue with patients regarding their traumatic experiences.

The conceptual definitions of the five CTQ subscales and the items composing each scale are as follows: Emotional abuse refers to verbal assaults on a child's sense of worth or well-being, or any humiliating, demeaning, or threatening behavior directed toward a child by an older person. The items in the Emotional Abuse Scale are as follows: (1) People in my family called me things like "stupid," "lazy," or "ugly"; (2) I thought that my parents wished I had never been born; (3) People in my family said hurtful or insulting things to me; (4) I felt that someone in my family hated me; and (5) I believe that I was emotionally abused.

Physical abuse is defined as "bodily assaults on a child by an older person that pose a risk of, or result in, injury" (1998, 2). The items that compose the Physical Abuse Scale of the CTQ are as follows: (1) I got hit so hard by someone in my family that I had to see a doctor or go to the hospital; (2) People in my family hit me so hard that it left me with bruises or marks; (3) I was punished with a belt, a board, a cord, or some other hard object; (4) I believe that I was physically abused; and (5) I got hit or beaten so badly that it was noticed by someone like a teacher, neighbor, or doctor.

Sexual abuse refers to sexual contact or conduct between a child and an older person. Explicit coercion is viewed as a frequent but not essential feature of such experiences. The items composing the Sexual Abuse Scale include the following: (1) Someone tried to touch me sexually or tried to make me touch them; (2) Someone threatened to hurt me or tell lies about me unless I did something sexual with them; (3) Someone tried to make me do sexual things or watch sexual things; (4) Someone molested me; and (5) I believe that I was sexually abused.

Emotional neglect was defined as the failure of caretakers to provide a child's basic psychological and emotional needs, such as love, encouragement, belonging, and support. The items composing the Emotional Neglect Scale are as follows: (1) There was someone in my family who made me feel important or special (reversed); (2) I felt loved (reversed); (3) People in my family looked out for each other (reversed); (4) People in my family felt close to each other (reversed); and (5) My family was a source of strength and support (reversed).

Physical neglect refers to the failure of caregivers to provide a child's basic physical needs, including food, shelter, safety and supervision, and health. The items composing the Physical Neglect Scale include the following: (1) I didn't have enough to eat; (2) I knew there was someone to take care of me and protect me (reversed); (3) My parents were too drunk or high to take care of the family; (4) I had to wear dirty clothes; and (5) There was someone to take me to the doctor if I needed it (reversed).

Bernstein and colleagues (2003) validated the short form of the CTQ on a total of 1,978 individuals in four different samples: adult substance abusers (predominantly male) enrolled in inpatient and outpatient treatment programs in New York City (n = 378); female and male adolescent psychiatric inpatients (n = 396); female and male substance abusers in a community sample from Texas (n = 625); and a normative sample of female and male community members from the Los Angeles area (n = 579). Bernstein factor analyzed the responses to the twenty-five-item CTQ in each of the four samples separately. The factor structures obtained for each of the four samples conformed to the a priori item groupings, with the five items composing each subscale loading on the expected factor in each sample. This finding supports the convergent and discriminant validity of the instrument and also demonstrates the instrument's measurement invariance across diverse populations. The five subscales were also internally consistent in all four samples. Alpha coefficients ranged from .84 to .89 for the emotional abuse subscale; from .81 to .86 for physical abuse; from .92 to .95 for sexual abuse; from .85 to .91 for emotional neglect; and from .61 to .78 for physical neglect.

As a further demonstration of the validity of the twenty-five-item CTQ, Bernstein and his colleagues (2003) obtained therapists' ratings of the abuse experienced by a subsample of 179 of the adolescent inpatients. For each of these adolescents, the therapist rated physical abuse, sexual abuse, emotional abuse, and neglect. The scores of these adolescents on the five subscales of the CTQ were correlated with the therapists' ratings in each of these four domains. The correlation between the CTQ score on physical abuse and the therapist's rating of physical abuse was .59 ($p < .001$). The correlation between the CTQ score on sexual abuse and the therapist's rating of sexual abuse was .75 ($p < .001$). The correlation between the CTQ score on emotional abuse and the therapists' rating of emotional abuse was .48 ($p < .001$). The correlation between the CTQ score on emotional neglect and the therapist's rating of neglect was .36 ($p < .001$); and the correlation between the CTQ score on physical neglect and the therapist's rating of neglect was .50 ($p < .001$). These substantial and significant validity coefficients provide compelling evidence of the utility of the CTQ for clinicians. Moreover, the CTQ was designed to be self-administered in five minutes or less. The CTQ is available commercially in an easily scored form from the Psychological Corporation.

Measures of Abuse-Related Symptoms and Personality Disturbances

Omnibus Personality Measures

At the beginning of this chapter we referred to Allen, Coyne, and Huntoon (1998), who argued that because survivors of childhood abuse display such a broad range of symptoms, they are best assessed using an omnibus measure of personality, such as the Millon Multiaxial Clinical Inventory (MCMI-III) (Millon 1994). Several studies employing the MCMI-I and MCMI-II have indicated that adult survivors of physical and/or sexual abuse tend to have scores in the clinically significant range on several MCMI personality and symptom syndrome scales, including the avoidant, dependent, passive–aggressive, and borderline personality scales, and the anxiety, somatoform, thought disorder, major depression, and delusional disorder syndrome scales (Allen et al. 1998; Bryer, Nelson, Miller, and Krol 1987; Busby, Glenn, Steggell, and Adamson 1993; Fisher, Winne, and Ley 1993).

However, in discussing the relevance of the MCMI for assessing survivors of childhood abuse, Briere (2004) pointed out that

> A potential problem associated with interpreting abuse survivors' responses to the MCMI is whether high scores on a given scale indicate that the survivor, in fact, "has" the relevant disorder or personality style. For example, clinical experience suggests that adults abused as children who have elevated scores on the MCMI scales that involve psychosis (i.e., Thought Disorder and Delusional Disorder) do not necessarily show psychotic symptoms, nor do all of those with a clinical Borderline scale score necessarily have borderline personality disorder. Instead, the psychotic scales may tap the posttraumatic symptoms (especially reexperiencing and avoidance), dissociation, and chaotic internal experience of survivors of severe abuse, whereas the Borderline scale may be affected by the greater identity, affect regulation, and interpersonal difficulties of the severely abused. (546)

Thus the use of the MCMI with survivors of childhood abuse has the potential of generating "false positive" assessments—leading the clinician to identify symptom areas for a given patient which are in fact not clinically problematic. Clinicians who choose to employ the MCMI are therefore cautioned to use test results as the basis for exploration with the patient, rather than as a definitive indicator of areas that must necessarily be addressed in treatment. The same caution is warranted in using any omnibus personality measure to assess adult survivors of childhood abuse.

Measures of Symptoms Related to Traumatic Experiences

More relevant to the assessment of symptoms among survivors of childhood abuse are measures specifically designed to measure posttraumatic symptomatology. These include: (1) measures of symptoms of PTSD experienced in relation to a specific traumatic event; (2) measures of posttraumatic symptoms that may be derived from various traumatic experiences that occurred during adulthood or childhood; (3) measures designed specifically to assess the range of symptoms associated with complex PTSD; and (4) more detailed measures of specific areas of posttraumatic stress, such as dissociative symptoms.

The following discussion of assessment tools considers each of these categories but focuses specifically on two assessment techniques that we consider particularly valuable to clinicians working with patients who may be survivors of childhood abuse, the Traumatic Symptom Inventory (TSI) (Briere

1995) and the Structured Interview for Disorders of Extreme Stress (SIDES) (van der Kolk and Pelcovitz 1999).

Measures of Symptoms of PTSD Experienced
in Relation to a Specific Traumatic Event
There are at least two different self-report measures which assess the respondent's experience of symptoms of PTSD in relation to a specific traumatic event, the revised Impact of Event Scale (IES-R) (Weiss and Marmar 1997), and the Detailed Assessment of Posttraumatic Stress (DAP) (Briere 2001).

The Impact of Event Scale (IES) (Horowitz, Wilner, and Alvarez 1979) and the revised Impact of Event Scale (IES-R) (Weiss and Marmar 1997) were developed to measure the individual's symptomatic response to a specific traumatic experience. The original IES is a fifteen-item scale that assessed two dimensions of posttraumatic symptomatology, intrusive cognitions and affects (seven items) and avoidance, denial, or blocking of thoughts and images (eight items). The IES-R added seven items aimed primarily at assessing the symptoms of hyperarousal described in the DSM as criteria for the diagnosis of PTSD. The instructions of the IES-R state:

> Below is a list of difficulties people sometimes have after stressful life events. Please read each item, and then indicate how distressing each difficulty has been for you DURING THE LAST SEVEN DAYS with respect to _____. How much were you distressed or bothered by these difficulties?

Thus the respondent is expected to indicate the event which is the source of the distress, and then to rate the degree of distress experienced during the last week as a result of this event. Each item is a symptom, and respondents rate the degree of distress associated with the symptom on five-point Likert-type scales having response options ranging from 0 (not at all) to 4 (extremely).

Weiss and Marmar (1997) reported excellent internal consistency and stability coefficients for the three subscales of the IES-R in samples responding to the scale when administered in English as well as when translated into several different languages. The alpha coefficients for the three subscales in the English language norming sample were .89 for the intrusion subscale, .84 for the avoidance subscale, and .82 for the hyperarousal subscale. The divergent validity of the subscales was indicated by moderate subscale intercorrelations across the several norming samples. The authors do not provide cut-off points indicating clinically significant symptom levels in each area, nor do they recommend that the IES-R be substituted for clinical interviews in making the diagnosis of PTSD.

The IES-R provides a good measure of three important dimensions of PTSD symptomatology. It does not assess the symptoms of complex PTSD that we have seen to characterize survivors of prolonged severe abuse in general and prolonged severe childhood abuse in particular. Therefore, the clinician working with a patient who may be a survivor of childhood abuse will probably not turn to the IES-R as the first step in assessing the symptoms experienced by that adult survivor. However, the IES-R could provide a useful index of the severity of PTSD symptoms that may be experienced by the survivor, particularly when that survivor has been exposed to revictimization or to additional traumatic events as an adult.

The Detailed Assessment of Posttraumatic Stress (DAPS) (Briere 2001) is a 105-item inventory that contains scales that measure an individual's (1) immediate cognitive, emotional, and dissociative reactions to a specific traumatic event (peritraumatic distress); (2) subsequent posttraumatic stress symptoms (reexperiencing, avoidance, and hyperarousal); and (3) level of experienced disability (posttraumatic impairment). The DAPS allows respondents to complete the measure in the context of childhood sexual abuse and childhood physical abuse. Therefore it allows patients to rate their posttraumatic symptoms in the context of their history of traumatic events experienced during childhood. However, the symptom dimensions assessed do not fully represent the range of difficulties associated with severe and prolonged childhood abuse. Therefore this measure, like the IES-R, will be used by the clinician seeking to assess the distress experienced by an adult survivor of childhood abuse primarily as an ancillary tool to assist in his or her understanding the entire history of the patient's traumatic experiences and related symptoms. The DAPS is available commercially through Psychological Assessment Resources.

Measures of Posttraumatic Symptoms Associated with
Traumatic Events Experienced during Childhood and/or Adulthood
    Foremost among the measures of posttraumatic symptoms that may derive from either trauma experienced during childhood or adult traumatic experiences is the Trauma Symptom Inventory (TSI) (Briere 1995). This is a hundred-item measure of posttraumatic stress and other psychological sequelae of traumatic events. The TSI manual describes the TSI as "intended for use in the evaluation of acute and chronic traumatic symptomatology, including, but not limited to, the effects of rape, spouse abuse, physical assault, combat, major accidents, and natural disasters, as well as the lasting seque-

lae of childhood abuse and other early traumatic events" (Briere 1995, 1). Each item of the TSI represents a symptom that the respondent may have experienced. Responses to each item of the TSI are made on a four-point scale having response options ranging from 0 (never) to 3 (often).

The TSI yields scores on ten clinical scales, which include not only scales measuring the symptoms commonly associated with Posttraumatic Stress Disorder (PTSD) and Acute Stress Disorder (ASD), but also scales assessing some of the intra- and interpersonal difficulties associated with chronic psychological trauma. The ten clinical scales of the TSI are as follows:

1. The Anxious Arousal (AA) Scale measures symptoms of anxiety, especially symptoms associated with posttraumatic hyperarousal, such as jumpiness and tension. Individuals with high scores on this scale tend to report periods of trembling or shaking, nervousness, excessive worrying, and fears of bodily harm. They describe themselves as tense, and they tend to exhibit exaggerated startle responses. Patients with high AA scores are prone to both generalized anxiety and to panic attacks.

2. The Depression (D) Scale assesses both depressed mood state and depressive cognitive distortions. Individuals with high scores on this scale frequently experience feelings of sadness and unhappiness and a pervasive sense of being depressed. They tend to perceive themselves as useless and inadequate. They tend to view the future as hopeless, and they have thoughts about death and dying. Behaviorally, they tend to experience periods of tearfulness; and they tend to isolate themselves from others. Elevated D scores should warn the clinician of the possibility of self-injurious behavior and suicidal thoughts. Briere (1995) recommended that when a patient's D score is elevated, the clinician should conduct a follow-up interview to review the patient's responses to specific items regarding suicidal behavior (item 25) and thoughts of death (items 30 and 90)

3. The Anger/Irritability (AI) Scale assesses self-reported anger and irritable affect, as well as related angry cognitions and behaviors. High scores may reflect either the irritability associated with PTSD or a more chronic angry state. The AI scale measures the presence of angry cognitions, such as wanting to hurt someone or wanting to tell them off, and also the presence of angry behavior, such as yelling, argumentativeness, and starting fights. Individuals who score high on the AI scale often experience their anger as an intrusive and unwanted experience that is not within their control. These individuals often experience pervasive feelings of irritability, annoyance, and bad temper. Minor difficulties or frustrations may lead to inappropriately angry reactions. Briere (1995) recommended that when a patient has an elevated score on the AI scale, the clinician should consider and discuss with the patient the response to TSI item 19, which concerns fantasies about hurting someone.

4. *The Intrusive Experiences (IE) Scale* measures the intrusive symptoms of PTSD, such as flashbacks, upsetting memories that are easily triggered by current events, nightmares, and intrusive thoughts. These intrusive symptoms are unwanted and are frequently experienced unexpectedly, as if they came "out of nowhere." Individuals who score high on the IE scale often feel out of control and may fear that they are psychotic.

5. *The Defensive Avoidance (DA) Scale* measures posttraumatic avoidance of cues that remind one of experienced trauma, including both cognitive avoidance (e.g., pushing painful memories from one's mind) and behavioral avoidance (e.g., avoiding situations containing stimuli that remind one of the traumatic event(s)). Respondents who score high on the DA scale tend to report that they consciously engage in efforts to neutralize negative feelings associated with prior traumatic experiences. For example, they tend to endorse TSI item 87, "Trying not to have any feelings about something that once hurt you." Briere (1995) noted that "DA responses do not represent dissociation, repression, or other similar psychological defenses as much as they represent the conscious, intentional process of cognitive and behavioral avoidance as a way of managing posttraumatic distress" (14).

6. *The Dissociation (DIS) Scale* measures dissociative symptoms. Dissociation is defined as a "largely unconscious defensive alteration in conscious awareness, developed as an avoidance response to overwhelming, often posttraumatic, psychological distress" (Briere 1995, 14). The dissociative experiences tapped by the DIS scale include cognitive disengagement, depersonalization, derealization, out-of-body experiences, and psychic numbing. These symptoms represent the most common dissociative responses and do not include the more extreme dissociative symptoms such as fugue states and/or Dissociative Identity Disorder. Briere (1995) suggested that individuals who score high on the DIS Scale tend to report that they are highly distractible, tend to "space out," and feel out of touch with themselves and their bodies. The experience of depersonalization is aversive and may generate substantial anxiety. Briere (1995) suggested that when a patient has an elevated score on the DIS Scale, the clinician may want to explore this area in greater detail through the use of a more comprehensive dissociation inventory such as the Dissociative Experiences Scale (DES) (Bernstein and Putnam 1986).

7. *The Sexual Concerns (SC) Scale* measures self-reported sexual distress, including sexual dissatisfaction, negative thoughts and feelings experienced during sex, sexual dysfunction, unwanted sexual preoccupation, and feelings

of shame regarding sexual activities or responses. The scale does not assess issues surrounding sexual orientation. Individuals who score high on the SC scale frequently experience anxiety and fearfulness regarding sex.

8. *The Dysfunctional Sexual Behavior (DSB) Scale* assesses sexual behavior that is dysfunctional, either because it is indiscriminant or potentially harmful, or because it is used inappropriately to achieve nonsexual goals. Indiscriminate and potentially harmful sex may involve promiscuity, failure to practice safe sex, and/or the tendency to be attracted to dangerous or abusive partners. Inappropriate sex for nonsexual goals includes entering into sexual relationships to ward off loneliness or internal distress, as well as prostitution or otherwise using sex as a commodity. Elevated scores on the DSB scale are closely associated with childhood sexual victimization.

9. *The Impaired Self-Reference (ISR) Scale* measures problems related to an inadequate sense of self and personal identity. These problems include the inability to distinguish between one's own needs and the needs of others, confusion regarding one's purpose and goals for life, an inability to understand one's own behavior, a feeling of emptiness, reliance on others to provide structure and direction, and the inability to say no to requests/demands made by others. Individuals who score high on the ISR scale tend to lack self-knowledge and self-confidence. They are subject to manipulation and tend to handle stressful situations poorly.

10. *The Tension-Reduction Behavior (TRB) Scale* measures the respondent's tendency to employ external methods of reducing internal tension or distress. Externalizing distress may be accomplished through self-mutilation, suicidal tendencies, aggressive behavior, and/or indiscriminate sexuality. Since the externalization of distress is accomplished through various forms of acting out, elevated scores on the TRB scale indicate a risk of dangerous behavior that may potentially result in harm to self and/or others. High scores on the TRB scale should be discussed with patients to further assess the potential for harm.

The TSI manual (1995) provides T-score and percentile equivalents for respondents' raw scores on each of the TSI clinical scales. A T-score of 65 or above is considered clinically significant for each scale. This T-score corresponds to a point 1.5 standard deviations above the mean for the standardization sample, or a percentile rank of approximately 93.3.

The TSI also includes three validity scales: (1) the Response Level (RL) Scale, which measures the respondent's defensiveness and/or need to appear symptom free; (2) the Atypical Response (AR) Scale, which reflects psychosis, extreme distress, and/or an attempt to appear particularly disturbed or dysfunctional; and (3) the Inconsistent Response (IR) Scale, which reflects random responding, attention or concentration problems, and/or reading or language difficulties.

Briere (1995) provided clinicians with important guidelines for interpreting TSI profiles. He noted that factor analytic studies of the TSI in both standardization and clinical samples indicated the presence of two principal symptom dimensions, representing trauma symptoms and self-dysfunction. The TSI scales loading primarily on the trauma symptoms factor were Anxious Arousal, Depression, Intrusive Experiences, Defensive Avoidance, and Dissociation. However, the Impaired Self-Reference and Tension Reduction Behavior Scales also had moderately high loadings on the trauma symptoms factor. The TSI scales loading primarily on the self-dysfunction factor were Sexual Concerns, Dysfunctional Sexual Behavior, and Tension Reduction Behavior. The Impaired Self-Reference Scale also had moderately high loadings on this factor.

Briere recommended that clinicians "may wish to see traumatic events as external challenges to the individual's internal equilibrium, and the self as a set of resources that allow the individual to deal with such challenges" (1995, 16). Viewed from this perspective, elevations on the AA, D, IE, DA, and DIS scales are seen as reflecting distress associated with the impact of traumatic events, whereas elevations on the TRB, DSB, and ISR scales are seen as indicating that the respondent has insufficient self-resources to "modulate or otherwise address such distress" (1995, 16). Therefore

> (1) a respondent with trauma symptom elevations but not unusually prominent self-difficulties tends to present more as a classic/uncomplicated trauma victim, often in response to a relatively recent stressor; (2) a respondent with relatively low trauma symptomatology but with multiple self-difficulties would be seen as someone more likely to have the identity and affect regulation difficulties often associated with dysfunctional personality traits; and (3) a person with both trauma and self-disturbance indicators would be most likely to present as a complex trauma victim: chronically distressed, overwhelmed by intrusive symptoms, and potentially more likely to act out painful internal states by virtue of lesser self-resources. (1995, 16)

Thus a patient demonstrating clinically significant elevations on both TSI scales representing the trauma dimension and TSI scales representing the self-dysfunction dimension would be most likely to have been the victim of severe and extended childhood abuse.

In addition to the interpretation of elevated scores on scales reflecting the two major TSI dimensions of trauma symptoms and self-dysfunction, Briere

(1995) noted that the TSI contains twelve "critical items" which clinicians should consider individually. These items include seven that constitute components of one or more of the ten clinical scales, and five additional items which have been included because they individually represent "critical issues in the evaluation of traumatized individuals" (16). These items are as follows: (19) thoughts or fantasies about hurting someone; (25) threatening or attempting suicide; (28) getting into trouble because of sex; (30) wishing you were dead; (40) using drugs other than marijuana; (48) intentionally hurting yourself (e.g., by scratching, cutting, or burning) even though you weren't trying to commit suicide; (50) sexual fantasies about being dominated or overpowered; (58) getting into trouble because of your drinking; (65) hearing someone talk to you who wasn't really there; (90) feeling like life wasn't worth living; (92) seeing people from the spirit world; and (99) thinking someone was reading your mind. Briere (1995) recommended that a nonzero response to any of these items represents a potentially serious clinical problem that should be explored with the patient.

The TSI manual also presents several illustrative TSI test profiles, along with descriptions of the presenting symptoms and histories of the patients who had these profiles. An example of such a test profile that is particularly relevant for clinicians working with survivors of childhood abuse is that of a forty-six-year-old woman who sought treatment for relationship problems and self-destructive impulses. This woman had clinically significant elevations on all of the TSI clinical scales relevant to the self-dysfunction factor (SC, DSB, TRB, and ISB). She also had clinically significant elevations on the D and DIS scales within the trauma symptom cluster. In addition, she endorsed two of the twelve critical items noted above—getting into trouble because of sex and self-mutilation. Briere interpreted this profile as indicating that the patient has significant disturbances in the areas of identity and self-awareness, and that she tends to externalize her internal distress through self-mutilation and by acting out sexually. The fact that her scores were not within the clinical range on IE or DA suggests an absence of formal PTSD. Briere (1995) noted that this profile is common among adults who have experienced severe and chronic childhood sexual abuse. The combination of a clinically significant elevation on the DIS scale, along with the significant elevations on the SC and DSB scales, suggests that this patient may regard her indiscriminant or maladaptive sexual behavior as shameful, though uncontrollable. She may well be dissociated when engaging in these behaviors.

The TSI is a highly useful tool for clinicians working with clients who might be survivors of childhood abuse. The profiles of scores on the TSI clinical scales may be used to develop hypotheses regarding a possible history of childhood abuse. The TSI has cutoff scores that indicate clinically significant elevations in each of the ten symptom dimensions. The use of T-scores provides an element of comparability across the ten clinical scales that may be used roughly along with feedback from the patient to help in identifying the symptom areas that may be most immediately in need of clinical attention. In addition, the twelve designated critical questions of the TSI provide an important safeguard to reduce the chances that potentially harmful or even life-threatening symptoms will be overlooked or underestimated. The validity and reliability data for the TSI is good, and the validity scales provide the clinician with important indications of denial or defensive response style. The TSI is available commercially from Psychological Assessment Resources.

Measures Assessing Symptoms of Complex PTSD

As we discussed in the previous chapter, survivors of severe and prolonged childhood abuse tend to manifest symptoms beyond those of simple PTSD. Several measures have been developed specifically to assess either the entire range of symptoms associated with complex PTSD, or specific aspects of complex PTSD. The Structured Interview for Disorders of Extreme Stress (SIDES) (Pelcovitz et al. 1997; van der Kolk and Pelcovitz 1999; Zlotnick and Pearlstein 1997), considered above in connection with our discussion of the DESNOS diagnosis, represents the state of the art in the assessment of the symptoms of complex PTSD that are not included in the DSM-IV-TR criteria for the diagnosis of simple PTSD. The Trauma and Attachment Belief Scale (TABS) (Pearlman 2003) and the Inventory of Altered Self Capacities (IASC) (Briere 2000) have been developed to assess the attachment and self-related personality disturbances that are characteristic of complex PTSD in general and specifically characteristic of adult survivors of severe and prolonged childhood abuse.

Structured Interview for Disorders of Extreme Stress

As described above (chapter 9, pp. 223), the SIDES measures twenty-seven specific symptoms of complex PTSD that fall within seven major symptom categories. Thus the SIDES provides the clinician with a finely tuned assessment of the symptoms that an adult survivor of severe child abuse might be experiencing. Within the area of regulation of affect/impulses, the SIDES assesses six specific areas, including inability to regulate affect, inability to modulate anger, self-destructive behavior, suicidal preoccupation, preoccupation with sexual thoughts and behaviors, and excessive risk taking. Within the area of alterations in attention and or consciousness, the SIDES measures both amnesia and episodic dissociation/depersonalization. Within the area of dysfunctional self-perceptions, the SIDES indicates the extent to which the respondent experiences feelings of ineffectiveness, perceives the self as permanently damaged, feels guilty and responsible for the traumatic experiences to which he or she has been exposed, feels shame, believes no one can understand, and minimizes the trauma. Within the area of alterations in the respondent's perceptions of the perpetrator(s) of traumatic experiences, the SIDES assesses distorted beliefs regarding the perpetrator and/or the reasons why the traumatic experiences occurred, idealization of the perpetrator, and preoccupation with harming the perpetrator. With respect to the potential impact of severe childhood abuse on relationships with others, the SIDES assesses inability to trust others, the tendency toward revictimization, and the tendency to victimize others. The somatic symptoms assessed by the SIDES include digestive disorders, chronic pain, cardiopulmonary symptoms, conversion reactions, and sexual dysfunction. Finally, within the area of altered systems of meaning associated with severe childhood abuse, the SIDES measures both the foreshortened sense of the future and the loss of previously held beliefs that characterize survivors of prolonged severe trauma.

The SIDES measures many symptoms that adult survivors of childhood abuse may experience that are not measured by the TSI. Van der Kolk and Pelcovitz (1999) reported good internal consistency and interrater reliability coefficients for the seven subscales of the SIDES. Zlotnick and associates (1996) reported that the subscales of the SIDES were correlated significantly with other instruments designed to measure similar constructs. Zlotnick and others (1997) found that the subscales of the SIDES significantly differentiated a sample of female survivors of childhood sexual abuse from an otherwise comparable sample of women without histories of sexual abuse. Roth and associates (1997) reported that women who had experienced both physical and sexual abuse during childhood tended to have higher symptom scores on the SIDES subscales than women who had experienced one form of abuse only.

Van der Kolk and Pelcovitz (1999) stressed the utility of the SIDES for determining the most appropriate treatment for adult survivors of childhood abuse. They suggested that the conceptualization of PTSD embodied in the DMS-IV-TR tends to emphasize unbidden and intrusive thoughts and feelings, against which the sufferer defends himself by avoiding stimuli reminiscent of the trauma. This emphasis suggests the efficacy of treatment involving desensitization to the traumatic memories, with "the goal that the patient can habituate to the conditioned stimuli that precipitate traumatic reexperiences" (1999, 23). However, the symptoms of complex PTSD assessed by the SIDES, including dissociation, somatization, affect dysregulation, and altered relationships with self and others, would not be expected to be ameliorated through desensitization procedures. Therefore, van der Kolk and Pelcovitz noted that

> For the past several years we have used the SIDES in our clinical evaluations of a wide variety of traumatized populations. After taking a careful, developmentally based trauma history we use the SIDES to elicit information regarding the overall effects of the trauma. It has been particularly valuable in identifying the most critical areas of psychological impairment which need to be addressed for effective treatment planning. Post-traumatic patients with high degrees of difficulties on the dimensions of affect regulation, dissociation, or somatization may require a different treatment approach than patients who suffer from "simple" PTSD. (1999, 24)

Van der Kolk and Pelcovitz (1999) suggested that many patients who are diagnosed with PTSD primarily seek treatment not for their intrusive symptoms, but for symptoms of complex PTSD, such as affect dysregulation, dissociative problems, and difficulties with trust and intimacy. But such issues may respond better to dynamic therapy than to approaches emphasizing desensitization. The developers of the SIDES concluded that "fully effective treatment may require a strategically staged, multimodal treatment approach" (24) and they suggested that the assessment of the patient's complex adaptation to traumatic life experiences may provide the clinician with the data necessary to make decisions regarding the components of such treatment.

Trauma and Attachment Belief Scale

The Trauma and Attachment Belief Scale (TABS) (Pearlman 2003) is an eighty-four-item scale that measures five dimensions of the respondent's schemas regarding self and others, including safety, trust, esteem, intimacy, and control. Pearlman used the TABS to measure the impact of traumatic experiences (including childhood abuse) on samples of college students, outpatients, battered women, and homeless individuals. Briere (2004) suggested that because this scale focuses on aspects of attachment and relationships that are affected by histories of trauma, "the TABS is likely to be helpful in understanding important assumptions that the client carries in his or her relationships to others, including the therapist, and in formulating more relational (i.e., not just symptom focused) treatment goals" (Briere 2004, 554).

Inventory of Altered Self Capacities

The Inventory of Altered Self Capacities (IASC) (Briere 2000) is a sixty-three-item test that yields scores on seven scales representing different types of "self-related" personality disturbances that are characteristic of survivors of severe childhood abuse. The seven IASC subscales are: (1) interpersonal conflicts; (2) idealization–disillusionment; (3) abandonment concerns; (4) identity impairment (with two different subscales, self-awareness and diffusion); (5) susceptibility to influence; (6) affect dysregulation (with two different subscales, instability and skills deficits), and (7) tension reduction activities. Briere (2000) reported that the IASC predicts self-reported child abuse history, adult attachment style, borderline and antisocial personality features, relationship problems, suicidal tendencies, and substance abuse. Furthermore, Briere argued that this test can forewarn clinicians of possible obstacles to the treatment process associated with such self–other issues as abandonment fears, idealization/devaluation, and hypersusceptibility to interpretation, which might otherwise disrupt or derail the client–therapist relationship.

CHAPTER ELEVEN

~

Individual Therapy with Survivors of Childhood Abuse

Presenting Problems

Patients almost never enter therapy stating that they need help with issues related to abuse they experienced during childhood. Patients typically seek treatment for specific symptoms or interpersonal problems. Initial inquiries regarding the patient's complaints may suggest that some of the difficulties reported are associated with histories of childhood abuse. These symptoms may include indicators of inadequate or dysfunctional self-concept, such as feelings of inadequacy, ineffectiveness, guilt, shame, an inability to trust, or a chronic inability to maintain meaningful intimate relationships. These symptoms may also include posttraumatic symptoms, such as affect dysregulation and impulsivity, dissociative experiences, and somatic disorders. When a patient presents with initial complaints that represent both impaired self-capacities and posttraumatic symptoms, our experience suggests a strong likelihood that the patient has a history of childhood abuse. In most cases, such patients have experienced severe abuse over an extended period of time.

However, it is unusual for a patient to enter treatment and immediately identify symptoms that represent both impaired self-capacities and posttraumatic symptoms. Most patients initially disclose difficulties in only one of these two areas. Perhaps the patient actually has difficulties in only one of the two areas. For example, patients who have impaired or inadequate self-concept but no posttraumatic symptoms may have experienced childhood neglect or other forms of inadequate caretaking behavior, but no discrete instances of severe traumatic experiences, as these experiences are defined in the DSM-IV-TR. These patients may manifest insecure adult attachment patterns that are clearly dysfunctional but not experience posttraumatic symptoms. In contrast, a patient who reports posttraumatic stress symptoms but no indications of inadequate or dysfunctional self-concept may have experienced a traumatic episode or episodes in the context of an otherwise secure and nurturing childhood environment.

Other patients who initially report only symptoms representing impaired or dysfunctional self-concept or posttraumatic symptoms may in fact have symptoms in both domains, but they may be aware of symptoms in one domain only. Alternatively, the patient may be aware of problems in both areas but is not prepared to disclose symptoms in one area or the other when beginning treatment.

Fortunately, these diverse possibilities have the same implication for the clinician. If there is any indication of a possible history of childhood abuse or trauma, the clinician should proceed on the assumption that other indications may be present, and should set about establishing a secure and trusting relationship with the patient that will facilitate the disclosure of additional symptoms, as well as the disclosure of the childhood experiences that may have given rise to these symptoms.

Establishing Security and Trust in the Therapeutic Relationship

As they work to establish a relationship in which the patient feels secure, clinicians should be aware that clients who are survivors of childhood abuse may not remember being abused. Failure to remember abuse may represent an avoidance strategy, implemented through dissociation or repression. If patients do remember negative childhood experiences, they may not characterize these experiences as abuse. The failure to identify abusive experiences as such may reflect denial, or it may represent a perception that the negative experiences are not unusual or are even normative in our society. Furthermore, even if patients do enter treatment knowing that they were abused as children, they may not connect the abusive experiences to the problems that led them to seek treatment. Therefore it may not initially occur to them to relate these experiences to the therapist. Finally, even if patients do recognize that they were abused and suspect that the abuse may have interfered with their normal development, they may be reluctant to disclose the experiences, due to feelings of shame or guilt and lack of trust.

Clinicians working with patients who are known to be or suspected of being survivors of childhood abuse should strive first to establish a relationship in which the patient feels safe. Briere (1992a) suggested that establishing safety begins with negotiating the structural parameters of the therapeutic relationship, including such pragmatic issues as scheduling and fees, as well as the focus and boundaries of the relationship. He argued that "because child abuse inherently involves violation of physical and/or psychological integrity, the survivor may grow to expect invasion in a variety of other relationships—especially those involving intimacy or unequal power" (89). For this reason the therapist must make it clear to the patient that he or she has the right to feel safe, including the right to choose the issues that are discussed. Therapist and client must each agree that the therapeutic relationship will function solely to promote the psychological growth and development of the patient, and that neither the therapist nor the client will seek to exploit the relationship by allowing it to become sexual or romantic.

Similarly, in discussing the treatment of victims of incest, Price (1994) argued that patients enter treatment "with fear, trepidation and ambivalence" (216). Therefore patients must be reassured that the therapeutic relationship will not recapitulate the betrayal and exploitation of the original abusive relationship. In his discussion of men who were sexually abused as children, Gartner (1999) suggested that the patient may have less need for insight regarding his history of abuse and its aftereffects and more for "a relationship that permits him to let himself be known intimately without fear of surrendering himself to the other person" (237).

In her discussion of complex PTSD, Herman (1992b) argued that the core experiences of psychological trauma are "disempowerment and disconnection from others" (134). For this reason, Herman suggested that the first principle of recovery is the empowerment of the survivor. The patient's participation in negotiating and agreeing on the parameters of the therapeutic relationship represents a first step toward empowerment. In contrast to the helplessness that the survivor may have experienced during traumatic childhood experiences, this negotiation communicates to the patient that his or her needs are valued and carry weight. Although discussing frequency and length of sessions and fee policies may seem mundane, the fact that the therapist is soliciting the patient's input represents a dramatic shift away from the dynamics of the abusive relationship experienced during childhood.

Initial Inquiries Regarding Symptoms and Abuse History

As the patient begins to experience a sense of security in the therapeutic relationship, the therapist may begin to make observations and appropriately paced inquiries aimed at developing a complete picture of the patient's current psychosocial functioning and history. We have found that this process will proceed most smoothly if the therapist focuses initially on identifying all of the patient's symptoms. On the one hand, the process of assessment should be organic, and the patient's efforts to self-disclose should be reinforced when such efforts occur. On the other hand, specific therapist inquiries regarding possible history of childhood abuse are most appropriately made after the therapist has an idea of both the range of symptoms experienced by the patient and the severity of these symptoms. There are at least four reasons for focusing our inquiry initially on current symptoms.

First, patients tend to be more aware of their current experience than they are of their histories of abuse. They are likely to be aware of feelings of anxiety, both generalized anxiety and acute occurrences of startle responses, flashbacks, and nightmares. They may not be aware of chronic low grade depression to the extent that they would spontaneously volunteer the conclusion that they are depressed, but their responses to the therapist's specific questions regarding indicators of depression and their responses to self-report instruments measuring depression are likely to indicate such depression. Similarly, they may not be completely aware of dissociative symptoms that they may experience, but these too may be identified through appropriate diagnostic interview questions and/or self-report instruments. In contrast, patients may not have immediate access to memories of childhood abuse, because these have been repressed or denied.

Second, inquiries about how the patient is feeling and the patient's satisfaction with life communicate the therapist's concern for the patient and thus help foster the growth of the therapeutic relationship. Third, if the patient's status as a survivor of childhood abuse is not immediately clear, developing a complete picture of the patient's symptoms will provide the clinician with valuable data that may be used to draw inferences regarding both the likelihood that the patient is in fact a survivor of childhood abuse and the likely severity of such abuse. This in turn will help the clinician frame subsequent inquiries regarding abuse histories. Finally, the assessment of the degree to which the patient may respond to trauma-related cues with extreme negative conditioned emotional responses (e.g., panic reactions) will provide the therapist with guidance regarding the appropriate pacing of inquiries regarding abuse history.

In most cases, we recommend that clinicians assess the full range and severity of symptoms by working off the complaints that the patient reports initially. An appropriate inquiry would suggest that individuals who have the problems reported by the patient sometimes experience other difficulties as well, and it is important to identify all the problems the patient may be experiencing, as well as get a sense of the positive and negative aspects of his or her relationships with family, friends, and business associates. In addition to allowing the patient to report any additional difficulties that may come to mind during a treatment session, we sometimes give patients a homework assignment of listing the most satisfying and least satisfying aspects of their lives. This allows them adequate time to recognize and record areas of discomfort that might not come to mind immediately during the session. In addition, we recommend that clinicians who suspect a history of childhood abuse make use of instruments designed to measure the symptoms that have been shown to be associated with such abuse, such as the Trauma Symptom Inventory (TSI) and the Structured Interview for Disorders of Extreme Stress (SIDES). (See chapter 10.) These assessments both provide reliable measures of the entire range of symptoms associated with complex PTSD.

As the assessment of symptoms proceeds, the therapist may become more convinced that a history of childhood abuse is a factor. Once the clinician has a reasonably good picture of the patient's psychosocial functioning and symptoms, the next step in the assessment process is to elicit all the data relevant to the patient's childhood experiences. If the patient has not already mentioned his or her childhood, we tend to introduce this topic with a general observation such as, "Adults who come into treatment mentioning some of the same sources of dissatisfaction that you have mentioned frequently find over time that these difficulties may be related to experiences they had as children. Can you tell me what you remember about your childhood?" This inquiry, followed by appropriate probes, may be sufficient to elicit reports of childhood experiences that constitute abuse. In assessing responses to such an inquiry, the clinician should be sensitive to the patient's subjective experience of the events that he or she relates.

First and foremost, in eliciting data on childhood abuse experiences, the clinician must be acutely sensitive to possible negative emotional responses in the patient that may be triggered by recalling these experiences. In the event of such negative responses, it may be necessary for the therapist to temporarily discontinue efforts at eliciting trauma related information and focus on bolstering the patient's sense of security in the relationship with the therapist and/or the patient's ability to regulate affect. We have found that when we sense that a patient is becoming upset while attempting to relate aspects of his or her childhood experience, it is often very helpful to point out to the patient that the material seems disturbing and to explicitly suggest that we back off for a while in order to restore the patient's emotional balance. In such cases we explicitly tell the patients that we are not here to upset them and will only discuss troubling subjects when we are sure that they can handle it safely. We have found that patients are often unaware that they are becoming upset at the point where we intervene. This suggests that they may come to treatment with inadequate self-monitoring skills. Such deficits render them vulnerable to being overwhelmed before they can take steps to cope with impending negative emotional states.

Sometimes patients have only scattered or fragmented memories of abuse, possibly indicating the effects of dissociation that may have occurred at the time of the abuse. Often patients relate clearly traumatic events in quite neutral terms, possibly the result of defensive adaptations such as distancing or depersonalization.

When the patient employs defenses like denial and distancing, it may be necessary for the clinician to inform the patient that the events described seem to be quite traumatic, and to indicate that the patient's subjective reactions seem quite mild under the circumstances. This observation will allow the clinician to introduce the idea that the events described appear to constitute abuse, as well as the concept that children who experience abuse of this nature frequently employ certain self-protective strategies in order to survive during periods of abuse. These strategies include amnesia, dissociation, and distancing, which may explain the patient's incomplete recollections of childhood events. The strategies may also include efforts to externalize or numb the psychological pain associated with the abuse, including self-injurious behavior, impulsive risk-taking behavior, and substance abuse.

The therapist should explain further that these strategies may actually be functional in the context of the abusive childhood relationship, but they often prove dysfunctional when carried over into adulthood. The therapist may also acknowledge that some people, perhaps even the patient himself, may consider these coping behaviors to be entirely pathological. However, the therapist may also emphasize that these adaptations are in reality signs of strength, healthy accommodations to real threats posed in the environment during childhood. Therefore, the patient should regard therapy not as an attempt to be cured of some defect, but rather as a process through which a better, more satisfying way of living within the patient's current reality can be achieved.

Reframing the therapeutic endeavor in this manner is meant to free the patient to discuss both perceived dysfunctional behavior patterns and the childhood events that may have led to the development of these patterns. By regarding current symptoms as the result of adaptive responses to forces beyond the survivor's control, the therapist may help ameliorate the patient's experience of shame, guilt, or feelings of ineffectiveness in disclosing and describing these symptoms. Giving the patient this perspective on his or her dysfunctional behaviors also provides the basis for the primary work of therapy, which typically involves reworking attachment schemas and ameliorating posttraumatic symptoms.

Goals for Treatment

We have conceptualized the effects of childhood abuse in terms of insecure adult attachment patterns and posttraumatic symptoms. We have suggested that various forms of neglect and inconsistent parenting predict later insecure attachment. We have also suggested that exposure to traumatic events, particularly repeated traumatic events that begin early in the course of development and continue for some time, predict the emergence of posttraumatic symptoms that persist into adulthood. We have argued that complex PTSD, which involves both the interpersonal deficits associated with insecure attachment and specific posttraumatic symptoms, frequently results from the combination of neglect and/or inconsistency on the part of early caregivers, and the experience of trauma associated with childhood physical and/or sexual abuse that began early and persisted over time.

Given this conceptualization of complex PTSD, the goals for the treatment of survivors of various forms of childhood abuse will involve (1) goals relevant to attachment schemas and concomitant cognitions and behaviors and/or (2) goals focused on reducing posttraumatic symptoms. Goals falling into the first category are pursued through the use of the therapeutic relationship, a process referred to by Gartner (1999) as "relational reconstruction in the therapeutic dyad" (236). Goals in the second category are pursued behaviorally through the desensitization of conditioned emotional responses to traumatic cues, and through the development of behavioral skills aimed at improving the patient's ability to regulate affect and control the tendency to respond impulsively to negative emotional states.

In the event that a patient is experiencing both manifestations of insecure attachment and posttraumatic symptoms, the general rule that clinicians should follow is to address the attachment issues first, and then proceed to interventions aimed at reducing posttraumatic symptoms (Courtois 1991; Linehan 1993; van der Hart, Steele, Boon, and Brown 1993). This admonition has been summarized by Briere (1992a) in the phrase, "self before trauma" (188). The reason that we proceed in this order is that the essence of insecure attachment lies in negative internal representations of self and negative expectations regarding the manner in which one is likely to be treated by others. The abused child will understandably conclude that he or she is worthless and deserving of punishment or maltreatment and can expect neglect, abuse, and/or abandonment. Such negative representations of self and others disrupt the individual's ability to form and maintain intimate personal relationships. In addition, they leave the individual feeling powerless, helpless, and vulnerable to the stress associated with the conditioned negative emotional responses that will arise in the process of accessing and reworking traumatic memories. Thus, before the survivor can begin to access and rework traumatic memories, he or she must develop a positive sense of the self as capable of dealing with stressful stimuli. In addition, the survivor must develop sufficient trust in the therapist to rely on the support of the therapist during the reworking process.

Altering Dysfunctional Attachment Schemas and Developing Self-capacities

Pearlman (2001) noted that severe or chronic breakdowns in responsive early caregiving make it impossible for children to learn the lessons that form the basis for internal stability and self-care during adulthood. As adults, these children "may not feel worthy of love and affection, or even of life. They may not be able to feel anything or may feel everything intensely, without modulation. They do not have internalized images of loving others to draw upon in difficult times" (Pearlman 2001, 212). As a result of their inability to deal with the inevitable disappointments and injuries of life, these adult survivors experience a variety of symptoms in adulthood. Some use alcohol or other drugs to help them cope. Some dissociate when they feel fear, anxiety, or shame. Others experience somatic complaints (Rothschild 2000; van der Kolk 1994), sexual dysfunction (Briere and Elliot 1994; Maltz 1991; Miller 1994), or eating disorders (de Groot and Rodin 1999; Kent and Waller 2000). Still others inflict harm on their bodies to distract themselves from painful internal feelings or to punish themselves for being worthless and inadequate (Connors 2000; Deiter, Nicholls, and Pearlman 2000).

But the same failure to develop internalized images of loving others that has made it impossible for these survivors to cope effectively with the vicissitudes of life before entering treatment also makes it difficult for them to cope with the therapeutic process of reworking abusive experiences to reduce conditioned emotional responses to trauma-related cues. Therefore the first focus of therapy must be on restructuring dysfunctional attachment schemas and developing the associated internal coping resources of the patient.

Dysfunctional Attachment Schemas

As discussed in chapter 3 of this volume, secure attachment requires that the individual's experience with early caretakers has resulted in the development of positive schemas regarding both self and others. Bartholomew and Horowitz (1991) argued that various forms of insecure attachment develop when early caretaking is inadequate, leading the child to develop a negative view of the self as unworthy of love, and/or a negative view of others as capable of providing love. Bartholomew and Horowitz suggested that *dismissive adult attachment* results when the child develops a positive view of self as worthy of being loved, but negative expectations regarding others as a source of that love. They suggested that *preoccupied adult attachment* results when the child develops positive expectations regarding others as the potential source of love but a negative view of the self as unworthy of being loved. And they suggested that *fearful adult attachment* results when the child not only views the self as unworthy of being loved but also views others as undependable or potentially hurtful rather than loving.

In conceptualizing the forms of insecure attachment we observe in survivors of child abuse, we have modified the four category attachment typology offered by Bartholomew and Horowitz (1991) to encompass the effects of the nature and severity of the abuse the child may have experienced. We have concluded that children have an innate tendency to view themselves positively, as valuable, worthy of being taken care of, and, as development proceeds, increasingly capable of seeing to it that they are in fact taken care of, either through their own devices or through their relationships with attachment figures. Thus the development of self schemas is highly resilient with respect to simple neglect on the part of primary caregivers. Being ignored or even abandoned does not necessarily destroy a child's innate sense of self as worthy of being loved. This must almost literally be beaten out of the child (or destroyed through sexual abuse or verbal assault).

Therefore, in the absence of specific acts of abuse, the child will develop positive self schemas associated with either secure attachment or dismissive attachment. Among children who develop these positive self schemas, whether the overall attachment pattern is secure or dismissive will depend on the extent to which the caretaker is responsive to the child. If the caretaker is present and regularly responsive to the needs of the child, secure attachment will result. As adults, these children will expect to be taken care of, and they will be willing to depend on others to do so. On the other hand, if the caretaker is regularly absent, neglectful, or unresponsive, but does not commit specific acts of physical, sexual, or emotional abuse toward the child, dismissive attachment will result. As adults, these children will also feel that

270 ~ Chapter Eleven

they deserve to be taken care of, but they will logically conclude that they will have to take care of themselves.

Just as children have an innate tendency to view themselves as worthy of being taken care of, they have a natural tendency to view attachment figures as capable of providing nurturance and care. Thus the development of schemas regarding the possibility of receiving nurturance from others is highly resilient to discrete instances of abuse. Even if the child is beaten, sexually abused, or verbally assaulted by early caregivers, the child will probably maintain the hope that these caregivers are potential sources of nurturing and love. This hope can only be eliminated through the complete absence of nurturing, as occurs when caregivers ignore and neglect their children.

Therefore, unless the early caregivers have been uniformly and completely unresponsive to the needs of the child, the child will develop schemas that predispose him or her to seek attachment to others to meet the innate need to be nurtured. Among these children, the overall attachment pattern may be secure, preoccupied, or fearful, depending on the consistency with which the child's needs have been met and the nature and extent of any acts of physical, sexual, or emotional abuse that the caregivers may have perpetrated on the child.

If early caregivers have been erratic in response to the attachment behaviors and the demands of the child, sometimes responding appropriately to the needs of the child but at other times either ignoring the child's needs or responding with milder forms of abuse, such as demanding that the child display an inappropriately high level of self-reliance or criticizing the child for seeking the caretaker's attention, then the child will be likely to develop the preoccupied attachment pattern. These children will crave the attention of the caregiver but will always have a vague fear of not being loved, and they may be constantly anxious at the possibility of being abandoned at any time. Preoccupied children often go to great lengths to please their caregivers. As adults, they may go to extraordinary lengths to elicit and maintain the love of attachment figures, often reaching the point of fawning obsequiousness or pathetic self-denigration. They may also develop sicknesses or make suicidal gestures to elicit sympathy and caretaking behavior from their loved ones. Paradoxically, as we saw in the case study of Karen presented in chapter 3 of this volume, the extreme neediness of preoccupied adults may undermine the very attachment relationships that they seek to guarantee. As patients, these preoccupied individuals need to learn to value themselves. They need to have demonstrated to them through the relationship with the therapist that they are worthy of being taken care of and that they will not be abandoned.

Finally, if early caregivers have committed serious acts of physical, sexual, or emotional abuse, the child is likely to develop fearful attachment. These children may still consider the caregiver to be a potential source of nurturance, but their predominant reaction to the caregiver is likely to be one of fear and dread. In fact, they come to associate nurturance and love with fear and injury. As adults, they may be attracted to individuals who are dangerous. They may unconsciously assume that getting beaten, raped, and or verbally abused is the price that worthless beings such as themselves pay to receive any little crumb of nurturing. As patients, fearful adults, like preoccupied adults, need to learn that they are worthy of being taken care of. In addition, they need to be disabused of the notion that one must be hurt in order to be loved.

Dysfunctional attachment schemas are addressed through the relationship with the therapist in two primary ways: (1) by giving the patient an experience with a relationship that is different from the abusive childhood relationship with the caregiver that created the dysfunctional schemas and (2) by identifying the dysfunctional schemas, demonstrating their negative impact on the patient's adult psychosocial adjustment, and suggesting more appropriate schemas.

In purpose and structure the therapeutic relationship contradicts and offers alternatives to the dysfunctional schemas of self and others that underlie the various types of insecure attachment manifested by adult survivors of childhood abuse. For preoccupied and fearful patients, whose history of abuse has led to the development of a negative concept of the self as not deserving to be taken care of, the therapeutic relationship promotes the development of a positive view of self. The whole purpose of the therapeutic relationship is to "take care of" the patient by addressing his or her most pressing needs. For dismissing patients, whose history of neglect or abandonment has led them to operate on the assumption that relationships with others offer little potential for being taken care of, the relationship with the therapist represents a dramatic contrast. For preoccupied patients, whose experience with attachment figures has been unpredictable, the structure of the therapeutic relationship offers a model of a relationship that can be relied on, and the therapist offers a model of an attachment figure that the patient can trust. For fearful patients who associate intimacy with being physically harmed, sexually exploited, and/or emotionally battered, the therapeutic relationship offers safety.

With respect to the identification and exploration of specific dysfunctional schemas regarding self and others, we have found that as the patient gains trust, we as therapists are able to point out the faulty assumptions that

**Adult Attachment Patterns in Relation to Childhood Histories
of Neglect and Physical, Sexual, and Emotional Abuse**

Secure Attachment. These children have caretakers who (1) are regularly responsive to their needs and (2) do not commit acts of abuse in the form of physical, sexual, or emotional abuse. As adults, these individuals feel that they are worthy of being well taken care of, and they are willing to form close relationships with significant others on whom they can depend to meet their needs for affection and nurturance.

Dismissive Attachment. These children are regularly ignored and/or neglected by their caregivers, but they are not actively abused. These children maintain a relatively positive view of self as worthy of being taken care of, but they expect little from the others. They take care of themselves. This will likely carry over into adulthood as a general expectation that there is little to gained from close relationships. Such individuals are most likely to report little need for close relationships. Instead, they are likely to express a high need for independence and self-reliance, which they tend to frame as an indicator of their personal strength and competence. However, such individuals may eventually come to a point where they feel that their lives are empty and lacking in real meaning. Often this occurs during midlife, and this realization is frequently the reason they report for seeking treatment. As patients, these dismissive individuals must learn the value of connection with others, first through their relationship with the therapist and later through specific efforts aimed at developing meaningful relationships with other individuals.

Preoccupied Attachment. These children experience erratic behavior on the part of caretakers. Sometimes the caretaker is appropriately responsive and loving, but at other times the caretaker may be unresponsive, absent, or even abusive. This attachment pattern is common among children of caretakers who have substance abuse problems which cause radical shifts in their behavior toward their children. It is also common among children whose caregivers suffer from psychoses or extreme fluctuations in affect such as those associated with Manic Depressive Disorder. The children of such caregivers will tend to try to preserve the internal image of the attachment figure as positive, since the attachment figure can at times provide love. In order to maintain the positive image of the caregiver, these children are likely attribute the periods of abuse to some personal defect or misdeed. These children may resort to prodigious efforts to make themselves perfect in order to maintain their positive attachment to the caregiver. As adults, these individuals will similarly go to great lengths to maintain proximity to attachment figures. They may obsequiously do whatever is asked of them by the attachment figure, without ever considering their own wants or needs. They may interpret the slightest negative comment on the part of the attachment figure as a sign that they will soon be abandoned. They may develop psychosomatic illnesses or even make suicidal overtures in response to perceived abandonment. They often alienate attachment figures with their neediness. As patients, these preoccupied individuals need to learn that they are worthy of being taken care of and that the therapist may be depended on not to abandon them.

Fearful Attachment. These children may receive some nurturing from their primary caregivers, but they also experience severe physical, sexual, and/or emotional abuse. As a result, the predominant schema that they develop with respect to potential attachment figures is apprehension, fear, and dread. They would like to have intimate adult relationships, but at the same time they fear such relationships. Often fear and apprehension become associated with nurturance. In this case, the adult with fearful attachment may be attracted only to individuals who are dangerous. Fearful individuals may behave as if they believe that being beaten, raped, and/or insulted is the price that they must pay to receive love and nurturing. As patients, fearful adults must be shown through the relationship with the therapist that they are worthy of being taken care of and respected without being abused. Then they must be taught appropriate self-protective and assertiveness skills, so that they can insist on being treated with the respect they deserve.

appear to underlie specific problematic orientations and behaviors. For example, when Karen (our case representing dysfunctional preoccupied adult attachment presented in chapter 3) complained that she felt lonely and anxious when her husband occasionally worked late or played golf with his friends, we reserved comment at first. But in due course we explored Karen's underlying dysfunctional schemas of personal unworthiness and inevitable abandonment by others.

Self-capacities

Pearlman (2001) used the term "self-capacities" to refer to the domain of the attachment-related abilities that are frequently dysfunctional among survivors of childhood abuse. The self-capacities are based on assumptions regarding self and others that are formed early in life. Pearlman described self-capacities as "inner abilities that allow individuals to manage their intrapersonal world

[and] to maintain a coherent and cohesive sense of self" (211). She identified three specific self-capacities that are normally developed through early interactions with responsive caregivers, but fail to develop adequately in the absence of responsive caregiving or in the presence of physical, sexual, and/or emotional abuse. These are (1) connection (or object constancy), which is the ability to maintain an inner sense of positive connection with others; (2) self-worth, which is the ability to maintain a sense of self as viable, benign and positive; and (3) affect tolerance, which is the ability to experience, tolerate, and integrate feelings.

There are specific indicators of inadequate development with respect to each of these three self-capacities. Problems in the area of connection are indicated by expressions of disdain regarding the value of relationships with others, social isolation, feelings of being "different," and unconscious efforts to avoid intimacy by hiding or desexualizing the self (as we see in eating disorders). Problems in the area of self-worth are manifested in self-deprecation, lack of self-care, helplessness and lack of initiative, lack of appropriate assertiveness, and repeatedly allowing oneself to be used by others sexually or otherwise. Inadequate affect tolerance capacities are indicated by affective lability, dissociation, psychic numbing, substance abuse, impulsive aggressive or risk-taking behavior, self-mutilation, and suicidal tendencies.

The first step in addressing deficits in self-capacities is promoting self-awareness. Self-awareness involves recognizing how we are feeling and understanding some of the possible bases for negative feelings. We make it a point to explore patients' feelings in each session. We ask about both the patient's overall emotional state and specific physical symptoms that may reflect somatization. In many cases, patients who are survivors are out of touch with their feelings. They may not be aware of feeling anything at all, and/or they may be alexithymic—unable to articulate their feelings.

In many cases, simply inquiring regularly about the patient's feelings is sufficient to open the door to self-awareness. We initiate the discussion of the patient's feelings at or near the beginning of the session. After we make this inquiry in several successive sessions, patients tend to report their feelings spontaneously in subsequent sessions. Once patients become aware that they have not been paying attention to how they feel, we begin to teach them why it is important to be aware of feelings. We explain that feelings which are unnamed may find expression in somatic symptoms, such as anxiety responses, headaches, upset stomachs, and muscle tension and pain. When patients are ready, we point out that unresolved emotional distress may also lead us to engage in a variety of dysfunctional behaviors, including substance abuse, self-mutilation, bingeing and purging, and compulsive sexual activity.

We teach patients that simply being able to identify their feelings and the origins of these feelings can help to prevent somatization and dysfunctional self-injurious behaviors. We also make patients aware of specific steps that they can take to cope with negative affect without resorting to self-injurious activities. These steps include various relaxation techniques, exercising, meditation, and participation in enjoyable recreational activities.

Although these steps are aimed most directly at developing the self-capacity of affect regulation, they clearly impact all three of the deficits in self-capacities mentioned above. The implicit assumption underlying the focus on the patient's feelings is that the well-being of the patient is important. This assumption helps to develop and reinforce the patient's feelings of self worth. Furthermore, the fact that this work is going on in the context of the therapeutic relationship reinforces the value of connection with others. Thus the therapist's sensitivity to the mood states of the patient serves the dual purpose of developing the capacity for intimacy and improving the patient's ability to regulate affect.

Deconditioning Negative Emotional Responses to Trauma Cues

As the patient begins to develop affect regulation skills, the therapist may begin to address posttraumatic symptoms in the patient. The technique we use to ameliorate posttraumatic symptoms is an example of systematic desensitization. The desensitization process is aimed at extinguishing the negative conditioned emotional responses that the traumatized patient experiences when exposed to cues that remind the patient of traumatic experiences from childhood. These responses include intense anxiety and feelings of extreme fear and helplessness similar to those the patient experienced at the time of the original trauma. The intensity of these feelings leads the patient to feel as if he or she is actually reexperiencing the trauma. In order to reduce or extinguish such responses to cues that recall the original trauma, the patient must experience these anxiety-eliciting cues in a controlled situation where the patient may maintain a relaxed and calm state. These relaxed responses are incompatible with the conditioned anxiety responses.

We hasten to point out, however, that our conceptualization of the process of ameliorating posttraumatic symptoms according to a desensitization paradigm is in no way inconsistent with a more dynamically oriented description of the process as "working through" the traumatic experiences. We feel that the main difference between these conceptualizations is semantic. The patient allows himself or herself to be exposed once again to memories of the abuse, but this time under conditions that guarantee safety and security, so as to break the connection leading from trauma-related cues to overwhelming anxiety reactions. The conditions of safety and security depend on both the immediate presence of the trusted and reassuring therapist and the patient's growing capacity to regulate his or her affective states.

As we begin the desensitization process, our efforts to develop the client's affect regulation skills have already included relaxation training through progressive muscle relaxation and controlled breathing techniques. We have also instructed patients on how to employ soothing self-statements and images of tranquil scenes to alleviate anxiety. These are the tools that the patient uses to maintain a calm state while thinking of cues related to the trauma. We teach these skills early in the treatment process, beginning as soon as we have a sense that the patient has a problem with anxiety and fear responses. This often occurs even before we have completely assessed the extent of the patient's trauma history and the specific trauma-related cues that elicit conditioned negative emotional responses. We begin to teach affect regulation skills early because the early assessment of trauma-related cues can itself be anxiety provoking. The therapist must always strive to maintain a balance between actions that increase the patient's real or imagined exposure to anxiety-producing cues (including aspects of the assessment process) and factors that increase the patient's capacity to maintain affective balance in the face of such cues (including both the reassuring presence of the therapist and the increasing individual capacity of the patient to regulate affect).

Among the actions that increase the patient's exposure to anxiety-producing cues are the very efforts we make to assess trauma history and identify a hierarchy of stimuli that evoke anxiety responses. Therefore the dual therapeutic tasks of building affect regulation skills and gradually exposing the patient to trauma-related cues are reciprocal in nature, and they must occur alternately in small incremental steps throughout the course of treatment. We cannot neatly develop the patient's affect regulation skills, declare him ready to confront his demons, and then proceed to work through the memories of the trauma. We must recognize that some of the most important affect regulation skills can be taught only in the context of trauma-related cues. The most delicate aspect of the therapist's work is the continual balancing of the available affect regulation resources against the strength of the anxiety-inducing material to which the patient is exposed.

Resistance

Briere (2002) emphasized that survivors of childhood abuse have perfected avoidance responses to protect themselves from negative emotional responses to trauma-related cues. They have employed such responses throughout life to reduce their awareness of trauma-related cues present in their environment, disrupt their memories of the trauma, and dampen the activation of negative emotional responses to these cues and memories. Accordingly, survivors are likely to continue to use these avoidance responses during treatment, especially when the strength of conditioned responses to trauma-related cues threatens to overwhelm the factors promoting the maintenance of tolerable affect. Therefore, in spite of his or her best efforts to provide the patient with a sense of safety and security, and in spite of his or her continuing efforts to validate the patient's response to the abuses the patient experienced, the clinician may from time to time encounter resistance. Such resistance may take the commonly encountered forms of missing sessions or forgetting previously remembered material; or it may take more dramatic forms, including significant dissociative manifestations that occur during sessions.

In describing the appropriate response of the therapist to the self-protective defenses that survivors are likely to employ, Briere (2002) stressed that

> avoidance defenses are viewed as necessary survival responses by some survivors, and overly enthusiastic or heavy-handed attempts by a therapist to remove such resistance, denial, or dissociative symptoms may be seen as potential threats to the client's internal equilibrium. For this reason, the psychotherapeutic process must proceed carefully to avoid overwhelming the client and reinforcing the use of additional avoidance responses that otherwise would further impede therapeutic progress. (186)

Briere used the term "therapeutic window" to refer to the point where affect regulation resources are sufficient to allow the patient to be exposed to trauma-related cues without being overwhelmed and therefore resorting to the use of avoidance defenses that disrupt the progress of treatment. He suggested that the therapist's interventions should be "neither so nondemanding as to provide inadequate exposure and processing nor so evocative or powerful that the client's delicate balance between trauma activation and self-capacity is tipped toward the former" (2002, 186).

Specific Case Context: Treating Claire

The foregoing discussion of the treatment objectives of altering dysfunctional attachment schemas, developing self-capacities, and deconditioning negative emotional responses to trauma-related cues is generally applicable to patients who are survivors of childhood abuse. However, patients don't often come in telling us that they are survivors of childhood abuse that has precipitated a variety of symptoms. Rather, they tend to come in for help with a particular problem, and both their survivor status and related symptoms become clear as treatment progresses.

Each patient we treat has a unique context in which the principles described in this chapter can be applied. In the case of many of the patients we treat who are survivors of childhood abuse, an outsider viewing a therapy session might not immediately recognize that we had firmly in mind at all times the survivor status of the patient, or that we were working toward the goals of altering dysfunctional attachment schemas, developing self-capacities, and deconditioning negative emotional responses. An outside observer might well conclude that the session was focused quite specifically on the patient's presenting problems. To illustrate this, we consider here some of the early work with Claire, whose case was described in chapter 9 as an example of a survivor of severe and prolonged childhood abuse who manifested both classic symptoms of PTSD and the character disturbances of complex PTSD.

Claire sought treatment for a "midlife crisis" arising from a period of introspection precipitated by her second divorce. Claire came into treatment with a written list of problems that she had identified during her self-analysis. These problems included a lack of close interpersonal relationships, a pervasive sense of life as lacking in purpose, chronic depression, lack of enjoyable leisure time activities, problems with substance abuse and eating disorders, problems with anger management, and an inability to control her sexual behavior. Given a list of problems of this scope and seriousness, the therapist immediately suspected that Claire had a history of childhood neglect and serious physical and/or sexual abuse. However, he did not suggest this possibility initially.

Instead, he encouraged Claire to describe each of the problems on her list and her emotional response to each one. For example, he asked Claire to talk about the lack of close personal relationships. She said that throughout her life she had always been self-reliant and had never felt there was much to be gained from relying on others or becoming vulnerable to subsequently injury by "letting your guard down" and "revealing weaknesses that could be used against you later on." However, Claire also volunteered that since her second divorce she had begun to feel that this was not the right way to think about other people. She explained that she was beginning to see that most people derived much joy and comfort from their relationships with others, and so she was beginning to think of her extreme independence and self-reliance not as a strength, but rather as a problem that needed to be worked on.

Given Claire's incipient recognition of a potential problem in the area of interpersonal relationships, the therapist noted that many adults shared

Claire's lack of appreciation for the value of close relationships, as well as her apprehension that becoming close may leave one vulnerable to being hurt. He suggested that these ideas typically reflected one's past experiences, particularly experiences that occurred during childhood. Without mentioning words like "neglect" or "abuse," he asked whether Claire could remember anything about her childhood that might have led her to become an adult who tended to place little value on relationships with others, rather than one of the larger group of adults who considered relationships to be very important.

When the therapist made this inquiry initially during the session, Claire responded immediately that she didn't think that either her father or her stepmother had taken a very great interest in her, since they were so wrapped up in their own careers and their own social lives. She complained that they didn't pay much attention to what was going on in her life and didn't praise her very much for being such a good student. She complained that she could never get any help with homework and that she couldn't get them attend or even to take her to sports programs and social events. In the session following this discussion, Claire mentioned that she had been thinking about the question and she had realized that (1) her own mother had died; (2) her father was quite old when he had her, and he had already gone through the "soccer dad" role with his kids from his first marriage; and (3) her stepmother had kids of her own to worry about. She said that she had pretty much "fallen between the cracks."

When Claire brought back these observations, her therapist attempted to help her get in touch with how painful this neglect must have been for her. However, when he asked Claire how it felt not to have anyone help with homework or take her to soccer games, she had trouble responding. Claire had a good deal more difficulty describing her emotional response to the neglect that she had experienced than she did recognizing on a purely cognitive level that her parents were unavailable to her. Therefore Claire understood quickly that the absence of her parents might explain why she would place less value on close relationships than other people might, people who had really been nurtured by their parents when they were young. However, Claire had more difficulty appreciating how the neglect that she experienced might lead her to avoid forming close relationships, in order to avoid developing a hope for nurturance that would inevitably lead to disappointment and pain.

Recognizing that it might take a while for Claire to allow herself to get in touch with the pain she felt arising from her parents' neglect, the therapist praised Claire for her efforts to understand how her past experiences may have contributed to the belief that there is little to be gained from seeking out and maintaining close relationships. Furthermore, he used the data that Claire provided as the basis for a brief intervention aimed at developing more positive schemas toward others and an enhanced capacity for connectedness. The therapist asked Claire to pick an individual at work whose opinion she respected and ask that person whether she had seen a certain movie that had just been released. The purpose of this exercise was simply to get Claire to engage another individual in conversation, in order to demonstrate to her that such intercourse can be fun. Much to Claire's surprise, the woman she approached seemed delighted to have her opinion sought out, and they had quite a long conversation. Over time, Claire became rather good friends with this colleague.

At this same point early in Claire's treatment, her therapist strongly suspected that there was much more than simple emotional neglect involved in Claire's history, but he did not push the issue at this time. He noted that she had been so highly motivated that she had gone home and thought about the question of her childhood experiences, and that she had come up with several important insights as a result. He also noted the difficulty she had even appreciating how painful it must have been to be neglected. He therefore concluded that she was probably not ready at that early point in treatment to begin to contemplate and/or disclose any experiences she may have had with physical, sexual, or emotional abuse. Therefore he did not push for disclosure of possible abusive experiences, but rather focused on the work of developing the self-capacity of connectedness.

In a similar manner, concurrently and consecutively, the therapist explored the other problems that Claire had included in her initial list. In each case the therapist attempted to identify the dysfunctional attachment schemas that might be contributing to the problem, as well as any aspects of her childhood experience that might have contributed to the development of such dysfunctional schemas. He considered her use of substances, her bouts with bulimia, her impulsive outbursts of anger, and her inability to politely decline unwanted sexual advances. During their discussion of substance abuse, several sessions into the treatment, Claire first mentioned being abused sexually.

The therapist was helping Claire explore the functions served by her use of alcohol and cocaine. She remarked that of all the problems she had listed out, this one was absolutely the clearest. She used substances when she had sex. She said that often when men would ask her for a date, they would take her out to dinner and make sure she had a great deal to drink. She said that she knew this was a cheap old trick, but in her case it worked very well. Claire said that the trick worked for two reasons: first, because she didn't like to refuse the offer of wine or liquor, any more than she liked to refuse a request to have sex; and, second, because she only enjoyed sex when she was high. Claire thought about this explanation for a minute, then she said that she had mischaracterized the situation slightly. It wasn't that she didn't *like* to refuse a man's offer of a drink or sex, but she was *unable* to refuse. She said that she didn't generally have difficulty saying no, but when it came to either of these areas, she never felt that she had a choice.

Then Claire suddenly blurted out her older stepsister made her take her first drink, and she lost her virginity when her older stepbrother raped her while her younger stepbrother held her down. She hesitated a moment, then she said that she had been given alcohol and abused sexually by her stepsiblings for many years, and over that time she had learned that being raped was a lot better when you were drunk. In fact, she learned eventually that "if I were drunk enough to forget what was actually happening, I could even enjoy it . . . or at least become aroused and have an orgasm."

Claire made this disclosure without displaying any indications of being upset. She had learned to use the alcohol not only to anesthetize the painful affect associated with being held down and raped, but also to allow her to be sexually responsive while enduring trauma which would otherwise have inhibited sexual arousal. Claire immediately recognized that the childhood connection between substance use and sexuality was replicated in her adult life. At this point in the session, the therapist asked Claire how she was feeling. He said that she had shown a great deal of courage in sharing these experiences with him, and he wanted to make sure that she was okay. Claire indicated that she felt all right, except that she was embarrassed because she had not "put two and two together before" to figure out why she couldn't say no and why she always used substances before having sex.

The therapist suggested to Claire that they should probably use the few minutes remaining to them on that day practicing relaxation techniques. He pointed out that Claire had made some important disclosures and had taken an important step forward in treatment, and that when this occurs it is important for the therapist and the patient to proceed cautiously and consolidate their gains. This cautious response on the part of the therapist illustrates not only the importance of avoiding the possibility of overloading the patient either during or between sessions, as well as the importance of respecting the patient's rights by sharing his concerns and motivations and enlisting Claire as a full partner in the therapy process.

In the following session Claire indicated that she had experienced some distress between sessions. She was worried that the therapist would look down on her, first for being promiscuous and second for failing to figure out why. In response to these admissions, the therapist stressed that Claire was right when she told him in the last session that she had no choice regarding either the alcohol or the sex that were forced on her as a child. Further, her use of alcohol to help her forget what was happening to her was actually adaptive. It helped her survive. The fact that she became responsive sexually was adaptive as well. It helped her live through the abuse without losing her mind, and it probably minimized the physical injuries that she experienced as a result of the repeated rapes. The therapist stressed to Claire that her survival was remarkable in and of itself, and he explained that her continued use in adulthood of some of the strategies that she had developed to survive her abusive childhood was to be expected, even though it created problems that they would need to work on in order to improve her adjustment and make her happier.

Subsequent sessions were dedicated to developing a variety of skills to replace the dysfunctional behaviors that Claire had been employing with respect to sexual activity. These included (1) helping Claire realize that she can be interested in a man for various reasons other than sex, as well as for sex; (2) helping her identify the qualities in a man that would make the man sexually desirable or undesirable; (3) teaching her how to politely but assertively decline the sexual advances of a man in whom she has no interest; (4) teaching her how to take the initiative in approaching a man in whom she does have a sexual interest; and (5) teaching her that when you are with a man that you really want to be with, drugs are not a necessary prerequisite to good sex.

Conclusion

Claire's therapy was necessarily intense and time-consuming. The skills listed above pertain to only one of Claire's original list of presenting problems. Patients come to grasp the general principle that adaptations which are functional in the context of childhood abuse may be dysfunctional when carried over into adulthood. Nevertheless, most patients require a therapist's help to apply this general principle to the diverse adjustment difficulties that bring the patients to treatment. Moreover, interventions aimed at altering dysfunctional schemas, procedures designed to decondition emotional responses to trauma-related cues, and efforts to build skills to replace dysfunctional behavior patterns must all be planned and executed individually and specifically, while maintaining overall sensitivity to the diverse areas of dysfunction that may have been created by the experience of childhood trauma.

CHAPTER TWELVE

Group Treatment for Adult Survivors of Childhood Abuse

We feel that group therapy can be an important adjunct to the individual treatment of adult survivors of child abuse. We do not recommend that survivors participate in group treatment only, because of the critical importance of maintaining the patient's safety and security that we discussed in the previous chapter. We feel that even highly structured groups for survivors have at least some potential of producing material which may overload the traumatized survivor's developing affect regulation capacities. Such an overload can elicit excessive, uncontrolled emotional responses to trauma-related cues, and these responses may have the effect of retraumatizing the survivor. Alternatively or additionally, such an overload may trigger the patient's return to the utilization of dissociative defenses that serve to reduce his or her awareness of these trauma-related cues. Either of these outcomes represents a setback to treatment, and we feel that patients who participate in groups should have access to an individual therapist who can monitor the patient's experience with the group, prepare the patient for possible discomforting disclosures that might be made by other group members, and provide a reassuring presence and backup safety net if an event that occurs in the group proves to be particularly stressful to the patient.

That said, however, it is clear that groups can be valuable in our work with survivors. After all, survivors of childhood abuse typically develop not only posttraumatic symptoms such as reexperiencing, avoidance, and emotional numbing, but also characterological disturbances based on the formation of dysfunctional attachment schemas regarding self and others, the inadequate development of self-capacities, and inadequate affect regulation skills. These characterological disturbances typically give rise to impaired interpersonal relationships, which may take such forms as: (1) failing to ever establish any close interpersonal relationships or even see the need for such relationships (dismissive attachment); (2) experiencing chronic anxiety in relation to maintaining proximity to attachment figures and chronic fear of abandonment (preoccupied attachment); or (3) repeatedly being attracted to dangerous individuals who predictably exploit or abuse (fearful attachment). But groups are based on interpersonal relationships, and participation in various forms of group treatment can be helpful in the construction of positive schemas regarding self and others, the development of the inclination and ability to connect with others, and the improvement of the social skills that are necessary to make connections with others rewarding rather than punishing. In the following section of this chapter, we consider the advantages of group work for adult survivors of childhood abuse.

Advantages of Group Treatment
for Survivors of Childhood Abuse

In his book on dynamically oriented treatment for sexually abused men, Gartner (1999) observed that "since sexual betrayal in early intimate relationships disrupts the sexually abused man's ability to form and maintain relationships, therapy must engender a capacity for interpersonal connections" (295). In making this observation, Gartner did not employ the terminology of dysfunctional attachment schemas and inadequately developed self-capacities employed by Herman (1992a) and Pearlman (2001) in their discussions of PTSD. However, he was nevertheless focusing clearly on the characterological disturbances of survivors of severe and prolonged abuse that make adult interpersonal functioning problematic. Gartner is making the simple point that childhood abuse leads to inadequate interpersonal functioning that carries over into adulthood, and he is stressing the potential value of group therapy in helping to develop interpersonal relationship skills.

Gartner (1999) argued that groups composed entirely of survivors of childhood abuse and focused specifically on their unique issues can be particularly helpful, because exposure to individuals who have had similar experiences will reduce isolation and tend to ameliorate the feelings of shame that frequently plague male survivors of sexual abuse. Similarly, in discussing the use of group approaches with male and female survivors of physical and or sexual abuse, Buchele (2000) noted that "the psychotherapy group, with its intimate yet public atmosphere, affords opportunities to safely dilute the sense of shame and secrecy by hearing about others' experiences and sharing one's own" (172). In his discussion of the treatment of adults who were molested as children, Briere (1996) argued that among the advantages of groups for survivors of childhood abuse are the "benefits of lessened isolation and stigmatization, reduced shame [and] the opportunity to help as well as be helped—a process that supports self-esteem and lessens the sense of being a deviant, passive recipient of treatment" (170). And in his discussion of the treatment of homosexual males with a history of childhood sexual abuse, Parker (1990) noted that group therapy had the "power to reduce isolation, enhance self-esteem, and provide a boundary laboratory where stereotypes and dysfunctional patterns of intimacy can be met with a more appropriate systemic response" (187).

Scott (1999) and Gerrity and Peterson (2004) both noted that group psychotherapy is useful in addressing symptoms associated with each of the four "traumagenic dynamics" of childhood sexual abuse—powerlessness, stigmatization, betrayal, and traumatic sexualization. Finkelhor (1986) pointed out that survivors of severe childhood sexual abuse that took place repeatedly over a prolonged period of time often manifest a profound sense of personal powerlessness derived from their inability as children to protect themselves or otherwise avoid being abused. Scott (1999) noted that this sense of powerlessness tends to manifest itself in the process of group therapy in the form of ambivalence about participation in the group, passivity, allowing oneself to detach from the group process through the use of dissociative defenses, and a generally defeatist attitude. Horowitz (1977) observed that a psychotherapy group has great potential to overcome these manifestations of powerlessness, since the members of the group will tend to encourage a reluctant group member to engage in the group process. In addition, group members who feel powerless are likely to benefit from the modeled behavior of fellow group members who have already made some improvements in psychosocial adjustment as a result of their efforts to modify dysfunctional cognitions and behaviors and develop new adaptive behaviors.

Scott (1999) noted that survivors of childhood physical and sexual abuse tend to feel stigmatized on a number of levels. Of course, they are likely to feel shame based on taboos regarding incest and/or homosexual behavior. In addition, however, survivors may also feel stigmatized by the manifestations of complex PTSD that they may have experienced, including substance abuse, self-mutilation, eating disorders, uncontrolled angry outbursts, and/or dissociative experiences. Survivors may even feel stigmatized simply by virtue of their social isolation and their failure to develop normative family relationships. Scott pointed out that participating in a group with other survivors who share these feelings and experiences may help the survivor to understand that he or she is not alone and that the symptoms he or she is experiencing are the predictable results of the traumatic experiences they had in childhood.

Finkelhor and his associates (Browne and Finkelhor 1986; Finkelhor 1986; Finkelhor and Browne 1985) discussed the traumatic dynamic of betrayal in terms of the inability to trust others following the obvious betrayal of trust committed by the attachment figure who perpetrated the abuse. This notion may also be described in the language of attachment theory in terms of the development of negative schemas regarding attachment figures as undependable and/or potentially dangerous. These schemas lead survivors to preoccupied or fearful attachment patterns, as indicated by the dysfunctional cognitions that "the people I love always wind up leaving me," or "the people I love always wind up exploiting me or hurting me." The survivor's participation in group psychotherapy can provide him or her with experiences that contradict these cognitions and ultimately help alter dysfunctional attachment schemas.

Finally, Finkelhor (1986) observed that being sexually abused as a young child leads to "traumatic sexualization." Finkelhor used this term to refer specifically to the process of shaping the child's sexual feelings and sexual attitudes in a developmentally inappropriate manner. For example, if the child is rewarded for sexual behavior by receiving affection and nurturance from the perpetrator, the child may come to believe that the only way to obtain affection is through sex. This view can lead to promiscuity in adulthood, with the survivor offering sex to anyone who will pay some attention to the survivor and provide affection and nurturance. Additionally, if the child is rewarded for sexual behavior by tangible gifts, the child may come to view sex as a commodity. This may be reflected in subsequent participation in prostitution. Finally, if the abused child has been beaten, restrained, or physically threatened while being abused sexually, the child may come to associate the experience of physical pain with the sexual response. In adulthood, these forms of childhood abuse may lead to repeated victimization, because the survivor is unconsciously attracted to dangerous and abusive partners. Childhood sexual abuse involving violence and restraint may also leave survivors unable to achieve orgasm unless there is a sadomasochistic element in their sexual activities. Participation in group treatment with fellow survivors of childhood abuse is likely to expose the survivor to peers who have shared some of these same dysfunctional cognitions regarding the nature of sexuality and some of these same inclinations with respect to sexual behavior, but have come to recognize that the beliefs are faulty and the behaviors are counterproductive and possibly dangerous.

Scott (1999) expanded broadly on Finkelhor's concept of traumatic sexualization to encompass all situations in which a sexually abused child confuses his or her own needs with those of the perpetrator. He suggested that this dynamic tends to reappear in adulthood in the form of "boundary disturbances," in which personal boundaries become diffuse and survivors feel that their own survival is dependent on the emotional status of their attachment figures. This dynamic might be reflected in a survivor who has little or no sense of his or her own sexual needs and desires, but instead functions sexually solely to gratify the needs of a partner. This mode of behaving is most often observed among survivors with preoccupied adult attachment, who fear that any failure to anticipate and meet the needs of the partner may result in abandonment. Scott suggested that group feedback regarding such dysfunctional cognitions can help the survivor recognize the problem of inadequately developed self-boundaries and become more aware of his or her own needs. These observations made by Scott (1999) and by Gerrity and Peterson (2004) indicate additional unique advantages of participation in group therapy for survivors of childhood abuse.

However, group therapy is not only useful for survivors because of its emphasis on developing interpersonal relationships and relationship skills. Nor is the usefulness of group therapy for survivors of childhood abuse confined to the relevance of group feedback regarding dysfunctional cognitions arising from traumagenic sexualization. On the contrary, group treatment for survivors is also useful for a pragmatic reason.

Group treatment is generally a useful adjunct to individual treatment simply because almost every time we are treating adult survivors, we find that there is a tremendous volume of work to be done. As was illustrated in our description of our treatment of Claire in the previous chapter, the survivor may be experiencing a wide variety of psychological symptoms and dysfunctional behavior patterns; and any one of these symptoms or dysfunctional behaviors may require a series of specific interventions aimed at altering underlying attachment schemas, replacing negative cognitions and self-statements with positive ones, and teaching adaptive behaviors that may be substituted for current dysfunctional behaviors. In this regard, in their discussion of groups for survivors of childhood physical and sexual abuse, Gerrity and Peterson (2004) noted that "CSA treatment is usually long term, multimodal, and multidimensional because of the pervasive effects of abuse, the compounded consequences due to the delayed treatment of abuse, and the complexities of the posttraumatic responses" (498). Put simply, given the large amount of work to be done, the addition of group treatment to individual treatment adds an additional vehicle to the treatment mix, a vehicle that can be used to accomplish a portion of the work.

Structuring Group Psychotherapy for Survivors of Childhood Abuse

Just as the therapist who is conducting individual psychotherapy with survivors must carefully structure the therapeutic relationship to guarantee the safety of the patient, so those who lead groups for survivors of childhood abuse must provide clear structure and firm boundaries (Braun 1986; Chu 1988; Courtois 1988; Kluft 1993; Putnam 1989). Scott (1999) stressed that "providing a clear treatment frame [is necessary] to ensure emotional safety, to reduce confusion and retraumatization, and to provide adequate structure for the therapeutic process" (40).

In groups, a key aspect of structure is the establishment of ground rules regarding the topics that may be discussed, as well as the manner in which these topics may be discussed. Of particular concern is the discussion of patients' personal experiences with physical and sexual abuse. In keeping with the idea of reworking traumatic experiences in a safe and supportive environment to reduce the power of negative conditioned emotional responses, many groups for survivors have an explicit goal of self-disclosure, including the description of the patients' abuse histories, their initial reactions to the trauma they experienced, their perceptions of how these experiences shaped their adaptive capacities, and the problems that have plagued them as adults (Cole and Barney 1987; Goodwin and Talwar 1989). However, the goal of self-disclosure may not be appropriate in the case of patients who have extreme anxiety and hyper-arousal in response to trauma-related cues, or in the case of patients whose avoidance defenses involve serious manifestations of dissociative phenomena such as Dissociative Identity Disorder. For such patients, either attempting to describe one's own abusive experiences or hearing the stories of abuse suffered by other members of the group may be overwhelming.

For this reason, groups composed of patients who are particularly fragile may adopt a rule discouraging members from describing graphic details of their personal abuse histories. Scott (1999) presented a model of group treatment appropriate for seriously disturbed survivors of childhood abuse who are inpatients in hospital or residential settings and who have been determined to represent a threat to themselves or to others. In group therapy with this fragile population, "clients rarely discuss specific aspects of their abuse and are usually restrained from such disclosures. . . . Instead, they are encouraged to refer to earlier abuse generally and to focus on its impact on their current lives" (Scott 1999, 40).

In these groups for the most fragile survivors, the focus is on managing the most immediate posttraumatic symptoms and building the rudimentary capacity to benefit from the support of the group. Treatment is focused specifically on the dissociative impulse to withdraw psychologically or physically from the group discussion. Patients are taught self-soothing skills to help them tolerate negative affect and grounding strategies to help them reduce dissociative symptoms. Self-soothing skills include stretching, changing one's body position, and deep breathing. Grounding strategies include reminding oneself to keep one's eyes open and to stay awake, touching objects in the room, making eye contact with the therapist or with the group member who is currently speaking, and reminding oneself of the time, date, and place. Patients agree to make a good faith effort to remain in the room throughout each session, despite any urge they may feel to withdraw. This facilitates their exposure to the support of the group and begins to open up the possibility of developing connectedness.

However, most outpatient groups for survivors of childhood abuse are intended for persons who have developed at least rudimentary self capacities in the areas of connection, self-worth, and affect regulation. Accordingly, these groups aim at helping members confront the reality of the abuse they experienced by describing the abuse to other members of the group, and by sharing their emotional responses to the abuse, both their responses at the time that it occurred and their current responses to trauma-related cues. It is expected that sharing this material with others who have had similar experiences will reduce the patient's feelings of isolation and stigmatization and generate feedback indicating that his or her responses to the abuse were predictable and adaptive at the time the abuse occurred, and understandable if dysfunctional now.

This expectation is based on the assumption that the patient has sufficient resources available to regulate and tolerate negative affect that may be experienced in connection with recalling his or her own abusive experiences, or in connection with hearing about the abuse experienced by other group members. The group leader has the difficult task of monitoring the status of the various group members while difficult material is being discussed, to make sure that none of the members are being overwhelmed or responding with dissociative avoidance reactions. This task represents the group therapy analogue of Briere's (2002) recommendation that the therapist conducting individual treatment always make sure that the patient remains within the "therapeutic window," where exposure to trauma-related cues is matched by sufficient affect regulation capacity on the part of the patient to avoid the activation of dissociative avoidance defenses.

This task of the group therapist is simplified to the extent that (1) the participants all have some capacity for connection and affect regulation; and (2) all of the participants are willing to exercise a degree of restraint in their descriptions of their experiences, if called upon to do so by another group member or by the therapist. These conditions imply that group leaders must carefully assess potential group members to determine if they are too fragile to tolerate the predictable level of affective distress that will arise from time to time during the course of treatment. Ideally, a patient will not be referred to group treatment by the individual therapist until that therapist has had an adequate opportunity to determine the patient's strengths and resiliency. Ideally as well, the prospective group leader and the patient's individual therapist share a common view with respect to the need to be certain that none of the members of a group are too fragile to benefit from participation. This implies that groups work best when the members are quite homogeneous with respect to the level of development of their self-capacities.

The group leader must also assess potential group members from the opposing perspective—the leader must make certain that anyone included in the group will be willing and able to modulate or postpone his or her recounting of childhood traumatic experiences if called upon to do so by the leader. This can be problematic, since some survivors will have had the experience of being silenced by their abusers with threats. Other survivors may have had the experience of disclosing their abusive experiences to other family members or to authority figures, only to have their experience invalidated by not being believed or by suggestions that their reports are distorted or exaggerated. Therefore, when it is necessary for a therapist to "put the brakes" on a patient who may be disclosing graphic details of abuse that may be causing some group members to experience severe anxiety or to activate dissociative avoidance responses, there is the potential for the patient who has been interrupted to experience a transference reaction to the therapist, confounding the current behavior of the therapist with the internalized image of the perpetrator, since both are viewed as silencing the victim.

Ideally, through the recruitment of group members who are homogeneous with respect to the capacity for self-regulation, as well as through adequate explanation and discussion of the rules of the group and the rationale for these rules, groups for survivors can function within the therapeutic window without being disrupted by either patients who are completely unable to tolerate even mild affective discomfort or by patients who display disruptive, transferentially based anger toward the efforts of the group leader to turn the discussion away from dangerous emotionally charged descriptions of trauma that might elicit dissociative avoidance responses even among group members who do have some capacity for affective self-regulation.

Herman's Stage Model of Recovery Applied to Group Psychotherapy

Herman (1992b) proposed a stage model to describe the process of recovery from the effects of trauma. She suggested that recovery from complex PTSD proceeds through three stages: "The central task of the first stage is the establishment of safety. The central task of the second stage is remembrance and mourning. The central task of the third stage is reconnection with ordinary life" (155).

Herman suggested that specific types of group psychotherapy experiences are appropriate for survivors in each of these three different stages of recovery. She suggested that for survivors in the first stage of recovery, who have not yet addressed issues of interpersonal connection, safety, and trust, the ideal therapy group is cognitively oriented and highly structured. She suggested that didactic groups which focus primarily on self-care are most appropriate at this stage of recovery because they facilitate the exchange of information on the impact of trauma, symptoms, and self-care strategies. Herman suggested further that these groups should focus on developing the coping abilities of the survivor while strictly protecting the survivor from being overwhelmed. She stressed that the group process in such psycho-educational groups is focused on maintaining boundaries and providing support. The group leader will endeavor to steer clear of confrontation and the complexities of interpersonal relationships among group members.

Survivors who have established some sense of personal safety and have developed a support network in their lives (e.g., outpatients who are functioning adults even though they are aware of one or more issues that bring them into treatment) are likely to have amassed the personal and interpersonal resources necessary to work through their histories of abuse. Thus Herman argued that "while exploring traumatic experiences in a group can be highly disorganizing for a survivor in the first stage of recovery, the same work can be extremely productive once the survivor reaches the second stage" (221). At the second stage of recovery, Herman suggested that trauma-focused groups are appropriate, since these groups allow the survivor to tell the story of the abuse to a small group of others. At this stage, she suggested,

A well-organized group provides both a powerful stimulant for reconstruction of the survivor's story and a stimulating source of emotional support during mourning. As each survivor shares her unique story, the group provides a profound experience of giving it social as well as personal meaning. When the survivor tells her story only to one other person, the confessional, private aspect of the testimony is paramount. Telling the same story to a group represents a transition toward the judicial, public aspect of testimony. The group helps each individual survivor enlarge her story, releasing her from her isolation with the perpetrator and readmitting the fullness of the larger world from which she has been alienated. (1992b, 221–22)

Herman recommended that groups for survivors at this second stage of recovery should be highly structured and clearly focused toward the work of remembrance and mourning. She suggested that these groups should be time limited and focused on traumatic events that took place during childhood. The time-limited aspect of the group fosters a climate of emotional intensity while assuring the participants that the intensity will not last forever.

Herman argued further that having time limitations in groups for stage 2 survivors promotes rapid bonding among group members, while discouraging the possibility that participants will develop a limited and dysfunctional "survivor identity." The latter term pertains in situations where survivors participate in long term, open-ended therapy groups that are composed only of members who share histories of abuse. In this situation, Herman and others have cautioned that extended psychotherapy in homogeneous groups composed only of traumatized persons can lead members to develop an identity as a survivor that they become reluctant to move beyond (Buchele 1994, 2000; Ganzarain and Buchele 1988). Nicholas and Forrester (1999) have argued that treatment for survivors can be considered complete only after the factors that caused the abuse and the effects of the abuse on the survivor have been addressed in interaction with nontraumatized individuals. This notion suggests that the survivor's final experience in group treatment should occur in a heterogeneous group that is not composed only of survivors.

Consistent with Herman's contention that the experience of severe and prolonged abuse is disempowering and leads to the development of learned helplessness, the trauma-focused stage 2 groups focus on personal goals selected by the individual participants. This focus is designed to empower the survivor. Often the goals selected by the participants involve recovering memories or simply being able to tell their stories to others. Having established such goals, recounting the story of one's traumatic experiences takes on a purpose beyond simple catharsis. It takes on a new meaning as a step toward developing a sense of self-efficacy and personal mastery.

Herman (1992b) suggested that these stage 2 groups should focus on sharing experiences of past trauma rather than current interpersonal difficulties. She argued that discussing conflicts among group members diverts the group from its primary tasks of remembrance and mourning. She recommended that the group leader(s) intervene actively to promote sharing and minimize conflict. She suggested that one of the key tasks of the group leader(s) in these groups is to make certain that each member has the opportunity to tell her story, rather than allowing the members to negotiate time-sharing among themselves.

Herman also noted that the emotional intensity of these groups creates a situation where members can quickly become dependent on each other. For this reason, the leader(s) should require a commitment from each participant to attend each meeting and not leave the group before the group has run its course. In addition, Herman suggested that no new participants should be admitted to such trauma-focused groups once they had begun.

The emotional intensity of the second stage group also demands that the therapist(s) screen participants carefully. Herman suggested that participation in these groups requires a high degree of readiness and motivation, and that the "inclusion of a member who is not ready to engage in concentrated uncovering work can demoralize the group and damage that individual" (1992b, 224). Herman recommended that a survivor is ready for a trauma-focused group

> when her safety and self-care are securely established, her symptoms are under reasonable control, her social supports are reliable, and her life circumstances permit engagement in a demanding endeavor. Beyond this, however, she must be willing to commit herself to faithful attendance throughout the life of the group, and she must feel reasonably sure that her desire to reach out to others outweighs her dread and fear of a group. (224)

Although she did not use terminology reflecting the development of the survivor's self-capacity, as we did in the previous section of this chapter, it seems clear that Herman's description of the first two stages of recovery from trauma as well as her descriptions of the types of groups that are relevant for survivors at each of these stages roughly parallel our recommendations for very fragile survivors who are almost completely lacking in self-regulation skills as opposed to survivors who have developed sufficient self-capacities to tolerate a reasonable level of exposure to trauma-related cues.

Reflecting her ideas regarding the different tasks for survivors at stage 2 and stage 3 of the recovery process, Herman (1992b) recommended different group experiences as appropriate for survivors at these two stages. Herman conceptualized the third stage of recovery in terms of reconnecting with ordinary life. This involves altering the dysfunctional modes of relating to others that have developed as a result of the survivor's self-protective adaptations to the experiences of childhood abuse. Herman suggested that for this purpose, "different types of groups may be useful, depending on how she [the survivor] defines her priorities" (1992b, 233). Herman suggested that a trauma-focused group might still be the most appropriate group modality for a survivor in stage 3, if the survivor is seeking to address a specific trauma-related problem that is interfering with the development and maintenance of satisfying interpersonal relationships. For example, Herman suggested that

> a survivor of childhood abuse . . . might wish to resolve the residual issue of secrecy, which presents a barrier to more authentic relationships within her family. The task of preparing a family disclosure is well suited to a time-limited, trauma-focused survivors' group. Group members have an almost uncanny ability to understand the dynamics of each other's families, and while they may feel immobilized and helpless with their own relatives, they have no such inhibitions regarding other families. The resourcefulness, imagination, and humor of other survivors offer invaluable aid to the individual who is attempting to negotiate changes in entrenched family relationships. (1992b, 233)

Herman noted several other examples of specific issues for a stage 3 survivor that might be amenable to focused, time-limited group therapy, including sexual dysfunction and lack of assertiveness.

However, Herman argued that even though a trauma-focused group might be useful for addressing certain circumscribed residual problems in the third stage of recovery, "the survivor's broader difficulties in relationships are better addressed in an interpersonal psychotherapy group" (1992b, 234). Herman suggested that survivors, particularly those who have endured prolonged, repeated trauma, are often aware that the abuse to which they were exposed has left them with a severely impaired capacity to relate to other people. However, recognizing the existence of dysfunctional interpersonal relationship patterns is not enough to eliminate those patterns. Survivors must learn new modes of relating, and they must practice these new behaviors. Herman argued that an open-ended interpersonal therapy group provides the stage 3 survivor with a safe place in which to carry out this practice. The interpersonal therapy group provides the survivor with both support and feedback. Herman suggested that "group support makes it possible for each participant to acknowledge her own maladaptive behavior without excessive shame and to take the emotional risk of relating to others in new ways" (1992b, 234).

Herman argued that interpersonal groups differ from trauma-focused groups in that the interpersonal groups are not time limited and membership in interpersonal therapy groups is not limited to individuals who share a particular traumatic history. In addition, whereas membership in trauma-focused groups is unchanging over the fixed duration of the group, the membership of the interpersonal therapy group typically changes over time. Finally, whereas trauma-focused groups tend to discourage conflict, "interpersonal groups allow and encourage such conflict to develop, within safe limits" (1992b, 235). Herman argued that in fact conflict is essential to the therapeutic task of the group, since it is through understanding and resolving conflict that insight and change occur.

Alternative Models for the Group Treatment of Survivors of Childhood Abuse

In discussing his clinical work with sexually abused men, Gartner (1999) took issue with Herman's sharp distinction between the highly structured, time-limited, homogeneous trauma-focused group that she felt was appropriate for survivors in stage 2 of recovery and the less structured, open-ended, heterogeneous interpersonal therapy group that she recommended for survivors in stage 3 of recovery. Gartner stated,

> I concur [with Herman] that structured, psychoeducational, or time-limited groups can all be very useful for men, particularly those in the early stages of dealing with their abuse. I believe, however, that all of Herman's goals may also be addressed at one time or another in open-ended, psychodynamic groups such as those I have run. (1999, 297)

The groups that Gartner described are composed entirely of members who are survivors of childhood sexual abuse, but these groups are not time limited. Gartner argued that an open-ended format has an advantage over the time-limited format, since the survivor will be "willing to take risks if he trusts that the group will be there for him should he get in trouble" (1999, 298).

Gartner suggested that such open-ended groups may include psychoeducational components, particularly during the early stages of the group. He noted further that

> The main work of my groups has combined, first, work on trying to remember the abuse and mourn it, which is accomplished by concentrating on past experiences; and second, addressing relational patterns, achieved by emphasizing the interpersonal events in the group itself. In my experience, combining these goals has not presented a problem. (1999, 297)

Our experience with groups for survivors supports Gartner's view that both of these objectives can be achieved in a single group. We also agree with Gartner that such a group may be composed entirely of survivors, even for stage 3 recovery work. While Herman's distinction between stage 2 and stage 3 of the recovery process is conceptually useful, we have found that it is very difficult in practice to confine the topics of discussion in a group to just the events of the past. Issues surrounding what is going on in the group in the here and now tend to arise spontaneously, and when they do arise they need to be addressed at that time. In addition, some survivors take longer than others to feel safe enough in the group to share their traumatic experiences. For these individuals it may be necessary to have interaction with other group members before they can fully engage in the task of remembering and mourning. Thus from time to time in the survivor group, the stage 2 goal of remembrance and mourning and the stage 3 goal of reconnection with ordinary life can be pursued simultaneously, and making progress toward each of these two goals can be mutually reinforcing.

There are also practical reasons for using a single group. Depending on where one's practice is located, it may not be easy or even possible to find a time-limited trauma-focused group that is appropriate for a given patient at stage 2 of recovery, and then find a dynamically oriented, open-ended, interpersonal group with heterogeneous membership to take up the goals of stage 3 recovery. We feel that an open-ended psychodynamic group composed of survivors is generally a perfectly acceptable vehicle through which to pursue the goals of stage 2 and stage 3 recovery.

Evidence of the Efficacy of Group Therapy for Survivors of Childhood Abuse

There is a good deal of empirical evidence supporting the efficacy of various forms of group treatment for adult survivors of childhood abuse. These studies consider (1) time-limited psychoeducational groups; (2) process-oriented psychodynamic groups; and (3) group experiences having a cognitive–behavioral orientation.

Psychoeducational Groups

Several studies have been reported focusing on the effectiveness of groups designed specifically for survivors who correspond to Herman's description of stage 1 recovery (Talbot, Houghtalen, Cyrulik, Betz, Barkun, Duberstein, and Wynne 1998; Talbot, Houghtalen, Duberstein, Cox, Giles, and Wynne 1999). These groups are known as the Women's Safety in Recovery Groups.

The groups were designed to educate members regarding trauma and self-care, in order to help the women establish safety and self-control. These groups meet three times a week for three weeks, with one week devoted to each of three content areas. During the first week the topic is control of the body. This unit focuses on the physical health of the survivor. The content areas covered in the first week include substance abuse, self-harming behaviors, distorted perceptions of the body, and sexuality. The second week of the intervention focuses on control of the environment. This unit aims to teach participants how to make good decisions regarding their personal safety, including judgments about whom they can trust and under what circumstances. The third week focuses on control of emotions. The topics covered during this week include posttraumatic stress disorder, dissociation, anger, and guilt. In this unit participants are helped to identify the stimuli that trigger their negative emotional reactions. In addition, they are taught affect-regulation strategies, including relaxation techniques, seeking social support, engaging in physical activities, and participating in psychotherapy. Talbot and associates (1998, 1999) reported that the Women's Safety in Recovery Groups resulted in significant reductions in measured anxiety, hostility, interpersonal sensitivity, phobic anxiety, and paranoid ideation.

Dynamic Process-Oriented Groups

Carver, Stalker, Stewart, and Abraham (1989) studied fifty-seven adult female survivors of childhood sexual abuse who participated in process-oriented groups for periods ranging from ten to fifteen weeks. The investigators administered the SCL-90 before and after treatment. The results indicated that the participants improved significantly from pretreatment to posttreatment on every subscale of the SCL-90 except the paranoid ideation subscale. They also reported that the participants perceived the group experience as extremely helpful, particularly with respect to being able to disclose their abuse histories, being understood, and not feeling different. Members also reported feeling less guilty following their participation in the group.

Alexander and associates studied sixty-five adult female survivors who were participants in groups that were either "process-oriented" or employed an interpersonal transaction (IT) model (Alexander, Neimeyer, and Follette 1991; Alexander, Neimeyer, Follette, and Moore 1989). In the process-oriented groups, members shared their abuse histories, after which the group focused on interactions among group members. The IT groups employed a new disclosure topic each week, such as feeling different, perceptions of self, helplessness, and family secrets. Each of the two types of groups ran for ten weeks. Each session was an hour and a half in duration. Alexander and associates measured social adjustment, depression, and general distress at pretreatment, posttreatment, and six months after the conclusion of treatment. They also assessed a wait-for-treatment control at pretreatment and posttreatment. They found that participants in each of the two types of therapy groups demonstrated significantly greater improvements from pretreatment to posttreatment than did the wait-for-treatment controls on all three of the adjustment measures. They also found that the pretreatment to posttreatment gains in psychosocial adjustment were maintained six months later.

Richter, Snider, and Gorey (1997) studied 115 adult women survivors of childhood sexual abuse who participated in process-oriented groups containing four to ten members each for a period of fifteen weeks. They measured the participants at pretreatment, posttreatment, and six months following treatment on depression and self-esteem. They reported significant decreases in depression and significant increases in self-esteem from pretreatment to posttreatment, and they reported that participants continued to improve in each of these areas during the six-month follow-up period.

Bagley and Young (1998) studied a group of twenty-nine adult women who were survivors of childhood sexual abuse who participated in multimodal group treatment for fifteen weeks. The group met once a week for an hour. They compared this sample to a sample of twenty-eight adult female survivors who had individual psychotherapy for the same period of time, and to a sample of sixty adult women with no history of abuse. The women in these three samples were measured on social isolation, self-esteem, depression, and suicidal ideation before the start of treatment and again six years later. Bagley and Young reported that the women in each of the two samples with histories of sexual abuse demonstrated significant decreases over the six-year period in depression, social isolation, and suicidal ideation. The women in each of the two groups with histories of child sexual abuse also demonstrated significant increases in self-esteem over the same period. However, at the six-year mark, the women in the two abused samples still had lower self-esteem and higher scores on depression, social isolation, and suicidal ideation than the women in the comparison group who had no history of abuse.

Longstreth, Mason, Schrieber, and Tsao-Wei (1998) evaluated the progress of nineteen women who participated in process-oriented psychotherapy groups for sixteen weeks. These groups met once per week for an hour and a half. The participants were assessed pre- and posttreatment as well as in a follow-up one year after the conclusion of the treatment. The authors reported that the women demonstrated significant gains in self-image and relationship satisfaction. The participants also demonstrated significant symptom reductions on each of the SCL-90 symptom scales, and on a measure of self-blame. These gains were largely maintained at the time of the one-year follow-up.

While not all of these studies are methodologically strong, taken together they represent substantial support for the view that process-oriented therapy in groups consisting of survivors of similar traumatic experiences can improve the psychosocial adjustment of adult survivors of childhood abuse.

Cognitive–Behavioral Groups

Several investigators have examined the efficacy of therapy groups that have a cognitive-behavioral orientation. Chard, Weaver, and Resnick (1997) studied fifteen women diagnosed with PTSD who participated in a combination of individual and group treatment for a period of seventeen weeks. This treatment, referred to as "cognitive processing therapy," involved learning to process feelings and cognitions while reconstructing, integrating, and processing memories of the abuse. At the conclusion of the treatment, none of the women continued to meet the diagnostic criteria for PTSD. The women reported decreases in negative cognitions, improvements in managing stress, improvements in interpersonal relationships, and improvements in sexual functioning.

DiVitto (1998) studied ten adult outpatients who participated in an eight-week cognitive–behavioral group that aimed to develop the self-capacity for affect regulation. DiVitto found that these women reported decreases in flashbacks, dissociation, suicidal ideation, self-harm, and panic attacks. They also reported increases in the anger they felt regarding the abuse they experienced, and increased ability to control these feelings.

Eclectic Group Treatment Models

Westbury and Tutty (1999) reported an evaluation of a group treatment for women survivors of childhood sexual abuse that they described as a "body-focused feminist model" (34). They described the groups as closed, with six to eight members, short-term, structured, and led by two co-therapists. Each group meets for two and a half hours weekly over ten to twelve weeks. The prerequisite to participation is six months of individual therapy focused on childhood sexual abuse issues. All potential participants are screened by the facilitators, and women are not admitted if they "are in current crisis, have suicidal ideation, or active substance abuse" (34).

Westbury and Tutty (1999) stated that the focus of their group treatment model is to have each woman tell her story in a supportive and safe environment. In this regard the group is similar to the trauma-focused group that Herman described as appropriate to the needs of the stage 2 survivor. However, the groups evaluated by Westbury and Tutty also employed integrative body therapy (IBP) (Rand, Rosenberg, and Assay 1985), a holistic approach that focuses on the cognitive, emotional, physical, and spiritual aspects of the patient. The approach stresses the need to balance all aspects of the patient's life. It stresses the importance of personal boundaries and the need to be "present" during group sessions. The latter characteristic refers to steps taken to prevent patients from utilizing dissociative defenses to withdraw from anxiety-producing aspects of the group process.

The IBP experiential techniques include body-focused relaxation exercises and personal boundary exercises. The women are taught to use deep breathing, and they are taught to become aware of all five senses to bring themselves back to the "here and now" during the group. Guided visualizations are used to explore themes of safety, inner wisdom, and containment. In addition, patients are taught to cope with dissociation and flashbacks outside group sessions by "stopping or getting away from whatever or whoever has triggered the reaction" (34). In addition,

> A number of feminist therapy techniques are utilized, including determining personal and societal goals, problem-solving, and developing interpersonal and life-management skills. The group provides a safe place for women to discuss the power structure of a patriarchal society and to perceive sexual abuse as a violent abuse of power while establishing their personal goals, group goals, and social goals. (1999, 34)

The authors found that, compared to wait-for-treatment controls (n = 10), women who participated in one of these groups (n = 22) demonstrated significantly greater reductions in depression, measured by the Beck Depression Inventory (BDI) (Beck and Steer 1987), and also significantly greater reductions in trauma symptoms, measured by the Trauma Symptoms Checklist (TSC-33) (Briere and Runtz 1989).

Conclusion

Our experience, the observations of other clinicians, and the empirical literature clearly indicate the efficacy of group treatments of various forms for adult survivors of childhood abuse. Group therapy can promote the development of self-capacities such as the ability to connect with others and the ability to regulate affect. It can facilitate the process of reworking traumatic childhood experiences to diminish the disruptive impact of intrusive memories. Group therapy can also facilitate the development of new patterns of interpersonal behavior to replace the dysfunctional patterns that resulted from the patient's early adaptations to the experience of abuse.

There may be times when these diverse therapeutic goals can be pursued, as Herman suggested, in the logical order suggested by her three stages of recovery from complex PTSD. It may also be possible under certain circumstances to provide patients with several different types of group experiences that parallel their current stage of recovery and focus on facilitating the work of that stage. However, it is also quite likely and by no means disastrous if the goals of recovery for stages 1, 2, and 3 cannot be neatly compartmentalized. It is also quite likely that a given adult survivor will be able to participate in only one group. This would typically be an open-ended group composed of fellow survivors. In this eventuality, much of the stage 1 recovery work of building self-capacity will take place in individual treatment, and group work will begin when the survivor has developed sufficient trust, safety, and affect regulation capacity to allow him or her to engage in the work of remembering and mourning.

The critical issue is keeping the patient at all times within the therapeutic window in which his or her self-capacities and support systems are sufficient to allow the survivor to tolerate the affective responses that are raised by group participation, including both the survivor's own efforts to disclose the traumatic history and the reminders associated with the related experiences of fellow group members. We strongly recommend that group treatment be conducted only in conjunction with individual treatment, in order to monitor the patient to ensure that he or she is being exposed only to a level of trauma-related cues that is consistent with his or her affect regulation capability and support network.

With respect to the question of whether the treatment of adult survivors can be considered complete if they work only in a group composed of fellow survivors and never move into a heterogeneous group, we have observed that many survivors form close attachments to their fellow participants in survivor groups and are reluctant to end a survivor group to begin a new interpersonal group experience with nontraumatized individuals. We believe that there is nothing wrong with continuing in a group with fellow survivors. We feel that survivors generally have ample opportunity to develop their interpersonal skills with the general public during their daily lives, which go on even as they continue to participate in their survivor group. We also tend to make group participants aware of other support systems that may be helpful to them with respect to specific issues (such as substance abuse issues, eating disorders, risky sexual activity or problems with sexual revictimization, and issues derived from parental alcoholism). Support groups focused on these issues tend to include both individuals who have identified themselves as survivors of childhood abuse and individuals who have not.

We also believe that it is possible for open-ended survivor groups to develop over time by taking on new members who are not survivors of childhood abuse or any particular experience with trauma, but who nevertheless feel that they have developed dysfunctional behavioral patterns that can be improved. In fact, we have found that it can be quite useful to have both survivors of childhood abuse who are working on stage 3 recovery issues to be in the same group as nonsurvivors.

Our review of the outcome research on group treatment for survivors of childhood abuse clearly indicates that group treatment of various types is effective. Kessler, White, and Nelson (2003) reported the results of a meta-analysis of thirteen outcome studies of group treatments for women who were sexually abused as children. They concluded that despite the methodological limitations of some of these studies, the overwhelming weight of the evidence indicated that group treatment for adult female survivors is effective.

CHAPTER THIRTEEN

~

Treating Survivors Who Have Posttraumatic Symptoms and Co-morbid Substance Use Disorders

The Self-Medication Hypothesis

In chapter 6 of this volume we considered the links between childhood physical, sexual, and emotional abuse and adult substance use disorders (SUD). We noted that there is substantial empirical evidence of the relationship between childhood abuse and adult substance abuse, and we discussed theoretical explanations for this relationship based on genetic factors, environmental factors, the self-medication hypothesis (Khantzian 1985, 1997, 2004), and the corollary of the self-medication hypothesis that views PTSD symptoms as mediating the relationship between childhood abuse and adult substance use disorders (Epstein et al. 1998; Kilpatrick et al. 2000; Stewart and Conrod 2003). With respect to the mediating role of posttraumatic symptoms, Stewart and Conrod (2003) concluded that "studies that have assessed patient perceptions of the factors that exacerbate or maintain their psychiatric symptoms suggest a self-medication process by which . . . drugs with central nervous system depressant properties are reportedly used as a way to cope with physical or emotional discomfort or to avoid exacerbation of PTSD symptoms" (54).

As we saw in chapter 9 of this book, survivors of severe and prolonged childhood abuse, including physical, sexual, and emotional abuse, tend to experience as adults not only the symptoms of simple PTSD, as referred to by Stewart and Conrod (2003), but also the symptoms of complex PTSD. Both sets of symptoms are uncomfortable physically and/or distressing psychologically, and we have observed that survivors who experience these symptoms do frequently self-medicate these symptoms by using alcohol or other addict-ing drugs. We see the self-medication hypothesis and the posttraumatic symptom corollary as explaining a substantial portion of the relationship be-tween childhood abuse and adult SUD. Specifically, we believe that adult substance abuse can result from the experience of childhood abuse via two distinct but by no means mutually exclusive pathways: (1) the child or ado-lescent who is experiencing abuse might begin to use substances *at the time of the abuse* to ease the current pain of the abuse, and this early substance use could grow into addiction over time; and (2) the child or adolescent who has experienced abuse may develop PTSD and/or complex PTSD which contin-ues into adulthood, carrying with it discomforting symptoms experienced in adulthood. These symptoms may lead the survivor to begin or to continue to use substances *as an adult* to ease the symptoms that he or she is experienc-ing as an adult. Either of these two pathways may operate separately and in-dependently, or they may coexist and be mutually reinforcing.

The self-medication hypothesis strongly suggests that adult patients who are experiencing the symptoms of PTSD and/or complex PTSD have a mo-tivation to continue to use substances that goes beyond the normal physical addictive processes of increasing tolerance and the potential for withdrawal symptoms. These survivors are motivated to continue to use substances (or to relapse during treatment) not only because they experience physical crav-ings, but because they have developed the behavioral pattern of coping with negative affect by using substances rather than employing less harmful affect regulation strategies to cope with the negative affect associated with their symptoms of PTSD and/or complex PTSD. For this reason, we have found that such individuals must be treated for both the substance use disorder and the deficits in self-capacities that exacerbate the substance abuse.

The Need to Treat Posttraumatic
Symptoms and SUD Simultaneously

We have found that patients who are survivors are frequently aware of the fact that they use substances for several different reasons, including both the gratification of physical cravings and the reduction of negative affect. We have also found that because both of these factors contribute to the maintenance of substance use, it is not a good idea to attempt to treat a sur-vivor who has both posttraumatic symptoms and an SUD for substance abuse only. Survivors with posttraumatic symptoms and co-morbid sub-stance abuse symptoms must be treated for both problems simultaneously. We emphasize this recommendation to clinicians because it has become standard procedure among some clinicians to require that survivors seeking treatment for symptoms of PTSD and/or complex PTSD who have a co-morbid SUD begin their treatment for the posttraumatic symptoms only af-ter they have been sober for a period of time, generally three to six months. This is not a good idea and generally does not work. In our experience, when these patients attempt to maintain sobriety, they become the "white-knuckled drunks" for whom sobriety is a constant struggle. Stressful life events in general and trauma-related stimuli in particular are likely to re-sult in relapses among these patients. They rarely achieve lasting sobriety in the absence of assistance with the PTSD symptoms that contribute to and support the maintenance of their substance use.

Our experience in this regard is supported by the results of several studies of the effectiveness of treatment for substance use disorders among patients with and without posttraumatic symptoms. For example, Brown, Recupero, and Stout (1995) studied male and female patients who sought treatment for a substance use disorder. The investigators compared the progress made by the SUD patients who were also diagnosed with PTSD to the progress made by SUD patients without PTSD. They found that the patients who were di-agnosed with PTSD did not do as well with their SUD treatment as the pa-tients without PTSD. The patients who were also diagnosed with PTSD re-ported more frequent relapse, as indicated by more readmissions to inpatient addiction programs over the course of their lifetimes. Brown and associates interpreted this finding as indicating that co-morbid PTSD symptoms exac-erbated the SUD, leading to more frequent relapse. Similarly, Brown, Stout, and Mueller (1996) reported that SUD inpatients with co-morbid PTSD di-agnoses relapsed more quickly following discharge than SUD inpatients dis-charged from the same program. The patients with PTSD also reported that they drank more on the occasions when they did drink, and they reported more instances of really heavy drinking.

Ouimette, Ahrens, Moos, and Finney (1997, 1998) reported the results of a study of SUD patients treated in fifteen different substance abuse programs at Veterans Administration facilities. They found that patients diagnosed with a Substance Use Disorder only demonstrated positive changes in ex-pectancies regarding the benefits of abstinence and the possibility of remain-ing abstinent, whereas patients with both a Substance Use Disorder and co-morbid PTSD did not. They also reported that patients with co-morbid PTSD tended to use the coping strategies of cognitive avoidance and emo-tional discharge more than patients with SUD only. The investigators inter-preted these findings as indicating that patients with co-morbid PTSD who are treated for SUD may be less motivated than patients without PTSD to maintain abstinence, because the patients with co-morbid PTSD are more likely to experience negative affect and less able to modulate this affect without resorting to the use of drugs.

Ouimette, Finney, and Moos (1999) reported the results of a two-year follow-up study of this same group of SUD patients. They reported that the patients with a co-morbid PTSD demonstrated more frequent and more serious substance use throughout the follow-up period. They also found that the relationship between a co-morbid PTSD diagnosis and poor substance-related outcomes was mediated by the tendency toward emotional discharge, a dimension of emotion-focused coping that reflects the extent to which an individual focuses on and vents his or her distress, rather than thinking about and enacting strategies aimed at reducing or resolving the distress.

Stewart and Conrod (2003) argued that the deficits in appropriate affective coping strategies that are displayed by patients with both PTSD and SUD "may actually reflect the effect of PTSD hyperarousal symptoms on coping [and that] hyperarousal symptoms may be the specific feature of PTSD that renders certain PTSD patients particularly likely to resort to substance abuse and prove additionally resistant to traditional SUD treatment" (54). We would add that the characterological dysfunctions associated with complex PTSD are similarly associated with both maladaptive coping strategies (e.g., isolation, outbursts of anger) and painful affect (e.g., loneliness, poor self-concept) that can contribute to ongoing substance abuse.

Clearly survivors who have both posttraumatic symptoms and a substance use disorder are not likely to make much progress toward lasting sobriety in a traditional substance use treatment that does not address the survivor's need to develop the capacity for affective self-regulation as well as the need to decondition negative emotional responses to trauma-related cues. Ouimette, Moos, and Brown (2003) concurred with our conclusion and observed that "most clinical researchers recognize that SUD and PTSD symptoms are interwoven and emphasize the need for concurrent treatment of both substance use problems and PTSD symptoms" (93). Several other groups of investigators have come to the same conclusion (Abueg and Fairbank 1991; Najavits, Weiss, and Liese 1996; Stine and Kosten 1995).

A Group Treatment Model for Survivors with Posttraumatic Symptoms and Co-morbid SUD

Group Composition

Our group treatment model for survivors of childhood abuse with posttraumatic symptoms and a co-morbid SUD employs groups composed of survivors. These groups often consist entirely of survivors who have substance abuse problems, but on other occasions the groups also contain some survivors who do not regard substance abuse as a personal issue for them. We have found that most survivors of severe and prolonged childhood abuse who seek treatment for symptoms of PTSD and/or complex PTSD will ultimately recognize that they do have a substance abuse issue of some kind. They may not come into treatment thinking about substance use as their primary problem, or a major problem, or even a significant problem. Nevertheless, we have found that when we begin discussing the means through which individuals can manage unpleasant affect, most survivors who have sought treatment for any posttraumatic symptom will recognize and acknowledge that they have on more than one occasion used alcohol or some other drug as a means of alleviating anxiety, soothing blows to their self-esteem, or otherwise distancing themselves from unpleasant emotional responses. These are unhealthy ways to use substances, even if the substance use has not proceeded to a point where addictive processes have initiated or the substance use has become clearly disruptive to normal functioning.

The principal exceptions to the generalization that survivors seeking treatment for posttraumatic symptoms will have used substances to alleviate uncomfortable affective states are those survivors of childhood abuse who have never used alcohol or any other drug. These individuals typically abstain from all drug use because they are afraid of drugs. They have seen and felt the impact of drugs on their caregivers or other family members, and they have therefore avoided drugs completely for fear of becoming addicted or becoming abusive toward their own children, as their caregivers were toward them.

Therefore most or all of the participants in the typical survivor group will relate to the issue of using substances inappropriately to manage affective responses, whether or not they themselves have a substance abuse problem. For this reason, in a group of survivors that contains a broad range of individuals with respect to self-perceptions of the existence and severity of personal substance use disorder symptoms, we find that even members who do not consider their personal substance use to be an issue are nevertheless responsive to group discussion of substance use issues. Thus we do not hesitate to treat a patient with both posttraumatic symptoms and a co-morbid SUD in a survivor group that has members who do not meet the criteria for a formal SUD diagnosis.

Treatment Goals

Within our survivor groups, including those composed entirely or largely of survivors with posttraumatic symptoms and a co-morbid SUD, we attempt to work toward the treatment goals described by Herman (1992a) as relevant to each of the three stages of recovery from trauma. These goals were reviewed in some detail in the preceding chapter of this volume. Here we simply note that initially we work on the stage 1 goals of establishing the patients' safety and security in the group, and developing their affect regulation skills. Later we direct the attention of the group members to the stage 2 tasks of remembering, disclosing, and working through their abuse experiences. Finally, we focus on the stage 3 task of developing the patients' repertoires of interpersonal skills. When a given group has survivors with a co-morbid SUD, the group processes reflecting the goals for each of the three stages of recovery will include discussions that address these goals in the specific context of substance abuse as well as discussions that address the same goals in relation to other specific problems.

Group Processes with Survivors with Substance Use Disorders

In our discussion of the process of group treatment with survivors in chapter 12, we indicated that we do not adhere to a rigid sequence of goals that would require, for example, that the process of development of self-capabilities must be completed before the process of remembering begins. The same principle applies in our group work when some or all of the survivor patients have problems with substance abuse. Moreover, we also remain flexible with respect to the timing and the relative emphasis placed on discussions of substance abuse versus other symptoms of PTSD or complex PTSD. Thus we do not employ a rigid schedule which requires that the problem of substance abuse be considered in any particular order relative to other problem areas as we work through the objectives for the three stages of recovery. However, for each of the stages of recovery, we do have a series of topics for discussion and a series of activities that pertain to the issue of substance abuse.

Stage 1: Safety and Security

Stage 1 work tends to be didactic in nature. We always dedicate a session early in the group treatment process to the issue of safety. We explain why it is only logical that survivors of severe and prolonged abuse have a strong need to feel safe, and we discuss the structure and rules of the group that have been designed and incorporated to guarantee patients' safety.

In this session also we always point out that for many survivors substance use represents both a serious threat to immediate physical and psychological safety, and a serious threat to the possibility of successful recovery from other posttraumatic symptoms. Along with substance abuse, we discuss bulimia, self-mutilation, and risky sexual behavior as other "unsafe" forms of behavior that many survivors engage in. With respect to substance abuse specifically, we teach patients that any use of substances for the purpose of insulating oneself from negative affect is potentially harmful, both because it can lead to addiction and because it can enable the survivor to avoid remembering and confronting the abuse that he or she experienced. We provide patients with information on substance abuse as well as information on the other forms of unsafe behavior. We discuss signs of severe difficulty in each of these domains of unsafe behavior, and we discuss the supports that are available to group members to help them achieve safety in each of these areas.

For example, with respect to substance abuse, we make patients aware that twelve-step programs are available, such as AA and NA. We also note the existence of similar sources of support for individuals with other serious symptoms of PTSD and complex PTSD. In making patients aware of these potential sources of support, we also caution them regarding the potential stresses associated with such groups. We urge each patient to consult with his or her individual therapist prior to joining any such mutual self-help group. We find that patients with an SUD are often quite fragile, and we are very careful to monitor their use of other supports. On the other hand, patients with eating disorders can be quite fragile as well. In fact, when patients in our survivor group seek support from an outside source for virtually any symptom, we try to have a sense of what is going on there and whether or not it may be stressful. We actually do this monitoring in our individual treatment sessions with our patients, where we also obtain feedback on their experience with the survivor group.

In the same way, we always schedule a group session fairly early in the course of group work in which discussion is focused on becoming aware of and identifying one's emotional states and the cues that elicit negative emotional responses. We encourage group members to consider the circumstances under which they have engaged in dysfunctional behaviors. We give homework assignments in which we ask group members to identify the behaviors they consider dysfunctional, and then try to recall the events that preceded these behaviors and their emotional states at the time. Obviously one area of dysfunctional behavior for many will be using alcohol or drugs inappropriately, and one of the activities toward which we direct patients is the identification of the negative emotional states that may have preceded such episodes.

Also in the service of our safety goal, we teach the patients in our survivor groups relaxation techniques that they can use to control negative affect when they begin to feel anxious or apprehensive. These techniques include progressive muscle relaxation, deep breathing, and visualization techniques.

These specific relaxation procedures have obvious relevance as alternatives to using addicting substances to reduce negative affect. When a patient feels anxious or experiences a disappointment that might precipitate substance use, we teach the patient to use one or more of the relaxation techniques instead. However, teaching these techniques also fosters patient safety by reducing the likelihood of binge eating, self-mutilation, and uncontrolled angry acting-out behavior. Early in the group process we also introduce patients to lifestyle activities that promote general relaxation, such as exercise, yoga, and the use of neurofeedback technology; and we discuss the potential affective benefits of environmental elements such as music, fragrance, fresh air, and lighting.

We attend to patient safety needs that are relevant to any substance abuse issues they may have at the same time that we are working on developing safety with respect to other symptom areas. Other issues that we consider early in the group process include grounding techniques that patients may use to keep from dissociating in order to withdraw from the group process, positive cognitions regarding the benefits of discontinuing substance abuse and other risky or self-injurious behaviors, and positive expectations regarding the benefits of sharing experiences with other group members.

Stage 2: Remembrance and Mourning

As in any survivor group, we monitor the developing self-capacities of the members of survivor groups containing patients with SUDs. When it appears that the patients' capacities for connectedness and their ability to monitor and regulate their affective states have developed sufficiently, we begin to open up the topic of childhood experiences with abuse. This process does not change in any fundamental way as a function of the number of patients in the group who are diagnosed with an SUD. However, in groups with patients with co-morbid SUDs, we spend some time discussing (1) the possible impact of caretaker substance abuse on the various forms of abuse that the caretaker(s) inflicted on the survivors who are in the group; (2) the genetic and environmental linkages between caretaker substance abuse and the development of substance use disorders among their children; and (3) the self-medication hypothesis and the PTSD and complex PTSD symptom corollary of the self-medication hypothesis.

Of course, among members of survivor groups for whom substance abuse is a significant issue, some portion of the material that they will remember and mourn will extend beyond the abuse that they suffered directly at the hands of their caretakers or other perpetrators to the additional negative experiences that have been inflicted upon them indirectly through their own substance abuse, which resulted from the childhood abuse. Again, we hasten to point out that in principle this multitiered process of remembrance is really no different from the experience of a patient whose primary presenting problem might be bulimia, since the patient with the eating disorder would be remembering and disclosing both the physical, sexual, and/or emotional abuse that she experienced directly at the hands of her caretaker(s) and the subsequent indirect abuse that has resulted from the experience of living with bulimia.

We have found that the substance-abusing survivors in our groups often report that their caretakers were substance abusers as well. This is to be expected, of course, because parental substance abuse is a significant predictor of various forms of child abuse. Maternal neglect is often attributed to maternal substance abuse. Physical and sexual abuse is often reported as occurring most frequently when dad was drunk. Secondary abuse is frequently described as occurring when either dad, or mom, or both were intoxicated. This means that many of the substance-abusing survivors in our groups (as well as some of the survivors who are not themselves substance abusers) are children of alcoholics or children of persons addicted to other substances.

As such, we have found that many of these survivor group members will seek out and join peer support groups for children of alcoholics. We have found that their participation in these groups is generally helpful in terms of feeling accepted and understanding the development of some of the dysfunctional interpersonal behaviors that are associated with complex PTSD. We therefore support such participation, but again we try to monitor each patient's experience with such groups so as to avoid the possibility of counterproductive emotional overload. Groups for children of alcoholics can also be useful during stage 3 of recovery, because the peers who participate in such groups are typically very good at identifying the dysfunctional interpersonal behavior patterns that are typically adopted by children of alcoholics as a result of the dysfunctional home environment, and then continue into adulthood.

Stage 3: Reconnection

The goal of reconnection with the world is substantially the same for all survivor groups, regardless of the number of group members who have co-morbid substance use disorders. The goal is to identify dysfunctional cognitions and interpersonal behavior patterns that have inhibited the patient's ability to form close, rewarding relationships and to substitute for these dysfunctional cognitions and behaviors new adaptive patterns of thinking and acting. When the survivor has a substance abuse issue, however, there are certain particular changes that need to be made.

Recovering addicts need to support their intention to remain sober by avoiding places where substances are readily available and by avoiding social contact with individuals who still use substances. Recovering addicts need to develop alternative interests and activities to take up the space in their lives that was occupied previously by substance use and related activities. Recovering addicts need to develop assertiveness skills that they can use to politely decline offers of substances or invitations to go to places where substances will be available. Peer support groups such as AA and NA can be very helpful in terms of structuring the addicted survivor's time and providing him with a social network composed of individuals who are substance free. Here again, we hasten to add that when the recovering substance abuser develops the ability to identify and to politely turn down offers that would be expected to lead to substance use, he is really doing exactly the same thing as the woman who has been repeatedly victimized sexually, when she learns to identify and extricate herself from situations that may be expected to end in unwanted sexual activity.

In a typical survivor group, there are likely to be a substantial number of members with substance use disorders. As a result, a substantial amount of group time will be spent discussing experiences that members may have had in AA or NA, and/or experiences they may have had in a peer support group for children of alcoholics. In addition, we typically spend a substantial amount of time discussing and rehearsing behavioral strategies that can be used to minimize the likelihood of relapse. In the typical survivor group that we have run, there tend to be proportionately fewer members who regard repeated sexual victimization as a primary posttraumatic symptom. Therefore it is likely that proportionately less time will be spent discussing and practicing behaviors aimed at preventing such revictimization.

However, in the groups that we run, both sets of alternative behaviors are likely to be discussed and practiced to some extent. Furthermore, group members will be aware that dysfunctional substance use and dysfunctional sexual revictimization are substantially analogous problems, representing responses to childhood abuse that may have served a purpose at the time but are now maladaptive. Group members will also understand that in order to eliminate the dysfunctional behaviors they must learn and practice appropriately assertive alternative responses. The survivor who has a co-morbid SUD may learn some of these behaviors in his child abuse survivor group and others at an AA meeting or in a peer support group for children of alcoholics. The sexually revictimized survivor may learn some of these behaviors in her child abuse survivor group and others in a woman's group, a rape victim support group, or a self-defense class.

The essential point here is that regardless of the particular dysfunctional behaviors that are most salient for the individual group member, the latter stages of the group process will be structured so as to identify the dysfunctional behaviors, learn how to avoid these behaviors, and develop the habit of using alternative adaptive behaviors to fill the void.

Evidence of the Efficacy of Combined Treatment for Posttraumatic Symptoms and SUD

Several treatment models have been developed to provide integrated treatment for PTSD symptoms and co-morbid SUD. In most instances these models have been applied to populations of alcohol-dependent military veterans who have also been diagnosed with simple PTSD as defined in the DSM-IV-TR. For example, Abueg and Fairbank (1991) developed a PTSD-relapse prevention program by selecting and adapting the elements of the relapse prevention training program developed by Marlatt and Gordon (1985) that they believed to be particularly relevant for SUD-PTSD patients. These elements included (1) training aimed at helping patients assess their emotional states and recognize that negative affect can precipitate substance use episodes; (2) training aimed at developing the patients' self-efficacy and the self-perception that they can in fact resist the temptation to resume substance use; and (3) training aimed at convincing patients that a single relapse does not represent a fatal blow to patients' ongoing efforts to achieve abstinence. Abueg and Fairbank (1991) reported that patients who completed this program were more likely than control patients to be abstinent at the conclusion of the twelve-week program. In addition, the patients who participated in the PTSD-relapse prevention program reported lower levels of alcohol use than controls at the time of a nine-month follow-up.

Other group treatment protocols for patients with PTSD and a co-morbid SUD have incorporated the principle of progressive exposure to trauma-related cues for the purpose of desensitizing the patient to conditioned negative emotional responses to these cues that constitute a defining characteristic of the DSM-IV-TR diagnosis of PTSD (Coffey, Dansky, and Brady 2003; Dansky and Brady 1998; Dansky, Brady, and Saladin 1998; Dansky, Saladin, Brady, Killeen, Becker, and Roitzsch 1994; Donovan and Padin-Rivera 1999; Donovan, Padin-Rivera, and Kowaliw 2001; Keane, Fairbank, Caddell, and Zimering 1989; Triffleman, Carroll, and Kellogg 1999). These protocols were all developed relatively recently, because until quite recently it was accepted practice to exclude patients with addiction problems from treatments for PTSD in general and from exposure treatments for PTSD specifically. Litz,

Blake, Gerardi, and Keane (1990) reported that 27 percent of the clinicians they surveyed considered a concurrent SUD a contraindication for exposure treatment for PTSD. According to Ouimette, Moos, and Brown (2003), "clinicians' reasons for reluctance to use exposure treatment for SUD-PTSD are based on the beliefs that such patients may experience overwhelming emotions that would lead to more substance abuse or that cognitive impairment associated with the SUD could impair the patient's ability to do the necessary imagery for exposure treatment" (98).

As we have already emphasized in our discussions of individual and group treatment of survivors of childhood abuse with PTSD and complex PTSD, the affect regulation capabilities of the patient must always be balanced against the potential of trauma-related cues to evoke overwhelming negative emotional responses. This is as true of the group situation in which patients remember and disclose their traumatic childhood experiences as it is when formal systematic desensitization is employed using imaginary stimuli to expose the patient to trauma-related cues. The leader will always strive to keep the patients in the group within the "therapeutic window" in which conditioned emotional responses to trauma-related cues can be extinguished. It may or may not be the case that patients with a co-morbid SUD are more vulnerable to being overwhelmed than other survivors of trauma who have developed PTSD and/or complex PTSD who do not have a co-morbid SUD. In either case, the group leader should begin exposure to trauma-related cues only after affect regulation capacities have developed substantially, and the leader should always monitor carefully the responses of all the group members to trauma-related cues that are presented in any form during the group.

Donovan, Padin-Rivera, and Kowaliw (2001) developed an exposure protocol for patients with combat-related SUD-PTSD co-morbidity. This protocol, referred to as the Transcend treatment, has two phases. First, there is a twelve-week period during which patients are partially hospitalized. This phase of treatment focuses on decreasing PTSD symptoms and promoting an addiction-free lifestyle. Treatment during this first phase includes behavioral skills training, exposure to trauma-related cues through written narratives, and peer social support. The second phase of the Transcend treatment involves weekly group meetings that continue for a minimum of six months following the completion of phase 1. These groups emphasize PTSD symptom management and relapse prevention. Donovan and associates (2001) reported that a group of five hundred male Vietnam veterans with SUD-PTSD demonstrated significant decreases in PTSD symptoms during phase 1 of the Transcend treatment, and they maintained these gains one year following the conclusion of phase 1.

Dansky and colleagues (Coffey et al. 2003; Dansky et al. 1998; Dansky, Roitzsch, Brady, and Saladin 1997) developed an exposure protocol that they employed with patients diagnosed with PTSD and co-morbid cocaine dependence. This concurrent treatment of PTSD and cocaine dependence (CTPCD) uses imaginal exposure procedures that require patients to repeatedly recall and relate their traumatic memories until the conditioned negative emotional responses to these cues diminish. The CTPCD treatment also involves a psychoeducational component through which patients are taught the basis for the connection between PTSD and substance abuse. In addition, patients are taught coping skills they can employ to support their efforts to remain abstinent. In addition to imaginal exposure to trauma-related cues, the CTPCD treatment program also employs in vivo exposure. This involves prolonged contact with objects, places, or people that symbolically represent or in some other way are associated with the traumatic experiences of the patient. As examples of the types of stimuli used to achieve in vivo exposure, Coffey and her associates (2003) cited holding pieces of clothing worn during an assault and visiting the site of a car accident. In the case of survivors of childhood abuse, relevant stimuli might include photographs of the perpetrator of physical, sexual, and/or emotional abuse, or visits to the home in which the survivor was abused.

Brady, Dansky, Back, Foa, and Carroll (2001) reported the results of a preliminary outcome study of CTPCD based on a sample of thirty-nine patients. They reported that the exposure treatment protocol was effective in reducing both substance use and symptoms of PTSD. Commenting on the results reported by Brady and her colleagues, Coffey et al. (2003) pointed out that the primary concern regarding the use of exposure-based techniques with PTSD patients who have a co-morbid SUD is the possibility of exposure-related relapse. In this regard they noted that in the study reported by Brady and her associates (2001), "drug use did not escalate during the second half of treatment, when the majority of the exposure sessions occurred" (Coffey et al. 2003, 140). Coffey and her associates concluded that CTPCD is an effective treatment for co-occurring PTSD and cocaine dependence, and that the treatment does not appear to increase the risk of substance use relapse in this co-morbid population. They also pointed out that CTPCD is appropriate for patients of both genders and for patients with diverse trauma histories.

Another protocol for treating PTSDD and substance dependence was developed by Triffleman, Carroll, and Kellogg (1999). This treatment, known as substance dependence PTSD therapy (SDPT), employs elements of coping skills training (CST) (Monti, Rohsenow, Colby, and Abrams 1995), stress inoculation training (SIT) (Meichenbaum and Deffenbacher 1988;

Meichenbaum and Novaco 1985), and in vivo exposure. SDPT is a highly structured intervention of five months' duration. Treatment occurs two times per week. Phase 1 of SDPT lasts twelve weeks and aims at establishing sobriety and informing patients of the relationship between PTSD and substance use. Phase 2 runs for eight weeks and focuses on the reduction of PTSD symptoms. Patients are taught coping skills that will enable them to approach trauma-related stimuli; then in vivo exposure is used to reduce the patients' cognitive, emotional, and physiological reactivity to trauma-related stimuli. Preliminary data suggest that SDPT is well tolerated by patients with an SUD, and that it is effective in reducing symptoms of PTSD.

The available outcome data for combined PTSD-SUD treatment protocols has been limited to patients with PTSD as defined in the DSM-IV-TR—simple PTSD. Comparable data are not available for patients with complex PTSD (although one could argue that a substance use disorder is itself a symptom of complex PTSD). Coffey and her associates (2003) have stressed that combined treatment protocols involving exposure to trauma-related cues is appropriate to patients with diverse trauma histories. Triffleman and associates (1999) also suggested that SDPT is appropriate for individuals with diverse trauma histories, although they cautioned that individuals with histories of prolonged childhood physical and/or sexual abuse typically require continued therapy at the conclusion of the five-month SDPT intervention.

We feel that these combined treatment protocols are appropriate for survivors with complex PTSD, although they do not represent a sufficient response to the dysfunctional interpersonal adjustment that characterizes survivors with complex PTSD. We run groups with patients who have symptoms of complex PTSD which often include substance abuse issues. In these groups we employ many of the same techniques as these protocols during the earlier stages of the group work. However, as the open-ended groups continue and become more cohesive, the focus shifts increasingly to interpersonal issues. This represents a response to the stage 3 recovery issues faced by survivors of severe childhood abuse. Of course, we hasten to stress once again that group work always takes place in conjunction with ongoing individual treatment.

References

Aahrens, M., Cameron, T., Roizen, J., et al. 1978. *Alcohol, Casualties, and Crime.* Berkeley: Social Research Group.

Abraham, S., and Llewellyn-Jones, D. 2001. *Eating Disorders.* 5th ed. Oxford: Oxford University Press.

Abueg, F. R., and Fairbank, J. A. 1991. Behavioral treatment of the PTSD substance abuser: A multidimensional stage model. In P. Saigh, ed., *Posttraumatic Stress Disorder: A Behavioral Approach to Assessment and Treatment,* 111–46. New York: Pergamon.

Ackard, D. M., and Neumark-Sztainer, D. 2003. Multiple sexual victimizations among adolescent boys and girls: Prevalence and associations with eating behaviors and psychological health. *Journal of Child Sexual Abuse* 12, no. 1: 17–37.

Ackard, D. M., Neumark-Sztainer, D., Hannan, P., French, S., and Story, M. 2001. Binge and purge behavior among adolescents: Associations with sexual and physical abuse in a nationally representative sample: The Commonwealth Fund. *Child Abuse and Neglect* 16: 101–18.

Adam, B. S., Everett, B. L., and O'Neal, E. 1992. PTSD in physically and sexually abused psychiatrically hospitalized children. *Child Psychiatry and Human Development* 23: 3–8.

Adams-Tucker, C. 1981. A socioclinical overview of 28 sex-abused children. *Child Abuse and Neglect* 5: 361–67.

———. 1982. Proximate effects of sexual abuse in childhood: A report on 28 children. *American Journal of Psychiatry* 139: 1252–56.

Ainsworth, M. D. S., Blehar, M. C., Waters, E., and Wall, S. 1978. *Patterns of attachment: A psychological study of the strange situation.* Hillsdale, NJ: Erlbaum.

Albach, F., and Everaerd, W. 1992. Posttraumatic stress symptoms in victims of child-hood incest. *Psychotherapy Psychosomatics* 57: 143–51.

Alexander, P. C. 1993. The differential effects of abuse characteristics and attach-ment in the prediction of long-term effects of sexual abuse. *Journal of Interpersonal Violence* 8, no. 3: 346–62.

Alexander, P. C., Neimeyer, R. A., and Follette, V. M. 1991. Group therapy for women sexually abused as children: A controlled study and investigation of indi-vidual differences. *Journal of Interpersonal Violence* 6: 218–31.

Alexander, P. C., Neimeyer, R. A., Follette, V. M., and Moore, M. K. 1989. A com-parison of group treatments of women sexually abused as children. *Journal of Con-sulting and Clinical Psychology* 57: 479–83.

Alfaro, J. 1978. *Summary Report on the Relationship between Child Abuse and Neglect and Later Socially Deviant Behavior*. New York: Select Committee on Child Abuse.

Allen, J. G., Coyne, L., and Console, D. A. 1998. Dissociative detachment relates to psychotic symptoms and personality decompensation. *Comprehensive Psychiatry* 38: 327–34.

Allen, J. G., Coyne, L., and Huntoon, J. 1998. Complex Posttraumatic Stress Disor-der in women from a psychometric perspective. *Journal of Personality Assessment* 70, no. 2: 277–98.

Allers, C. T., Benjack, K. J., White, J., and Rousey, J. T. 1993. HIV vulnerability and the survivor of sexual abuse. *Child Abuse and Neglect* 17: 291–98.

American Academy of Pediatrics and the American Academy of Pediatric Dentistry. 2003. *Oral and Dental Aspects of Child Abuse and Neglect*. Medem: Medical Library/American Medical Association Website.

American Humane Association. 1981. *National Study on Child Neglect and Abuse Re-porting*. Denver: AHA.

American Psychiatric Association. 1994. *Diagnostic and Statistical Manual of Mental Disorders*. 4th ed. Washington, DC: American Psychological Association.

———. 2000. *Diagnostic and Statistical Manual of Mental Disorders*. 4th ed. Text revi-sion. Washington, DC: APA.

American Psychological Association. 1999. *Understanding Child Sexual Abuse: Edu-cation, Prevention, and Recovery*. www.apa.org/releases/sexabuse.

Anderson, J. C., Martin, J. L., Mullen, P. E., Romans, S. E., and Herbison, P. 1993. The prevalence of childhood sexual abuse experiences in a community sample of women. *Journal of the American Academy of Child and Adolescent Psychiatry* 32: 911–19.

Anderson, L. 1981. Notes on the linkage between the sexually abused child and the suicidal adolescent. *Journal of Adolescence* 4: 157–62.

Araji, S., and Finkelhor, D. 1986. Abusers: A review of the research. In D. Finkelhor, ed., *A Sourcebook on Child Sexual Abuse*, 89–118. Beverly Hills: Sage.

Arata, C. M. 1999a. Coping with rape: The roles of prior sexual abuse and attribu-tions of blame. *Journal of Interpersonal Violence* 14: 62–78.

———. 1999b. Repeated sexual victimization and mental disorders in women. *Jour-nal of Child Sexual Abuse* 7: 1–17.

———. 1999c. Sexual revictimization and PTSD: An exploratory study. *Journal of Child Sexual Abuse* 8, no. 91: 49–66.

Arata, C. M., and Lindeman, L. 2002. Marriage, child abuse, and sexual revictimization. *Journal of Interpersonal Violence* 17: 953–71.

Ards, S., Chung, C., and Myers, S. L. 1998. The effects of sample selection bias on racial differences in child abuse reporting. *Child Abuse and Neglect* 22, no. 2: 103–15.

Babcock, J. C., Waltz, J., and Jacobson, N. S. 1993. Power and violence: The relation between communication patterns, power discrepancies, and domestic violence. *Journal of Consulting and Clinical Psychology* 61: 40–50.

Bachman, K. M., Moggi, F., and Stirnemann-Lewis, F. 1994. Mother–son incest and its long-term consequences: A neglected phenomenon in psychiatric practice. *Journal of Nervous and Mental Disease* 182: 723–25.

Bagley, C., and Ramsey, R. 1986. Sexual abuse in childhood: Psychosocial outcomes and implications for social work practice. In J. Gripton and M. Valentich, eds., *Social Work Practice in Sexual Problems*, 33–47. New York: Haworth.

Bagley, C., and Young, L. 1998. Long-term evaluation of group counseling for women with a history of CSA: Focus on depression, self-esteem, suicidal behaviors, and social support. *Social Work with Groups* 21: 63–73.

Bancroft, J., and Vukadinovic, A. 2004. Sexual addiction, sexual compulsivity, sexual impulsivity, or what? Toward a theoretical model. *Journal of Sex Research* 41, no. 3: 225–47.

Bander, K. W., Fein, E., and Bishop, G. 1982. Child sex abuse treatment: Some barriers to program operation. *Child Abuse and Neglect* 6: 185–91.

Banning, A. 1989. Mother–son incest: Confronting a prejudice. *Child Abuse and Neglect* 13: 563–70.

Baron, R. M., and Kenny, D. A. 1986. The moderator–mediator variable distinction in social psychological research: Conceptual, strategic, and statistical considerations. *Journal of Personality and Social Psychology* 51, no. 6: 1173–82.

Barth, R. J., and Kinder, B. N. 1987. The mislabeling of sexual impulsivity. *Journal of Sex and Marital Therapy* 13: 15–23.

Bartholomew, K., and Horowitz, L. M. 1991. Attachment styles among young adults: A test of the four-category model. *Journal of Personality and Social Psychology* 61: 226–44.

Bass, E., and Davis, L. 1994. *The Courage to Heal*. 3rd ed. New York: Harper & Row.

Beautrais, A. L. 2000. Risk factors for suicide and attempted suicide among young people. *Australian and New Zealand Journal of Psychiatry* 34, no. 3: 420–36.

Beck, A., and Steer, R. 1987. *Beck Depression Inventory Manual*. San Antonio: Psychological Corporation/Harcourt Brace.

Beckinsale, P., Martin, G., and Clark, S. 1999. Sexual abuse and suicidal issues in Australian young people: An interim report. *Australian Family Physician* 28, no. 12: 1298–1303.

Bendixen, M. Muus, K. M., and Schei, B. 1994. The impact of child sexual abuse: A study of a random sample of Norwegian students. *Child Abuse and Neglect* 8: 837–47.

Bensley, L. S., Van Eenwyk, J., and Simmons, K. W. 2000. Self-reported childhood sexual and physical abuse and adult HIV-risk behaviors and heavy drinking. *American Journal of Preventative Medicine* 18: 151–58.

Bensley, L. S., Van Eenwyk, J., Spieker, S. J., and Schoder, J. 1999. Self-reported abuse history and adolescent problem behaviors, I: Antisocial and suicidal behaviors. *Journal of Adolescent Health* 24: 163–72.

Berger, L. M. 2005. Income, family characteristics, and physical violence toward children. *Child Abuse and Neglect* 29: 107–33.

Bernstein, D. P., Ahluvalia, T., Pogge, D., and Handelsman, L. 1997. Validity of the Childhood Trauma Questionnaire in an adolescent psychiatric population. *Journal of the American Academy of Child and Adolescent Psychiatry* 36: 340–48.

Bernstein, D. P., and Fink, L. 1998. *Manual for the Childhood Trauma Questionnaire.* New York: Psychological Corporation.

Bernstein, D. P., Fink, L., Handelsman, L., Foote, J., Lovejoy, M., et al. 1994. Initial reliability and validity of a new retrospective measure of child abuse and neglect. *American Journal of Psychiatry* 151: 1132–36.

Bernstein, D. P., Stein, J. A., Newcomb, M. D., Walker, E., Pogge, D., Ahluvalia, T., Stokes, J., Handelsman, L., Medrano, M., Desmond, D., and Zule, W. 2003. Development and validation of a brief screening version of the Childhood Trauma Questionnaire. *Child Abuse and Neglect* 27: 169–90.

Bernstein, E. M., and Putnam, F. W. 1986. Development, reliability, and validity of a dissociation scale. *Journal of Nervous and Mental Disease* 174, no. 12: 727–35.

Berrick, J. D. 1999. Entitled to what? Welfare and child welfare in a shifting policy environment. *Children and Youth Services Review* 21, no. 9–10: 709–17.

Bess, B. E., and Janssen, Y. 1982. Incest: A pilot study. *Hillside Journal of Clinical Psychiatry* 4: 39–52.

Blumberg, M. L. 1978. Child sexual abuse: Ultimate in maltreatment syndrome. *New York State Journal of Medicine* 78: 612–16.

———. 1981. Depression in abused and neglected children. *American Journal of Psychotherapy* 35: 342–55.

Blume, E. S. 1990. *Secret Survivors: Uncovering Incest and Its Aftereffects in Women.* New York: Wiley.

Bolen, R. 2002. Child sexual abuse and attachment theory: Are we rushing headlong into another controversy? *Journal of Child Sexual Abuse* 11, no. 1: 95–124.

Bonner, B. 1998. Children with sexual behavior problems. Paper presented at the International Congress on Child Abuse and Neglect, Auckland, New Zealand.

Boudewyn, A., and Liem, J. 1995. Childhood sexual abuse as a precursor to depression and self-destructive behavior in adulthood. *Journal of Traumatic Stress* 8: 445–59.

Bowlby, J. 1969. *Attachment and Loss.* Vol. 1, *Attachment.* New York: Basic.

———. 1982. Attachment and loss: Retrospect and prospect. *American Journal of Orthopsychiatry* 52: 664–78.

———. 1988a. *A Secure Base.* New York: Basic.

———. 1988b. Developmental psychiatry comes of age. *American Journal of Psychiatry* 145: 1–10.

Brandt, R., and Tiza, V. 1977. The sexually misused child. *American Journal of Orthopsychiatry* 47: 80–90.

Brassard, M. R., Tyler, A., and Kehle, T. J. 1983. Sexually abused children: Identification and suggestions for intervention. *School Psychology Review* 12: 93–97.

Bratton, M. 1999. *From Surviving to Thriving: A Therapist's Guide to Stage II Recovery for Survivors of Childhood Abuse.* New York: Haworth.

Braun, B. G. 1986. Group therapy in treatment of Multiple Personality Disorder. In B. G. Braun, ed., *Treatment of Multiple Personality Disorder*, 145–56. Washington, DC: American Psychiatric Press.

Brett, E. A. 1992. Classification of PTSD in DSM-IV as an anxiety disorder, dissociative disorder, or stress disorder. In J. Davidson and E. Foa, eds., *PTSD in Review: Recent Research and Future Directions.* Washington, DC: American Psychiatric Press.

Briere, J. 1984. The long-term effects of childhood sexual abuse: Defining a postsexual abuse syndrome. Paper presented at the Third National Conference on Sexual Victimization of Children, Washington, DC, April.

———. 1988. Long-term clinical correlates of childhood sexual victimization. *Annals of the New York Academy of Sciences* 528: 327–34.

———. 1992a. *Child Abuse and Trauma: Theory and Treatment of the Lasting Effects.* Newbury Park, CA: Sage.

———. 1992b. *Child Maltreatment Interview Schedule, Short Form CMIS-SF.* www.johnbriere.com. Accessed June 2, 2005.

———. 1995. *Trauma Symptom Inventory: Professional Manual.* Odessa, FL: Psychological Assessment Resources.

———. 1996. *Therapy for Adults Molested as Children: Beyond Survival.* New York: Springer.

———. 2000. *Inventory of Altered Self Capacities IASC.* Odessa, FL: Psychological Assessment Resources.

———. 2001. *Detailed Assessment of Posttraumatic Stress DAPS.* Odessa, FL: Psychological Assessment Resources.

———. 2002. Treating adult survivors of severe childhood abuse and neglect: Further development of an integrative model. In J. E. B. Myers, L. Berliner, J. Briere, C. T. Hendrix, C. Jenny, and T. A. Reid, eds., *The APSAC Handbook on Child Maltreatment*, 175–204. Thousand Oaks, CA: Sage.

———. 2004. Psychological assessment of child abuse effects in adults. In J. P. Wilson and T. M. Keane, eds., *Assessing Psychological Trauma and PTSD*, 538–64. 2nd ed. New York: Guilford.

Briere, J., and Elliott, D. M. 1994. Immediate and long-term impacts of child sexual abuse. *Future of Children* 4: 54–69.

———. 2003. Prevalence and psychological sequelae of self-reported childhood physical and sexual abuse in a general population sample of men and women. *Child Abuse and Neglect* 27: 1205–22.

322 ～ References

Briere, J., and Runtz, M. 1987. Postsexual abuse trauma: Data and implications for clinical practice. *Journal of Interpersonal Violence* 2: 367–79.

———. 1988. Multivariate correlates of childhood psychological and physical maltreatment among university women. *Childhood Abuse and Neglect* 12: 331–41.

———. 1989. The Trauma Symptom Checklist TSC-33: Early Data on a New Scale. *Journal of Interpersonal Violence* 8: 312–30.

———. 1990. Differential adult symptomatology associated with three types of child abuse histories. *Child Abuse and Neglect* 14: 357–64.

Briere, J., and Zaidi, L.Y. 1989. Sexual abuse histories and sequelae in female psychiatric emergency room patients. *American Journal of Psychiatry* 146: 1602–6.

Brown, G. R., and Anderson, B. 1991. Psychiatric morbidity in adult inpatients with childhood histories of sexual and physical abuse. *American Journal of Psychiatry* 148: 55–61.

Brown, J., Cohen, P., Johnson, J. G., and Smailes, E. M. 1999. Childhood abuse and neglect: Specificity of effects on adolescent and young adult depression and suicidality. *Journal of the American Academy of Child and Adolescent Psychiatry* 38: 1490–96.

Brown, P. 1994. Toward a psychobiological model of dissociation and Posttraumatic Stress Disorder. In S. J. Lynn and J. W. Rhue, eds., *Dissociation: Clinical and theoretical perspectives*. New York: Guilford.

Brown, P. J., Recupero, P. R., and Stout, R. L. 1995. PTSD substance abuse comorbidity and treatment utilization. *Addictive Behaviors* 20: 251–54.

Brown, P. J., Stout, R. L., and Mueller, T. 1996. Posttraumatic Stress Disorder and substance abuse relapse among women: A pilot study. *Psychology of Addictive Behaviors* 10: 124–28.

Browne, A., and Finkelhor, D. 1986. Impact of child sexual abuse: A review of the literature. *Psychological Bulletin* 99: 55–77.

Browning, C. R., and Laumann, E. O. 1997. Sexual contact between children and adults: A life course perspective. *American Sociological Review* 62: 540–60.

Browning, D., and Boatman, B. 1977. Incest: Children at risk. *American Journal of Psychiatry* 134: 69–72.

Bryant, S. L., and Range, L. M. 1995. Suicidality in college women who were sexually and physically abused and physically punished by parents. *Violence and Victims* 10: 195–201.

Bryer, J. B., Nelson, B. A., Miller, J. B., and Krol, P. A. 1987. Childhood sexual and physical abuse as factors in adult psychiatric illness. *American Journal of Psychiatry* 144: 1426–30.

Buchele, B. J. 1993. Object-relations theory and the treatment of sexual abuse victims. Paper presented at the Symposium on the Treatment of Sexual Abuse, Columbus, OH.

———. 1994. Innovative uses of psychodynamic group psychotherapy. *Bulletin of the Menninger Clinic* 58, no. 2: 215–23.

———. 2000. Group psychotherapy for survivors of sexual and physical abuse. In R. H. Klein and V. L. Schermer, eds., *Group Psychotherapy for Psychological Trauma*, 170–87. New York: Guilford.

Buddeberg, C., Buddeberg, F. B., Gnam, G., Schmid, J., and Christen, S. 1996. Suicidal behaviors in Swiss students: An 18-month follow-up survey. *Crisis* 17: 78–86.

Burgess, A. W., Hartman, C. R., and McCausland, M. P. 1984. Response patterns in children and adolescents exploited through sex rings and pornography. *American Journal of Psychiatry* 141: 656–62.

Burnam, M. A., Stein, J. A., Golding, I. M., Siegel, J. M., Sorenson, S. B., Forsythe, A. B., and Telles, C. A. 1988. Sexual assault and mental disorders in a community population. *Journal of Consulting and Clinical Psychology*, 56, 843–850.

Busby, D. M., Glenn, E., Steggell, G. L., and Adamson, D. W. 1993. Treatment issues for survivors of physical and sexual abuse. *Journal of Marital and Family Therapy* 19: 377–92.

Bushnell, J. A., Wells, J. E., and Oakley-Browne, M. 1992. Long-term effects of intrafamilial sexual abuse in childhood. *Acta Psychiatrica Scandinavia* 85: 136–42.

Butts, J. D. 1992. The relationship between sexual addiction and sexual dysfunction. *Journal of Health Care for the Poor and Underserved* 3: 128–35.

Cameron, C. 1994. Veterans of a secret war: Survivors of childhood sexual trauma compared to Vietnam War veterans with PTSD. *Journal of Interpersonal Violence* 9: 117–32.

Cardena, E., Classen, C., Koopman, C., and Spiegel, D. 1996. Psychometric review of the Stanford Acute Stress Reaction Questionnaire (SASRQ). In B. Stamm, ed., *Measurement of Stress, Trauma, and Adaptation*. Lutherville, MD: Sidran.

Cardena, E., Koopman, C., Classen, C., Waelde, L., and Spiegel, D. 1996. Psychometric properties of the Stanford Acute Stress Reaction Questionnaire SASRQ: A valid and reliable measure of acute stress. Manuscript.

Carlson, B. E. 1991. Outcomes of physical abuse and observations of marital violence among adolescents in placement. *Journal of Interpersonal Violence* 6: 526–34.

Carlson, V., Cicchetti, D., Barnett, D., and Braunwald, K. 1989. Disorganized/disoriented attachment relationships in maltreated infants. *Developmental Psychology* 25: 525–31.

Carmen, E. H., Rieker, P. P., and Mills, T. 1984. Victims of violence and psychiatric illness. *American Journal of Psychiatry* 141: 378–83.

Carnes, P. 1983. *Out of the Shadows: Understanding Sexual Addiction*. Minneapolis: CompCare Publishers.

Carver, C. M., Stalker, C., Stewart, E., and Abraham, B. 1989. The impact of group therapy for adult survivors of childhood sexual abuse. *Canadian Journal of Psychiatry* 34: 753–58.

Cashdan, S. 1988. *Object Relations Therapy: Using the Relationship*. New York: Norton.

Cavaiola, A. A., and Schiff, M. 1988. Behavioral sequelae of physical and/or sexual abuse in adolescents. *Child Abuse and Neglect* 12: 181–88.

Chandy, J. M., Blum, R. Wm., and Resnick, M. D. 1996a. Gender-specific outcomes for sexually abused adolescents. *Child Abuse and Neglect* 20: 1219–31.

———. 1996b. History of sexual abuse and parental alcohol misuse: Risk, outcomes, and protective factors in adolescents. *Child and Adolescent Social Work Journal* 13, no. 5: 411–32.

Chard, K. M., Weaver, T. L., and Resnick, P. A. 1997. Adapting cognitive processing therapy for child sexual abuse survivors. *Cognitive and Behavioral Practice* 4: 31–52.

Chu, J. A. 1988. Ten traps for therapists in the treatment of trauma survivors. *Dissociation* 1, no. 4: 24–31.

———. 1992. The revictimization of adult women with histories of childhood abuse. *Journal of Psychotherapy Practice and Research* 1: 259–69.

Chu, J. A., and Dill, D. L. 1990. Dissociative symptoms in relation to childhood physical and sexual abuse. *American Journal of Psychiatry* 147: 887–92.

Cicchetti, D. 1987. Developmental psychopathology in infancy: Illustration from the study of maltreated infants. *Journal of Consulting and Clinical Psychology* 55: 837–45.

Cinq-Mars, C., Wright, J., Cyr, M., and McDuff, P. 2003. Sexual at-risk behaviors of sexually abused adolescent girls. *Journal of Child Sexual Abuse* 12, no. 2: 1–18.

Classen, C., Field, N. P., Koopman, C., Nevill-Manning, K., and Spiegel, D. 2001. Interpersonal problems and their relationship to sexual revictimization among women sexually abused in childhood. *Journal of Interpersonal Violence* 16, no. 6: 495–509.

Coffey, S. F., Dansky, B. S., and Brady, K. T. 2003. Exposure-based, trauma-focused therapy for co-morbid Posttraumatic Stress Disorder–Substance Use Disorder. In P. Ouimette and P. Brown, eds., *Trauma and Substance Abuse: Causes, Consequences, and Treatment of Co-morbid Disorders*, 127–146. Washington, DC: American Psychological Association.

Cohen, F. S., and Densen-Gerber, J. 1988. A study of the relationship between child abuse and drug addiction in 178 patients: Preliminary results. *Child Abuse and Neglect* 6: 383–87.

Cole, C. H., and Barney, E. E. 1987. Safeguards and the therapeutic window: A group treatment strategy for adult incest survivors. *American Journal of Orthopsychiatry* 57, no. 4: 601–9.

Cole, P., and Putnam, F. W. 1992. Effect of incest on self and social functioning: A developmental psychopathology perspective. *Journal of Consulting and Clinical Psychology* 60: 174–84.

Coleman, E. 1992. Is your patient suffering from compulsive sexual behavior? *Psychiatric Annals* 22: 320–25.

Collins, M. E. 1998. Factors influencing sexual victimization and revictimization in a sample of adolescent mothers. *Journal of Interpersonal Violence* 13: 3–24.

Collings, S. J. 1995. The long-term effects of contact and noncontact forms of child sexual abuse in a sample of university men. *Child Abuse and Neglect* 19: 1–6.

Colman, R. A., and Widom, C. S. 2004. Childhood abuse and neglect and adult intimate relationships: A prospective study. *Child Abuse and Neglect* 28: 1133–51.

Condy, S. R., Templer, D. L., Brown, R., and Veaco, L. 1987. Parameters of sexual contact of boys with women. *Archives of Sexual Behavior* 16, no. 5, 379–94.

Connelly, C., and Straus, M. 1992. Mother's age and risk for physical abuse. *Child Abuse and Neglect* 16: 709–18.

Conners, M. E., and Morse, W. 1993. Sexual abuse and eating disorders: A review. *International Journal of Eating Disorders* 13: 1–11.

Conners, N. A., Bradley, R. H., Mansell, L. W., Liu, J. Y., Roberts, T. J., Burgdorf, K., and Herrell, J. M. 2004. Children of mothers with serious substance abuse problems: An accumulation of risks. *American Journal of Drug and Alcohol Abuse* 30: no. 1: 85–99.

Connors, R. E. 2000. *Self-injury: Psychotherapy with People Who Engage in Self-inflicted Violence*. Northvale, NJ: Jason Aronson.

Coons, P., Bowman, E., and Pellows, T. A. 1989. Post-traumatic aspects of the treatment of sexual abuse and incest. *Psychiatric Clinics of North America* 12: 325–37.

Coovert, D. L., Kinder, B. N., and Thompson, J. K. 1989. The psychosexual aspects of anorexia nervosa and bulimia nervosa: A review of the literature. *Clinical Psychology Review* 9: 169–80.

Courtois, C. 1979. The incest experience and its aftermath. *Victimology* 4: 337–47.

———. 1988. *Healing the Incest Wound: Adult Survivors in Therapy*. New York: Norton.

———. 1991. Theory, sequencing, and strategy in treating adult survivors. In J. Briere, ed., *Treating Victims of Child Sexual Abuse*, 47–60. San Francisco: Jossey-Bass.

———. 1999. *Recollections of Sexual Abuse: Treatment Principles and Guidelines*. New York: Norton.

Covington, S. S., and Kohen, J. 1984. Women, alcohol, and sexuality. *Advances in Substance Abuse* 4: 41–56.

Culbertson, J. L., and Willis, D. J. 1998. Interventions with young children who have been multiply abused. *Journal of Aggression, Maltreatment, and Trauma* 2, no. 1: 207–32.

Dansky, B. S., and Brady, K. T. 1998. *Exposure Therapy for Posttraumatic Stress Disorder and Substance Abuse*. Manuscript, Medical University of South Carolina.

Dansky, B. S., Brady, K. T., and Saladin, M. E. 1998. Untreated symptoms of PTSD among cocaine-dependent individuals: Changes over time. *Journal of Substance Abuse Treatment* 15: 499–504.

Dansky, B. S., Roitzsch, C. A., Brady, K. T., and Saladin, M. E. 1997. Intimate violence and Posttraumatic Stress Disorder and substance abuse: Use of research in a clinical setting. *Journal of Traumatic Stress* 10: 141–48.

Dansky, B. S., Saladin, M., Brady, K. T., Killeen, T., Becker, S., and Roitzsch, J. C. 1994. Concurrent treatment of PTSD and substance abuse in women. Presentation at the annual meeting of the International Society of Traumatic Stress Studies, Chicago.

Darche, M. A. 1990. Psychological factors differentiating self-mutilating and non-self-mutilating adolescent inpatient females. *Psychiatric Hospital, 21*, 31–35.

Davis, L. and Carlson, B. 1987. Observation of spouse abuse: What happens to children? *Journal of Interpersonal Violence*, 2: 278–91.

Deblinger, E., McLeer, S. V., Atkins, M. S., Ralphe, D., and Foa, E. 1989. Post-traumatic stress in sexually abused, physically abused, and nonabused children. *Child Abuse and Neglect* 13: 403–8.

De Groot, J., and Rodin, G. M. 1999. The relationship between eating disorders and childhood trauma. *Psychiatric Annals* 29, no. 4: 225–29.

Deiter, P. J., Nicholls, S. S., and Pearlman, L. A. 2000. Self-injury and self capacities: Assisting an individual in crisis. *Journal of Clinical Psychology* 56, no. 9: 1173–91.

Demare, D. 1993. Childhood psychological maltreatment experiences as predictors of adult psychological symptomatology. Paper presented at the annual meeting of the American Psychological Association, Toronto, Canada.

De Paul, J., and Arruabarrena, M. I. 1995. Behaviour problems in school-aged physically abused and neglected children in Spain. *Child Abuse and Neglect* 19: 409–18.

Derogatis, L. P. 1983. *SCL-90-R Administration, Scoring, and Procedures Manual for the Revised Version*. Towson, MD: Clinical Psychiatric Research.

DeVoe, E. R., and Smith, E. L. 2003. Don't take my kids: Barriers to service delivery for battered mothers and their young children. *Journal of Emotional Abuse* 33–34: 277–94.

De Young, M. 1982. *The Sexual Victimization of Children*. Jefferson, NC: McFarland.

Deykin, E., Alpert, J., McNamarra, J. 1985. A pilot study of the effect of exposure to child abuse or neglect on suicidal behavior. *American Journal of Psychiatry* 142: 1299–1303.

Dhaliwal, G. K., Gauzas, L., Antonowicz, D. H., and Ross, R. R. 1996. Adult male survivors of childhood sexual abuse: Prevalence, sexual abuse characteristics, and long-term effects. *Clinical Psychology Review* 16: 619–39.

Dickinson, L., Verloin deGruy, F., Dickinson, W. P., and Candib, L. Health-related quality of life and symptom profiles of female survivors of sexual abuse. *Archives of Family Medicine* 8: 35–43.

Dimock, P. T. 1988. Adult males sexually abused as children: Characteristics and implications for treatment. *Journal of Interpersonal Violence* 3: 203–16.

DiScala, C., Sege, R., Guohua, L., and Reece, R. 2000. Child abuse and unintentional injuries: A ten-year retrospective. *Archives of Pediatric and Adolescent Medicine* 154: 16–22.

DiVitto, S. 1998. Empowerment through self-regulation: Group approach for survivors of incest. *Journal of the American Psychiatric Nurses Association* 4, no. 3: 77–86.

Dodge, B., Reece, M., Cole, S., and Sandfort, G. M. 2004. Sexual compulsivity among heterosexual college students. *Journal of Sex Research* 41, no. 4: 343–59.

Dong, M., Anda, R. F., Felitti, V. J., Dube, S. R., Williamson, D. F., et al. 2004. The interrelatedness of multiple forms of childhood abuse, neglect, and household dysfunction. *Child Abuse and Neglect* 28, no. 7: 771–84.

Donovan, B. S., and Padin-Rivera, E. 1999. Transcend: A program for treating PTSD and substance abuse in Vietnam combat veterans. *National Center for PTSD Clinical Quarterly* 8: 51–53.

Donovan, B. S., Padin-Rivera, E., and Kowaliw, S. 2001. Transcend: Initial outcomes from a Posttraumatic Stress Disorder/substance abuse treatment program. *Journal of Traumatic Stress* 14: 757–72.

Drake, B., and Pandey, S. 1996. Understanding the relationship between neighborhood poverty and specific types of child maltreatment. *Child Abuse and Neglect* 20, no. 11: 1003–18.

Dube, S. R., Anda, R. F., Felitti, V. J., Croft, J. B., Edwards, V. J., and Giles, W. H. 2001. Growing up with parental alcohol abuse: Exposure to childhood abuse, neglect, and household dysfunction. *Child Abuse and Neglect* 25: 1627–40.

Dube, S. R., Anda, R. F., Felitti, V. J., Edwards, V. J., and Croft, J. B. 2002. Adverse childhood experiences and personal alcohol abuse as an adult. *Addictive Behaviors* 27, no. 5: 713–25.

Dube, S. R., Felitti, V. J., Dong, M., Chapman, D. P., Giles, W. H., and Anda, R. F. 2003. Childhood abuse, neglect, and household dysfunction and the risk of illicit drug use: The adverse childhood experiences study. *Pediatrics* 110: 564–72.

Dubo, E. D., Zanarini, M. C., Lewis, R. E., and Williams, A. A. 1997. Relationship between lifetime self-destructiveness and pathological childhood experiences. In M. C. Zanarini, ed., *The Role of Sexual Abuse in the Etiology of Borderline Personality Disorder*, 107–30. Washington, DC: American Psychiatric Press.

Dutton, D., and Painter, S. L. 1981. Traumatic bonding: The development of emotional attachments in battered women and other relationships of intermittent abuse. *Victimology* 6: 139–55.

Dutton, K. A., and Hart, S. D. 1992. Evidence for long-term specific effects of childhood abuse and neglect on criminal behavior in men. *International Journal of Offender Therapy and Comparative Criminology* 36: 129–37.

Eckenrode, J., Laird, M., and Doris, J. 1993. School performance and disciplinary problems among abused and neglected children. *Developmental Psychology* 29: 53–62.

Egeland, B. 1985. The consequences of physical and emotional neglect on the development of young children. Paper presented at symposium of the National Center on Child Abuse and Neglect, Chicago.

Elhai, J. D., Klotz Flitter, J. M., Gold, S. N., and Sellers, A. H. 2001. Identifying subtypes of women survivors of childhood sexual abuse: An MMPI-2 cluster analysis. *Journal of Traumatic Stress* 14: 157–75.

Ellason, J. W., Ross, C. A., and Fuchs, D. L. 1995. Assessment of Dissociative Identity Disorder with the Millon Multiaxial Inventory-II. *Psychological Reports*, 76, 895–905.

Elliot, D. M., and Briere, J. 1992. Sexual abuse trauma among professional women: Validating the Trauma Symptom Checklist-40 TSC-40. *Child Abuse and Neglect* 16: 391–98.

————. 1995. Symptomatology associated with delayed recall of sexual abuse. *Journal of Traumatic Stress* 8: 629–47.

Elliot, M. 1994. *Female Sexual Abuse of Children.* New York: Guilford.

Ellis, E., Atkeson, B., and Calhoun, K. 1982. An examination of differences between multiple- and single-incident victims of sexual assault. *Journal of Abnormal Psychology* 91: 221–24.

Engel, B. 1989. *The Right to Innocence: Healing the Trauma of Childhood Sexual Abuse.* New York: Random House.

Epstein, J. N., Saunders, B. E., Kilpatrick, D. G., and Resnick, H. S. 1998. PTSD as a Mediator between Childhood Rape and Alcohol Use in Adult Women. *Child Abuse and Neglect* 22: 223–34.

Ethier, L., Palacio-Quintin, E., and Jourdan-Ionescu, C. 1992. Abuse and neglect: Two distinct forms of maltreatment? *Canada's Mental Health* 40: 13–19.

Evans, E., Hawton, K., and Rodham, K. 2005. *Child Abuse and Neglect* 29: 45–58.

Evans, K., and Sullivan, J. M. 1995. *Treating Addicted Survivors of Trauma.* New York: Guilford.

Everill, J., Waller, G., and Macdonald, W. 1995. Dissociation in bulimic and non-eating disordered women. *International Journal of Eating Disorders* 17, no. 2: 127–34.

Fairbairn, W. R. D. 1954. Observations on the nature of hysterical states. *British Journal of Medical Psychology* 27: 105–25.

Fairburn, C. G., Doll, H. A., Welchn, S. L., Hay, P. J., Davies, B. A., and O'Conner, M. E. 1998. Risk factors for Binge Eating Disorder: A community-based case control study. *Archives of General Psychiatry* 55: 425–32.

Famularo, R., Kinscherff, R., and Fenton, T. 1992. Parental substance abuse and the nature of child maltreatment. *Child Abuse and Neglect: The International Journal* 16: 475–83.

Famularo, R., Stone, K., Barnum, R., and Wharton, R. 1986. Alcoholism and severe child maltreatment. *American Journal of Orthopsychiatry* 56: 481–85.

Fantuzzo, J. W., and Mohr, W. K. 1999. Prevalence and effects of children's exposure to domestic violence. *Domestic Violence and Children* 9: 21–32.

Favazza, A. 1989. Why patients mutilate themselves. *Hospital and Community Psychiatry* 40: 137–45.

Favazza, A., and Conterio, K. 1988. The plight of chronic self-mutilation. *Community Mental Health Journal* 24: 22–30.

Favazza, A., and Rosenthal, R. 1993. Diagnostic issues in self-mutilation. *Hospital and Community Psychiatry* 44: 134–39.

Feeney, J. A., Noller, P., and Hanrahan, M. 1994. Assessing adult attachment. In M. B. Sperling and W. H. Berman, eds., *Attachment in Adults,* 128–54. New York: Guilford.

Feldman, R. S., Salzinger, S., Rosario, M., Alvarado, L., Carabello, L., and Hammer, M. 1995. Parent, teacher, and peer ratings of physically abused and nonmaltreated children's behavior. *Journal of Abnormal Psychology* 23: 317–34.

Fergusson, D. M., Horwood, L. J., and Lynskey, M. T. 1996. Childhood sexual abuse and psychiatric disorder in young adulthood, II: Psychiatric outcomes of childhood sexual abuse. *Journal of the American Academy of Child and Adolescent Psychiatry* 35, no. 10: 1365–74.

Fergusson, D. M., Horwood, J. L., and Lynskey, M. 1997. Childhood sexual abuse, adolescent sexual behaviors, and revictimization. *Child Abuse and Neglect* 21: 789–803.

Fergusson, D. M., and Lynskey, M. T. 1997. Physical punishment/maltreatment during childhood and adjustment in young adulthood. *Child Abuse and Neglect* 21: 617–30.

Fergusson, D. M., Lynskey, M. T., and Horwood, L. J. 1996. Childhood sexual abuse and psychiatric disorders in young adulthood, Part I: The prevalence of sexual abuse and the factors associated with sexual abuse. *Journal of the American Academy of Child and Adolescent Psychiatry* 35: 1355–64.

Fergusson, D. M. and Mullen, P. E. 1999. *Childhood Sexual Abuse: An Evidence-Based Perspective.* Thousand Oaks, CA: Sage.

Fine, C. G. 1990. The cognitive sequelae of incest. In R. P. Kluft, ed., *Incest-related Syndromes of Adult Psychopathology.* Washington, DC: American Psychiatric Press.

Finkelhor, D. 1979. *Sexually Victimized Children.* New York: Free Press.

———. 1980. Sex among siblings: A survey on prevalence, variety and effects. *Archives of Sexual Behavior* 9: 171–94.

———. 1982. Sexual abuse: A sociological perspective. *Child Abuse and Neglect* 6: 95–102.

———. 1983. Removing the child: Prosecuting the offender in cases of sexual abuse. *Child Abuse and Neglect* 7: 195–205.

———. 1984. *Child Sexual Abuse: New Theory and Research.* New York: Free Press.

———. 1986. *A Sourcebook on Child Sexual Abuse.* Beverly Hills: Sage.

———. 1990. Early and long-term effects of child sexual abuse: An update. *Professional Psychology: Research and Practice* 21: 325–30.

———. 1993. The main problem is still underreporting, not overreporting. In R. Gelles and D. R. Loseke, eds., *Current Controversies on Family Violence,* 182–96. London: Sage.

Finkelhor, D., and Baron, L. 1986. High-risk children. In D. Finkelhor, S. Arjac, A. Browne, S. Peters, and G. Wyatt, eds., *A Sourcebook on Child Sexual Abuse.* Beverley Hills: Sage.

Finkelhor, D., and Browne, A. 1985. The traumatic impact of child sexual abuse: A conceptualization. *American Journal of Orthopsychiatry* 55: 530–41.

Finkelhor, D., and Dzuiba-Leatherman, J. 1994. Children as victims of violence: A national study. *Pediatrics* 4: 413–19.

Finkelhor, D., Hotaling, G. T., Lewis, I. A., and Smith, C. 1989. Sexual abuse and its relationship to later sexual satisfaction, marital status, religion, and attitudes. *Journal of Interpersonal Violence* 4: 379–99.

Finkelhor, D., and Yllo, K. 1983. Rape in marriage: A sociological view. In D. Finkelhor, R. J. Gelles, G. T. Hotaling, and Straus, eds., *The Dark Side of Families: Current Family Violence Research,* 119–31. Beverly Hills: Sage.

Finn, S. E., Hartmann, M., Leon, G. R., and Lawson, L. 1986. Eating disorders and sexual abuse: Lack of confirmation for a clinical hypothesis. *International Journal of Eating Disorders* 5: 1051–60.

Fischer, B. 1995. Sexual addiction revisited. *Addiction Newsletter* 2, no. 3: 5–27.

Fisher, P. M., Winne, P. H., and Ley, R. G. 1993. Group therapy for adult women survivors of child sexual abuse: Differentiation of completers versus dropouts. *Psychotherapy* 30: 616–24.

Fleming, J. M. 1997. Prevalence of childhood sexual abuse in a community sample of Australian women. *Medical Journal of Australia* 166: 65–68.

Fleming, J., Mullen, P. E., Sibthorpe, B., and Bammer, G. 1999. The long-term impact of childhood sexual abuse in Australian women. *Child Abuse and Neglect* 23: 145–59.

Folette, V. M., Polusny, M. A., Bechtle, A. E., and Naugle, A. E. 1996. Cumulative trauma: The impact of child sexual abuse, adult sexual assault, and spouse abuse. *Journal of Traumatic Stress* 11, no. 4: 743–61.

Ford, J. D., and Kidd, P. 1998. Early childhood trauma and disorders of extreme stress as predictors of treatment outcome with chronic Posttraumatic Stress Disorder. *Journal of Traumatic Stress* 11, no. 4: 743–61.

Freeman-Longo, R. E. 1986. The impact of sexual victimization on males. *Child Abuse and Neglect* 10: 411–14.

French, S., Story, M., Downes, B., Resnick, M., and Blum, R. 1995. Frequent dieting among adolescents: Psychosocial and health behavior correlates. *American Journal of Public Health* 85, no. 5: 695–701.

Freud, S. 1954. *Beyond the Pleasure Principle.* In J. Strachey, ed. and trans., *The Standard Edition of the Complete Psychological Works of Sigmund Freud,* 18: 7–64. London: Hogarth. Originally published 1920.

Frick, P. J., Lahey, B. B., Loeber, R., Stouthamer-Loeber, M., Christ, M. A. G., et al. 1992. Familial risk factors to Oppositional Defiant Disorder and Conduct Disorder: Parental psychopathology and maternal parenting. *Journal of Consulting and Clinical Psychology* 60: 49–55.

Fridja, N. H. 1986. *The Emotions.* Cambridge: Cambridge University Press.

Friedrich, W. N. 1990. *Psychotherapy of Sexually Abused Children and Their Families.* New York: Norton.

———. 1996. An integrated model of psychotherapy for abused children. In J. Briere, L. Berliner, J. A. Bulkley, C. Jenny, and T. Reid, eds., *The APSAC Handbook on Child Maltreatment.* Thousand Oaks, CA: Sage.

Friedrich, W. N., and Chaffin, M. 2000. Developmental–systematic perspectives on children with sexual behavior problems. Paper presented at the Association for the Treatment of Sexual Abusers, San Diego.

Friedrich, W. N., and Luecke, W. 1988. Young school-age sexually aggressive children. *Professional Psychology Research and Practice* 19: 155–64.

Friedrich, W. N., Urquiza, S. J., and Beilke, R. 1986. Behavioral problems in sexually abused young children. *Journal of Pediatric Psychology* 11: 47–57.

Fritz, G. S., Stoll, K., Wagner, N. N. 1981. A comparison of males and females who were sexually molested as children. *Journal of Sex and Marital Therapy* 7, no. 1: 54–59.

Fromuth, M. 1983. The long-term psychological impact of childhood sexual abuse. Ph.D. dissertation, Auburn University, Alabama.

———. 1986. The relationship of childhood sexual abuse with later psychological and sexual adjustment in a sample of college women. *Child Abuse and Neglect* 10: 5–15.

Fromuth, M. E., and Burkhart, B. R. 1989. Long-term psychological correlates of childhood sexual abuse in two samples of college men. *Child Abuse and Neglect* 13: 533–42.

Gabel, S., and Shindledecker, R. 1993. Characteristics of children whose parents have been incarcerated. *Hospital and Community Psychiatry* 44: 656–60.

Ganzarin, R., and Buchele, J. 1988. *Fugitives of Incest: A Perspective from Psychoanalysis and Groups.* Madison, CT: International Universities Press.

Garbarino, J., Schellenbach, C., and Sebes, J. 1986. *Troubled Youth, Troubled Families: Understanding Families at Risk for Adolescent Maltreatment.* New York: Aldine.

Garbino, J., and Ebata, A. 1983. The significance of ethnic and cultural differences in child maltreatment. *Journal of Marriage and the Family* 11: 733–83.

Gartner, R. B. 1999. *Betrayed as Boys: Psychodynamic Treatment of Sexually Abused Men.* New York: Guilford.

Geffner, R. A., Igelman, R. S., and Zellner, J. 2003. Children exposed to interparental violence: A need for additional research and validated treatment programs. *Journal of Emotional Abuse* 31–32: 1–10.

Geffner, R., Jaffe, P. G., and Suderman, M., eds. 2000. *Children Exposed to Domestic Violence: Current Research, Interventions, Prevention, and Policy Development.* New York: Haworth.

Gelinas, D. J. 1983. The persisting negative effects of incest. *Psychiatry* 46: 312–32.

Gerrity, D. A., and Peterson, T. L. 2004. Groups for survivors of childhood sexual abuse, in J. L. DeLucia-Waack, D. A. Gerrity, C. R. Kalodner, and M. T. Riva eds., *Handbook of Group Counseling and Psychotherapy*, 497–517. Thousand Oaks, CA: Sage.

Giardino, E. R., and Giardino, A. P. 2003. *Nursing Approach to the Evaluation of Child Maltreatment.* St. Louis, MO: G. W. Medical.

Gidycz, C. A., Coble, C. N., Latham, L., and Layman, M. J. 1993. Sexual assault experience in adulthood and prior victimization experiences: A prospective analysis. *Psychology of Women Quarterly* 17: 151–68.

Gil, D. 1970. *Violence Against Children.* Cambridge: Harvard University Press.

Gil, E., and Johnson, T. C. 1993. *Sexualized Children: Assessment and Treatment of Sexualized Children and Children Who Molest.* Rockville, MD: Launch.

Gilmartin, P. 1994. *Rape, Incest, and Child Sexual Abuse: Consequences and Recovery.* New York: Garland.

Giovanni, J. 1988. Overview of issues on child neglect. In *Child Neglect Monograph: Proceedings from a Symposium*, 1–6. Washington, DC: Clearinghouse on Child Abuse and Neglect Information.

Glaser, D. 1998. Unfinished business: Erotophobia vs. erotophilia. Presentation at Trauma and Intimacy: Self/Other Adaptations, River Oakes Hospital, New York, NY.

Gold, S. N., and Heffner, C. L. 1998. Sexual addiction: Many conceptions, minimal data. *Clinical Psychology Review* 18: 303–14.

Gold, S. N., and Seifer, R. E. 2002. Dissociation and sexual addiction/compulsivity: A contextual approach to conceptualization and treatment. *Journal of Trauma and Dissociation* 3, no. 4: 59–82.

Goldman, L., Horan, D., Warshaw, C., Kaplan, S., and Hendricks-Matthews, M. 1995. *Diagnostic and Treatment Guidelines on Mental Health Effects of Family Violence.* www.ama-assn.org/ama/pub/category/3548.html.

Goldstein, G., van Kammen, V., and Shelly, C. 1987. Survivors of imprisonment in the Pacific theater during World War II. *American Journal of Psychiatry* 144: 1210–13.

Goodman, A. 1992. Sexual addiction: Designation and treatment. *Journal of Sex and Marital Therapy* 18: 303–14.

———. 1993. Diagnosis and treatment of sexual addiction. *Journal of Sex and Marital Therapy* 19: 225–51.

Goodman, L., Corcoran, C., Turner, K., Yuan, N., and Green, B. 1998. Assessing traumatic event exposure: General issues and preliminary findings for the stressful life events screening questionnaire. *Journal of Traumatic Stress* 11: 521–42.

Goodwin, J. 1985. Post-traumatic symptoms in incest victims. In S. Eth and R. S. Pynoos, eds., *Posttraumatic Stress Disorder in Children*, 155–68. Washington, DC: American Psychiatric Press.

———. 1988. Posttraumatic symptoms in abused children. *Journal of Traumatic Stress* 1: 475–88.

———. 1989. *Sexual Abuse: Incest Victims and Their Families.* Chicago: Mosby Yearbook.

———. 1993. *Rediscovering Childhood Trauma: Historical Casebook and Clinical Applications.* Washington, DC: American Psychiatric Press.

———. 1996. Adult survivors of child abuse and neglect. In S. J. Kaplan, ed., *Family Violence: A Clinical and Legal Guide*, 209–40. Washington, DC: American Psychiatric Press.

Goodwin, J. , and DiVasto, P. 1979. Mother–daughter incest. *Child Abuse and Neglect* 3: 953–57.

Goodwin, J. M., Cheeves, K., and Connell, V. 1990. Borderline and other severe symptoms in adult survivors of incestuous abuse. *Psychiatric Annals* 20: 22–32.

Goodwin, J. M., McMarty, T., and DiVasto, P. 1982. Physical and sexual abuse of the children of adult incest victims. In Goodwin, J., ed., *Sexual Abuse: Incest Victims and Their Families*, 139–54. Boston: John Wright.

Goodwin, J. M., and Talwar, N. 1989. Group Psychotherapy for Victims of Incest. *Psychiatric Clinics of North America* 12, no. 2: 279–93.

Goodwin, J. M., Zouhar, M. S., and Bergman, R. 1989. Hysterical seizures in adolescent incest victims. In J. Goodwin, ed., *Sexual Abuse: Incest Victims and Their Families*, 102–34. Chicago: Year Book Medical.

Goodyear-Smith, F. 1994. Medical considerations in the diagnosis of child sexual abuse. *Institute for Psychological Therapies* 6: 2.

Gorcey, M., Santiago, J. M., and McCall-Perez, F. 1986. Psychological consequences for women sexually abused in childhood. *Social Psychiatry* 21: 129–33.

Gormally, J., Black, S., Daston, S., and Rardin, D. 1982. The assessment of binge eating severity among obese persons. *Addictive Behaviors* 7: 47–55.

Gottman, J. M. 1997. *The Heart of Parenting: Raising an Emotionally Intelligent Child*. New York: Simon & Shuster.

Graham-Berman, S. A. and Edelson, J. L. 2001. *Domestic violence in the lives of children: The future of research, intervention, and social policy*. Washington, DC: American Psychological Association.

Graham-Bermann, S. A., and Levendosky, A. A. 1998. Traumatic Stress Symptoms in Children of Battered Women. *Journal of Interpersonal Violence* 13: 111–28.

Graham, D. L., Rawlings, E., and Rimini, N. 1988. Survivors of terror: Battered women, hostages, and the Stockholm syndrome. In K. Yllo and M. Bograd, eds., *Feminist Perspectives on Wife Abuse*. Beverley Hills: Sage.

Gray, A. 1996. Precursors to sexual aggression: Research implications for changing treatment of sexual misbehavior in young children. Paper presented at the Annual Conference of the Association for the Treatment of Sexual Abusers, Chicago.

Gray, A., Pithers, W. D., Busconi, A., and Houchens, P. 1999. Developmental and etiological characteristics of children with sexual behavior problems: Treatment implications. *Child Abuse and Neglect* 23: 601–21.

Green, A. H. 1978. Self-destructive behavior in battered children. *American Journal of Psychiatry* 135: 579–82.

———. 1996. Overview of child sexual abuse. In S. J. Kaplan, ed., *Family Violence: A Clinical and Legal Guide*. Washington, DC: American Psychiatric Press.

Green, B. 1996. Trauma history questionnaire. In B. H. Stamm and E. M. Varra, eds., *Measurement of Stress, Trauma, and Adaptation*, 366–68. Lutherville, MD: Sidran.

Gross, J. J. 1999. Emotion regulation: Past, present, and future. *Cognition and Emotion* 13: 551–73.

Grossman, D. C., Milligan, B. C., and Deyo, R. A. 1991. Risk factors for suicide attempts among Navajo adolescents. *American Journal of Public Health* 81: 870–74.

Groth, A. N. 1982. The incest offender. In S. M. Sgroi, ed., *Handbook of Clinical Intervention in Child Sexual Abuse*. Lexington, MA: Lexington.

Gunderson, J. G., Kolb, J. E., and Austin, V. 1981. The diagnostic interview for borderline patients. *American Journal of Psychiatry* 138: 896–903.

Gunderson, J., and Sabo, A. N. 1993. The phenomenological and conceptual interface between borderline personality and PTSD. *American Journal of Psychiatry* 150: 19–27.

Hagan, T. 1988. A retrospective search for the etiology of drug abuse: A background comparison of a drug-addicted population of women and control group of nonaddicted women. NIDA Research Monograph no. 81, 254–61.

Hall, D. K. 1999. "Complex" Posttraumatic Stress Disorder/disorders of extreme stress CP/DES in sexually abused children: An exploratory study. *Journal of Child Sexual Abuse* 8, no. 4: 51–71.

Hall, R. C. W., Tice, L., Beresford, T. P., Wooley, B., and Hall, A. K. 1989. Sexual abuse in patients with anorexia nervosa and bulimia. *Psychosomatics* 30: 73–79.

Halperin, D. S., Bouvier, P., Jaffe, P. D., Mounoud, R., Pawlak, C. H., Laederach, J., Rey Wicky, H., and Astie, F. 1996. Prevalence of child sexual abuse among adolescents in Geneva: Results of a cross-sectional survey. *British Medical Journal* 312: 1326–29.

Hamarman, S. and Bernet, W. 2000. Evaluating and reporting emotional abuse in children: Parent-based action focused aids in clinical decision-making. *Journal of the American Academy of Child and Adolescent Psychiatry*, 37, no. 7: 928–30.

Hampton, R., and Newberger, E. 1985. Child abuse incidence and reporting by hospitals: Significance of severity by class and race. *American Journal of Public Health* 75: 56–60.

Harrison, H. 1993. Female abusers: What children and young people have told Childline. In M. Elliott, ed., *Female Sexual Abuse of Children: The Ultimate Taboo*, 95–98. London: Longman Information and Reference.

Harrison, P. A., Edwall, G. E., Hoffman, N. G., and Worthen, M. D. 1990. Correlates of sexual abuse amongst boys in treatment for chemical dependency. *Journal of Adolescent Chemical Dependency* 1, no. 1: 53–67.

Haviland, M. G., Sonne, J. L., and Woods, L. R. 1995. Beyond Posttraumatic Stress Disorder: Object relations and reality testing disturbances in physically and sexually abused adolescents. *Journal of American Academy of Child and Adolescent Psychiatry* 34: 1054–59.

Hazan, C., and Shaver, P. 1987. Romantic love conceptualized as an attachment process. *Journal of Personality and Social Psychology* 52, no. 3: 511–24.

Hendricks-Mathews, M. K. 1993. Survivors of abuse: Health care issues. *Primary Care* 20: 391–406.

Herman, J. 1981. *Father–Daughter Incest*. Cambridge: Harvard University Press.

Herman, J. 1988. Considering sex offenders: A model of addiction. *Signs: A Journal of Women, Culture, and Society* 13: 695–724.

Herman, J. 1992a. Complex PTSD: A syndrome in survivors of prolonged and repeated trauma. *Journal of Traumatic Stress* 53: 377–91.

———. 1992b. *Trauma and Recovery*. New York: Basic.

Herman, J. 1993. Sequelae of prolonged and repeated trauma: Evidence for a complex PTSD syndrome DESNOS. In J. R. T. Davidson and E. B. Foa, eds., *Posttraumatic Stress Disorder: DSV-IV and Beyond*, 213–28. Washington, DC: American Psychiatric Press.

Herman, J. 1997. *Trauma and Recovery: The Aftermath of Violence: From Domestic Abuse to Political Terror*. New York: HarperCollins.

Herman, J., and Hirschman, L. 1981. Families at risk for father–daughter incest. *American Journal of Psychiatry* 138: 967–70.

Herman, J. L., Perry, J. C., and Van der Kolk, B. A. 1989. Childhood trauma in Borderline Personality Disorder. *American Journal of Psychiatry* 146: 490–95.

———. 1987. Traumatic antecedents of Borderline Personality Disorder. In B. A. van der Kolk, ed., *Psychological Trauma*, 111–26. Washington, DC: American Psychiatric Press.

Hernandez, J. T., Lodico, M., and DiClemente, R. J. 1993. The effects of child abuse and race on risk taking in male adolescents. *Journal of the National Medical Association* 85: 593–97.

Higgins Kessler, M. R., While, M. B., and Nelson, B. S. 2003. Group treatments for women sexually abused as children: A review of the literature and recommendations for future outcome research. *Child Abuse and Neglect* 27: 1045–61.

Hilberman, E. 1980. The "wife beater's wife" reconsidered. *American Journal of Psychiatry* 137: 1336–47.

Himelein, M. J. 1995. Risk factors for sexual victimization in dating. *Psychology of Women Quarterly* 19: 31–48.

Horowitz, L. 1977. A group-centered approach to group psychotherapy. *International Journal of Group Psychotherapy* 27: 423–39.

Horowitz, M. D., Wilner, N., and Alvarez, W. 1979. Impact of Event Scale: A measure of subjective stress. *Psychosomatic Medicine* 41: 209–18.

Horowitz, M. J. 1975. Intrusive and repetitive thoughts after experimental stress. *Archives of General Psychiatry* 134: 1381–85.

———. 1978. *Stress Response Syndromes*. Northvale, NJ: Jason Aronson.

———. 1986. *Stress Response Syndromes*. 2nd ed.. Northvale, NJ: Jason Aronson.

Horowitz, L., Rosenberg, S., Baer, B., Ureno, G., and Villasenor, V. 1988. Inventory of interpersonal problems: Psychometric properties and clinical applications. *Journal of Consulting and Clinical Psychology* 56: 885–92.

Hotaling, G., and Sugarman, D. 1986. An analysis of risk markers in husband to wife violence: The current state of knowledge. *Violence and Victimology* 1: 101–24.

Humphreys, J. 1997. Nursing care of battered women. *Pediatric Nursing* 23: 122–28.

Hunter, J. A. 1991. A comparison of the psychosocial maladjustment of adult males and females sexually molested as children. *Journal of Interpersonal Violence* 6: 205–17.

Hunter, M. 1990. *Abused Boys: The Neglected Victims of Sexual Abuse*. New York: Random House.

Hussey, D. L., and Singer, M. 1993. Psychological distress, problem behaviors, and family functioning of sexually abused adolescent inpatients. *Journal of the American Academy of Child and Adolescent Psychiatry* 32: 954–61.

Irwin, H. J. 1994. Proneness to dissociation and traumatic childhood events. *Journal of Nervous and Mental Diseases* 182: 456–60.

———. 1999. Violent and nonviolent revictimization of women abused in childhood. *Journal of Interpersonal Violence* 14: 1095–1110.

Jaffe, P. G., Wolfe, D. A., Wilson, S. K. 1990. *Children of Battered Women.* Newbury Park, CA: Sage.

James, J., and Meyerding, J. 1977. Early sexual experience and prostitution. *American Journal of Psychiatry* 6: 67–76.

Jehu, D., and Gazan, M. 1983. Psychosocial adjustment of women who were sexually victimized in childhood or adolescence. *Canadian Journal of Community Mental Health* 2, no. 2: 1–15.

Johnson, C. F. 2000. Abuse and neglect of children. In R. Behrman, ed., *Nelson Textbook of Pediatrics,* 110–19. 16th ed. Philadelphia: Saunders.

Johnson, R. L., and Shrier, D. 1987. Past sexual victimization by females of male patients in an adolescent medicine clinic population. *American Journal of Psychiatry* 144, no. 5: 650–53.

Johnson, T. C. 1988. Child perpetrators: Children who molest other children—Preliminary findings. *Child Abuse and Neglect* 12: 219–29.

———. 1989. Female child perpetrators: Children who molest other children. *Child Abuse and Neglect* 13: 571–85.

———. 2002. Some considerations about sexual abuse and children with sexual behavior problems. *Journal of Trauma and Dissociation* 3, no. 4: 83–105.

Jones, I. F. 1992. Social factors in adolescent suicide ideation and behavior. Ph.D. dissertation, University of North Texas.

Jouriles, E. N., McDonald, R., Norwood, W. D., Ware, S. H., Spiller, L. C., and Swank, P. R. 1998. Knives, guns, and interparental violence: Relations with child behavior problems. *Journal of Family Psychology,* 12, 2: 178–94.

Kaplan, S. J. 1996. Physical abuse of children and adolescents. In S. J. Kaplan, ed., *Family Violence: A Clinical and Legal Guide,* 1–35. Washington, DC: American Psychiatric Press.

Kaplan, S., Montero, G., and Pelcovitz, D. 1986. Psychopathology of parents of abused and neglected children. Paper presented at the International Congress of Child Psychiatry and Allied Professions, Paris, France.

Kaplan, S., Pelcovitz, D., and Salzinger, S. 1983. Psychopathology of parents of abused and neglected children. *Journal of American Academy of Child Psychiatry* 22: 238–44.

Kaufman, J., and Zigler, E. 1987. Do abused children become abusive parents? *American Journal of Orthopsychiatry* 57: 186–92.

Keane, T. M., Fairbank, J. A., Caddell, J. M., and Zimering, R. T. 1989. Implosive flooding therapy reduces symptoms of PTSD in Vietnam combat veterans. *Behavior Therapy* 20: 245–60.

Kearney-Cooke, A. 1988. A group treatment of sexual abuse among women with eating disorders. *Women and Therapy* 7: 5–22.

Kearney-Cooke, A., and Striegel-Moore, R. H. 1994. Treatment of childhood sexual abuse in anorexia nervosa and bulimia nervosa: A feminist psychodynamic approach. *International Journal of Eating Disorders* 15: 305–19.

Kempe, R., and Kempe, C. 1978. *Child Abuse*. Cambridge: Harvard University Press.

Kench, S., and Irwin, H. J. 2000. Alexithymia and the childhood family environment. *Journal of Clinical Psychology* 56: 737–45.

Kendall-Tacket, K. A., and Eckenrode, J. 1996. The effects of neglect on academic achievement and disciplinary problems: A developmental perspective. *Child Abuse and Neglect* 20: 161–69.

Kendall-Tackett, K. A., Williams, L. M., and Finkelhor, D. 1993. Impact of sexual abuse on children: A review and synthesis of recent empirical studies. *Psychological Bulletin* 113: 164–80.

Kent, A., and Waller, G. 2000. Childhood emotional abuse and eating psychopathology. *Clinical Psychology Review* 20, no. 7: 887–903.

Kessler, B. L., and Bieschke, K. J. 1999. A retrospective analysis of shame, dissociation, and adult victimization in survivors of childhood sexual abuse. *Journal of Counseling Psychology* 46: 355–641.

Khantzian, E. J. 1985. The self-medication hypothesis of addictive disorders: Focus on heroin and cocaine dependence. *American Journal of Psychiatry* 142: 1259–64.

———. 1997. The self-medication hypothesis of substance use disorders: A reconsideration and recent applications. *Harvard Review of Psychiatry* 4: 231–44.

———. 2004. Book forum: Substance abuse and co-morbidity. *American Journal of Psychiatry.* 161: 587–88.

———. 2005. Addiction: Disease, symptom, or choice. *Counselor: The Magazine for Addiction Professionals.* www.counselormagazine.com.

Kilpatrick, D. G., Acierno, R., Saunders, B., Resnick, H. S., Best, C. L., et al. 2000. Risk factors for adolescent substance abuse and dependence: Data from a national sample. *Journal of Consulting and Clinical Psychology* 68: 19–30.

Kinard, E. 1980. Emotional development in physically abused children. *American Journal of Orthopsychiatry* 50: 689–96.

Kinzie, J. D., Boehnlein, J. K., and Leung, P. K. 1990. The prevalence of Posttraumatic Stress Disorder and its clinical significance among Southeast Asian refugees. *American Journal of Psychiatry* 147: 913–17.

Kinzl, J. F., Traweger, C., and Biefl, W. 1995. Sexual dysfunctions: Relationship to childhood sexual abuse and early family experiences in a nonclinical sample. *Child Abuse and Neglect* 19: 785–92.

Kirby, J. S., Chu, J. A., and Dill, D. L. 1993. Correlates of dissociative symptomatology in patients with physical and sexual abuse histories. *Comprehensive Psychiatry* 34: 258–63.

Kirmayer, L., and Carroll, J. 1987. A neurobiological hypothesis on the nature of chronic self-mutilation. *Integrative Psychiatry* 5: 212–13.

Kiser, L. J., Ackerman, B. J., Brown, E., et al. 1988. Posttraumatic Stress Disorder in young children: A reaction to purported sexual abuse. *Journal of the American Academy of Child and Adolescent Psychiatry* 27: 645–49.

Kiser, L. J., Heston, J., Milsap, P. A., and Pruitt, D. B. 1991. Physical and sexual abuse in childhood: Relationship with Posttraumatic Stress Disorder. *Journal of the American Academy of Child and Adolescent Psychiatry* 30: 776–83.

Kline, D., and Christiansen, J. 1975. *Educational and Psychological Problems of Abused Children: Final Report.* ERIC document ED121041.

Kluft, R. P. 1985. *Childhood Antecedents of Multiple Personality.* Washington, DC: American Psychiatric Press.

Kluft, R. P. 1989. Treating patients sexually exploited by a previous therapist. *Psychiatric Clinics of North America* 12: 483–500.

Kluft———. 1990a. Incest and subsequent revictimization: The case of therapist–patient sexual exploitation, with a description of the sitting duck syndrome. In R. P. Kluft, ed., *Incest-Related Syndromes of Adult Psychopathology,* 263–87. Washington, DC: American Psychiatric Press.

———. 1990b. Dissociation and subsequent vulnerability: A preliminary study. *Dissociation* 3: 167–73.

———. 1993. Basic principles in conducting the psychotherapy of Multiple Personality Disorder. In R. Kluft and C. Fine, eds., *Clinical Perspectives on Multiple Personality Disorder,* 19–50. Washington, DC: American Psychiatric Press.

Knittle, B. J., and Tuana, S. 1980. Group therapy as primary treatment for adolescent victims of intrafamilial sexual abuse. *Clinical Social Work Journal* 8: 236–42.

Koopman, C., Gore-Felton, C., Classen, C., Kim, P., and Spiegel, D. 2001. Acute stress reactions to everyday stressful events among sexual abuse survivors with PTSD. *Journal of Child Sexual Abuse* 10, no. 2: 83–99.

Korte, K., Horton, C. B., and Graybill, D. 1998. Child sexual abuse and bulimic behaviors: An exploratory investigation of the frequency and nature of a relationship. *Journal of Child Sexual Abuse* 7, no. 1: 53–64.

Koss, M. P., and Gidycz, C. A. 1985. Sexual Experiences Survey: Reliability and validity. *Journal of Consulting and Clinical Psychology* 53: 422–23.

Koss, M. P., and Dinero, T. E. 1989. Discriminant analysis of risk factors for sexual victimization among a national sample of college women. *Journal of Clinical and Consulting Psychology* 57: 242–50.

Kovach, J. A. 1983. The relationship between treatment failures of alcoholic women and incestuous histories with possible implications for Posttraumatic Stress Disorder symptomatology. Ph.D. dissertation, Wayne State University, 1983.

Koverola, C., Foy, D., Heger, A., and Lytle, C. 1990. Posttraumatic stress disorder as a sequela of child sexual abuse. Paper presented at the annual meeting of the International Society for Traumatic Stress Studies, New Orleans.

Krahe, B., Scheinberger-Olwig, R., Waizenhofer, E., and Kolpin, S. 1999. Childhood sexual abuse and revictimization in adolescence. *Child Abuse and Neglect* 23, no. 94: 383–94.

Krugman, S., Mata, L., and Krugman, R. 1992. Sexual abuse and corporal punishment during childhood: A pilot retrospective survey of university students in Costa Rica. *Pediatrics* 90: 157–61.

Krystal, H. 1982. Alexithymia and the effectiveness of psychoanalytic treatment. *International Journal of Psychoanalytic Psychotherapy* 9: 353–78.

Kunitz, S. J., Levy, J. E., McCloskey, J., and Gabriel, K. R. 1998. Alcohol dependence and domestic violence as sequelae of abuse and conduct disorder in childhood. *Child Abuse and Neglect* 22: 1079–91.

Kurtz, P. D., Gaudin, J. M., Wodarski, J. S., and Howing, P. T. 1993. Maltreatment and the school-age child: School performance consequences. *Child Abuse and Neglect* 17: 581–89.

Ladwig, G. B., and Anderson, M. D. 1989. Substance abuse in women: Relationship between chemical dependency of women and past reports of physical and/or sexual abuse. *International Journal of Addiction* 24: 739–54.

Langeland, W., and Hartgers, C. 1998. Child sexual and physical abuse and alcoholism: A review. *Journal of Studies of Alcohol* 59: 336–48.

Latimer, J. 1998. *The Consequences of Child Maltreatment: A Reference Guide for Health Practitioners.* Ottawa, Ont.: National Clearinghouse on Family Violence, Health Canada www.phac-aspc.gc.ca/nc-cn. Accessed November 20, 2004.

Laumann, E. O., Gagnon, J. H., Michael, R. T., and Michaels, S. 1994. *The Social Organization of Sexuality: Sexual Practices in the United States.* Chicago: University of Chicago Press.

Lawrence, K. J., Cozolino, L., and Foy, D. W. 1995. Psychological sequelae in adult females reporting childhood ritual abuse. *Child Abuse and Neglect* 19: 975–83.

Leibenluft, E., Gardner, D. L., and Cowdry, R. W. 1987. The inner experience of the borderline self-mutilator. *Journal of Personality Disorders* 1: 328–33.

Lesnik-Oberstein, M., Coers, A. J., and Cohen, L. 1994. Parental hostility and its sources in psychologically abusive mothers: A test of the three-factor theory. *Child Abuse and Neglect* 19: 33–34.

Levin, M. P., and Troiden, R. R. 1988. The myth of sexual compulsivity. *Journal of Sex Research* 25: 347–63.

Lewis, D. 1985. Biopsychosocial characteristics of children who later murder: A prospective study. *American Journal of Psychiatry* 142: 1161–67.

Lewis, M., and Sarrell, P. 1969. Some psychological aspects of seduction, incest, and rape in childhood. *Journal of the American Academy of Child Psychiatry* 8: 606–19.

Liebschutz, J., Savetsky, J. B., Saitz, R., Horton, N. J., Lloyd-Travaglini, C., and Samet, J. H. 2002. The relationship between sexual and physical abuse and substance abuse consequences. *Journal of Substance Abuse Treatment* 22: 121–28.

Lindberg, F., and Distad, L. 1985. Posttraumatic Stress Disorders in women who experienced childhood incest. *Child Abuse and Neglect* 9: 329–34.

Lindsey, D. 1994. *The Welfare of Children.* New York: Oxford University Press.

Lindholm, K., and Willey, R. 1983. *Child Abuse and Ethnicity: Patterns of Similarities and Differences.* Occasional paper no. 18. Los Angeles: UCLA Spanish-Speaking Mental Health Research Center.

Linehan, M. M. 1993. *Cognitive–Behavioral Treatment of Borderline Personality Disorder.* New York: Guilford.

Links, P. S., Boiago, I., Huxley, G., et al. 1990. Sexual abuse and biparental failure as etiological models in the Borderline Personality Disorder. In P. S. Links, ed., *Family Environment and Borderline Personality Disorder*, 105–20. Washington, DC: American Psychiatric Press.

Links, P. S., Steiner, M., Offord, D. R., et al. 1988. Characteristics of borderline personality disorder: A Canadian study. *Canadian Journal of Psychiatry* 33: 336–40.

Lisak, D., and Miller, P. M. 2003. Childhood trauma, Posttraumatic Stress Disorder, substance abuse, and violence. In P. Ouimette and P. J. Brown, eds., *Trauma and Substance Abuse: Causes, Consequences, and Treatment of Co-morbid Disorders*.

Litz, B. T., Blake, D. D., Gerardi, R. G., and Keane, T. M. 1990. Decision-making guidelines for the use of direct therapeutic exposure in the treatment of Posttraumatic Stress Disorder. *Behavior Therapist* 13: 91–93.

Livingston, R. 1987. Sexually and physically abused children. *Journal of the American Academy of Child and Adolescent Psychiatry* 27: 413–15.

Livingston, R., Lawson, L., and Jones, J. G. 1993. Predictors of self-reported psychopathology in children abused repeatedly by a parent. *Journal of the American Academy of Child and Adolescent Psychiatry* 32: 948–53.

Lodico, M. A., and DiClemente, R. J. 1994. The association between childhood sexual abuse and prevalence of HIV-related risk behaviors. *Clinical Pediatrics* 33: 498–502.

Long, P. J. 1999. *Assessing a History of Childhood Sexual Abuse in Adults: The Life Experiences Questionnaire*. Norman: Oklahoma State University Press.

Longdon, C. 1993. A survivor's and therapist's viewpoint. In M. Elliott, ed., *Female Sexual Abuse of Children: The Ultimate Taboo*, 50–60. London: Longman Information and Reference.

Longstreth, G. F., Mason, C., Schrieber, I. G., and Tsao-Wei, D. 1998. Group psychotherapy for women molested in childhood: Psychological and somatic symptoms and medical visits. *International Journal of Group Psychotherapy* 48: 533–41.

Loos, M. E., and Alexander, P. C. 1997. Differential effects associated with self-reported histories of abuse and neglect in a college sample. *Journal of Interpersonal Violence* 12: 340–60.

Ludolph, P. H., Westen, D., Misle, B., et al. 1990. The borderline diagnosis in adolescents: Symptoms and developmental history. *American Journal of Psychiatry* 147: 470–76.

Lukianowicz, N. 1972. Incest. *British Journal of Psychiatry* 120: 301–13.

Lundberg-Love, P. K., Marmion, S., Ford, K., Geffner, R., and Peacock, L. 1992. The long-term consequences of childhood incestuous victimization upon adult women's psychological symptomatology. *Journal of Child Sexual Abuse* 1: 81–102.

Lusk, R., and Waterman, J. 1986. Effects of sexual abuse on children. In K. MacFarlane and J. Waterman, eds., *Sexual Abuse of Young Children: Evaluation and Treatment*, 101–18. New York: Guilford.

Luster, T., and Small, S. A. 1997. Sexual abuse history and number of sex partners among female adolescents. *Family Planning Perspectives* 29: 204–11.

Lystad, M. L., Rice, M., and Kaplan, S. J. 1996. Domestic violence. In S. J. Kaplan, ed., *Family Violence: A Clinical and Legal Guide*, 139–80. Washington, DC: American Psychiatric Press.

MacVicar, K. 1979. Psychotherapy of sexually abused girls. *Journal of the American Academy of Child Psychiatry* 27: 342–53.

Malinosky-Rummell, R., and Hansen, D. J. 1993. Long-term consequences of childhood physical abuse. *Psychological Bulletin* 114: 68–79.

Mallinckrodt, B., McCreary, B. A., and Robertson, A. K. 1995. Co-occurrence of eating disorder and incest: The role of attachment, family environment, and social competencies. *Journal of Counseling Psychology* 42, no. 2, 178–86.

Maltz, W. 2001. *The Sexual Healing Journey: A Guide for Survivors of Sexual Abuse.* New York: HarperCollins.

Manion, I. G., and Wilson, S. K. 1995. *An Examination of the Association between Histories of Maltreatment and Adolescent Risk Behaviours.* Ottawa, Ont.: Supply and Services Canada.

Mannarino, A. P., Cohen, J. A., and Gregor, M. 1989. Emotional and behavioral difficulties in sexually abused girls. *Journal of Family Violence* 4: 437–51.

Marlatt, G. A., and Gordon, J. R., eds. 1985. *Relapse Prevention.* New York: Guilford.

Martin, G. 1996. Reported family dynamics, sexual abuse, and suicidal behaviors in community adolescents. *Archives of Suicide Research* 2, no. 3, 183–95.

Martin, G., Bergen, H. A., Richardson, A. S., Roeger, L., and Allison, S. 2004. Sexual abuse and suicidality: Gender differences in a large community sample of adolescents. *Child Abuse and Neglect* 28: 491–503.

Martin, H., and Beezley, P. 1977. Behavioral observations of abused children. *Developmental Medicine and Child Neurology* 13: 373–87.

Masterson, J. F., and Klein, R. 1989. *Psychotherapy of the Disorders of the Self: The Masterson Approach.* New York: Brunner/Mazel.

Mathias, J. L., Mertin, P., and Murray, A. 1995. The psychological functioning of children from backgrounds of domestic violence. *Australian Psychologist*, 30, 1: 47–56.

Matthews, R., Matthews, L. K. and Speltz, K. 1989. *Female Sexual Offenders: An Exploratory Study.* Orwell, VT: Safer Society Press.

Mayall, A., and Gold, S. R. 1995. Definitional issues and mediating variables in the sexual revictimization of women sexually abused as children. *Journal of Interpersonal Violence* 10: 26–42.

McBean, A. 1987. Another secret out in the open: Female sex offenders. *Looking Ahead: Innovation and Inquiry in Family Sexual Abuse Prevention* 1, no. 1: 5–6.

McCann, I. L., and Pearlman, L. A. 1990. *Psychological Trauma and the Adult Survivor: Theory, Therapy, and Transformation.* New York: Brunner/Mazel.

McCarthy, B. 1994. Sexually compulsive men and inhibited sexual desire. *Journal of Sex and Marital Therapy* 20: 200–209.

McClellan, J., Adams, J., Douglas, D., McCurry, C., and Storck, M. 1995. Clinical characteristics related to severity of sexual abuse: A study of seriously mentally ill youth. *Child Abuse and Neglect* 19: 1245–54.

McFarlane, A. C. 1986. Posttraumatic morbidity of a disaster: A study of cases presenting for psychiatric treatment. *Journal of Mental and Nervous Disorders* 174: 4–14.

———. 1988. The etiology of Posttraumatic Stress Disorder following a natural disaster. *Journal of Nervous and Mental Diseases* 152: 116–21.

———. 1990. Vulnerability to Posttraumatic Stress Disorder. In M. E. Wolf and A. D. Misname, eds., *Posttraumatic Stress Disorder: Etiology, Phenomenology, and Treatment*, 2–20. Washington, DC: American Psychiatric Press.

McFarlane, J. M., Groff, J. Y., O'Brien, J. A., and Watson, K. 2003. Behaviors of children who are exposed and not exposed to intimate partner violence: An analysis of 330 black, white, and Hispanic children. *Pediatrics* 1123: 202–7.

McKay, M. M. 1994. The link between domestic violence and child abuse: Assessment and treatment considerations. *Child Welfare* 73, no. 1: 29–39.

McLeer, S. V., Callaghan, M., Henry, D., and Wallen, J. 1994. Psychiatric disorders in sexually abused children. *Journal of the American Academy of Child and Adolescent Psychiatry* 33: 313–19.

McLeer, S. V., Deblinger, E., Atkins, M., et al. 1988. Posttraumatic Stress Disorder in sexually abused children. *Journal of the American Academy of Child and Adolescent Psychiatry* 27: 650–54.

McLeer, S. V., Deblinger, E., Henry, D., and Orvaschel, H. 1992. Sexually abused children at high risk for Posttraumatic Stress Disorder. *Journal of the American Academy of Child and Adolescent Psychiatry* 31: 875–79.

Meichenbaum, D. H., and Deffenbacher, J. L. 1988. Stress inoculation training. *Counseling Psychologist* 16: 69–90.

Meichenbaum, D. H., and Novaco, R. 1985. Stress inoculation: A preventative approach. *Issues in Mental Health Nursing* 7: 419–35.

Meiselman, K. C. 1978. *Incest: A Psychological Study of Causes and Effects with Treatment Recommendations*. San Francisco: Jossey-Bass.

Messman, T. L., and Long, P. J. 1996. Child sexual abuse and its relationship to victimization in adult women: A review. *Clinical Psychology Review* 16: 397–420.

Messman-Moore, T. L., and Long, P. J. 2000. Child sexual abuse and revictimization in the form of adult sexual abuse, adult physical abuse, and adult psychological maltreatment. *Journal of Interpersonal Violence* 15, no. 5: 489–502.

Meston, C. M., Heiman, J. R., and Trapnell, P. D. 1999. The relation between early abuse and adult sexuality. *Journal of Sex Research* 36, no. 4: 385–409.

Mian, M., Marton, P., and LeBaron, D. 1996. The effects of sexual abuse on 3- to 5-year-old girls. *Child Abuse and Neglect* 20: 731–45.

Miletski, H. 1995. *Mother–Son Incest: The Unthinkable Broken Taboo: An Overview of Findings*. Brandon, VT: Safer Society Press.

Miller, B. A., Downs, W. R., Gondoli, D. M., and Keil, A. 1987. The role of child-hood sexual abuse in the development of alcoholism in women. *Journal of Violence and Victimology*, 2: 157–71.

Miller, B. A., Downs, W. R., and Testa, M. 1993. The interrelationships between victimization experiences and women's alcohol use. *Journal of Studies on Alcohol*, suppl. 11, 109–17.

Miller, D. 1994. *Women Who Hurt Themselves: A Book of Hope and Understanding*. New York: Basic Books.

Miller, D. A. F., McCluskey-Fawcett, K., and Irving, L. M. 1993. The relationship between childhood sexual abuse and subsequent onset of bulimia nervosa. *Child Abuse and Neglect* 17: 305–14.

Miller, J., Moeler, D., Kaufman, A., DiVasto, P., Pathak and Christy, D. 1978. Recidivism among sex assault victims. *American Journal of Psychiatry* 135: 1103–4.

Miller, J., Moeller, D., and Kaufman, A. 1987. Recidivism among sexual assault victims. *American Journal of Psychiatry* 135: 1103–4.

Millon, T. 1994. *Millon Multiaxial Inventory III Manual*. Minneapolis: National Computer Systems.

Mineka, S., and Suomi, S. J. 1978. Social separations in monkeys. *Psychological Bulletin* 85: 1376–1400.

Moeller, T. P., Bachman, G. A., and Moeller, J. R. 1993. The combined effects of physical, sexual, and emotional abuse during childhood: Long-term health consequences for women. *Child Abuse and Neglect* 17: 623–40.

Molnar, B. E., Berkman, L. F., and Buka, S. L. 2001. Psychopathology, childhood sexual abuse, and other adversities: Relative links to subsequent suicidal behavior in the U.S. *Psychological Medicine* 31, no. 6: 965–77.

Monteleone, J. A. 1998. *A Parent's and Teacher's Handbook on Identifying and Preventing Child Abuse*. St. Louis, MO: G.W. Medical.

Monti, P. M., Rohsenhow, D. R., Colby, S. M., and Abrams, D. B. 1995. Coping and social skills training. In R. K. Hester and W. R. Miller, eds., *Handbook of Alcoholism Treatment Approaches: Effective Alternatives*, 221–41. Needham Heights, MA: Simon & Schuster.

Morrison, D., Zaslow, M., and Dion, R. 1998. Completing the portrayal of parenting behavior with interview-based measures. In M. Zaslow and C. Eldred (Eds.), *Parenting behavior in a sample of young mothers in poverty*. New York: Manpower Demonstration Research Corp.

Moyer, D., DiPietro, L., Berkowitz, R., and Stunkard, A. 1997. Childhood sexual abuse and precursors of binge eating in an adolescent female population. *International Journal of Eating Disorders* 21, no. 1: 23–30.

Mullen, P. E., and Fleming, J. 1998. Long-term effects of child sexual abuse. *Issues in Child Abuse Prevention* 9: 1–19.

Mullen, P. E., Martin, J. L., Anderson, J. C., Romans, S. E., and Herbison, G. P. 1993. Childhood sexual abuse and mental health in later life. *British Journal of Psychiatry* 163: 721–32.

———. 1994. The effect of child sexual abuse on social, interpersonal, and sexual function in adult life. *British Journal of Psychiatry* 165: 35–47.

Muller, R. T., and Lemieux, K. E. 2000. Social support, attachment, and psychopathology in high-risk formerly maltreated adults. *Child Abuse and Neglect* 24, no. 7: 883–900.

Murphy, J. M., Jellinek, M., Quinn, D., Smith, G., Poitrast, F. G., and Goshko, M. 1991. Substance abuse and serious child mistreatment: Prevalence, risk, and outcome in a court sample. *Child Abuse and Neglect: The International Journal* 15: 197–211.

Najavits, L. M., Weiss, R. D., and Liese, B. S. 1996. Group cognitive–behavioral therapy for women with PTSD and Substance Use Disorder. *Journal of Substance Abuse Treatment* 13: 98–104.

National Clearinghouse on Child Abuse and Neglect Information. 2004. *What Is Child Abuse and Neglect?* nccanch.acf.hhs.gov/pubs/factsheets/whatiscan.cfm.

Nay, P., Fung, T., and Wickett, A. 1992. Causes of child abuse and neglect. *Canadian Journal of Psychiatry* 36: 401–5.

Neumann, D., Housekamp, B., Pollock, V., and Briere, J. 1996. The long-term sequelae of childhood sexual abuse in women: A meta-analytic review. *Child Maltreatment* 1: 6–16.

Neumark-Sztainer, D., Story, M., Hannan, P., Beuhring, T., and Resnick, M. 2000. Disordered eating among adolescents: Associations with sexual/physical abuse and other familial/psychosocial factors. *International Journal of Eating Disorders* 28, no. 3, 249–56.

Nicholas, M., and Forrester, A. 1999. Advantages of heterogeneous therapy groups in the psychotherapy of the traumatically abused: Treating the problem as well as the person. *International Journal of Group Psychotherapy* 49, no. 3: 323–42.

Noll, J. G., Horowitz, L. A., Bonanno, G. A., Trickett, P. K., and Putnam, F. W. 2003. Revictimization and self-harm in females who experienced childhood sexual abuse. *Journal of Interpersonal Violence* 18, no. 12: 1452–71.

Nordling, N., Sandnabba, N. K., and Santtila, P. 2000. The prevalence and effects of self-reported childhood sexual abuse among sadomasochistically oriented males and females. *Journal of Child Sexual Abuse* 9, no. 1: 53–64.

Norris, F. 1990. Screening for traumatic stress: A scale for use in the general population. *Journal of Applied Social Psychology* 20: 409–18.

Norris, F. H., and Hamblen, J. L. 2004. Standardized self-report measures of civilian trauma and PTSD. In J. P. Wilson and T. M. Keane, eds., *Assessing Psychological Trauma and PTSD*, 63–102. 2nd ed. New York: Guilford.

Oates, R. K. 2004. Sexual abuse and suicidal behavior. *Child Abuse and Neglect* 28: 487–89.

———. 1996. *The Spectrum of Child Abuse: Assessment, Treatment, and Prevention.* New York: Brunel/Mazel.

Ogilvie, B.A. 1996. *Why Didn't She Love Me?* Vancouver, B. C.: Hazeldine.

———. 2004. *Mother–Daughter Incest.* New York: Haworth.

Ogilvie, B., and Daniluk, J. 1995. Common themes in the experiences of mother–daughter incest survivors: Implications for counseling. *Journal of Counseling and Development* 73: 598–602.

O'Keefe, M. 1994. Racial/ethnic differences among battered women and their children. *Journal of Child and Family Studies* 3: 283–305.

Okun, L. 1986. *Women Abuse: Facts Replacing Myths*. New York: State University of New York Press.

Olson, P. E. 1990. The sexual abuse of boys: A study of the long-term psychological effects. In M. Hunter, ed., *The Sexually Abused Male*. Vol. 1, *Prevalence, Impact, and Treatment*, 137–52. Lexington, MA: Lexington.

O'Neill, K., and Gupta, K. 1991. Posttraumatic Stress Disorder in women who were victims of childhood sexual abuse. *Irish Journal of Psychological Medicine* 8: 124–27.

Onyskiw, J. E. 2003. Domestic violence and children's adjustment: A review of research. *Journal of Emotional Abuse* 3, no. 1–2: 11–45.

Oppenheimer, R., Howells, K., Palmer, R. L., and Chaloner, D. A. 1985. Adverse sexual experiences in childhood and clinical eating disorders: A preliminary description. *Journal of Psychiatric Research* 19: 357–61.

Orgata, S. N., Silk, K. R., Goodrich, S., et al. 1990. The childhood experience of the borderline patient. In P. S. Links, ed., *Family Environment and Borderline Personality Disorder*, 87–103. Washington, DC: American Psychiatric Press.

Osuch, E. A., Noll, J. G., and Putnam, F. W. 1999. The motivations for self-injury in psychiatric inpatients. *Psychiatry: Interpersonal and Biological Processes* 64: 334–46.

Ouimette, P. C., Ahrens, C., Moos, R. H., and Finney, J. W. 1997. Posttraumatic Stress Disorder in substance abuse patients: Relationship to one-year posttreatment outcomes. *Psychology of Addictive Behaviors* 11: 34–47.

Ouimette, P. C., Ahrens, C., Moos, R. H., and Finney, J. W. 1998. During treatment changes in substance abuse patients with Posttraumatic Stress Disorder: The influence of specific interventions and program environments. *Journal of Substance Abuse Treatment* 15: 555–64.

Ouimette, P. C., Finney, J. W., and Moos, R. H. 1999. Two-year posttreatment functioning and coping of substance abuse patients with Posttraumatic Stress Disorder. *Psychology of Addictive Behaviors* 13: 105–14.

Ouimette, P. C., Moos, R. H., and Brown, P. J. 2003. Substance Use Disorder–Posttraumatic Stress Disorder co-morbidity: A survey of treatments and proposed practice guidelines. In P. Ouimette and P. Brown, eds., *Trauma and Substance Abuse: Causes, Consequences, and Treatment of Co-morbid Disorders*, 91–110. Washington, DC: American Psychological Association.

Pagliaro, A. M., and Pagliaro, L. A. 1996. *Substance Use among Children and Adolescents: Its Nature, Extent, and Effects from Conception to Adulthood*. New York: Wiley.

Paivio, S. C. 2001. Stability of retrospective self-reports of child abuse and neglect before and after therapy for child abuse issues. *Child Abuse and Neglect* 25: 1053–1068.

Paivio, S. C., and Cramer, K. M. 2004. Factor structure and reliability of the Child-hood Trauma Questionnaire in a Canadian undergraduate student sample. *Child Abuse and Neglect* 28: 889–904.

Paivio, S. C., and McCulloch, C. R. 2004. Alexithymia as a mediator between child-hood trauma and self-injurious behaviors. *Child Abuse and Neglect* 28: 339–54.

Paris, J., and Frank, H. 1989. Perceptions of parental bonding in borderline patients. *American Journal of Psychiatry* 146: 1498–99.

Paris, J., and Zweig-Frank, H. 1997. Parameters of childhood sexual abuse in female patients. In M. C. Zanarini, ed., *Role of Sexual Abuse in the Etiology of Borderline Personality Disorder*, 15–28. Washington, DC: American Psychiatric Press.

Parker, S. 1990. Healing Abuse in Gay Men: The Group Component. In M. Hunter, ed., *The Sexually Abused Male*, 2:177–98. Lexington, MA: Lexington.

Paxson, C., and Waldfogel, J. 1999. Parental resources and child abuse and neglect. *American Economic Review* 89, no. 2: 239–51.

Pearlin, L. I., Menaghan, E. G., Lieberman, M. A., and Mullan, J. T. 1981. The stress process. *Journal of Health and Social Behavior*, 25: 337–56.

Pearlman, L. A. 2001. Treatment of persons with complex PTSD and other trauma-related disruptions of the self. In J. P. Wilson, M. J. Friedman, and J. D. Lindy, eds., *Treating Psychological Trauma and PTSD*, 205–36. New York: Guilford.

———. 2003. *Trauma and Attachment Belief Scale TABS Manual*. Los Angeles: Western Psychological Services.

Pearlman, L. A., and McCann, I. L. 1994. Integrating structured and unstructured approaches to taking trauma history. In M. B. Williams and J. Sommer Jr., eds., *Handbook of Posttraumatic Therapy*, 38–48. Westport, CT: Greenwood.

Pelcovitz, D., Kaplan, S., Goldenberg, B., Mandel, F., Lehane, J., and Guarrera, J. 1994. Posttraumatic Stress Disorder in physically abused adolescents. *Journal of the American Academy of Child and Adolescent Psychiatry* 33: 305–12.

Pelcovitz, D., van der Kolk, B. A., Roth, S. H., Mandel, F. S., Kaplan, S. J., and Resnick, P. A. 1997. Development of a criteria set and a Structured Interview for Disorders of Extreme Stress (SIDES). *Journal of Traumatic Stress* 10, no. 1: 3–16.

Pelton, L. 1994. The role of material factors in child abuse and neglect. In G. Melton and F. Barry, eds., *Protecting Children from Abuse and Neglect*, 131–81. New York: Guilford.

Peluso, E., and Putnam, N. 1996. Case study: Sexual abuse of boys by females. *Journal of the American Academy of Child and Adolescent Psychiatry* 35: 51–54.

Perkins, D., and Luster, T. 1999. The relationships between sexual abuse and purging: Findings from community-wide surveys of female adolescents. *Child Abuse and Neglect* 23, no. 4: 371–82.

Perry, J. C., and Cooper, S. H. 1986. A preliminary report on defenses and conflicts in Borderline Personality Disorder. *Journal of the American Psychoanalytic Association* 34: 863–93.

Perry, J. C., Herman, J. L., and van der Kolk, B. A., et al. 1990. Psychotherapy and psychological trauma in Borderline Personality Disorder. *Psychiatric Annals* 20: 33–43.

Peters, D. K., and Range, L. M. 1995. Childhood sexual abuse and current suicidality in college women and men. *Child Abuse and Neglect* 19: 335–41.

Peters, S. D. 1988. Child sexual assault and later psychological problems. In G. E. Wyatt and G. J. Powell, eds., *Lasting Effects of Child Sexual Abuse*. Newbury Park, CA: Sage.

Peterson, C., and Seligman, M. E. P. 1983. Learned helplessness and victimization. *Journal of Social Issues* 2: 103–6.

Peterson, R. A., and Reiss, S. 1992. *Anxiety Sensitivity Index Manual*. 2nd ed. Worthington, OH: International Diagnostic Systems.

Petrie, T. A., and Tripp, M. 2001. Sexual abuse and eating disorders: A test of a conceptual model. *Sex Roles: A Journal of Research*, 17–28.

Petrovich, M., and Templar, D. I. 1984. Heterosexual molestation of children who later become rapists. *Psychological Reports* 54: 810.

Pfeffer, C. R. 1986. *The Suicidal Child*. New York: Guilford.

Polusny, M. A., and Follette, V. M. 1995. Long-term correlates of child sexual abuse: Theory and review of the empirical literature. *Applied and Preventive Psychology* 4: 75–88.

Pope, K. S., and Bouhoutsos, J. C. 1986. *Sexual Intimacy between Therapists and Patients*. New York: Praeger.

Pope, H. G., Jr., and Hudson, J. I. 1992. Is childhood sexual abuse a risk factor for bulimia nervosa. *American Journal of Psychiatry* 149, no. 4: 455–63.

Prescott, C. A., and Kendler, K. S. 1999. Genetic and environmental contributions to alcohol abuse and dependence in a population-based sample of male twins. *American Journal of Psychiatry* 156: 34–40.

Pribor, E. F., and Dinwiddie, S. H. 1992. Psychiatric correlates of incest in childhood. *American Journal of Psychiatry* 149: 52–56.

Price, M. 1994. Incest: Transference and countertransference implications. *Journal of the American Academy of Psychoanalysis* 22: 211–29.

Price, J. H., Islam, R., Gruhler, J., Dove, L., Knowles, J., and Stults, G. 2001. Public perceptions of child abuse and neglect in a Midwestern urban community. *Journal of Community Health* 26, no. 4: 271–80.

Putnam, F. W. 1985. Dissociation as a response to extreme trauma. In R. P. Kluft, ed., *Childhood Antecedents of Multiple Personality*, 65–97. Washington, DC: American Psychiatric Press.

———. 1989. *Diagnosis and Treatment of Multiple Personality Disorder*. New York: Guilford.

———. 1993. Dissociative disorders in children: Behavioral profiles and problems. *Child Abuse and Neglect* 17: 39–45.

———. 1997. *Dissociation in Children and Adolescents*. New York: Guilford.

———. 2000. Dissociative disorders. In A. J. Sameroff and M. Lewis, eds., *Handbook of Developmental Psychopathology*, 739–54. 2nd ed. Dordrecht, Netherlands: Kluwer Academic.

Putnam, F. W., Helmers, K., Horowitz, L. A., and Trickett, P. K. 1995. Hypnotizability and dissociativity in sexually abused girls. *Child Abuse and Neglect* 19: 645–55.

Pynoos, R. S. 1993. Traumatic stress and developmental psychopathology in children and adolescents. In J. Oldham, M. Riba, and A Tasman, eds., *Review of Psychiatry* 12: 205–38. Washington, DC: American Psychiatric Press.

Raj, A., Silverman, J. G., and Amaro, H. 2000. The relationship between sexual abuse and sexual risk among high school students: Findings from the 1997 Massachusetts Youth Risk Behavior Survey. *Maternal and Child Health Journal* 4: 125–34.

Rand, M., Rosenberg, J., and Assay, D. 1985. *Body, Self, and Soul.* Atlanta, GA: Humanics.

Ray, S. L. 2001. Male survivors' perspectives of incest/sexual abuse. *Perspectives in Psychiatric Care* 37, no. 2: 49–66.

Renn, D. 2000. The emotional abuse of the child. *Adolescence* 35, no. 139: 1–5.

Resnick, H. S., Kilpatrick, D. G., Dansky, B. S., Saunders, B. E., and Best, C. L. 1993. Prevalence of civilian trauma and Posttraumatic Stress Disorder in a representative national sample of women. *Journal of Consulting and Clinical Psychology* 61: 984–91.

Rey Gex, C., Narring, F., Ferron, C., and Michaud, P. A. 1998. Suicide attempts among adolescents in Switzerland: Prevalence, associated factors, and co-morbidity. *Acta Psychiatrica Scandinavia* 98: 28–33.

Richter, N. L., Snider, E., and Gorey, K. M. 1997. Group work interventions with female survivors of childhood sexual abuse. *Research on Social Work Practice* 7, no. 1: 53–69.

Roche, D. M., Runtz, M. G., and Hunter, M. A. 1999. Adult attachment: A mediator between child sexual abuse and later psychological adjustment. *Journal of Interpersonal Violence* 14, no. 2: 184–207.

Rodriguez, N., Ryan, S. W., Rowan, A., and Foy, D. W. 1991. Trauma exposure and PTSD: Adult survivors of childhood sexual abuse. Paper presented at the annual meeting of the International Society for Traumatic Stress Studies, Washington, DC.

Rodriguez, N., Vande Kemp, H., and Foy, D. W. 1998. Posttraumatic Stress Disorder in survivors of childhood sexual and physical abuse: A critical review of the empirical research. *Journal of Child Sexual Abuse* 7, no. 2: 17–45.

Rodriguez-Srednicki, O. 2001. Childhood sexual abuse, dissociation, and adult self-destructive behavior. *Journal of Child Sexual Abuse* 10, no. 3: 75–90.

Roesler, T. A., and McKenzie, N. 1994. Effects of childhood trauma on psychological functioning in adults sexually abused as children. *Journal of Nervous and Mental Disease* 182: 145–50.

Rohsenow, D. J., Corbett, R., and Devine, D. 1988. Molested as children: A hidden contribution to substance abuse? *Substance Abuse Treatment* 5: 13–18.

Romans, S., Martin, J., Anderson, J. C., Herbison, G. P., Mullen, P. E., and Phil, M. 1995. Sexual abuse in childhood and deliberate self-harm. *American Journal of Psychiatry* 152: 1336–42.

Romeo, F. F. 2000a. Child abuse and report cards. *Education* 120, no. 3: 438–43.

———. 2000b. The educator's role in reporting the emotional abuse of children. *Journal of Instructional Psychology* 27, no. 3: 183–89.

Roosa, M. W., and Tein, J. Y. 1997. The relationship of childhood sexual abuse to teenage pregnancy. *Journal of Marriage and the Family* 59: 119–30.

Root, M. P. 1991. Persistent disordered eating as a gender-specific, posttraumatic stress response to sexual assault. *Psychotherapy* 28: 96–102.

Root, M. P., and Fallon, P. 1988. The incidence of victimization experiences in a bulimic sample. *Journal of Interpersonal Violence* 3: 161–73.

———. 1989. Treating the victimized bulimic: The functions of binge–purge behavior. *Journal of Interpersonal Violence* 4: 90–100.

Rorty, M., Yager, J., and Rossotto, E. 1994. Childhood sexual, physical and psychological abuse in bulimia nervosa. *American Journal of Psychiatry* 151: 1122–26.

Rosenberg, M. S., and Rossman, B. B. 1998. Multiple victimization of children: Remaining issues. *Journal of Aggression, Maltreatment, and Trauma* 2, no. 1: 317–22.

Rosencrans, B. 1997. *The Last Secret: Daughters Sexually Abused by Mothers.* Brandon, VT: Safer Society Press.

Rosenthal, P. A., and Rosenthal, S. 1984. Suicidal behavior by preschool children. *American Journal of Psychiatry* 141: 520–25.

Rosenzweig, H. D., and Kaplan, S. J. 1996. Child and adolescent neglect and emotional maltreatment. In S. J. Kaplan, ed., *Family Violence: A Clinical and Legal Guide*, 37–72. Washington, DC: American Psychiatric Press.

Ross, C. A., Anderson, G., Herber, S., and Norton, G. R. 1990. Dissociation and abuse among multiple personality patients, prostitutes, and exotic dancers. *Hospital and Community Psychiatry* 41: 328–30.

Ross, C. A., Miller, S. D., and Reagor, P. 1990. Structured interview data on 102 cases of Multiple Personality Disorder from four centers. *American Journal of Psychiatry* 147: 596–601.

Rossman, B. B. R., Hughes, H. M., and Rosenberg, M. S. 2000. *Children and Interparental Violence: The Impact of Exposure.* New York: Taylor & Francis.

Roth, S., Newman, E., Pelcovitz, D., van der Kolk, B., and Mandel, F. 1997. Complex PTSD in victims exposed to sexual and physical abuse: Results from the DSM-IV field trial for Posttraumatic Stress Disorder. *Journal of Traumatic Stress* 10, no. 4: 539–55.

Rotheram, M. J., and Bradley, R. 1987. Evaluation of imminent danger for suicide among youth. *American Journal of Orthopsychiatry* 57: 102–10.

Rothschild, B. 2000. *The Body Remembers: The Psychophysiology of Trauma and Trauma Treatment.* New York: Norton.

Rowan, A. B., and Foy, D. W. 1993. Posttraumatic Stress Disorder in child sexual abuse survivors: A literature review. *Journal of Traumatic Stress* 6: 3–20.

Rowan, A. B., Foy, D. W., Rodriguez, N., and Ryan, S. 1994. Posttraumatic stress disorder in a clinical sample of adults sexually abused as children. *Child Abuse and Neglect* 18: 51–61.

Rowe, J. 1989. Nursing assessment of children of alcoholics. *Journal of Pediatric Nursing* 4: 248–54.

Rubo-Stipec, M., Bird, M., Canino, G., Bravo, M., and Alegria, M. 1991. Children of alcoholic parents in the community. *Journal of Studies on Alcohol* 52: 78–88.

Rush, F. 1980. *The Best Kept Secret: Sexual Abuse of Children*. New York: McGraw-Hill.

Russ, M. J., Shearin, E. N., and Clarkin, J. F. 1993. Subtypes of self-injurious patients with BPD. *American Journal of Psychiatry* 150: 1869–71.

Russell, D. E. H. 1983. The incidence and prevalence of intrafamilial and extra-familial sexual abuse of female children. *Child Abuse and Neglect* 7: 133–46.

Russell, D. 1984. *Sexual Exploitation: Rape, Child Sexual Abuse, and Workplace Harassment*. Beverly Hills: Sage.

Russell, D. 1986. *The Secret Trauma: Incest in the Lives of Girls and Women*. New York: Basic.

Rutter, M. 1985. Resilience in the face of adversity: Protective factors and resistance to psychiatric disorder. *British Journal of Psychiatry* 147: 598–611.

Sadeh, A., Hayden, R. M., McGuire, J. P. D., Sachs, H., and Clivita, R. 1994. Somatic, cognitive, and emotional characteristics of abused children in a psychiatric hospital. *Child Psychiatry and Human Development* 24: 191–200.

Salzinger, S., Kaplan, S., and Artemyeff, C. 1983. Mother's personal social network and child maltreatment. *Journal of Abnormal Psychology* 22: 58–64.

Salzinger, S., Kaplan, S., and Pelcovitz, D. 1984. Parent–teacher assessment of children's behavior in child maltreating families. *Journal of the American Academy of Child Psychiatry* 23: 58–64.

Salzinger, S., Feldman, R., and Hammer, M. 1993. The effects of physical abuse on children's social relationships. *Child Development* 64: 169–87.

Salzman, J. P. 1988. Primary attachment at adolescence and female identity: An extension of Bowlby's perspective. Ph.D. dissertation, Harvard University.

———. 1990. Save the world, save myself. In C. Gilligan, N. Lyons, and T. Hanmer, eds., *Making Connections*, 110–46. Cambridge: Harvard University Press.

Salzman, J. P., Salzman, C., and Wolfson, A. N. 1997. Relationship of childhood abuse and maternal attachment to the development of Borderline Personality Disorder. In M. C. Zanarini, ed., *The Role of Sexual Abuse in the Etiology of Borderline Personality Disorder*, 71–92. Washington, DC: American Psychiatric Press.

Sandberg, D., Lynn, S. J., and Green, J. P. 1994. Sexual abuse and revictimization: Mastery, dysfunctional learning, and dissociation. In S. J. Lynn and J. W. Rhue, eds., *Dissociation: Clinical and Theoretical Perspectives*, 242–67. New York: Guilford.

Sandberg, D. A., Matorin, A., and Lynn, S. J. 1999. Dissociation, posttraumatic symptomatology, and sexual revictimization: A prospective examination of mediator and moderator effects. *Journal of Traumatic Stress* 12: 127–138.

Sanders, B., and Giolas, M. H. 1991. Dissociation and childhood trauma in psychologically disturbed adolescents. *American Journal of Psychiatry* 148: 50–54.

Sansonnet-Hayden, H., Haley, G., Marriage, K., and Fine, S. 1987. Sexual abuse and psychopathology in hospitalized adolescents. *Journal of the American Academy of Child Psychiatry* 26: 753–57.

Sarrel, P., and Masters, W. 1982. Sexual molestation of men by women. *Archives of Sexual Behavior* 11, no. 2: 117–31.

Saunders, B. E., Villeponteaux, L. A., Lipovsky, J. A., Kilpatrick, D. G., and Veronen, L. J. 1992. Child sexual assault as a risk factor for mental disorders among women. *Journal of Interpersonal Violence* 7: 189–204.

Schaaf, K. K., and McCanne, T. R. 1994. Childhood abuse, body image disturbance, and eating disorders. *Child Abuse and Neglect* 18: 607–15.

Schengold, L. 1979. Child abuse and deprivation: Soul murder. *Journal of the American Psychoanalytic Association* 27: 533–99.

Scher, D., and Twaite, J. A. 1999. The relationship between child sexual abuse and alexithymic symptoms in a population of recovering substance abusers. *Journal of Child Sexual Abuse* 8, no. 2: 25–40.

Schinke, S. P., Botvin, G. J., and Orlandi, M. A. 1991. Patterns of substance abuse among adolescents. In S. P. Schinke, G. J. Botvin, and M. A. Orlandi, eds., *Substance Abuse in Children and Adolescents: Evaluation and Intervention*, 1–17. Newbury Park, CA: Sage.

Schnurr, P., Spiro, A., Vielhauer, M., Findler, M., and Hamblen, J. 2002. *The Brief Trauma Questionnaire*. White River Junction, VT: National Center for PTSD.

Schoenborn, C. A. 1995. *Exposure to Alcoholism in the Family: United States, 1988*. Advance Data no. 205. Hyattsville, MD: National Center for Health Statistics. *Vital Health Statistics* DHHS Publication no. PHS-95-1880.

Schwartz, M., Galperin, L., and Masters, W. 1995a. Sexual trauma within the context of traumatic and inescapable stress, neglect, and poisonous pedagogy. In M. Hunter, ed., *Adult Survivors of Sexual Abuse: Treatment Innovations*, 1–17. Thousand Oaks, CA: Sage.

———. 1995b. Dissociation and treatment of compulsive reenactment of trauma: Sexual compulsivity. In M. Hunter, ed., *Adult Survivors of Sexual Abuse: Treatment Innovations*, 42–55. Thousand Oaks, CA: Sage.

Scott, K. D. 1992. Childhood sexual abuse: Impact on a community's mental health status. *Child Abuse and Neglect* 16: 285–95.

Scott, W. 1999. Group therapy for survivors of severe childhood abuse: Repairing the social contract. *Journal of Child Sexual Abuse* 7, no. 3: 33–54.

Seagull, E. A. 1997. Family assessment. In M. E. Helfer, R. S. Kempe, and R. D. Krugman, eds., *The Battered Child*, 150–74. 5th ed. Chicago: University of Chicago Press.

Sedlak, A. S., and Broadhurst, D. D. 1996. *Third National Incidence Study of Child Abuse and Neglect*. Washington, DC: United States Department of Health and Human Services.

Seidner, A. L., and Calhoun, K. S. 1984. Child sexual abuse: Factors related to differential adult adjustment. Paper presented at the Second National Family Violence Research Conference, Durham, NH.

Sgroi, S. M., Blick, L. C., and Porter, F. S. 1982. A conceptual framework for child sexual abuse. In S. M. Sgroi, ed., *Handbook of Clinical Intervention in Child Sexual Abuse*, 1–12. Lexington, MA: Lexington.

Sgroi, S. M., and Sargent, N. M. 1993. Impact and treatment issues for victims of childhood sexual abuse by female perpetrators. In M. Elliott, ed., *Female Sexual*

Abuse of Children: The Ultimate Taboo, 15–38. London: Longman Information and Reference.

Shapiro, D. L., and Levendosky, A. A. 1999. Adolescent survivors of childhood sexual abuse: The mediating role of attachment style and coping in psychological and interpersonal functioning. *Child Abuse and Neglect* 23, no. 11: 1175–92.

Shapiro, S. 1987. Self-mutilation and self-blame in incest victims. *American Journal of Psychotherapy* 41: 46–54.

Sharkansky, E. J., Brief, D. J., Peirce, J. M., Meehan, J. C., and Mannix, L. M. 1999. Substance abuse patients with Posttraumatic Stress Disorder (PTSD): Identifying specific triggers of substance abuse and their associations with PTSD symptoms. *Psychology of Addictive Behaviors* 13: 89–97.

Shearer, S. L., Peters, C. P., Quaytman, M. S., et al. 1990. Frequency and correlates of childhood physical and sexual abuse histories in adult female borderline patients. *American Journal of Psychiatry* 147: 214–16.

Shirk, S. R., and Eltz, M. J. 1998. Multiple victimization and the process and outcome of child psychotherapy. *Journal of Aggression, Maltreatment, and Trauma* 2, no. 1: 233–51.

Shull, J. R. 1999. Emotional and psychological child abuse: Notes on discourse, history, and change. *Stanford Law Review* 51, no. 6: 1665–1706.

Siegel, J. M., Sorenson, S. B., Golding, J. M., Burnham, M. A., and Stein, J. A. 1987. The prevalence of childhood sexual assault: The Los Angeles Epidemiologic Catchment Area Project. *American Journal of Epidemiology* 126, no. 6, 1141–53.

Sifneos, P. E. 1973. The prevalence of alexithymic characteristics in psychosomatic patients. *Psychotherapy and Psychosomatic Medicine* 22: 255–62.

———. 1975. Problems of psychotherapy of patients with alexithymic characteristics and physical disease. *Psychotherapy and Psychosomatic Medicine* 26: 65–70.

Silbert, M. H., and Pines, A. M. 1981. Sexual child abuse as an antecedent to prostitution. *Child Abuse and Neglect* 5: 407–11.

Silk, K. R., Nigg, J. T., Westen, D., and Lohr, N. E. 1997. Severity of childhood sexual abuse, borderline symptoms, and familial environment. In M. C. Zanarini, ed., *The Role of Sexual Abuse in the Etiology of Borderline Personality Disorder*, 131–63. Washington, DC: American Psychiatric Press.

Silverman, A. B., Reinherz, H. Z., and Giaconia, R. M. 1996. The long-term sequelae of child and adolescent abuse: A longitudinal community study. *Child Abuse and Neglect* 20: 709–23.

Singh, M. 1994. Validation of a measure of session outcome in the resolution of unfinished business. Ph.D. dissertation, York University, Toronto.

Solomon, Y., and Farrand, J. 1996. Why don't you do it properly: Young women who self-injure. *Journal of Adolescence* 19: 111–19.

Sorsoli, L. 2004. Hurt feelings: Emotional abuse and the failure of empathy. *Journal of Emotional Abuse* 4, no. 1: 1–26.

Spencer, J. 1978. Father–daughter incest: A clinical view from the corrections field. *Child Welfare* 57: 581–90.

Spiegel, D. 1990. Trauma, dissociation, and hypnosis. In R. Kluft, ed., *Incest-Related Syndromes of Adult Psychopathology*, 247–61. Washington, DC: American Psychiatric Press.

———. 1994. Multiple personality as a Posttraumatic Stress Disorder. *Psychiatric Clinics of North America* 7: 101–10.

Spiegel, D., and Cardena, E. 1991. Disintegrated experience: The dissociative disorders revisited. *Journal of Abnormal Psychology* 100: 366–78.

Spitzer, R. L., Williams, J. B. W., and Gibbon, M. 1987. *Structured Clinical Interview for DSM-III-R Personality Disorders SCID-II*. New York: New York State Psychiatric Institute.

Sroufe, L. A. 1995. *Emotional Development: The Organization of Emotional Life in the Early Years*. Cambridge: Cambridge University Press.

Stalker, C. A., and Davies, F. 1995. Attachment organization and adaptation in sexually abused women. *Canadian Journal of Psychiatry* 40, no. 5: 234–40.

Steiger, M., and Zanko, M. 1990. Sexual trauma among eating disordered, psychiatric, and normal female groups. *Journal of Interpersonal Violence* 5: 74–86.

Stein, J. A., Golding, J. M., Siegel, J. M., Burnam, M. A., and Sorenson, S. B. 1988. Long-term sequelae of child sexual abuse. In G. E. Wyatt and G. J. Powell, eds., *Lasting Effects of Child Sexual Abuse*, 135–54. Newbury Park, CA: Sage.

Steinberg, M. 1995. *Handbook for the Assessment of Dissociation: A Clinical Guide*. Washington, DC: American Psychiatric Press.

Stepakoff, S. 1998. Effects of sexual victimization on suicidal ideation and behavior in U.S. college women. *Suicide and Life-threatening Behavior* 28: 107–26.

Sterne, M., Schaefer, S., and Evans, S. 1983. Women's sexuality and alcoholism. In P. Golding, ed., *Alcoholism: Analysis of a Worldwide Problem*. Lancaster, U.K.: MTP Press.

Stewart, S. H., and Conrod, P. J. 2003. Psychosocial models of functional associations between Posttraumatic Stress Disorder and substance use disorder. In P. Ouimette and P. J. Brown, eds., *Trauma and Substance Abuse: Causes, Consequences, and Treatment of Co-morbid Disorders*, 29–56. Washington, DC: American Psychological Association.

Stewart, S. H., Conrod, P. J., Samoluk, S. B., Pihl, R. O., and Dongier, M. 2000. Posttraumatic Stress Disorder symptoms and situation-specific drinking in women substance abusers. *Alcoholism Treatment Quarterly* 18: 31–47.

Stewart, S. H., Samolul, S. B., Conrod, P. J., Pihl, R. O., and Dongier, M. 2000. Psychometric evaluation of the short form Inventory of Drinking Situations IDS-42 in a community-recruited sample of substance-abusing women. *Journal of Substance Abuse* 11: 305–21.

Stice, E. 2001. Risk factors for eating pathology: Recent advances and future directions. In R. H. Striegel-Moore and L. Smolak, eds., *Eating Disorders: Innovative Directions in Research and Practice*, 51–74. Washington, DC: American Psychological Association.

Stine, S. M., and Kosten, T. R. 1995. Complications of chemical abuse and dependency. In M. J. Friedman, D. S. Charney, and A. Y. Deutsch, eds., *Neurobiological and Clinical Consequences of Stress: From Normal Adaptation to PTSD*, 447–64. Philadelphia: Lippincott-Raven.

Stock, J., Bell, M., Boyer, D., and Connell, F. 1997. Adolescent pregnancy and sexual risk taking among sexually abused girls. *Family Planning Perspectives* 29: 200–203.

Straus, M. A. 1979. Measuring intrafamily conflict and violence: The Conflict Tactics CT Scales. *Journal of Marriage and the Family* 41: 75–88.

———. 1991. New theories and old canards about family violence research. *Social Problems* 38: 180–97.

———. 1992. Children as witnesses to marital violence: A risk factor for lifelong problems among a nationally representative sample of American men and women. In D. F. Schwartz, ed., *Children and Violence: Report on the 23rd Ross Roundtable on Critical Approaches to Common Pediatric Problems*, 98–104. Columbus, OH: Ross Laboratories.

Straus, M. A., and Gelles, R. 1986. Societal change and change in family violence from 1975 to 1985 as revealed by two national surveys. *Journal of Marriage and the Family* 48: 465–79.

———. 1990. *Physical Violence in American Families: Risk Factors and Adaptations to Violence in 8,145 Families*. New Brunswick, NJ: Transaction.

Straus, M. A., Gelles, R. J., and Steinmetz, S. K. 1980. *Behind Closed Doors: Violence in the American Family*. New York: Anchor.

Straus, M. A., and Kantor, G. K. 1994. Corporal punishment of adolescents by parents: A risk factor in the epidemiology of depression, suicide, alcohol abuse, child abuse, and wife beating. *Adolescence* 29: 543–61.

———. 2005. Definition and measurement of neglectful behavior: Some principles and guidelines. *Child Abuse and Neglect* 29: 19–29.

Summit, R. 1983. The child sexual abuse accommodation syndrome. *Child Abuse and Neglect* 7: 177–93.

Surrey, J., Swett, C., Michaels, A., and Levin, S. 1990. Reported history of physical and sexual abuse and severity of symptomatology in women psychiatric outpatients. *American Journal of Orthopsychiatry* 60: 412–17.

Swett, C., and Halpert, M. 1993. Reported history of physical and sexual abuse in relation to dissociation and other symptomatology in women psychiatric outpatients. *Journal of Interpersonal Violence* 8: 545–55.

Talbot, N. L., Houghtalen, R. P., Cyrulik, S., Betz, A., Bakun, M., Duberstein, P. R., and Wynne, L. C. 1998. Women's safety in recovery: Group therapy for patients with a history of childhood sexual abuse. *Psychiatric Services* 49: 213–17.

Talbot, N. L., Houghtalen, R. P., Duberstein, P. R., Cox, C., Giles, D. E., and Wynne, L. C. 1999. Effects of group treatment for women with a history of childhood sexual abuse. *Psychiatric Services* 50: 686–92.

Tam, T. W., Zlotnick, C., and Robertson, M. J. 2003. Longitudinal perspective: Adverse childhood events, substance use, and labor force participation among homeless adults. *American Journal of Drug and Alcohol Abuse* 29, no. 4: 829–46.

Tardif, M., Auclair, N., Jacob, M., and Carpentier, J. 2005. Sexual abuse perpetrated by adult and juvenile females: An ultimate attempt to resolve a conflict associated with maternal identity. *Child Abuse and Neglect* 29: 153–67.

Taylor, C. 1991. Diagnosed intellectual and emotional impairment among parents who seriously mistreat their children: Prevalence, type, and outcome in a court sample. *Child Abuse and Neglect* 15: 389–401.

Taylor, G. J., Bagby, R. M., Ryan, D. P., and Parker, J. D. A. 1990. Validation of the alexithymia construct: A measurement-based approach. *Canadian Journal of Psychiatry* 35: 290–97.

Taylor, G. J., Ryan, D. P., and Bagby, R. M. 1985. Toward the development of a new self-report alexithymia scale. *Psychotherapy and Psychosomatic Medicine* 44: 191–99.

Taylor, S., Koch, W. J., and McNally, R. J. 1992. How does anxiety-sensitivity vary across the anxiety disorders? *Journal of Anxiety Disorders* 6: 249–93.

Teicher, M. H., Ito, Y., and Glod, C. A. 1987. Early abuse, limbic system dysfunction, and BPD. In K. R. Silk, ed., *Biological and Neurobehavioral Studies of Borderline Personality Disorder*, 173–90. Washington, DC: American Psychiatric Press.

Texas Department of Human Services. 2003. Child Sexual Abuse. www.texaspolice central.com.childsex.html.

Texas Women's University Counseling Center. 2003. Incest and child sexual abuse misconceptions and facts. www.twu.edu/o-sl/counseling/SH055.html.

Thelen, M. H., Farmer, J., Wonderlich, S., and Smith, M. 1991. A revision of the Bulimia Test: The BULIT-R. *Psychological Assessment* 3: 119–24.

Theriault, C., Cyr, M., and Cinq-Mars, C. 1997. *The Sexual Abuse History Questionnaire: An Adaptation of the Incest History Questionnaire Coutois, 1988.* Montreal: Department of Psychology, University of Montreal.

Theriault, C., Cyr, M., and Wright, J. 1996. *The Inventory of Family Problems.* Montreal: Department of Psychology, University of Montreal.

Timms, R. J., and Connors, P. 1992. Adult promiscuity following childhood sexual abuse: An introduction. *Psychotherapy Patient* 8: 19–27.

Tjaden, P., and Thoennes, N. 2000. *Full Report of the Prevalence, Incidence, and Consequences of Violence against Women: Findings from the National Violence Against Women Survey.* Washington, DC: National Institute of Justice.

Tolman, R. M. 1989. The development of a measure of psychological maltreatment of women by their male partners. *Violence and Victims* 4: 159–77.

Tong, L. K., Oates, K., and McDowell, M. 1987. Personality development following sexual abuse. *Child Abuse and Neglect* 11: 371–83.

Tremblay, C., Hebert, M., and Piche, C. 2000. Type I and Type II Posttraumatic Stress Disorder in sexually abused children. *Journal of Child Sexual Abuse* 9, no. 1: 65–90.

Triffleman, E., Caroll, K., and Kellogg, S. 1999. Substance dependence posttraumatic stress disorder therapy: An integrated cognitive–behavioral approach. *Journal of Substance Abuse Treatment* 17: 3–14.

Triffleman, E. G., Marmar, C. R., Delucchi, K. L., and Ronfeldt, H. 1995. Childhood trauma and Posttraumatic Stress Disorder in substance abuse inpatients. *Journal of Nervous and Mental Disease* 183: 172–76.

Truscott, D. 1992. Intergenerational transmissions of violent behavior in adolescent males. *Aggressive Behavior* 18: 327–35.

Tsai, M., Feldman-Summers, S., and Edgar, M. 1979. Childhood molestation: Variables related to differential impact of psychosexual functioning in adult women. *Journal of Abnormal Psychology* 88: 407–17.

Tsai, M., and Wagner, N. 1981. Therapy groups for women sexually molested as children. *Journal of Abnormal Psychology* 88: 407–17.

Tufts New England Medical Center, Division of Child Psychiatry. 1984. *Sexually Exploited Children: Service and Research Project*. Final Report for the Office of Juvenile Justice and Delinquency Prevention. Washington, DC: U.S. Department of Justice.

Twaite, J. A., and Rodriguez-Srednicki, O. 2004. Childhood sexual and physical abuse and adult vulnerability to PTSD: The mediating effects of attachment and dissociation. *Journal of Child Sexual Abuse* 13, no. 1: 17–38.

Twaite, J. A., Silitsky, D., and Luchow, A. K. 1998. *Children of Divorce*. Northvale, NJ: Jason Aronson.

Urquiza, A., and Capra, M. 1990. The impact of sexual abuse: Initial and long-term effects. In M. Hunter, ed., *The Sexually Abused Male*. Vol. 1, *Prevalence, Impact, and Treatment*. Lexington, MA: Lexington.

Urquiza, A. J., and Goodlin-Jones, B. L. 1994. Child sexual abuse and adult revictimization with women of color. *Violence and Victims* 9: 223–32.

U.S. Department of Health and Human Services. 1988. *Study Findings: Study of National Incidence and Prevalence of Child Abuse and Neglect*. Washington, DC: U.S. Government Printing Office.

———. 1995. *Maltreatment 1993: Reports from the States to the National Center on Child Abuse and Neglect*. Washington, DC: U.S. Government Printing Office.

———. 2003. HHS launches effort to help children who witness domestic violence. News release. www.hhs.gov/news/press/2003pres/20031008.html.

U.S. Department of Health and Human Services. Administration on Children, Youth, and Families. 2000. *Child Maltreatment 1998: Reports from the States to the National Child Abuse and Neglect Data System*. Washington, DC: U.S. Government Printing Office.

———. 2002. *Child Maltreatment 2000: Reports from the States to the National Child Abuse and Neglect Data System*. Washington, DC: U.S. Government Printing Office.

Van der Hart, O., Steele, K., Boon, S., and Brown, P. 1993. The treatment of traumatic memories: Synthesis, realization, and integration. *Dissociation: Progress in Dissociative Disorders* 6: 162–80.

Van der Kolk, B. A. 1987. *Psychological Trauma*. Washington, DC: American Psychiatric Press.

———. 1989. The compulsion to repeat trauma: Reenactment, revictimization, and masochism. *Psychiatric Clinics of North America* 12: 389–411.

———. 1994. The body keeps the score: Memory and the evolving psychobiology of posttraumatic stress. *Harvard Review of Psychiatry* 1: 253–65.

———. 1996. The complexity of adaptation to trauma: Self-regulation, stimulus discrimination, and characterological development. In B. A. van der Kolk, A. C. McFarlane, and L. Weisaeth, eds., *Traumatic Stress: The Effects of Overwhelming Experience on Mind, Body, and Society*, 182–213. New York: Guilford.

Van der Kolk, B. A., and Fisler, R. E. 1994. Child abuse and neglect and loss of self-regulation. *Bulletin of the Menninger Clinic* 58: 145–68.

Van der Kolk, B. A., and Greenburg, M. S. 1987. The psychobiology of the trauma response: Hyperarousal, constriction, and the addiction to traumatic reexposure. In B. A. van der Kolk, ed., *Psychological Trauma*, 63–87. Washington, DC: American Psychiatric Press.

Van der Kolk, B. A., and Kadish, W. 1987. Amnesia, dissociation, and the return of the repressed. In B. A. van der Kolk, ed., *Psychological Trauma*. Washington, DC: American Psychiatric Press.

Van der Kolk, B. A., and Pelcovitz, D. 1999. Clinical applications of the structured interview for Disorders of Extreme Stress (SIDES). *National Center for Posttraumatic Stress Disorder* 8, no. 2: 21–26.

Van der Kolk, B. A., Pelcovitz, D., Roth, S. H., Mandel, F. S., McFarlane, A. C., and Herman, J. L. 1996. Dissociation, somatization, and affect dysregulation: The complexity of adaptation to trauma. *American Journal of Psychiatry* 153, no. 7: 83–93.

Van der Kolk, B. A., Perry, J. C., and Herman, J. L. 1991. Childhood origins of self-destructive behavior. *American Journal of Psychiatry* 148, no. 12: 1665–71.

Van der Kolk, B. A., Roth, S., Pelcovitz, D., and Mandel, F. S. 1993. *Complex PTSD: Results of the PTSD Field Trials for DSM-IV*. Washington, DC: American Psychiatric Press.

Vanderlinden, J., Vandereycken, W., van Dyck, R., and Vertommen, H. 1993. Dissociative experiences and trauma in eating disorders. *International Journal of Eating Disorders* 13: 187–93.

Vander Mey, B. J., and Neff, R. L. 1982. Adult–child incest: A review of the research and treatment. *Adolescence* 17: 717–35.

Varia, R., Abidin, R. R., and Dass, P. 1996. Perceptions of abuse: Effects on adult psychological and social adjustment. *Child Abuse and Neglect* 20: 511–26.

Vogeltanz-Holm, N. D., Wonderlich, S. A., Lewis, B. A., Wilsnack, S. C., Harris, T. R., Wilsnack, R. W., and Kristjanson, A. F. 2000. Longitudinal predictors of binge eating, intense dieting, and weight concerns in a national sample of women. *Behavior Therapy* 31: 221–35.

Volkan, K. 1994. *Dancing among the Maenads: The Psychology of Compulsive Drug Use*. San Francisco: Lang.

Vrana, S., and Lauterbach, D. 1994. Prevalence of traumatic events and posttraumatic psychological symptoms in a nonclinical sample of college students. *Journal of Traumatic Stress* 7: 289–302.

Wagman Borowsky, I., Resnick, M. D., Ireland, M., and Blum, R. W. 1999. Suicide attempts among American Indian and Alaska native youth. *Archives of Pediatric and Adolescent Medicine* 153: 573–80.

Waldfogel, J. 1998. *The Future of Child Protection: How to Break the Cycle of Abuse and Neglect* 17: 197–212.

Walker, L. E. 1979. *The Battered Woman*. New York: Harper & Row.

———. 1981. Battered Women: Sex Roles and Clinical Issues. *Professional Psychology* 12: 81–91.

———. 1984. *The Battered Woman Syndrome*. New York: Springer.

Walker, L. E., and Browne, A. 1985. Gender and victimization by intimates. *Journal of Personality* 53, no. 2: 179–95.

Waller, G. 1992. Sexual abuse and bulimic symptoms in eating disorders: Do family interaction and self-esteem explain the links? *International Journal of Eating Disorders* 12: 235–40.

Walser, R. D., and Kern, J. M. 1996. Relationships among childhood sexual abuse, sex guilt, and sexual behavior in adult clinical samples. *Journal of Sex Research* 33: 321–26.

Waterman, J., and Lusk, R. 1986. Scope of the problem. In K. MacFarlane and J. Waterman, eds., *Sexual Abuse of Young Children*, 3–12. New York: Guilford.

Waters, E., Merrick, S., Treboux, D., Crowell, J., and Albersheim, L. 2000. Attachment security in infancy and early adulthood: A twenty-year longitudinal study. *Child Development* 71, no. 3: 684–89.

Watkins, W., and Bentovim, A. 1992. The sexual abuse of male children and adolescents: A review of current research. *Journal of Child Psychology and Psychiatry* 33: 197–248.

Weeks, R., and Widom, C. S. 1998. Self-reports of early childhood victimization among incarcerated adult male felons. *Journal of Interpersonal Violence* 13: 346–61.

Weiss, D. S., and Marmar, C. R. 1997. The Impact of Event Scale–Revised. In J. P. Wilson and T. M. Keene, eds., *Assessing Psychological Trauma and PTSD*, 399–411. New York: Guilford.

Westbury, E., and Tutty, L. M. 1999. The efficacy of group treatment for survivors of childhood abuse. *Child Abuse and Neglect* 23: 31–44.

Westen, D., Ludolph, P., Misle, B., et al. 1990. Physical and sexual abuse in adolescent girls with Borderline Personality Disorder. *American Journal of Psychiatry* 60: 55–66.

Wheeler, J. R., and Berliner, L. 1988. Treating the effects of sexual abuse on children. In G. E. Wyatt and G. J. Powell, eds., *Lasting Effects of Child Sexual Abuse*, 227–47. Newbury Park, CA: Sage.

Whipple, E. E., and Webster-Stratton, C. 1991. The role of parental stress in physically abusive families. *Child Abuse and Neglect* 17: 539–47.

Widom, C. S., and Ames, M. A. 1994. Criminal consequences of childhood sexual victimization. *Child Abuse and Neglect* 18, no. 4: 303–18.

Williamson, J., Bordwin, C., and Howe, B. 1991. The ecology of adolescent maltreatment: A multilevel examination of adolescent physical abuse, sexual abuse, and neglect. *Journal of Consulting and Clinical Psychology* 59: 449–57.

Wilsnack, S. C., Vogeltanz, N. D., Klassen, A. D., and Harris, T. R. 1997. Childhood sexual abuse and women's substance abuse: National survey findings. *Journal of Studies on Alcohol* 58, no. 3: 264–83.

Wilson, J. P. 2004. PTSD and complex PTSD. In J. P. Wilson and T. M. Keane, eds., *Assessing Psychological Trauma and PTSD*, 7–44. New York: Guilford.

Wind, T. W., and Silvern, L. 1992. Type and extent of child abuse as predictors of adult functioning. *Journal of Family Violence* 7: 261–81.

Winfield, I., George, L. K., Swartz, M., and Blazer, D. G. 1990. Sexual assault and psychiatric disorders among a community sample of women. *American Journal of Psychiatry* 147: 335–41.

Wolfe, D. A., Sas, L., and Wekerle, C. 1994. Factors associated with the development of Posttraumatic Stress Disorder among child victims of sexual abuse. *Child Abuse and Neglect* 18: 37–50.

Wolfe, J., Kimerling, R., Brown, P. J. Chrestman, K. R. and Levin, K. 1996. Psychometric review of the Life Stressor Checklist–Revised. In B. H. Stamm, ed., *Measurement of Stress, Trauma, and Adaptation*, 198–201. Lutherville, MD: Sidran.

Wolfe, D. A., Zak, L., Wilson, S. and Jaffe, P. 1986. Child witnesses to violence between parents: Critical issues in behavioral and social adjustment. *Journal of Abnormal Child Psychology*, 14, 1: 95–104.

Wolfner, G. D., and Gelles, R. J. 1993. A profile of violence toward children: A national study. *Child Abuse and Neglect: The International Journal* 15: 197–211.

Wonderlich, S. A., Brewerton, T. D., Jocic, Z., Dansky, B. S., Abbott, D. W. 1997. Relationship of childhood sexual abuse and eating disorders. *Journal of American Academy of Child and Adolescent Psychiatry* 36, no. 8: 1107–15.

Wonderlich, S., Crosby, R., Mitchell, J., Thompson, K., Redin, J., Demuch, G., and Smyth, J. 2001. Pathways mediating sexual abuse and eating disturbances in children. *International Journal of Eating Disorders* 29: 270–79.

Wood, J. 1999. Emotional abuse: An in-depth review. suite101.com/article .cfm/ domestic violence.

Woodside, M., Coughey, K., and Cohen, R. 1993. Medical costs of children of alcoholics: Pay now or pay later. *Journal of Substance Abuse* 5: 281–87.

Wyatt, G. E. 1985. The sexual abuse of Afro-American and white-American women in childhood. *Child Abuse and Neglect* 9: 507–19.

Wyatt, G. E., Guthrie, D., and Notgrass, C. M. 1992. Differential effects of women's child sexual abuse and subsequent sexual revictimization. *Journal of Consulting and Clinical Psychology* 60: 167–73.

Wyatt, G. E., Newcomb, M. D., and Riederle, M. H. 1993. *Sexual Abuse and Consensual Sex*. Newbury Park: CA: Sage.

Yama, M. F., Fogas, B. S., Teegarden, L. A., and Hastings, B. 1993. Childhood sexual abuse and parental alcoholism: Interactive effects in adult women. *American Journal of Orthopsychiatry* 63: 300–305.

Yandow, V. 1989. Alcoholism in women. *Psychiatric Annals*, 243–47.

Yates, A. 1982. Children eroticized by incest. *American Journal of Psychiatry* 139: 482–85.

Yawney, D. 1996. Resiliency: A strategy for survival of childhood trauma. In M. Russell, J. Hightower, and G. Gutman, eds., *Stopping the Violence: Changing Families, Changing Futures*. Canada: Benwell Atkins.

Yehuda, R. 1998. Resilience and vulnerability factors in the course of adaptation to trauma. *National Center for Posttraumatic Stress Disorder Clinical Quarterly* 8, no. 1: 1–6.

Yehuda, R., and McFarlane, A. C. 1995. Conflict between current knowledge about Posttraumatic Stress Disorder and its original conceptual basis. *American Journal of Psychiatry* 152, no. 12: 1705–13.

Young, L. 1992. Sexual abuse and the problem of embodiment. *Child Abuse and Neglect* 16: 89–100.

Ystgaard, M., Hestetun, I., Loeb, M., and Mehlum, L. 2004. Is there a specific relationship between childhood sexual and physical abuse and repeated suicidal behavior? *Child Abuse and Neglect* 28: 863–75.

Zanarini, M. C., Dubo, E. D., Lewis, R. E., and Williams, B. S. 1997. Childhood factors associated with the development of Borderline Personality Disorder. In M. C. Zanarini, ed., *The Role of Sexual Abuse in the Etiology of Borderline Personality Disorder*, 29–44. Washington, DC: American Psychiatric Press.

Zanarini, M. C., and Gunderson, J. B. 1987. Childhood abuse common in borderline personality. *Clinical Psychiatry News* 6: 1.

Zanarini, M. C., Gunderson, J. G., and Frankenburg, F. R., et al. 1989a. The Revised Diagnostic Interview for Borderlines: Discriminating BPD from other Axis II disorders. *Journal of Personality Disorders* 3: 10–18.

Zanarini, M. C., Gunderson, J. G., Marino, M. F., et al. 1989b. Childhood experiences of borderline patients. *Journal of Comparative Psychiatry* 30: 18–25.

Zellman, G. 1992. The impact of case characteristics on child abuse reporting decisions. *Child Abuse and Neglect* 16: 57–74.

Zlotnick, C., Begin, A., Shea, M. T., Pearlstein, T., Simpson, E., and Costello, E. 1994. The relationship between characteristics of sexual abuse and dissociative experiences. *Comprehensive Psychiatry* 35: 465–70.

Zlotnick, C., and Pearlstein, T. 1997. Validation of the structured interview for disorders of extreme stress. *Comprehensive Psychiatry* 38: 243–47.

Zlotnick, C., Shea, M. T., Pearlstein, T., Simpson, E., Costello, E., and Begin, A. 1996. The relationship between dissociative symptoms, alexithymia, impulsivity, sexual abuse, and self-mutilation. *Comprehensive Psychiatry* 37: 12–16.

Zlotnick, C. Shea, M. T., Rosen, K. H., Simpson, E., Mulrenin, K., Begin, A., and Pearlstein, T. 1997. An affect-management group for women with Posttraumatic

Stress Disorder and histories of childhood sexual abuse. *Journal of Traumatic Stress* 10: 425–36.

Zlotnick, C., Zakrisky, A. L., Shea, M. T., Costello, E., Begin, A., Pearlstein, T., and Simpson, E. 1996. The long-term sequelae of sexual abuse: Support for a complex Posttraumatic Stress Disorder. *Journal of Traumatic Stress* 9, no. 2: 195–205.

Zuravin, S. 1988. Child abuse, child neglect, and maternal depression: Is there a connection? In *Child Neglect Monograph: Proceedings from a Symposium*. Washington, DC: Clearinghouse on Child Abuse and Neglect Information.

Zweig-Frank, H., and Paris, J. 1997. Relationship of childhood sexual abuse to dissociation and self-mutilation in female patients. In M. C. Zanarini, ed., *The Role of Sexual Abuse in the Etiology of Borderline Personality Disorder*, 93–106. Washington, DC: American Psychiatric Press.

Index

~

About the Authors

Ofelia Rodriguez-Srednicki, Ph.D is an associate professor of Psychology at Montclair State University in Montclair, New Jersey. She is also a clinician in private practice at Upper Montclair Psychological Associates in Upper Montclair, New Jersey. She has authored articles on sexual abuse, family-work-conflict, multicultural issues in treatment and school psychology. She is a frequent invited presenter for numerous conferences at hospitals, schools and community centers. Dr. Rodriguez-Srednicki is married to Dr. Henry J. Srednicki and has two sons—Mario and Joshua.

James A. Twaite is a psychologist and statistician in private practice in Milford, Pennsylvania. He is also the Director of Research at Neurodynamics, Inc., Tenafly, New Jersey, a neurofeedback treatment center. He has taught courses in psychology, statistics, and psychometrics at Teachers College, Columbia University, at Barnard College, and at the College of New Rochelle. He is the author of three previous professional books: *Introductory Statistics*; *The Black Elderly: Satisfaction in Later Life*; and *Children of Divorce*. His scholarly articles have appeared in *The Journal of Psychiatry and Law*, *The Journal of Child Sexual Abuse*, *Social Work*, and *The American Journal of Orthopsychiatry*.